Yellowjackets! The 361st Fighter Group in World War II - P-51 Mustangs over Germany *Paul B. Cora.* A narrative history of a combat unit attached to the U.S. 8th Air Force in the ETO from December 1943 through the end of the war in Europe. More than a narrow unit history, *Yellowjackets*! places the experiences of the Group's personnel in perspective with the larger context of the war, and also presents the human side, speaking, at times, from the intensely personal standpoint of the pilots and personnel.
Size: 8.5"x11" • over 130 b/w & color photographs, color aircraft profiles • 152 pp. • ISBN: 0-7643-1466-1 • hard cover • $39.95

The 370th Fighter Group in World War II - in Action over Europe with the P-38 and P-51 *Jay Jones.* The history of the 370th Fighter Group in World War II, conveyed in the words and photos of the veterans. The 370th was organized in 1943 to fly the P-47 Thunderbolt. When the group arrived in England in early 1944, they were assigned to the 9th Air Force and converted to fly P-38 Lightnings. They were involved in every major Allied offensive from D-Day onward. The group supported Operation Cobra, flew missions over the Falaise Gap, and flew cover over Operation Market Garden. On missions after the weather cleared, the men could actually watch from the base as their planes made dive-bombing runs on German armored columns. The group converted to P-51 Mustangs in March 1945, just in time for cover missions during Operation Varsity, the Rhine River crossing. This is one of the most thorough and comprehensive group histories written and is a must for veterans, their families, and enthusiasts.
Size: 8.5"x11" • over 700 black and white and color photos, color aircraft profiles • 448 pp. • ISBN: 0-7643-1779-2 • hard cover • $59.95

We are always interested in working with authors or collectors on wonderful book ideas. Contact us at **www.schifferbooks.com**, and page down to "For Authors – Submit a Book Proposal." Or call or write to us about your proposal.

Talk with your local bookseller. Their knowledge is one of the best tools in finding the correct book, and we all need to support them.

** Peter Schiffer and Team **

Designed & composed in America.

Printed in China.

Printed in China

High Noon over Haseluenne

Lt. Robert Shoens' Crew and Ground Crew taken upon completion of the crew's last combat sortie on the May 1, 1944, mission to St Omer. Standing: From left to right Nels Davidson (Ground Crew), Arnold Schluter (Ground Crew), Ed Silverstone (Ball Turret Gunner), Virgil Warders (Right Waist Gunner), William Wright (Left Waist Gunner), Don Hammond (Radio Operator), Charles Killebrew (Ground Crew), Frank Stevens (Ground Crew who painted *Our Gal Sal* and the mission markings), Dewey Nelson (Ground Crew), and Harold Wildrick (Crew Chief). Kneeling: From left to right Don Blair (Tail Gunner), Glenn Hudson (Bombardier and Navigator), Duncan Shand (Co-pilot), Bob Shoens (Pilot), and Bill Eresman (Top Turret - Engineer).

High Noon over Haseluenne

The 100th Bombardment Group over Berlin
March 6, 1944

Luc Dewez & Michael P. Faley

Schiffer Military History
Atglen, PA

Dedication

To the men and women assigned to or associated with the Army Air Forces during the Second World War

This book is dedicated to your service and to those who never returned from Berlin.

Roger Anthony Freeman
The quintessential English gentleman farmer whose intoxicating enthusiasm to understand the American presence on his 'side of the pond' has not only led to that generation's profound understanding of their place in history, but also preserves for this and generations yet to be born a compelling understanding as to what the 'boys of yesterday' and their Mighty Eighth accomplished in the face of tyranny.

Milo and Virginia "Ginger" Faley
Members of the "Greatest Generation" and my heroes. They are survivors of the Great Depression, World War II, and five Children. Thanks for being always being there.

Mr. & Mrs Dewez
"Even though my parents were deeply involved in resistance acts against the Germans, they told me very little about their activities (they were both awarded the Belgian Croix de Guerre). After all, Mom and Dad thought that all they had done was just their duty. They were more inclined to speak about the others, and mostly about the Allied soldiers. My parents remembered vividly the endless formations of U.S. heavy bombers cruising slowly over Belgium, looking like small crosses shining in the sun, but sometimes smoking. After the war, my father was with the Allied occupation forces in Germany. In the forest one day, hidden among the trees, he found the tail of a Flying Fortress. He was deeply impressed by the overall dimensions of the thing, which was as big as a fighter! This began my interest in the history of World War II." Luc Dewez

Cover Painting: "High Noon" by Robert Bailey. Depicting the 100th Bomb Group "B" Group over Hasaluenne at noon on March 6, 1944. Prints of this painting are available for purchase at www.baileyprints.com.

Book Design by Ian Robertson.

Library of Congress Control Number: 2009924132

Printed in China.
ISBN: 978-0-7643-3237-1

We are interested in hearing from authors with book ideas on related topics.

Published by Schiffer Publishing Ltd.
4880 Lower Valley Road
Atglen, PA 19310
Phone: (610) 593-1777
FAX: (610) 593-2002
E-mail: Info@schifferbooks.com.
Visit our web site at: www.schifferbooks.com
Please write for a free catalog.
This book may be purchased from the publisher.
Please include $5.00 postage.
Try your bookstore first.

In Europe, Schiffer books are distributed by:
Bushwood Books
6 Marksbury Avenue
Kew Gardens
Surrey TW9 4JF
England
Phone: 44 (0) 20 8392-8585
FAX: 44 (0) 20 8392-9876
E-mail: Info@bushwoodbooks.co.uk.

Contents

Introduction

This monograph had a modest beginning in January 2007 when Luc Dewez, a Belgian associate researcher, asked the 100th Bomb Group Association if there was any interest in posting on its website the results of his research on the March 6, 1944, Berlin Mission. His research, conducted many years ago, captured important information while many of the details were still fresh in the minds of the surviving 100th BG aircrews. We responded positively to Dewez's kind offer and in return received a remarkable piece of literature. Clearly, Luc's efforts could have been added to the web site without any further review and the story would have stopped there.

Those reading the manuscript were quickly convinced Luc's efforts provided a sound foundation for a more complete study of the 100th Bomb Group's (100BG) role during the 3, 4, 6, and 8 March 1944 missions to Berlin. We did miscalculate just how much time and effort would be required to make this transition. Moreover, initially, we were not even thinking about publishing the research as a book. All of us are volunteers who work full time jobs. Yet all of us are committed to one simple and direct objective; make High Noon Over Haseluenne the most complete and accurate account to date of the 100BG's involvement in the missions to Berlin. We did not foresee the "some small changes here and there" turning into over 18 months of "additional intensive research." The effort was unquestionably worthwhile. Luc and I uncovered many new and never before revealed facts and insights about the crews and the events surrounding all four of these missions to Berlin. We incorporated a cross section of first hand witness accounts with the historical facts through words and photos. We hope you enjoy the book as much as we did putting it together. Both authors encourage you to read Jeff Ethell's and Alfred Price's book Target: Berlin to give you an overall understanding of the 8th Air Force/Luftwaffe perspective for what you are about to read. Wherever possible, we have used the B-17 serial number along with the nickname associated with that plane to describe the aircraft flown on the missions.

As with any endeavor, High Noon Over Haseluenne is the result of a cooperative effort between the authors and those who witnessed the history, as well as those who research the history. In recognizing those who lent their special talents, the risk is inevitable that the efforts of some individuals may inadvertently be omitted. Any omission is a result of an oversight to which we ask in advance forgiveness. In combat and historical records you will find discrepancies, and we have tried in many circumstances to correct these, yet we have duplicated personal diaries "as is" so you will find that the frenzy of combat has clouded some of the facts. We have tried as much as possible to let the participants tell the stories of the missions as they unfolded.

First and foremost, we recognize the many individuals assigned to the 100BG, for they made the history to which we are committed to preserving for future generations. On a tiny little speck in East Anglia called Thorpe Abbotts, the ground echelon of the 100BG worked tirelessly in countless support activities to ensure the successful pursuit of the war effort in general, and more specifically to their friends, air crews composed of the young boys of yesterday, who climbed into their B-17s and flew the hazardous missions over occupied Europe between June 1943 and April 1945. Even if briefed as such, everyone knew there was no such thing as a 'milk run.' Death and tragedy, jointly associated with warfare, was present, just waiting to happen.

We appreciated the enthusiastic and kind responses to our inquiries. Robert Shoens, Don Hammond, and Ed Stone—who had shortened his name after the war from Silverstone—together provided additional insights to the inner workings of the combat crew of *Our Gal Sal*. This book really would not have come together without their recollections. The crew of *Our Gal Sal* have been and always will be linked historically to this one moment in time. We thank Bob, Ed, and Don for sharing their memories of the Berlin Missions. We also wish to thank John Gibbons and Frank Buschmeier from *Miss Irish*, who unhesitantly provided additional information on the 4 and 6 March missions to Berlin.

The following individuals also unselfishly provided important background information:

Paul West, Historian Emeritus, 100th Bomb Group Foundation.
Charles Harris, past President, 100th Bomb Group Foundation.
David E. Dorsey and Albert T. Keeler, 95th Bomb Group Association.
John S. Warner, 390th Memorial Museum Foundation.
Pat Foley, Mohave Museum of History and Arts.
Ron and Carol Bately, Thorpe Abbotts Tower Museum, Station 139, Diss, England.
William Cully, President 100th Bomb Group Foundation

We recognize the following individuals for their insights, contributions, and proof reading skills:

Paul M. Andrews, Project Bits and Pieces.
Mark Copeland, Historian for the 8th Air Force Historical Society
Ian Hawkins, Historian and Writer
Robert Shoens, Pilot *Our Gal Sal*
Jan Riddling, Historian and Membership, 100th Bomb Group Foundation
Cindy Goodman, Editor "Splasher 6," 100th Bomb Group Foundation Newsletter
Brian Thrailkill, B-17 Historian and sincere friend of the 100th Bomb Group
John Gilbert, 918th Bomb Group Living Memorial
Nancy Putnam, daughter of Capt. Gerald Putnam and a Historian

Finally, we thank all those who allowed us to probe deep into the recesses of their memories, stirring up images and voices from the past they might have rather left undisturbed.

Luc Dewez
Research Associate

Michael P. Faley
100th Bomb Group Historian
100th Bomb Group Photo Archivist
13th Combat Wing Historian

Prologue

For the young men who served in the Eighth Air Force (8AF) during World War II, one target evoked a sense of fear and weakness that made even the bravest man weak in the knees. "If you were an atheist, you found religion fast, if you were healthy as an ox before briefing, you were sick to your stomach when it ended." You sat there as the cigarette smoke hung like a pall over the room while the briefing officer pulled the curtain back further and further. Your eyes followed the red ribbon as it stretched from your base in England all the way across Germany.

Berlin was a target of strategic, political, and psychological importance. Air Marshall Sir Arthur 'Bomber' Harris and his Royal Air Force Bomber Command had already launched massive night bombing operations on Berlin. On the evening of November 18-19, 1943, the RAF dispatched 444 planes to Berlin. This was the first in what would be a series of 16 RAF Bomber Command attacks against the German capital. But where were the Americans and their 8th Air Force in England and 15th Air Force in the Mediterranean? When were they going to prove their theory of daylight precision bombing and hit Berlin? The enormous value of daylight operations against Berlin could not be ignored. The "around-the-clock" bombing of Berlin would bring convincingly the war to Hitler's very doorstep, to the city he envisioned to be the architectural showcase of the Third Reich, and to the very people that Hitler had promised "guns and butter."

Roland Knight and Operations officer Jack Kidd brief the 100th Bomb Group. Your Target for Today is...... Then you saw where it ended and your heart sank, that fresh egg breakfast was making its way back up, you fumbled for another cigarette, snapped open the Zippo, fired up, and took a deep drag as the operations officer announced: "Your target for today gentlemen is *Berlin!*"

The first 8AF alert for a mission against Berlin came in the evening of November 22, 1943. Even though there would be slightly more than 8 hours of daylight, the following morning the Crews were briefed for **Big B**. A round trip mission to Berlin would last over eight hours, so the Group would be landing in darkness, which was hazardous even in the best of weather conditions. One operations officer in the 8th AF remembered the experience this way:

"The night before the mission, the Squadron CO came up to me in the officers club and tells me I am flying tomorrow. It was our turn to lead so in that circumstance, the squadron CO or squadron operations officer flies the mission so I thought nothing more about it.[1] That is until the following morning at briefing. The next day was 23 Nov 43, we get to the briefing room and the curtain is pulled back, and there it is, Big-B Berlin! The legend goes that Brig. General Curtis LeMay was quoted as saying that "if only one plane returns from the mission, I will consider it a success."[2] I was so mad at my CO that I went up to him after briefing and said, "You knew the target was Berlin when you asked me to fly lead!" Well I am going to be that "one" plane that returns and I'm "going to kick your butt!" The planes took off but the mission was recalled due to bad weather. Upon returning to base, the young operations officer had cooled off enough to make the right career move. He could no longer work under his current CO so he went to the Group Operations officer and requested immediate transfer to another Squadron."[3]

Bad weather, lack of long-range fighter support, and limited daylight eventually compelled the operations planners to recall the mission. For the moment, the 8AF had dodged a big bullet.

PINETREE[4] was not to be denied, and again on December 12, 1943, the 100BG crews were briefed for Berlin. This time 10 minutes after briefing the operation was again cancelled. They were called back and briefed for Bremen, and this operation was scrubbed. Bad weather and dwindling daylight hours of winter compelled the mission planners to file the Berlin target folder away until late winter.

The winds of change were coming to the 8AF, making it possible to consider once again Berlin as a target. General 'Ike' Eisenhower was now the Supreme Commander of all Allied Forces in Europe. From his experience with General James H. Doolittle in North Africa and Operation Torch, Eisenhower knew that any success in a European invasion required command of the air. Eisenhower, on January 6, 1944, assigned General Ira Eaker to take command of the four air forces in the Mediterranean Theater of Operations and appointed General James H. Doolittle to be the Commanding General of the 8AF.[5] The edict to Doolittle: "Clear the skies." Without command of the air the anticipated invasion of Europe, scheduled for late spring or early summer of 1944, would become problematic. To accomplish this objective, Doolittle already started receiving sufficient numbers of the long-range P-51 fighter. Along with the P-47 and P-38, the P-51 afforded the 8AF the means to provide fighter escort to the heavy bombers to and from targets deep into Germany. When not defending the heavy bombers, this troika of fighters could bring the air war to the Luftwaffe in the air and on the ground.

General Doolittle also realized that he needed to lure the Luftwaffe up into the sky in order to destroy it, and the way to accomplish this was to strike at the very heart of the Third Reich. The air campaign took on a new tactic: bomb the strategic targets, such as aircraft manufacturing, industrial targets, and oil refineries on the ground, thereby taunting the Luftwaffe to come up to defend their country. Once the Luftwaffe was committed, the fighter escort along with the gunners in the bombers would deplete the Germans of irreplaceable combat tested pilots. To this end, a number of heavy bomber crews—B-17s and B-24s—saw themselves as the bait! Targets were now selected that would put extreme pressure on the German High Command and the Luftwaffe to defend their homeland.

On February 20, 1944, the plan went into full-scale effect with missions against the German aircraft facilities. Between 20 and 25 February 1944, the 8AF launched 3,300 sorties and released 6,000 tons of bombs on aircraft factories and airfields in what came to be known as **Big Week**. From the perspective of General Adolf Galland, one of the most famous German aces and a senior fighter leader, the "German Air Force lost over 1000 of its most experienced pilots between January and April 1944." He also stated that every bombing mission cost the vaulted Luftwaffe fifty pilots and machines. Galland understood that replacing experienced fighter pilots would further weaken the Luftwaffe's ability to defend strategic targets from the American bombers. He attributed these losses to the fine American pilots in the new long-range P-51 fighters and the "accuracy" of the gunners in the heavies. Albert Speer, German Minister of Armaments, expressed confidence in replacing the lost fighters, which he was able to accomplish.

Adolf Galland. (courtesy of Mark Copeland)

Ultimately, the lack of fuel limited the training of the new fighter pilots, which in turn exposed inexperienced, barely trained pilots to face the American daylight aerial onslaught of heavy bombers and fighters.

The 100BG's role during **Big Week** entailed hitting targets in Posen, Stettin, Alhorn, Vorden, Rostock, and Regensburg with a loss of only four crews. Operational fighter units equipped with sufficient numbers of P-51 fighters and long-range fuel drop tanks provided **PINETREE** mission planners with the means to provide fighter support to and from targets deep in Germany. The success of **Big Week** signaled that the time was near for **PINETREE** to readdress the target that got away from them in November and December 1943.

"No enemy bomber can reach the Ruhr. If one reaches the Ruhr, my name is not Göring. You may call me Meyer."

Reichsmarshall Herman Göring
September 1939

The RAF and the VIII Bomber Commands had long since reached the Ruhr, and many German citizens and political rivals had little if any difficulty in complying with Göring's boast, by calling the leader of the German Air Force Meyer. The time had arrived for the 8AF and the 100BG to accelerate the pressure on Göring and his Luftwaffe by bringing the war to Hitler's doorstep and taking command of the sky over occupied Europe. The time had come to strike **Big B**, Berlin!

Bomber Commands workhorse, a RAF Lancaster visits Thorpe Abbotts, Notice the quote by Goring. This Lancaster is now on display in the RAF museum at Hendon.

I

Lucky Strike!

2nd Lt Robert "Rosie" Rosenthal (2nd from Left) and 2nd Lt Gerald Putnam (3rd from Left) at Fort Meyers, Florida, 1943. (courtesy of Nancy Putnam)

On March 3, 1944, the 8AF was alerted for Berlin, only to have bad weather force the mission to be recalled after the heavy bombers had been dispatched. The "Hard Luck" group lived up to its name on this mission. Even with a recall, the 100BG lost three crews to enemy action. Through the heavy cloud cover and poor weather conditions some returning crews believed they witnessed a fiery explosion and concluded that there must have been a mid-air collision between two of the missing 100BG B-17s. Eventually the fate of 100BG B-17 231970 Berth'a the Blues, flown by Robert H. Lohof, was determined not to have been involved in a mid-air collision. The conclusion then was that the reported mid-air collision took place between Lt. John Gossage flying in 238017 One Mission Lulu and Lt. Robert Vollmer flying in 239817 Murderer's Row. Murderer's Row was named by Capt. Gerald Putnam for the famous batting order of the New York Yankees that included sluggers Babe Ruth and Lou Gerhig. Captain Putnam's Crew was originally assigned to the 100th BG in September 1943, along with another 2nd Lieutenant named Robert "Rosie" Rosenthal. Before coming overseas, both had served together at Ft Meyers as pilots for AT6 Gunnery training and accumulated a serious amount of stick time.

After completing about 20 missions, Lt Putnam was promoted to Captain (25 Jan 1944) and assigned as Operations Officer of the 349th BS. This required him to leave his original crew and be trained for Squadron and Group Leads. The 100th BG had four Squadrons (349, 350, 351, and 418), and whichever squadron was appointed to lead the 100th BG on any given mission it was the responsibility of the Squadron Commander or Operations Officer to fly along on the mission in the Lead plane (see Appendices A for squadron layout) and make sure everything went according to the mission "as briefed." Since the 349th BS was selected to lead the on March 3, 1944, Captain Gerald Putnam's responsibility was to be the 100BG Mission Leader. He was flying as Command Pilot with Captain Robert Lohof's seasoned lead Crew. Capt. Putnam recounts the mission as he saw it unfold:

"March 3 was the date, Berlin the target. The 100th lost three crews that day-Putnam/Lohof, Gossage, Vollmer. I remember the occasion well for obvious reasons but also because it was the first time I had served as acting Command Pilot as group leader-having flown Deputy Lead on two occasions prior to March 3. We were leading the 13th Combat Wing that day in a brand new plane with

Capt Gerald Putnam, 100th BG Command Pilot for March 3, 1944, mission to Berlin (courtesy of Nancy Putnam)

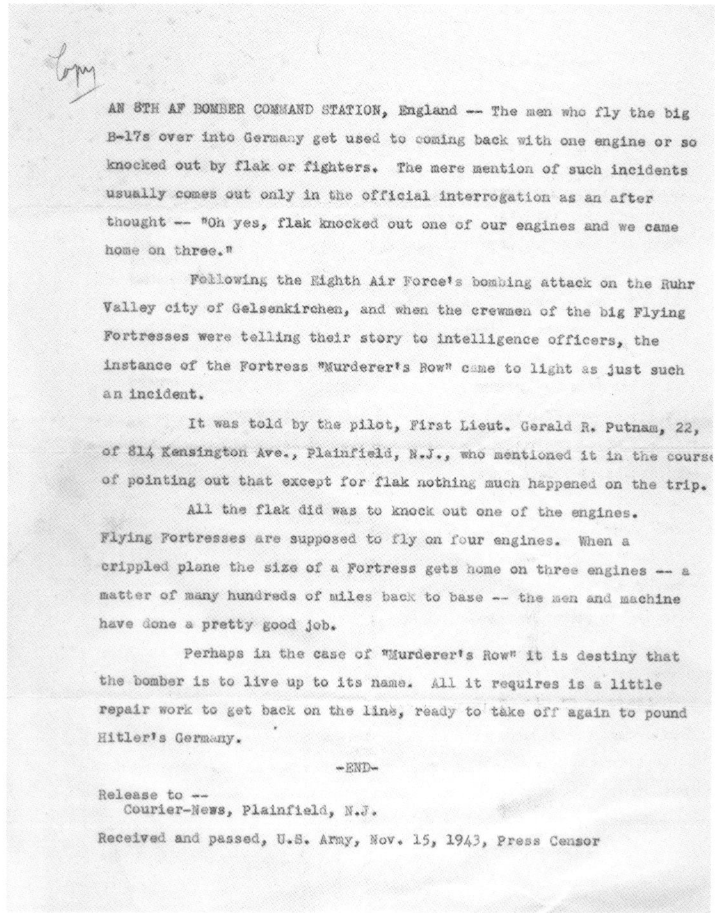

Copy

AN 8TH AF BOMBER COMMAND STATION, England -- The men who fly the big B-17s over into Germany get used to coming back with one engine or so knocked out by flak or fighters. The mere mention of such incidents usually comes out only in the official interrogation as an after thought -- "Oh yes, flak knocked out one of our engines and we came home on three."

Following the Eighth Air Force's bombing attack on the Ruhr Valley city of Gelsenkirchen, and when the crewmen of the big Flying Fortresses were telling their story to intelligence officers, the instance of the Fortress "Murderer's Row" came to light as just such an incident.

It was told by the pilot, First Lieut. Gerald R. Putnam, 22, of 814 Kensington Ave., Plainfield, N.J., who mentioned it in the course of pointing out that except for flak nothing much happened on the trip.

All the flak did was to knock out one of the engines. Flying Fortresses are supposed to fly on four engines. When a crippled plane the size of a Fortress gets home on three engines -- a matter of many hundreds of miles back to base -- the men and machine have done a pretty good job.

Perhaps in the case of "Murderer's Row" it is destiny that the bomber is to live up to its name. All it requires is a little repair work to get back on the line, ready to take off again to pound Hitler's Germany.

-END-

Release to --
Courier-News, Plainfield, N.J.

Received and passed, U.S. Army, Nov. 15, 1943, Press Censor

Putnam's vast flying experience and coolness under fire was evident by this official press release on only his second mission: 8th AF press release on *Murderer's Row.* (courtesy of Nancy Putnam)

the latest electronic and bombsight equipment but a very defective radio. When the recall went out, we did not receive it and very shortly found ourselves in thick soup over Germany. Afraid to turn the group back into the following waves, we decided to climb on course for ten minutes before turning and heading back. By that time, we had lost visual contact with all except our wingmen- Gossage and Vollmer. Before the 10 minutes were up, we started breaking out of the clouds, just in time to be met by three FW-190s coming at us from the sun. Nuff said, the rest is history."[6]

"One minute we were heading for home and the next we're bailing out!" That is how Sidney Goldenberg (TTE- Top Turret Engineer on Capt. Lohof's Crew) remembered the events of March 3, 1944:

"The pilot announced we were turning back, so I disconnected from my oxygen, grabbed a walk around oxygen bottle, and went to check on fuel. I heard gunfire...Pilot came on the intercom and said "We're Hit!" We're going down, Bail Out! There were

Murderer's Row 239817, flown by Lt Volmer Crew on March 3, 1944.

injuries. I had to push the Bombardier out the hatch. We were in clouds, didn't even know if we were over land or water. It was snowing heavily, difficult to breathe or see. Could see land just before hitting ground. Was met by angry civilians. During interrogation the Germans told me the whole crew was captured, that Capt. Putnam was not my regular pilot… I acted as if I did not know him."

All ten men on the Putnam/Lohof Crew safely parachuted into northern Germany and were taken prisoner. George Briggs, the tail gunner, died while in captivity. Although there seems to be a discrepancy as to the true nature of his passing, official records state:

"At 0200 on April 9, 1945 at a barn in Wohlen, Germany, S/Sgt George W.Briggs (Ser #39 193 615, TG of the Capt Robert H. Lohof crew, (which crashed March 3, 1944 @ Berlin), was suddenly overcome by violent shaking of the entire body & soon went into a coma."

But according to Sid Goldstein, as the War dragged on, the SS took over the POW camps from the Luftwaffe in late 1944. From that point on things got very serious, and tensions built rapidly on both sides inside the camp. It seems that during a curfew Briggs was sighted outside the barracks and shot by a guard. He died some days later of an infection that had set in. This event cannot be confirmed nor denied at this point and is still a question left unanswered 64 years later. The only thing certain is that this young man survived bailing out of a disintegrating airplane and over one year as a prisoner of war, only to die less than a month before the end of the War.

G.W.Briggs' headstone at Ardennes American Military Cemetery in Belgium.

March 3, 1944-BERLIN. Flying his 14th mission, Lt. Vollmer flew on Captain Lohof's left wing, # 3 position, on this day. Vollmer recalled picking up the recall message, but tried vainly to contact the lead plane via *'code gun'* in order not to break radio silence. Vollmer figured they had time to figure it all out, so elected to maintain radio silence. Hardly had the three planes emerged from the overcast than six FW-190s knocked Lt. Vollmer and Captain Lohof - Captain Putnam down on the first pass, and seriously damaged Lt. Gossage.[7] Front row, left to right: 2nd Lt. Edward G. Sullivan, NAV; 2nd Lt. Robert C. Vollmer, P; 2nd Lt. John W. Adams III, CP; 2nd Lt. Robert S. Connell, Bom. Back row, left to right: S/Sgt Thomas H. Mullerix, LWG; S/Sgt Donald W. Becker, RWG; S/Sgt George W. Wood, TG; T/Sgt Richard C. Hull, TTE; S/Sgt Don Guthrie, BTG; and T/Sgt Elias M. Johnson, ROG.

Based on research it is likely that Lohof-Putnam, Vollmer, and Gossage ran into the FW190s of I/JG 11 led by Hauptmann Rolf-Gunter Hermichen. His tally of confirmed victories includes shooting down a B-17 on March 3, 1944. Three days later, JG 11 would square off with the 100th BG again over Haseluenne.

Lt Robert Vollmer would find out about the 100th's famous reputation the hard way. On his first 48 hour leave to London someone asked him what unit he was with. When he told them, "they just shook their head and said, 'Too bad.'"

On 3 March his crew was flying in Capt Putnam's' old ride, *Murderer's Row*. They had just broken out of the never ending cloud bank when the FW190s attacked head on. The sky just lit up with 20mm shells heading for the three bombers. There was no time for any evasive action; Vollmer's ship was hit by 20mm cannon

Three photos of Lt Bill Vaden (navigator, Capt Robert H. Lohof's crew). Left, probably late 1942, at Victorville, CA; centre, unofficial portrait studio photo (stateside), right, POW photo, *Dulag Luft*, Frankfurt, Germany, approx. 6 Mar 1944 (shot down 3 Mar 1944).

Capt. Lohof's Crew Stateside.

shells that exploded in the cockpit and ignited hydraulic fluid and knocked out the oxygen system. At 31,000 feet, Lt Vollmer and co-pilot 2Lt John W. Adams III quickly lost consciousness before they could get to their walk-around oxygen bottles. For a period of time *Murderer's Row* flew itself, alternately diving and climbing. Vollmer recalled in his semi-conscious state vaguely feeling the Gs build at the bottom of a dive. Finally, the fire-weakened plane broke up and the unconscious Vollmer came to falling with aircraft debris all around him. He delayed pulling his D-ring for his chute, waiting instead to fall clear of the debris. He remembered the cold conditions, with snow literally blowing up at him as he fell. Finally he deployed his chute near the ground. As he came down, his chute was swinging almost 180 degrees back and forth. As he approached the ground, he pulled the lanyards in an attempt to better position himself for landing, but he swung out one final time, face to the ground, and just as his momentum built coming back down he hit. The wicked blow knocked him out cold and hurt his leg very badly. Five men failed to escape the wreck and were KIA. The remaining five were somehow able to escape the wreck and parachute down, only to be taken prisoner. Lt Vollmer was one of them. Next stop for him was the South Compound at Stalag Luft I (POW camp) in Barth, Germany, where he joined Capt Lohof and Capt Putnam.

A somewhat clearer picture of events is given in a letter from Lt Robert Vollmer to S/Sgt John Miller:[8]

"Our element remained together and broke out on top of the clouds at 31,000 feet. For the next five or ten minutes it looked like the mighty 8th Air Force, consisting now of only three B-17s,was going to try to make the first strike on Big B. It didn't last long. A bunch of FWs hit us from about 2 o'clock high and got all of us. Two shells exploded in the cockpit, starting a fire in front of the rudder pedals and causing flames to come through my oxygen mask. At that altitude, I was unable to secure the walk around bottle before losing consciousness. The plane then dived and climbed alternately until it finally broke up. I don't know how I got out, but I did parachute with debris falling all around me. Five of the men on my crew died that day. Bob Lohof was leading the 349th. John Gossage was on right wing, and I was on the left. Lohof was leading the 100th. His radio operator did not receive

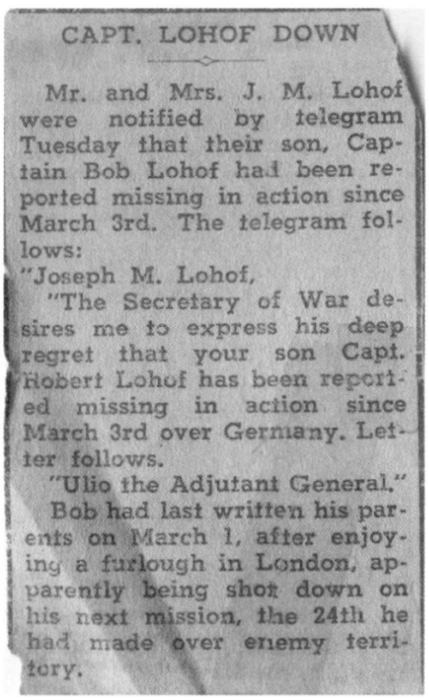

CAPT. LOHOF DOWN

Mr. and Mrs. J. M. Lohof were notified by telegram Tuesday that their son, Captain Bob Lohof had been reported missing in action since March 3rd. The telegram follows:

"Joseph M. Lohof,

"The Secretary of War desires me to express his deep regret that your son Capt. Robert Lohof has been reported missing in action since March 3rd over Germany. Letter follows.

"Ulio the Adjutant General."

Bob had last written his parents on March 1, after enjoying a furlough in London, apparently being shot down on his next mission, the 24th he had made over enemy territory.

Robert H. Lohof
349th BS
POW 3 Mar 44 Berlin

the recall message and we were unable to convince him, so we continued . . . . (Many years later, Bob showed distinct frustration over why Lohof/Putnam didn't pick up the recall message—What Vollmer did not know was that Lohof's radio was faulty)."

The break up of Vollmer's aircraft may well be the "fiery explosion" that returning crews presumed to be a mid-air collision. The wreckage of Vollmer's plane landed at Drage at 11:40hrs. That is near Iztehoe, in Holstein.

In a letter from 2nd Lt "Sully" Sullivan, navigator on Lt Vollmer's crew, to the Parents of John Adams:

"I am writing to you with deepest sympathy the details you have been so anxious to learn about Jack. It is very difficult for me to write this sad news, but knowing that Jack went fast, and there wasn't any long-suffering may ease your mind a little. Jack was gone on the first burst of enemy fire. It all happened in a matter of seconds. We were flying on the leaders' left wing in the clouds and the fighter attack was a complete surprise. It was from high on the right side. The Germans shot down all three planes in our element and Jack never knew our plane exploded in mid-air. Why some of us were spared that day is only a miracle.

All the words of praise will not bring him back. Whenever I speak of Jack, I tell of the fine courage and spirit he possessed. You can be very proud of him; he was a commendable officer and set an excellent example for our crew throughout the entirety of our flying days.

Again I wish to express my heartfelt sympathy to you and Jack's father for the unhealed scar this war has brought upon you.

Sincerely,
Sully"

John Miller, flying with Lt Cowan's Crew on March 3, 1944, recalled the action that day in a letter to Ed Adams, brother of Lt Vollmer's copilot, Lt John Adams III (see below).

The biggest mystery was the fate of Lt John Gossage and his Crew. The last anyone had heard, was that his B-17 was too damaged to return to England so he was setting a course for neutral Sweden. When word did not arrive from Sweden that the crew had been interned, everyone speculated that the Gossage Crew was shot down and either KIA or POW. It would not be until after the war that the true story could be sorted out.

Lt. John Gossage, flying in 238017 XR-O, *One Mission Lulu*, was damaged by fighters on the first pass and left T/Sgt Arthur Cooper (Top Turret Engineer) badly wounded. Over the VHF radio the pilot stated his intentions to take the damaged bomber to a safe haven in Sweden. Unfortunately, the crew mistook the Schleswig-Jagel air field in Germany to be Sweden and Lt. Gossage inadvertently delivered the Germans their first intact B-17G. Instead of hearing the sweet sound of "welcome to Sweden," they were greeted by a different refrain "for you the war is over." All ten became "guests" of the Luftwaffe in POW camps. *One Mission Lulu* was not the first B-17 acquired in flying condition by the Luftwaffe. This and other captured Allied aircraft were later operated by the Luftwaffe for training and to indoctrinate new crews on the best tactics to attack the B-17. It is also reported that some aircraft may have been flown operationally against 8AF bomber formations.

According to the German information available, the battle damage to *One Mission Lulu* was repaired and #1 engine was replaced by personnel of Nachtjagdgeschwader (NJG) 3 at Schleswig. Test trials on B-17G 238017 took place in Rechlin, Germany (this was the Luftwaffe's main testing ground for new aircraft designs), to find out the aircraft's capabilities. *One*

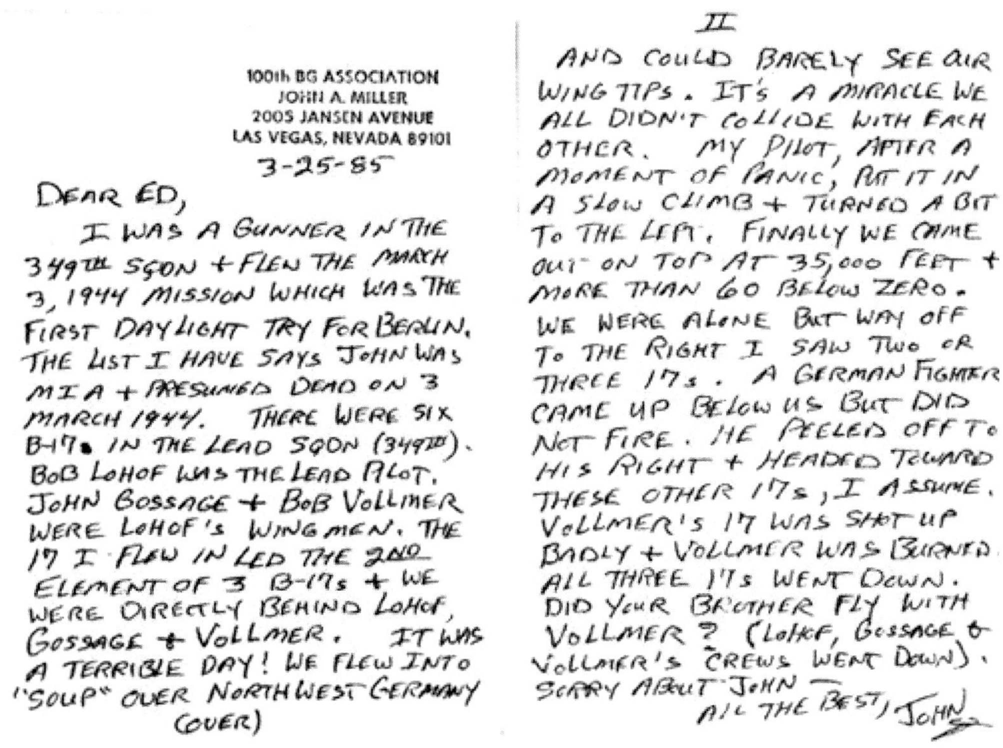
100th BG ASSOCIATION
JOHN A. MILLER
2005 JANSEN AVENUE
LAS VEGAS, NEVADA 89101
3-25-85

DEAR ED,
I WAS A GUNNER IN THE 349TH SQDN + FLEW THE MARCH 3, 1944 MISSION WHICH WAS THE FIRST DAYLIGHT TRY FOR BERLIN. THE LIST I HAVE SAYS JOHN WAS MIA + PRESUMED DEAD ON 3 MARCH 1944. THERE WERE SIX B-17s IN THE LEAD SQDN (349TH). BOB LOHOF WAS THE LEAD PILOT. JOHN GOSSAGE + BOB VOLLMER WERE LOHOF'S WINGMEN. THE 17 I FLEW IN LED THE 2ND ELEMENT OF 3 B-17s + WE WERE DIRECTLY BEHIND LOHOF, GOSSAGE + VOLLMER. IT WAS A TERRIBLE DAY! WE FLEW INTO "SOUP" OVER NORTHWEST GERMANY
(OVER)

II
AND COULD BARELY SEE OUR WING TIPS. IT'S A MIRACLE WE ALL DIDN'T COLLIDE WITH EACH OTHER. MY PILOT, AFTER A MOMENT OF PANIC, PUT IT IN A SLOW CLIMB + TURNED A BIT TO THE LEFT. FINALLY WE CAME OUT ON TOP AT 35,000 FEET + MORE THAN 60 BELOW ZERO. WE WERE ALONE BUT WAY OFF TO THE RIGHT I SAW TWO OR THREE 17s. A GERMAN FIGHTER CAME UP BELOW US BUT DID NOT FIRE. HE PEELED OFF TO HIS RIGHT + HEADED TOWARD THESE OTHER 17s, I ASSUME. VOLLMER'S 17 WAS SHOT UP BADLY + VOLLMER WAS BURNED. ALL THREE 17s WENT DOWN. DID YOUR BROTHER FLY WITH VOLLMER? (LOHOF, GOSSAGE & VOLLMER'S CREWS WENT DOWN). SORRY ABOUT JOHN —
ALL THE BEST, JOHN

S/Sgt John A. Miller's letter.

Lt Gossage's 238017 XR-O on March 3, 1944, at Schleswig-Jagel airfield in Germany.

Center, right and following: Lt Gossage's *One Mission Lulu* (238017 XR-O) at Schleswig-Jagel AF March 3, 1944. (all photos courtesy of Hans-Heiri Stapfer)

Mission Lulu was transferred to the Luftwaffe's top secret unit, Kampfgeschwader 200 (KG 200), in the spring of 1944 and probably coded A3+GE. This unit's mission was clandestine operations, which included dropping German agents behind enemy lines. Final disposition of this aircraft is still a mystery.[9]

The remainder of the 100BG jettisoned their bombs in the North Sea and returned to Station 139, Thorpe Abbotts. The crews knew what was coming next; they were turned back by weather today, but sooner or later they would be heading back to Berlin.

2nd Lt Robert W. Bailie, copilot on Lt Francis Malooly's Crew, collected his thoughts and wrote the following after the March 3, 1944, mission:

"Mission to Berlin. On way there ran into heavy cloud wall at 28,000 ft. Started through in formation. We broke through at 30,000 ft. alone, others having turned back because of a recall, which we didn't receive. A sqdn of FW were sitting there waiting for us. Saw a small formation of 17's at 2 o'clock about 5 mi. off. Trying to reach them, we were attacked several times. Looked back behind us and saw two B-17's break through clouds and collide exploding. No chutes seen. Made a diving turn to the left and had to drop bombs to keep from tearing wings off. It also helped us gain a little speed. This was about 20 mi west of Hamburg. Reached group of 8 ships of the 95th that were split from their group. Turned on heading home, and was attacked again by FW's and Me 109's. Shot our way through, dropping one Me 109.

Our P-47 and P-51 escort finally reached us and from there on didn't have any trouble.

On way back saw B-24 ditch in 'channel.' Circled ship and radioed position to Air Sea Rescue. Back home learned we lost 4 ships. Two groups ran together in clouds . Only 6 ships got out. Mission not complete and a very serious mistake was made by not recalling it sooner. We were very lucky to get back. I hope they won't all be this rough. It was to be the first time USAAF has ever

Original Gossage crew (left to right). Kneeling: John Gossage (P), William Grier (CP), Walter Nichols (NAV), and Theodore Don (BOM). Standing: William Humphrey (TTE would be shot down on Lt Vollmer's Crew on March 3, 1944), Ralph Schulte (RWG), Michael Gillen (ROG), Francis DeCooman (BTG), Clyde Lovell (LWG), and Bruce Alshouse (TG, would complete his 25th mission on March 6, 1944, flying with Lt Harrison's Crew).

bombed Berlin. On alert again for tomorrow. Time 71/2 hrs (of HELL)."

Lt Ed Stern described the action in Lt Massol's a/c *Fever Beaver* (238047) that day:[10]

"One of the biggest fiascos I can remember took place on March 3rd 1944; we were assigned Berlin as the target for the first time. I remember the combined gasp of surprise and dread that arose from the assembled airmen when the curtain was pulled back from the wall map and that long red ribbon stretched from the English coast to Berlin…

When the word to abort finally came, turning planes began to run into each other. Only with some luck and great skill by pilots Massol and Granger did we avert colliding with other aircraft. We tried to climb above the clouds, impossible! So Massol then took us down on the deck where the props were whipping up the water.

This was not the solution so we again climbed to altitude and broke out into the open over Holland, only to be pursued by FW 190's. We dove back into the clouds, changed course and headed back for England. We made it back to the base late in the day, short on fuel and completely unnerved and exhausted."

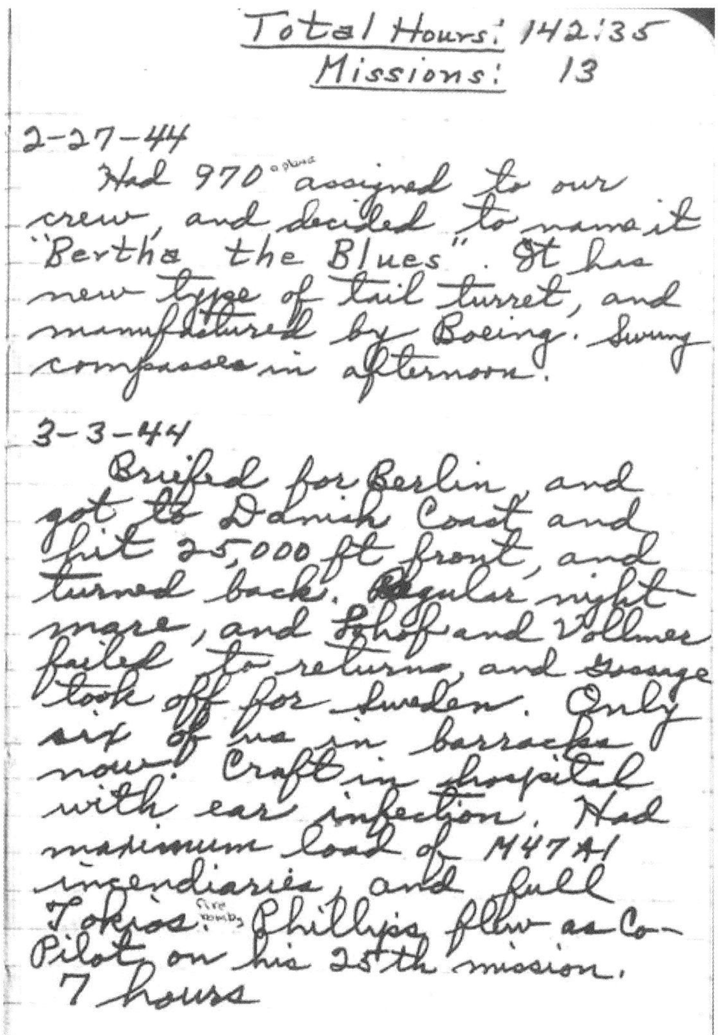

Total Hours: 142:35
Missions: 13

2-27-44
Had 970 (plane) assigned to our crew, and decided to name it "Bertha the Blues". It has new type of tail turret, and manufactured by Boeing. Swung compasses in afternoon.

3-3-44
Briefed for Berlin, and got to Danish Coast and hit 25,000 ft front, and turned back. Regular night-mare, and Lohof and Vollmer failed to return, and Gossage took off for Sweden. Only six of us in barracks now. Craft in hospital with ear infection. Had maximum load of M47A1 incendiaries and full Tokios (fire bombs). Phillips flew as Co-Pilot on his 25th mission. 7 hours

Upon his return to base, Lt. Orrin Heinrich, navigator on the Murray Crew, wrote in his diary:

"3-3-44

Briefed for Berlin and got to Danish coast and hit 25,000 ft front, and turned back. Regular nightmare, and Lohof and Vollmer failed to return and Gossage took of for Sweden. Only six of us in barracks now. Craft in hospital with ear infection. Had maximum load of M47 A-1 incendiaries and full Tokios. Phillips flew as Co-Pilot on his 25th mission. 7 hours."

The actual loss of 100 BG aircraft on March 3, 1944, was three planes. Twenty-five men were POWs while five were KIA.

Final notations on March 3, 1944: Lt Sam Barrick wrote the following in his Diary for March 3, 1944: "Group recalled on way in. Three B-17s missing."

Major Marvin "Red" Bowman, 100th BG S-2 Intelligence, entered in his diary: "Mar 3, 1944 Group took off for Berlin - ran into weather over France and returned. Gossage landed in Sweden - Vollmer and Lohof missing. Division Leader ordered a return at the Schleswig - Holstein coast."

Eighth Air Force Combat Chronology
Friday, 3 March 1944

STRATEGIC OPERATIONS (Eighth Air Force): Mission 246: 555 B-17s and 193 B-24s are dispatched to industrial areas and aviation industry plants at Berlin, Erkner, and Oranienburg, but deteriorating weather and dense contrails force the formations to abort or seek targets of opportunity, i.e.:

1. Nine of 555 B-17s are lost: 61 hit Wilhelmshaven and 14 hit targets of opportunity; casualties are 2 KIA, 3 WIA, and 83 MIA.
2. Two of 193 B-24s are lost and only 4 hit targets of opportunity; casualties are 3 KIA, 8 WIA, and 20 MIA. The bombers claim 3-1-1 Luftwaffe aircraft. Escort is provided by 89 P-38s, 484 Eighth and Ninth Air Force P-47s, and 130 Eighth and Ninth Air Force P-51s; claims and losses are:

1. One P-38 is lost and 1 damaged; 1 pilot is MIA.
2. One P-47 is damaged beyond repair and 13 damaged; 1 pilot is WIA.
3. P-51s claim 8-1-3 Luftwaffe aircraft; 6 P-51s are lost; 5 pilots are MIA. During a CARPETBAGGER mission on the night of 3/4 Mar, Two B-24s are lost.

With 3 March being a recall, the target that had been contemplated and briefed in November and December 1943 would again be assigned for the next day. Mission #247, March 4, 1944, the 8AF dispatched 502 B-17s heading towards the most heavily defended target in Germany—Berlin.

* * *

Exerpts from
"My Twenty-Fourth Mission
With The Hundredth Bomb Group"
by Earl L. Richardson, Major USAF (Retired)

"It was an early and dark March 4, 1944 at Thorpe Abbots, England. Day of the first Eighth Air Force maximum-effort bombing mission to Berlin. The ships were taking off one by one into the snowy morning gliding over the runway wet and slick. Pilot Barrick and crew craned their necks as the thirty-ton monster lifted into the air. The clouds formed a canopy at twenty-five thousand feet and the temperature was fifty-six below.

... This was my 24th mission, the first without Jack Flanigan's crew and without my lucky charm 'Royal Flush.' Fortunately, the pathfinder mission to Berlin went uneventful for our plane. The flak was heavy for there were over four hundred anti-aircraft guns."

Lt Earl Richardson is first person standing on the left in the back row. Seen here with Lt Flanigan's Crew in front of "lucky charm" *Royal Flush*.

Lt. Colonel Harry Griffin 'Griff' Mumford and his pilot, Lt. Alvin Brown, in 231320 *I'll Be Around* of the 95BG found themselves not part of 502 heavy bombers targeting Berlin, but instead leading a force of thirty-one ships (18 from the 95BG, 1 from the 482BG (Pathfinder), and 12 of the 100BG). As with a number of previous 8AF operations, weather forced yet another recall. Yet again, this recall was not complete. Nonetheless, Mumford and his force of thirty-one ships were determined to bomb 'Big-B.' Captain Magee Fuller, 100BG leader that day, confirmed, "thirty-one B-17s had gone over Berlin," with nine of them coming from the 350 Bomb Squadron. Many personal reports below will say anywhere from ten to thirteen aircraft participated from the 100BG on this mission. Twelve is what the authors and historians can verify. Lt. John P. '49 Missions' Gibbons of the 100BG, flying in 239830 *Berlin Playboy*, recalls:

"We were briefed that we would be flying as the low squadron with the 95th Bomb Group and would meet up with them over the designated radio beacon [called Bunchers]. I was concerned because I had flown only one mission prior to this and that was as a copilot to gain combat experience. We were now going to be flying with another group and I had not received much instruction on forming up over beacons so I was not sure I could locate the 95th."

The rendezvous did take place, and the 100BG was echeloned into the low position of the 95 **B** Group. Lt. Gibbons continues:

"Probably about 3 hours into the mission through tremendous clouds, half the time we never saw the flight in front of us, we started to receive a recall signal. My radio operator told me that we were being recalled. So I did everything with my copilot to motion to the flight leader that we had a recall."

It seems that just after the bomber stream entered Germany, a VHF recall signal was heard by all the B-17 radio operators. One by one, the formations started turning around and heading back to England. That is, all but one—Mumford's. It has been often reported that the group did not receive the correct recall signal. The radio operator in the lead plane, S/Sgt. Frank Atterbury, received the 'Return to Base' signal but informed Lt. Colonel Mumford the recall message did not meet with the Standard Operating Procedure (SOP). They thought the signal was a hoax, a German rouse to divert them from the target. Nonetheless, as the formations headed

Lt Harrison in *Messie Bessie* on March 4, 1944.

Lt Col Griff Mumford and Gen James Doolittle. (USAF)

back to England, Lt. Colonel Mumford and Lt. Brown, flying along with the rest of the crew in *I'll Be Around*, continued on to Berlin with the small composite task force.

Flying in the waist gun position in Gibbons' plane was S/Sgt. Frank Buschmeier, who remembered that the mission called for two forces to split off and hit Berlin from the North and South:

"Half way there I saw all these planes turn and thought it was part of the plan. I didn't know a damn thing was wrong until we hit Berlin."

In 231320 *I'll Be Around*, the 95BG lead plane, Lt. Colonel Mumford reflected on the thoughts that occurred to him as the small force of B-17s approached Berlin at 28,000 feet:

"Stinking weather, fighter attacks, and flak over Berlin so heavy it could be walked upon....God is it cold! . . . Minus 65 degrees! . . . Look at the flak!. . .The bastards must have all 2,500 guns operational today. . . .This has to be the longest bomb run yet. . . . Look at that gaping hole in the left wing of number three in the low element. . . .an 88mm must have gone right through. . . .Damn, won't we ever drop those bombs! . . .Boy, that was close, listen to the spent shrapnel hitting the airplane."[11]

In the Low Group, flying in 239830 *Berlin Playboy*, Lt. Gibbons relates what happened next:

"You see I was just a naïve 2nd Lieutenant so I didn't speak up more on the interphone when trying to reach the lead plane about the recall. I just figured he knew what he was doing. The recall was disregarded and we went onto Berlin. I think we were at 26,000 feet and the plane felt like mush through the air. The prettiest part of the mission was the site of two P-38's over Berlin.[12] That at least gave me the confidence that we were going to make it back. . . .maybe!"

Back in the waist, S/Sgt Frank Buschmeier heard Lt Sterling Blakeman, the Bombardier, yell out over the intercom:

"Jesus Christ! I have never seen so many fighters in all my damn life, 12 O'Clock High, 30 of em!"

As the German fighters came screaming down through the formation, Frank Buschmeier took aim and pressed the firing button. Click! Nothing! His gun would not fire. Even though the 50cal. worked over the North Sea[13] when the crew test fired all the guns, it now seemed the temperature at high altitude had caused the gun to freeze up. Now all he could do was keep his gun in motion to give the fighters the impression his gun was lethal, watch the show unfold in front of his window, and pray:

"What I remember most about the March 4th mission to Berlin was looking down at the enormous size of the city and seeing the flak coming up, how damn good the enemy fighter pilots were and how mad I was when my gun wouldn't fire!"

In the 100BG composite group, 239872 *Rubber Check*, piloted by Lt. Frank Granack, approached Berlin. T/Sgt. Harold Stearns, the top turret gunner, bracketed a fighter bearing down on *Rubber Check*. As Stearns recalled:[14]

"My pilot called out:

'Hal, a fighter is coming out of the sun at 12 O'clock high! Do you see him?'

The Franklin A. Granack crew after return from Berlin 4 Mar 44. Kneeling (Left to Right): Lloyd H. Rogers (Ball Turret Gunner), Glen D. Brown (Right Waist Gunner), Harold Stearns (Top Turret – Engineer), Robert L. Dunham (Copilot), and Grant D. Scott (Radio Operator - Gunner). Standing: George C. Christian (Tail Gunner), Murray Geisler (Navigator), Franklin A. Granack (Pilot), Joseph F. Kawiecki (Bombardier), and Edward T. Harrell (Left Waist Gunner).

I turned my turret around and again Frank called out:

'Hal do you see him?'

'I've got'em but he is too far out!'

At 700 yards I got'em in my sights and let off a short burst, then at 400 yards, I let out another burst! Lt. Murray Geisler, our navigator, said:

'You got'em Hal, he's on fire, he's going down!'"

S/Sgt. Brown "Brownie"(Waist Gunner) saw him go into the ground. T/Sgt. Stearns would be credited with shooting down the first fighter over Berlin by the 8th Air Force.

Buschmeiers' 50 cal was not the only thing frozen. While on the bomb run, the 95th BG lead squadron B-17, *I'll Be Around*, had a problem with its bomb-bay doors; they had frozen shut. Therefore, the honor of being the first crew to bomb Berlin went to Lt Bill Owen and his Pathfinder crew from the 482nd Bomb Group out of Alconbury. They were flying the number 2 position to the right of Mumford's aircraft. This was a very unusual procedure, since the Command Pilot for a mission usually flew in the PFF radar equipped aircraft. Lt. Colonel Mumford had requested that he fly with his own 95th BG lead crew and the PFF fly off his wing. This way if the weather was bad over Berlin, the PFF could take over and the group could bomb by radar. After bombs away, the group turned off the target and started the long trip back across Germany to England. The flying was tedious and nerve wracking. They were flying in horrendous weather, a solid layer of clouds

The First Heavy Bomber of the 8AF to Bomb Berlin March 4, 1944, B-17F 42-30731 equipped with RAF H2S "Stinky" radar, assigned to the 482BG (P). Standing: Ground Engineering Officer, Lt. Bill Owen (Pilot); T/Sgt. Don White (Top Turret/Engineer); and S/Sgt. Harlen "Hoppy" Sours (Waist Gunner). S/Sgt.George Moffat (Ball Turret Gunner), T/Sgt. Ed Aken (Radio Operator), S/Sgt. Ellsworth Beans (Waist Gunner), S/Sgt. John O'Neil (Tail Gunner, flew as Waist Gunner March 4th), Lt.Al Engelhardt (Navigator), Lt. Marshall Thixton (Bombardier), and Lt. Frank McAllister (Copilot). Kneeling: Ground Crew. Missing from the photo is 2nd Lt. Bill Milton who flew in the tail as a Formation Officer. (Photo: John O'Neil)

Lt Stanley Seaton, POW March 4, 1944, mission to Berlin. (courtesy of Robert Shoens)

S/Sgt. Leming Hull's headstone at Netherlands American Cemetery.

Seaton's *Sad Sack* 238016 over Berlin, March 4, 1944, by Ron Leigh.

with "squalls of fighters." In the ensuing battle, the 95BG lost the crews of Lt. Brownlow, Lt. Worthy, Lt. Dunham, and Lt. Roehm. The 100BG lost one crew, Lt. Stanley Seaton, flying in 238016 *Seaton's Sad Sack*.

According to the Toggler on Seaton's plane, T/Sgt. George Ofiesh, the plane fell behind the rest of the group because one of the incendiaries was "hung up" in the bomb bay:

"After jettisoning the hung up bomb over Berlin, a Me 109 came in from about two o'clock and unloaded on us. We sustained crippling damage to the engines."

Lt. Mark Wilson, flying in 23534 *Ol' Dad*, remembers seeing a fighter hitting *Seaton's Sad Sack* from the 7 o'clock position, raking the tail section with 20mm cannon fire, and Lt. Chadwick flying in 23413 *Hard Luck!* reported: "a B-17 about 1000 yards behind salvoed its bombs and turned back with #2 & #3 engines smoking." Lt. Seaton rang the bailout bell and the crew "hit the silk." Everyone that is except for tail gunner S/Sgt. Lemming Hull, who went down with the aircraft. The 20mm fire from the Me 109 most likely killed him.

A translation of a German report provides the following information:

"On 4 Mar 1944, at 1500 hours, a four engine enemy aircraft crashed, approximately 1 km north of the village of Kesseling [District of Ahrweiler]. The a/c exploded on the ground when it crashed. It burned completely and could not be salvaged. Type unknown. Leming Hull, 35671600 T 43 S Sgt. DEAD. The rest of the crew bailed out and were captured. They were sent to Vulag [Luft] Oberursel on 5 Mar 1944. The deceased was interred on 6 Mar 44, in the Community Cemetery in Kesseling."

Many years later, William Sapp, right waist gunner on *Snort Stuff*, received a copy of Lt Sam Barrick's diary kept during the war. The entry in Barrick's diary for 4 March reads:

"4 Mar 1944 6:00hrs A/C 994 Briefed target - Berlin, Germany

Force recalled, turned back near Kassel, Germany. Couldn't find B group, went in with 95th.

Two FW-190s and one Me-109 passed at us. P-47 escorts knocked them down. Some flak, not bad.

Alt 27,000'. Ten from 100th went over the target. Seaton down. Takeoff in snow storm and landed in snow storm. Richardson [Lt Earl Richardson] flew with us as Bombardier, Henry [Lt James M. Henry] in hospital."

On the way home Lt Col. Mumford reflected on just how lucky he was to be flying with Lt. Al Brown's crew. "This is as fine tuned a crew as any I have flown with." Upon touching down back at Station 119, Horham, home base for the 95BG, Mumford thought to himself: "We made it, Wonder what old 'Iron Ass' LeMay [Gen. Curtis E. LeMay, Commanding General of the 3rd Air Division] will think of the show his boys put on today."[15] LeMay thought enough of the show to award 'Griff' the Silver Star and Lt. Brown the Distinguished Flying Cross (DFC). Later in press reports, the raiders would complain about the six-mile high clouds that made formation flying hazardous, curse the cold, and give thanks to the fighter support that arrived in the nick of time. 'Griff' Mumford elaborates in *Stars and Stripes*:

"Goin in wasn't tough, the weather was pretty bad, clouds were broken and it was cold, down to 65 degrees below zero. My navigator Lt Malcolm Durr deserves all the credit; he saw enough ground points to set us up for the bomb run. Then the clouds closed in again and the bombing was done through the clouds (PFF). I am sure we hit the place.....How do I feel knowing we were the first Americans to bomb Berlin? Well, I know I felt a helluva lot of satisfaction… Fighters? I saw three Me 109's lined up and coming

Lt. Brown's crew with Lt. Colonel *'Griff'* Mumford in front of 231320 *I'll Be Around*. (Photo: USAF)

95th BG crews back from Berlin. (Photo: USAF)

into us when ZOOM! Down came a bunch of P-51's and that was the last I saw of the Luftwaffe on the whole trip."

Over at Thorpe Abbotts, the press interviewed and the photographers took photographs of T/Sgt. Stearns about his exploits over Berlin. The press would splash his photo and story on the front page of newspapers across America. On March 5, 1944, Harold wrote to his parents:

"Dearest Mother and Dad,

This has been a day of grace. I have had a pretty busy week. Don't be surprised when you read the papers. By the time you get this, you will know I have gotten credit for an enemy fighter.

Dad, remember what you told me about shooting straight. I've always gone up with those words pounding in my head. I'll write a letter tomorrow.

Love to All
Harold"

Brig, General Curtis LeMay pinning Silver Star on Lt. Colonel *'Griff'* Mumford for his role in the March 4, 1944, Berlin mission. (Photo: USAF)

T/Sgt. Harold Stearns, far right, after the March 4, 1944, mission to Berlin. (Photo: USAF)

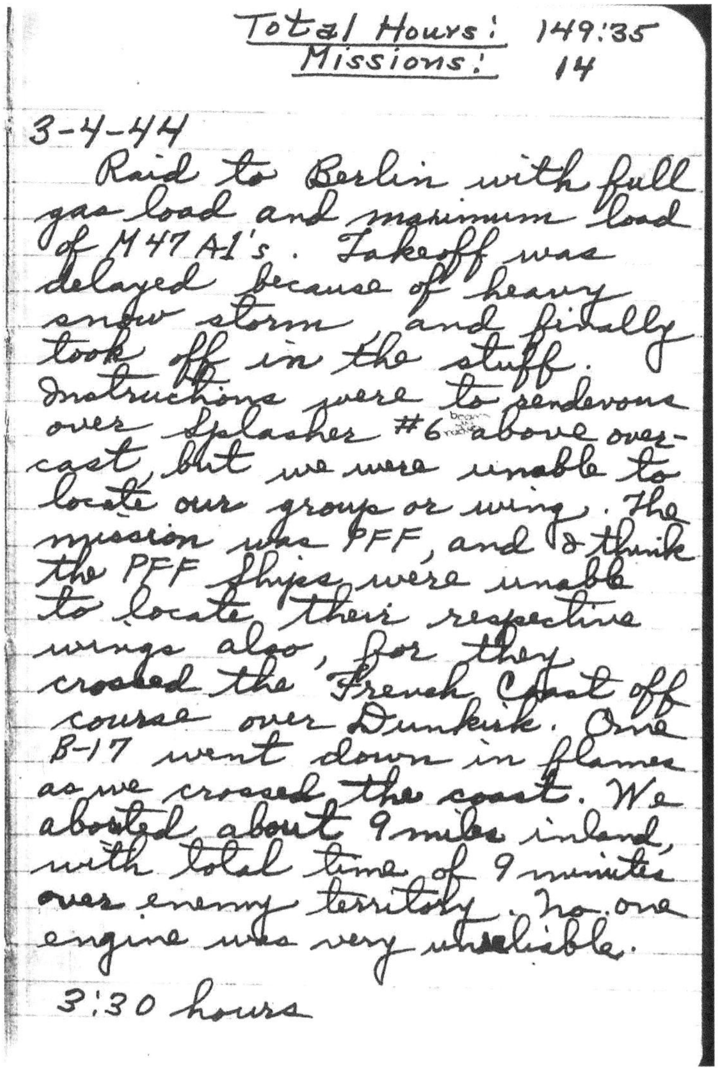

Total Hours: 149:35
Missions: 14

3-4-44
Raid to Berlin with full gas load and maximum load of M47 A1's. Takeoff was delayed because of heavy snow storm and finally took off in the stuff. Instructions were to rendevous over Splasher #6 above overcast, but we were unable to locate our group or wing. The mission was PFF, and I think the PFF ships were unable to locate their respective wings also, for they crossed the French Coast off course over Dunkirk. One B-17 went down in flames as we crossed the coast. We aborted about 9 miles inland, with total time of 9 minutes over enemy territory. No. one engine was very unreliable.
3:30 hours

As the men lit their cigarettes and fielded questions from the press, others went to get chow or celebrate their good luck at the officers and enlisted mens club with those who had been recalled earlier in the day. A few jotted down their experience as best they could for posterity. Upon his return from Berlin, Lt Robert Bailie, copilot on Lt Francis Malooly's Crew, jotted the following down in his personal diary:

"March 4/44, Mission to Berlin again. This time we got through. Over 900 ships started. Near Brunswick just north, all turned back because of high clouds up to 27,000 to 30,000 ft. All but 31 ships of us. We picked up very heavy and accurate flak at Magdeburg. Many ships were hit badly but managed to keep up.

From I.P. (Initial Point) to MPI (Mean Point of Impact) we were attacked by a large number of FW's and Me109's. Made nine passes at our ship alone. The temp. was -60 degrees at 27,000 ft. They cut the tail off of one of our bombers. We saw one FW blow up and two shot down. P-51 escorts shot a lot down. We had 4 head on attacks from 12 o'clock and 5 from 9 and 3 o'clock on our ship alone. Couldn't use chin turret it was froze up at 26,500 ft. As we reached target there was very heavy flak and our low squadron on left caught most of it. We lost one ship (Seaton) at target. He was in my barracks with me. We are the only crew left now in this barracks, the rest we have lost. Had a 8/10 undercast at target. After leaving target, we picked up a new escort and picked up some more heavy flak at Magdeburg. Had a good escort all the way back home. After leaving target we dropped down to 12,000 ft. About a 4/10 undercast, we could see small German towns and lots of snow on the ground. Oxygen ran out half way back from target. Came out through Belgium just about 4 mi. north of Dunkirk. Picked up moderate flak at Dunkirk. Near English coast, two FW's came out of clouds and followed a B-17, which dropped out of formation and headed back to Germany. Apparently, it was a captured US plane and the Jerrys were just following us in it. Back at the field, they had war correspondents at interrogation and by the looks and sounds of things, we made history. We were only 31 planes out of more than 900 to get to Berlin. We are damn lucky to be here now. At target it was a running gun fight. We just had to shoot our way through. It lasted at the longest point over the target for about 30 min. nine of the 13 planes from this field in the mission were from my squadron. One was lost. They took our pictures and we are to have a special interrogation by the war correspondents. Adding up everything and from reports, I guess we really did something big. The Major said that we would get a special citation but I doubt it. (Stand down tomorrow). This is the first time Berlin has ever been bombed in the daylight. The first USAAF had ever bombed Berlin. A very dangerous mission."

Major 'Red' Bowman, 100BG S-2 Intelligence Officer, recalled the March 4, 1944, mission this way:

"Mar 4, The 100th, led by Capt. Magee Fuller, flying with Lt. Herb Devore took off for Berlin. Increasing clouds forced the Commander of the First Division to cancel the mission. The Third Division, already well on it way to the target, was also recalled - part of the 13th Combat Wing failed to hear the recall and continued and bombed the target. The part that continued was two squadrons from the 95th and 13 planes from the 100th, mostly from the 350th Bomb Squadron (9 a/c coming from 350th)."[16]

As Lt. Orrin Heinrich, navigator on one of the 100BG planes, recalled on March 4, 1944, in his diary:

"3-4-44

Raid to Berlin with full gas load and maximum load of M47 A-1's. Take off was delayed because of heavy snow storm and finally took off in the stuff. Instructions were to rendezvous over Splasher #6 above overcast but we were unable to locate our group or wing. The mission was PFF, and I think the PFF ships were unable to locate their respective wings also, for they crossed the French coast off course over Denmark. One B-17 went down in flames as we crossed the coast. We aborted about 9 miles inland with total time of 9 minutes over enemy territory. No. one engine was very unreliable 3:30 hours."

Colonel Don Blakeslee, CO and "Chief Tenant" of the 4th Fighter Group, upon return from Berlin. (USAF)

Life magazine and history would go on to record that the 95th BG was the first 8AF bomb group to hit the Third Reich's capital by daylight. The cost in crews was relatively low—five in all—but it could have been much worse. According to John O'Neil, tail gunner on the 482nd BG PFF, the timely arrival of fighter escort, in particular the P-51s from Colonel Don Blakeslee's 4th Fighter Group out of Debden and Colonel Henry Spicer's 357th Fighter Group out of Leiston, saved the task force. "The Forts would not have made it back to England without the help of those P-51 pilots." Their help did not come without a high price, as 24 "Little Friends" failed to return to England.

The 95BG would receive their third Distinguished Unit Citation for the March 4, 1944, mission to Berlin. No other Bomb Group in the 8AF achieved the feat of receiving three Distinguished Unit Citations. The 95BG would forever be remembered as the "First Over Berlin." The 100BG's role in the mission was overshadowed by the events that would unfold two days later.

Mr Tettleys' Tenants, the P-51s of the 4th Fighter Group. (USAF)

Meanwhile, over at Debden (home of the Eagles of the 4th Fighter Group), Mr. Tettley's chief tenant exited his P-51 Mustang with a cascade of four letter superlatives. Seems his guns jammed as he was about to dispatch a Me109 on a one-way trip down to Berlin. "I'll be a sad sack, my goddamned guns wouldn't fire. There we were, I had the son of a bitch right in my sights and my guns jammed. I pulled up beside him and looked at the dumb sap. He must have thought I was crazy!"

One crew that was scheduled for the 3-4-1944 mission and later recalled was that of Lt Handorf. Lt Norman Rasmussen, bombardier on the crew, wrote this to his sweetheart back home:

Letter from 2nd Lt Norman Rasmussen to "Winnie," Feb 11, 1944:

"From Somewhere in England

Dear Winnie,

Come on, let's loosen up with that right hand of yours and jot me down a letter.

Ginny said she saw you at Christmas time but that's all she wrote. It isn't any fun to be over here and if I ever come back, I'll really be lucky. I've been raising a little hell everytime I bomb the bastards but the war keeps on and on. I've also seen things that scare the hell our to me and boy this is worse that running the 'old Wheel Scraper.' Ha! Ha! Lets laugh on that one. It isn't any use to complain over here because if I started in, I'd never get through. All I've got to do now is fight my way out of it and it isn't a paper sack that I'm in. I got a letter from Helen today and I also wrote to Dad. I remember the night I went to see him, he sure hated to see me go and he came out to the car and said 'SON, YOU'LL MAKE IT.'

First U.S. Bombs Dropped on Berlin; Air Force Hails Raiders of 'Big B'

Forts Beat Terrific Clouds, Cold to Paste Capital

By Bud Hutton
Stars and Stripes Staff Writer

A FORTRESS DIVISION HQ, Mar. 5—Flying Fortress crews who wouldn't quit were the envy of the Eighth Air Force today—they had gone to Big B.

Triumphant, shouting, cheered by anxious ground crews who had sweated them out, toasted (in one case by a general issue of double Scotches) and warm again, the first American airmen to bomb Berlin in daylight came home in Saturday's dusk from the job the whole Air Force had been waiting for.

In some bomber-station huts, however, there was disappointment. There, the air crews were unhappy because after the long, long wait for THE raid, they'd missed it.

Mostly, however, even the ones who didn't make it felt better. The tension of waiting at each briefing to see if this would be it was done now. Now Big B was just the same as any other tough target.

Most envied of all were the 11 men of the first American bomber to hit Berlin. Officially, the honor of being the first man over Big B went to 2/Lt. Marshall J. Phixton, of Mexia, Tex., the bombardier, whose place in the nose took him over the target before anyone else. For him and four others in the crew it was Mission No. 12B, "and a lot of us were sweating, but we got back," Phixton explained.

First enlisted man over the city was the ship's top-turret gunner, T/Sgt. Donald E. White, of North Bennington, Vt. The rest of the crew:

1/Lt. William V. Owens, Columbus, Ohio, pilot; S/Sgt. E. A. Beans, Pittsburgh, left waist; S/Sgt. Leo E. Moffatt, Grosse Point, Mich., ball turret; 2/Lt. Albert J. Englehardt, Chicago, navigator; 2/Lt. Frank L. McAllister, Omak, Wash, co-pilot; S/Sgt. Edmund R. Aken, Elkville, Ill., radio; S/Sgt. Harlin R. Sours, Page County, Va., tail; S/Sgt. John J. O'Neil, Malden, Mass., right waist, and 2/Lt. W. G. Milton, of Brooklyn, observer.

A Plenty Cold Job

Most of the things the Berlin raiders talked about were the masses of six-mile-

Among First U.S. Visitors to Berlin

U.S. Army Air Force Photos

The first enemy fighter shot down over Berlin by the Eighth Air Force was officially credited to T/Sgt. Harold Sterns (left), of Passaic, N.J., top turret gunner of the Fortress Rubber Check. Lt. Col. Donald J. M. Blakeslee (right), of Fairport, Ohio, former Eagle Squadron pilot, was given official credit for being the first American fighter pilot over Berlin while escorting heavy bombers.

Big New Pus[h] Near Odessa-

Russia's First Ukraine Army group bulge into Poland in January, has stru[ck] Odessa-Lwow trunk railroad and has b[...] miles deep in the Nazi defenses guardi[ng] announced last night in an order of th[e] Led by Marshal of the Soviet Union

U.S. Ignoring Farrell Regime

Argentine's New Govt. Not Recognized by Washington

Libs, B26s Hit France In a Follow-Up of Epochal Blow

American bomber fleets abruptly switched their attack to the west yesterday after Saturday's daylight penetration of the heart of Germany, in which Berlin for the first time felt the blast of American bombs.

Liberators, Marauders and endless relays of Allied medium and light bombers shuttled across the Channel in daylight yesterday to pound military objectives in France and to run the March box score to four heavy-bomber missions in five days. The Marauders were out twice, losing one plane.

Eighth Air Force Fortresses were grounded after their historic day's work on Saturday, which included the bombing of the Reich capital by one formation of several which carried out widespread attacks on targets in what officially was described as "eastern Germany."

Bonn, Cologne Hit, Nazis Say

In official broadcasts German radio said that Bonn and Cologne had been among the targets for the B17s, which struck deep into the Reich despite towering masses of clouds which made formation flying almost impossible.

Fourteen bombers were reported missing from the epochal attack, while preliminary reports that 26 of the escorting Eighth and Ninth AAF fighters had been lost were scaled down to 23.

Nine of the scattered few enemy fighters which got off the snow-covered ground and through the clouds were destroyed by Mustangs, Thunderbolts and Lightnings. Six more enemy planes which managed to get through the cordon of fighters were destroyed by bomber gunners.

For the Mustangs which circled over Berlin and even flew a little to the north in search of opposition, it was the longest haul yet—1,166 miles.

First reports of the Berlin attack—which, it was pointed out, was on one district of the city's metropolitan area—came from Nazi sources. The Germans claimed that it was the second successive day that U.S. bombers had tried to get through to the capital, and said that "only a small number reached the built-up area."

Stars and Stripes March 5, 1944, reporting on first Berlin strike. Note photo of Harold Sterns and Don Blakeslee in article.

A Plenty Cold Job

Most of the things the Berlin raiders talked about were the masses of six-mile-high clouds that made formation flying a nightmare, the temperature which got down past minus 50 and the U.S. fighters which swept along with them. They talked about 26-year-old Lt. Col. Harry C. Mumford, group leader from San Jose, Cal., who marshaled cloud-hidden planes into an attack formation and led them over the capital of Germany.

"Going in wasn't tough," the Colonel said. "The weather was pretty bad. Clouds were broken. And it was cold, damn cold—down to 55 degrees below zero.

"As we got near to the city the clouds were still broken. We caught some ground checks, even though we were nearly five miles up.

"My navigator, and believe me he deserves all the credit (he was 1/Lt. Malcolm D. Durr, 26, of Alton, Ill.), saw enough ground points to set us up for a visual bomb run. But then the clouds closed in again and the bombing was done through the clouds. I'm sure we hit the place.

"We had a little trouble on our ship

(Continued on page 2)

Forts Beat Terrific Clouds, Cold to Bomb Berlin 1st Time

(Continued from page 1)

getting the bomb-bay doors open. They were frozen tight. I never saw anyone work so hard as 'Brownie' (1/Lt. Albert H. Brown, of Decatur, Ill.) on the salvo handle to dump those bombs on Berlin. They went down all right.

"How did I feel knowing we were the first Americans to bomb Berlin? Well, I know I felt a helluva lot of satisfaction. But I kept wondering where the hell were the German fighters. We had to drop down, and the majority of the trip back was made entirely on instruments. We couldn't see the ground. Again that boy Durr did a beautiful job of navigation. Fighters? So help me, all I saw was three Mes. They were lined up coming into us when ZOOM! Down came a bunch of P51s and that was the last I saw of the Luftwaffe on the whole trip. Flak, too, was surprisingly weak. The trip was long, it was cold, but it was worth it."

The gunners back from Big B envied T/Sgt. Harold Stearns, 21-year-old top-turret man from Passaic, N.J., who was credited officially with getting the first Nazi fighter over the Reich's capital and biggest city.

"An Me109 came in out of the sun," Stearns said. "He came ramming in at 12 o'clock high. I got him in my sight at 800 yards. As he started to bore in at our nose I sweated him out for about 400 yards. Then I nailed him with about 150 rounds."

One Fortress scored the dubious honor of being the first bomber to come back from Berlin in trouble. S/Sgt. Junior Bucher, 25, of Cottonwood Falls, Kan., left-waist gunner, told about it:

"The Mustangs helped us along. We only had three engines. We saw some enemy fighters but the 51s kept 'em off. You can quote me on it, those Mustangs look beautiful any time you're in trouble. But over Berlin on three engines, they're wonderful."

Many of the crews were first-mission men. They'd climbed out of warm sacks in the pre-dawn darkness, chowed and gone to their first briefings to find their target for the day was Berlin, Big B. Some of them—and some veterans, too—frankly said they were scared, but even though the weather grew incredibly bad they pressed on.

Most of the men who bombed Berlin came back without seeing any more or as much of the German capital as the RAF airmen who go there by night. Clouds were almost solid, and they towered even above the bombers and their escorts. A few planes, however, stumbled onto gaps in the clouds and saw their bombs smash into buildings surrounded by trees, and saw the white blanket of snow which probably helped to keep down German fighters.

They lost their fighter escort just after that, and for a couple of hours flew westward alone. But most of them saw no signs of the enemy except the clumps of black flak which popped up through the clouds every once in a while, and when they got back to their bases and went to interrogation, the big maps on the walls of the interrogation rooms had grown, in eight or ten hours, a hell of a lot smaller.

We've sure been through Hell in our time but by golly this is the worse I've been in.

This War is a funny business; everything happens so fast in the air that I'm not scared till I get back on the ground. It never pays to think about it or a guy won't last in enemy territory. If you are looking for excitement, you should go along with me once and you'd know what I mean.

Ginny has a picture of my outfit, did you ever see it? I'd really appreciate a box of candy because us boys over here never get anything. People at home don't know how tough it is. Well I won't write anymore unless I hear from you, so goodbye.

Norman"

Eighth Air Force Combat Chronology
Saturday, 4 March 1944

STRATEGIC OPERATIONS (Eighth Air Force): Mission 247: 502 B-17s are dispatched to hit industrial areas in the suburbs of Berlin; bad weather forces aircraft to either turn back or hit targets of opportunity and only 1 wing attacks the primary target and a total of 249 bomb. 15 B-17s are lost, 1 is damaged beyond repair and 120 damaged; casualties are 3 KIA, 11 WIA and 141 MIA. Targets: 100 hit Bonn, 35 hit Cologne, 33 hit Dusseldorf, 30 hit Berlin/Klein Machnow, 7 hit Frankfurt and 33 hit other targets of opportunity. B-24s were also dispatched but abort because of the weather. Escort is provided by 86 P-38s, 563 Eighth and Ninth Air Force P-47s and 121 Eighth and Ninth Air Force P-51s; 24 fighters were lost. Details are:

1. P-38s: 4 lost, 2 damaged beyond repair, 1 damaged; casualties are 1 KIA and 4 MIA.
2. P-47s claim 3-1-3 Luftwaffe aircraft in the air and 1-0-0 on the ground; 4 P-47s are lost, 1 damaged beyond repair and 5 damaged; casualties are 3 MIA.
3. P-51s claim 5-2-1 Luftwaffe aircraft; 16 P-51s are lost, 1 damaged beyond repair and 1 damaged; casualties are 1 KIA and 16 MIA. CARPETBAGGER operations are flown during the night of 4/5 Mar.

The March 4, 1944, Berlin raid boosted morale all over occupied Europe and enraged Reichsmarshall Hermann Göring. Two days later Göring's Luftwaffe would make the 8th Air Force pay a heavy price for this target and T/Sgt. Harold Stearns would have to postpone that letter he promised to write home.

Captain Roland Knight and Lt. Colonel John B. Kidd look over the battle order for the Berlin mission of March 6, 1944.

Early morning fog rolls into Thorpe Abbotts while Ground Crew works on #4 engine.

* * *

On 5 March, just before 1900 hrs, the teletypes chattered to life at airbases all throughout East Anglia. They started to type Field Order #171 from the Third Bombardment Division HQ at Elveden Hall. At Horham, Framlingham, Rattlesden, Bury St. Edmunds, Snetterton Heath, Great Ashfield, Deopham Green, Knettishall, and Thorpe Abbotts the Air Executives and Operations Officers read the field order for Mission 250:

MAXIMUM FORCES WILL BE DISPATCHED AGAINST OBJECTIVES IN BERLIN AREA ON 6 MARCH, 1944

Every available B-17 and B-24 and their crews were to participate, including each flyable 100BG aircraft. Flight plans and all details of the mission were set into motion for the next morning. The alert that a mission was on for the next day was posted at each squadron HQ; officer and enlisted men's bars were closed early and the men were restricted to base. A flurry of messages began coming from operations officer Lt. Colonel John B. "Jack" Kidd that generated a flurry of activity at the base. Engineering, Ordnance, Armament, Communications, S-2 Intelligence, and Transportation were alerted. Soon began the fueling of each B-17 with 2,750 gallons of gas, loading 10-500 pound general purpose or incendiary bombs and boxes of 50 cal. ammunition. Along the flight line, ground crews knew this was going to be a deep penetration into Germany based on the fuel load, and speculation started to run rampant as to what the target would be. Over in the Nissen huts, sleep came at a premium for the combat crews; the tip of a lit cigarette could be seen in some of the bunks, while others tried to get that last letter in before getting 30 winks. Everyone wondered what the target would be, and they would not have to wait long to find out!

The Order of Battle for the mission to Berlin proposed on March 6, 1944, involved all three bombardment divisions. The First Bombardment Division would lead the 8AF to Berlin. They would be led by Colonel Ross Milton, the 91BG Air Executive, and would send 262 B-17s, divided into 5 Combat Wings, to bomb the VFK ball bearing plant at Erkner. Next, the Third Bombardment Division, led by Brigadier General Russell Wilson, Commanding Officer of the 4th Combat Wing in a 482 BG H2X radar-equipped B-17 23491, would send 242 B-17s consisting of 3 Combat Wings to bomb the Bosch electrical works. Flying "tail-end-Charlie," the Second Bombardment Division, led by 445BG Colonel Robert H. Terrill in a 482BG (814BS) B-24 pathfinder 128783 *Feather Merchant* piloted by Captain Henchman, would send 226 B-24s in 3 Combat Wings to bomb the Daimler Benz airplane engine plant at Genshagen.[17] Top cover for the 730 B-17s and B-24s would be provided by over 800 P-38, P-47, and P-51 fighters of the Eighth and Ninth Air Forces.

2700+ gallons of fuel meant a deep penetration mission into Germany.

Ken Lemmons working on #3 engine on *Skipper II* March 3, 1944.

Eighth Air Force Order of Battle
March 6, 1944

100 **A** Group

Major Albert 'Bucky' Elton was designated as Airborne Group Commander and **A** Group leader, who would sit in the right-hand seat with Lt. Herbert G. Devore's crew in 231981, leading 5 other A/C from the 350 Bomb Squadron (BS). Lt John A. Harrison in 231710 The Savage would be the High Squadron leader comprised of 9 B-17s from the 349 BS and 350 BS. The Low Squadron was to be led by James E. Wilkinson of the 390BG in 231974 Bomboogie and be comprised of 5 other 390BG, 570 BS B-17s.

100 **B** Group

Captain Jack Swartout (pictured at right and above), 351 BS Operations Officer, was the **B** Group leader and sat in the right seat with the Captain Frank Lauro crew flying in 231306 **Nelson King** leading 5 other A/C from 351 BS. Captain David Miner would be the High Squadron leader (nine 418 BS crews made up the High Squadron) and Lt. Norman Chapman in 239983 *Katie* was to lead the Low Squadron,[18] which was a composite squadron of 351, 349, and 418 crews.

The 100th BG was assigned to fly with the 95th and 390BGs, which comprised the 13th Combat Wing. Each Group would rotate, leading the Wing on a mission-by-mission basis. For March 6, 1944, the 13 **A** Wing would consist of 390BG and 95BG B-17s, and echeloned to the left and low would be the 100BG leading the 13 **B** Wing. Specifically for the 100BG, the 13 **B** Wing would consist of the 100BG **A** and **B** Groups. The 100BG **A** Group would fly Lead and consist of fifteen B-17s in the lead and high squadrons, while six B-17s from the 390BG filling in as the low squadron.

Major Bucky Elton

The **B** Group of the 13th **B** Wing would comprise of twenty B-17s from the 100BG. In total, the 100BG was to provide 35 aircraft. When stretched from beginning to end, the bomber stream would be approximately 84 miles long and headed for the heart of the Third Reich. Once penetrating occupied Europe, over Egmond, Holland, the stream would proceed to the target via a direct easterly route until it reached Celle, then East-Southeast to the respective Initial Points (IP) 18 miles of each target. At the IP, the formations started the bomb run into the wind. After bombs away, they would leave the flak zones as fast as possible to reach the Rally Point, over the small town of Kyritz, Northwest of Berlin.

Captain Jack Swartout

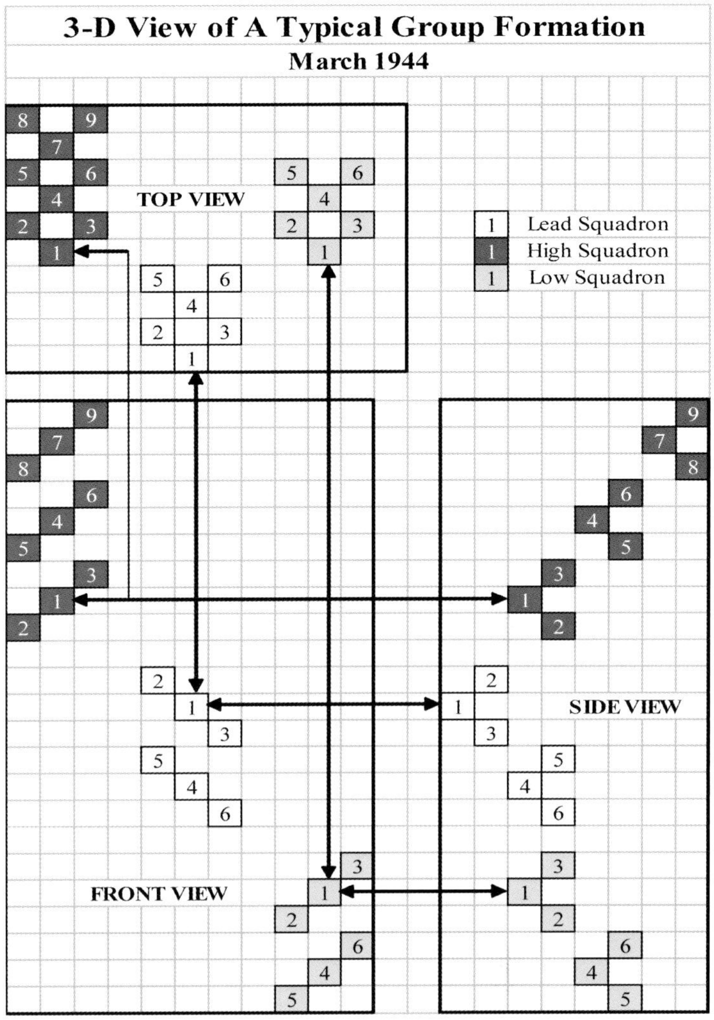

Since July 1943, a letter designation was now in use for each bomb group to make it easier to identify your bomb group and get into proper formation. The 100BG aircraft had a large Royal Insignia Blue **D** painted on a white square on the tail fin and on the upper surface of the right wing. Two large light blue-grey letters painted on the fuselage identified the squadron: **XR** for the 349th; **LN** for the 350th; **EP** for the 351st, and **LD** for the 418th. The individual aircraft identification letter was painted on the aft fuselage in blue-grey and on the tail fin in yellow. In the case of Robert Shoens' plane Our Gal Sal, the letter was **E**. Of the two other groups in the 13th Combat Wing, the 95BG, stationed at Horham, had a Square **B** on the tail of its aircraft, while the 390BG, stationed at Framlingham, had a Square **J** on its tail.

In March 1944, there generally existed a 21-plane formation, though various groups did experiment with this basic formation. Each formation, referred to as group, had lead, high, and low squadrons. Some "groups" even had a trail squadron, which flew directly behind and below the "lead" squadron. The term "group" refers to a formation not necessarily composed of aircraft assigned to the same numbered unit. This same caveat applies to the term "squadron." The terms "high" and "low" refer to the altitude of the "squadron" in relation to the altitude of the lead "squadron." Each "squadron" consists of smaller three aircraft "V" formations. The numbering system is straightforward. The first aircraft of the squadron is #1, the aircraft to the right is #2, and the aircraft to the left is #3. The lead aircraft of the next "V" is #4, and the aircraft to its right is #5 and so on. The same numbering system is employed for the high and low squadrons.

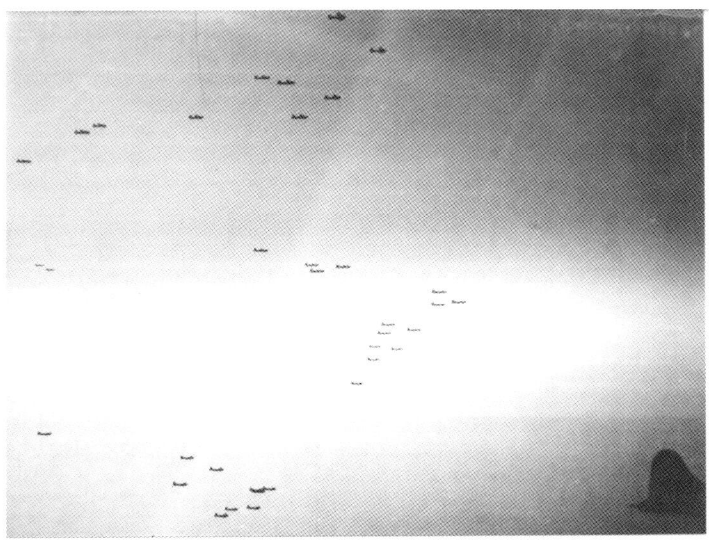
Side view of a very loose combat box.

II

Oh No! Big B!
Monday, March 6, 1944

It was still pitch black at Station 139, Thorpe Abbotts, home away from home for the 100BG personnel. They were known as the "hard luck" group. They were the "Bloody Hundredth." The group had earned this moniker due to high losses on individual missions: August 17, 1943, Regensburg with 9 aircraft missing; October 8, 1943, Bremen with 7 aircraft missing; and October 10, 1943, Munster with 12 aircraft missing. If those missions earned the moniker, then the 6 March mission to Berlin solidified it!

At 0200 hrs a door opened in a nissen hut, and the CQ (Charge of Quarters) turned his flashlight towards the sleeping crewmember:

"Drop your c—ks and grab your socks
Let's go Lieutenant!
Your crew is scheduled to fly!"

Dusk on March 5, 1944.

Like crews all around the base, Lt. Robert Shoens of the 351 BS started his 17th mission crawling out of bed, rubbing the sleep from his eyes, and hitting the latrines. Others, like Lt. Sam Barrick, were quartered in the dining hall of what had been a WAAF mess hall. He was part of the 56 officers from 14 replacement crews that joined the 100BG in November 1943. They were replacing some of the twenty aircrews lost over Hanau, Bremen, and Munster during the month of October. The number living in the WAAF mess hall dwindled as crews were assigned permanent quarters in their squadron areas while others had been lost in combat. The officers of 239994 *Snort Stuff*, Barrick's plane, and two other 418 bomb squadron crews remained in these "temporary" quarters. The enlisted men slept in different barracks, mainly nissen huts, but all were dingy and damp, and never seemed to keep out the cold nipping air of East Anglia.

Quarters at Thorpe Abbotts.

Over in the 350 Bomb Squadron site, Lt C.B. "Red" Harper was trying to get a few extra moments of shuteye when the orderly bursts in, waking everyone up flying the mission today. Using his best Hitler impersonation, the orderly rattles off the menu "you transient combat glamour boys are getting powdered eggs and salt peter in your coffee." He turns and slams the door on his way out. But not without the ominous "twenty-seven hundred gallons and ten five hundred pounders." "Red" Harper knows that means only one thing, "bad news—long trip ahead."[19]

At first glance, the pilot and copilot of *Our Gal Sal* often had their roles mistaken. At 6'1 inch tall, Lt. Duncan Shand, copilot, was a full 5 inches taller than Bob Shoens, the pilot. They both

Lt Robert Shoens in front of *Our Gal Sal*.

shaved and dressed quickly, putting on long underwear, standard wool shirt, pants, and the one-piece flight suit. Over this they wore a leather sheepskin lined B-3 jacket and heavy sheepskin boots. Other officers preferred the leather A2 flying jacket and G.I. high top boots. Crewmembers wore what they could, including the heating suit, to endure the biting cold. Most of the enlisted men had no such choice. Over the wool undercover they wore the Blue Bunny heating suit, and above all a heavy brown sheepskin jacket, trousers, and boots. The heated suit and clothing on top, along with a thin aluminum skin, is all that separated them for the intense cold 5 miles high, where temperatures could reach anywhere from minus 40 to minus 60+ degrees.

Representative Dress Procedure for Officers and Enlisted Men March 1944[20]

0200hrs.
Shaving important as not to get face chafed by hours of wearing Oxygen mask.
Get into class B uniform, flight jacket for breakfast & crew Briefing.
Officers Attend Pilots/Navigator/Bombardier briefing.
Gunners draw Browning .50 innards for installation in a/c.
Draw Kit Bag at the Quarter Master (QM)

All personal items turned in: cash, ID, etc. Bail out kits issued. Items not worn put into Aviator's Kit Bag.

Depending on unit and availability of flight gear, if items not personally issued, items may be issued by quartermaster, and worn over Class B uniform:

1. Electric heated, Type F-1 "Blue Bunny Suit." With electric heated booties and glove inserts.
2. Gabardine Flight suit.
3. A-2 jacket or Sheepskin B-3 jacket, A-6 boots and A-3 pants.
4. B-3 or B-4 Mae West.
5. Parachute Harness: QAC (Quick Attachable Chute) with corresponding Red or Yellow Group Parachute Pack. Or

Ready for combat (behind the oxygen mask is Lt Col John Bennett).

Backpack B-8 parachute. Parachutes not personally issued and fitted by rigger needed to be adjusted for proper fit NOTE: Although used early, Seat packs were not suitable for bomber crews, as they hampered easily egressing the a/c in an emergency, and were discontinued except on fighters and transport aircraft.

6. Headgear: personal preference including B-1 (sheepskin) or lightweight A-2 gabardine flight caps, Overseas cap, "50 mission" crush cap, or B-6 sheepskin flight helmet (with or without integral interphones).
7. Communication: HB-7 headphones, throat mike, and accompanying extension cords. Mask Microphones came out later in the war.
8. A-10 or A-14 oxygen mask and small bail out bottle in canvas case either strapped onto leg or on parachute harness.
9. Goggles (attached to Flight helmets) or sun glasses.
10. Flak Jacket and helmet.

Each crewmember approached or reflected upon the upcoming battle differently. Yet the notion of "good" luck and "bad" luck was not taken lightly. Lt. Shoens did not wear a talisman. However, he did exactly the same regimen before each mission, dressing in exactly the same way each time. Technical Sergeant Don Hammond, Shoens' radio operator, wore a red plaid scarf from his high school days. He also had another ritual; whenever he was flying, Hammond had Asa Spengler, radio operator on Lt. Massol's crew, hang onto his pocket book for safekeeping. The same would happen when Spengler flew; Hammond would hold on to Spengler's pocket book. On 6 March both men would be flying the mission, so it is not known whom they entrusted with their wallets. Men in the other crews were no different when it came to superstitions.

Lt. Harold Granger, Lt. Massol's copilot, wore exactly the same clothing on each mission. His special talisman was a large ragged piece of a nylon parachute that he cut roughly into a scarf. The scarf kept his neck from rubbing raw from constant turning to look for enemy fighters. Lt. Joe Carty, Chadwick's bombardier, preferred to stick to a more conventional talisman; a small scapular medal of St Theresa rode tucked inside his flying glove on each mission. He received it "on loan" from the Chaplain, who requested its return upon the completion of Carty's tour so that it could be passed on to a subsequent crewmember. Luck would be on his side this day even with the ominous name of the plane their crew was flying. This was the third day in a row they had set out in this aircraft for Berlin; it was an old "F" model, 23413, called *Hard Luck!*

23413 *Hard Luck!*, Lt.Randall Chadwick's aircraft on the March 3, 4, and 6, 1944, missions to Berlin.

Pilot Lt. Frank A. Granack always carried a Christian medal with the inscription "I am a Catholic in case of an accident call a priest." If he had something in his right pocket, S/Sgt. Sam J. LaFace never changed its location. Every crewman was going through his own ritual as fast as possible before heading to breakfast. There was always small talk to take some of the edge off on the walk from the barracks to the combat crew mess hall. The crews were heading now to get the best menu in the whole of East Anglia.

Breakfast consisted of fresh eggs and bacon, along with toast, pancakes, and syrup. They only got fresh eggs and bacon if they were flying a mission. "The better the chow, the rougher the mission." Even at that time of the morning, some had quite an appetite. One day Don Hammond and Bill Wright, from the Shoens crew, ate 9 and 12 eggs respectively! Not much coffee or orange juice though, for with the layers of flying clothing, relieving oneself could become a tricky task at 21,000 ft! They had a maximum of 30 minutes to get their breakfast. Some were wondering where today's mission would take them; others did not care to think about it. The 35 crews scheduled for the mission finished breakfast and caught a ride, biked, or walked to the briefing room. Scuttlebutt ran rampant with rumors of the target; flight crews knew it was going to be a rough one from the chow and a long one based on the fuel load. Now all they could do was await the scheduled briefing at 0300 hrs.

"At-ten-HUT."

The group brass was coming, namely Group CO Colonel Neil B. "Chick" Harding, the Air Exec and soon to be acting CO Lt. Colonel John Bennett, Group Operations Officer Lt. Colonel John B. Kidd, and the four Squadron Commanding Officers: Major Albert "Bucky" Elton (350), Leading the Group on this mission; Captain Sammy Barr (349); Lt. Colonel Ollie Turner (351); and Major Ev Blakely (418).

"Seats, men!"

After a few short opening remarks by Colonel Harding, the briefing officer, Lt. Mackesey from S-2 Intelligence, with a long pointer in his hand, pulled back the curtain covering the large European wall chart.[21]

On the huge map, a red ribbon started at Thorpe Abbotts and ran far into Germany:

"Your target for today is *BERLIN*."

It did not matter if you were on a seasoned crew or a new replacement, as Ed Silverstone, ball turret gunner on Lt. Shoens' crew, remembered: "when Berlin was announced as the target, the room went silent, dead silent!" But the silence did not last for long. Soon the mumbled cries could be heard:

"My aching back!"
"Big B!"

Also scattered throughout the briefing room:

"Oh, no!"
"Holy shit!"

Lt. C.B. "Red" Harper remembers hearing "who got drunk and dreamed that one up again," along with a "Jesus H. Christ!" and a few other choice expressions. Some bit their lips, swallowed hard, and tried to think of something else, anything else. Many expected it to be Berlin, since they had started twice for it on 3 and 4 March. Eventually they would have to try it again. Robert Shoens had good reason to dread this target, as two days earlier his friend through training and best man at his wedding Lt. Stanley Seaton had been shot down over Berlin.

S/Sgt Charles Allen, left waist gunner on Lt. Dean Radtke's crew, described the briefing:

"When we hit briefing that day, we thought we were going to Bremen or a No-Ball since we had been to Berlin on March 4th. Instead, the curtain is pulled back and there it is, 'Big B,' Berlin again! Well I just got a terrible feeling in my stomach and the responses in the room reflected that. That room got quiet really quick. We listened intently as if our lives depended on it, and it did! I looked for our position in formation, good, no 'tail end Charlie' for us, damn worst position to fly and we had seen our share of it lately! Enemy fighter, flak batteries, fighter rendezvous were all laid out for us."

The 8AF crews had already discovered what they knew to be inevitable; another daylight effort against Berlin was only a matter of time. There is little doubt that the German leadership, as much as it believed in the Third Reich's invincibility, also understood the inevitable. The outstanding question focused on the degree to which German defenses could meet the challenge posed by the heavy bombers of the Mighty Eighth. On a personal level, there is no doubt that many crew members shared Don Hammond's, radio operator gunner on Lt Shoens' crew, thoughts about their slim chances of returning to base that day.

T/Sgt Jack Robins, Radio Operator Gunner on Lt Barton's Crew, summed it up like this: "*I can't recall whether we fidgeted more over the sound of the name 'Berlin' or over the number of hours we would be in the air.*"

Lt. John A. Harrison thought Germany would probably not be very happy about this. His fill-in tail gunner that day, and flying his 25th and last mission, was S/Sgt Bruce 'Curly' Alshouse. Four days earlier Lt Harrisons' plane 231347 returned from Chartres, France, with flak damage to the hydraulic system. Unable to crank down the landing gear, Lt Harrison made a picture perfect belly landing alongside the runway. When the plane stopped, everyone scattered from the plane ASAP just in case there was an explosion from the remaining fuel in the gas tanks. Leading the way was 'Curly' Alshouse. When he stopped running, Sgt Robbins, the waist gunner, asked him sarcastically "*How many missions do you have left?*" Any new crewmember was looked upon with an air of suspicion and apprehension. "Bad luck" came in all forms, and none more so perceived than "fill-ins." Lt. John P. Gibbons, who had flown to Berlin two days earlier, was hoping he would at least have good weather for the mission. Others were convinced they would not be coming back and left their personal belongings in safe hands. The primary target for the 100 BG was the Robert Bosh electrical works at Klein Machnow. If clouds blanketed the target, a Pathfinder B-17G equipped with Radar "Mickey" from the 482nd BG based at Alconbury would guide the formation to the secondary target, the Friderichstrasse railway station. If both were

Berlin briefing. (Photo: USAF)

Major Albert M. "Bucky" Elton, 350th Bomb Squadron CO & Mission Commander for 100th BG on March 6, 1944.

March 6, 1944, Berlin
Scheduled formation, 13 B Wing

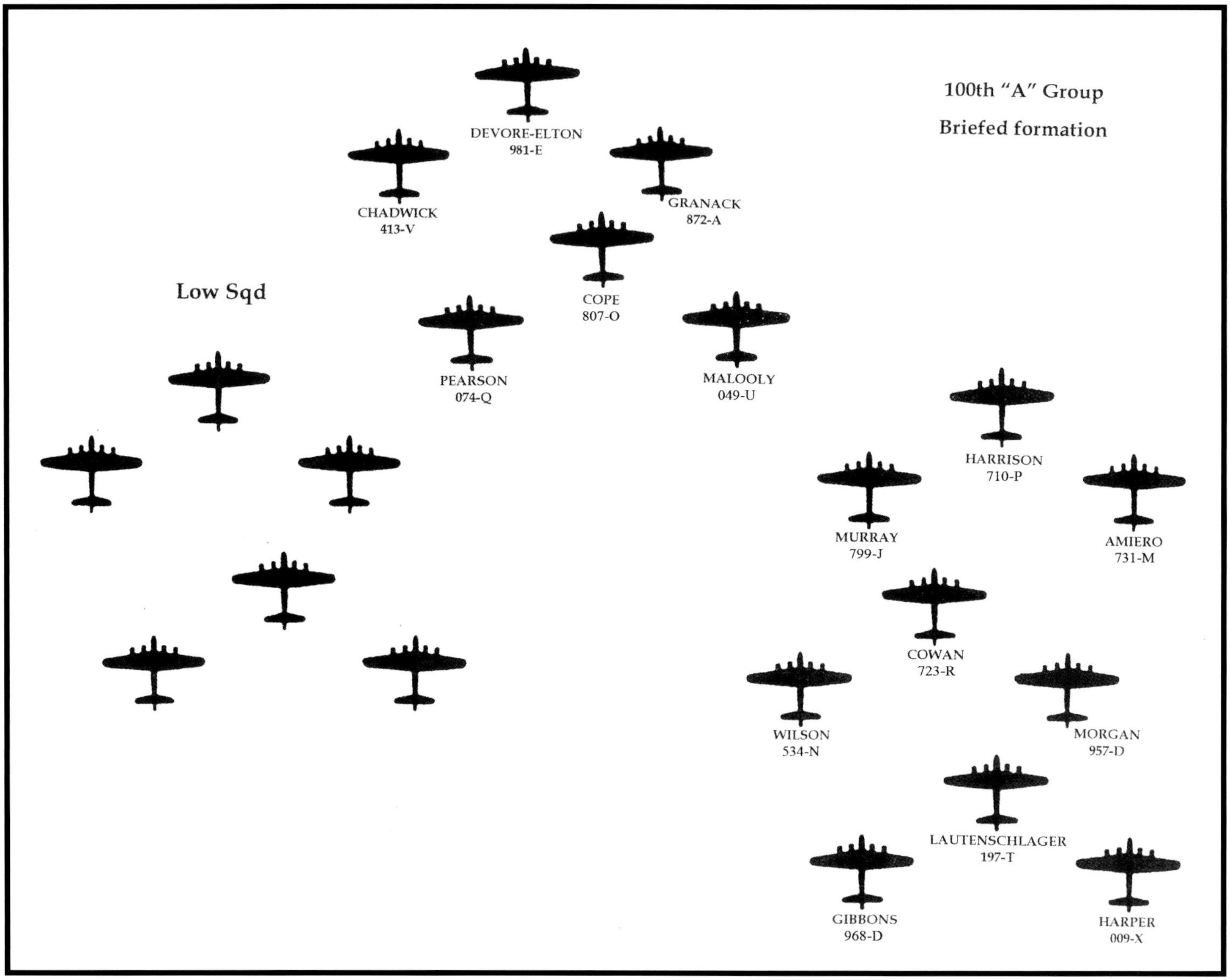

100th BG A formation chart at Briefing. (courtesy of Luc Dewez)

March 6, 1944, Berlin
Scheduled formation, 13 B Wing

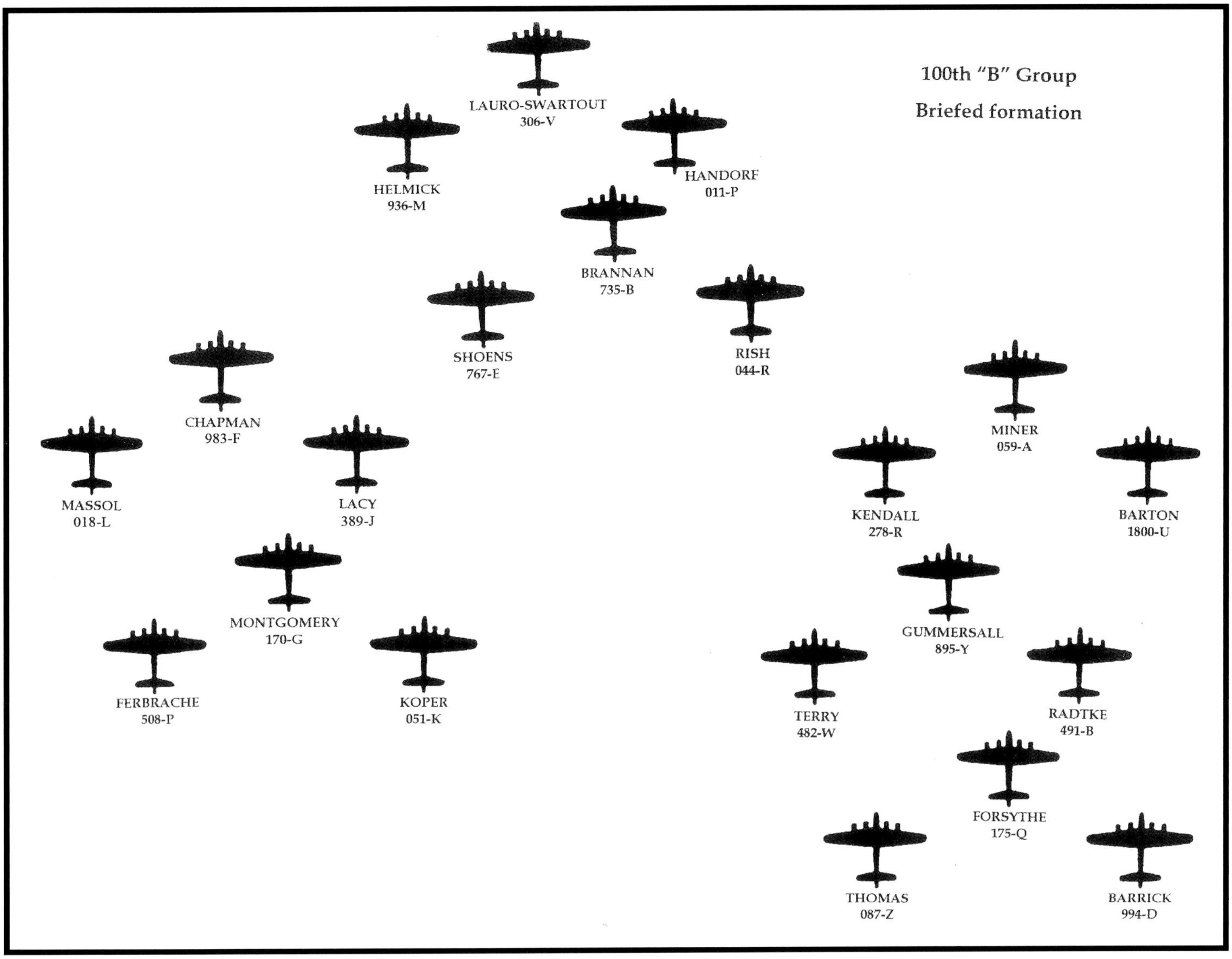

100th BG A formation chart at Briefing. (courtesy of Luc Dewez)

Major Ollie Turner (2nd from left), 351BS C.O., and Captain Jack R. Swartout (3rd from left) in front of 23307 *Skipper*.

covered, the group was to hit a "target of opportunity," which was any military objective positively identified as being in Germany that could be attacked without disrupting fighter support

It was now the turn of the Operations Officer, Lt. Colonel John B. 'Jack' Kidd, to describe the manner in which the force was to assemble. On the large wall map was posted the route to the target and back, while a blackboard showed the three last digits of the aircraft serial number with the pilot's name under each number. They were arranged in the shape of a group so each crew knew what position they flew (See Appendices A).

The S2 Intelligence Officer, Major Marvin 'Red' Bowman, outlined what the 100BG and the other groups would be facing. There was no avoiding the flak and the fighters. The routes into and out of the target area were designed to minimize exposure. It could not have been comforting to the crews to know that Berlin was protected with over 745 anti-aircraft guns and that the Luftwaffe could muster over one thousand fighters.

The plan called for more than 800 fighters ("Little Friends") to provide "top cover" all the way to and from the target. The map displayed the points where the successive groups of escorting fighters would rendezvous with the bomber stream. Weather Officer Captain Becker briefed the crews at to what they could expect for take-off, and over the target and return to base.

Colonel Harding gave a final pep talk along with the importance of the mission, while Lt. Colonel Kidd finished the briefing with the synchronization of the watches, or "Hack," after which the navigators and bombardiers went to separate briefings to obtain additional intelligence on the briefed course and target.

Lt. Glen Hudson, the bombardier on Shoens' crew, collected maps and "flimsies" to draw up his flight plan. When the crew lost their original navigator, Lt. Ray Hanson, after his 11th mission, the crew had been trying out a few Navigators and Togglers to see what combination worked best. Lt Shoens elaborates:

"Geez, I had forgotten about that mess! Lt Greenberg replaced Hanson for one raid on March 3rd. Then on Mar. 4th and 6th we had only Hudson. On Mar.8 we tried going with a togglier and Hudson as Nav. After we got back Hudson said I can do both. Since he had training in both, I decided to give it a try. I told Maj. Turner, and he said it was up to me and the crew. It worked for the rest of our tour." Consequently, they were a crew of nine for this mission.

Shoens and Shand went directly to the equipment room, where they picked up their parachute, flak suits, and escape kits. They did not attend a religious service but others did, meeting with their respective Chaplains to receive the Lord's blessing. The longer the ribbon was on the map of Europe in the Briefing Room, the more crewmen were kneeling in front of the Chaplain.

The crew of *Our Gal Sal* rode in the back of a Dodge 6x6 truck from the personal equipment shack to the aircraft dispersal hardstand. They usually arrived at their airplane 15 or 20 minutes before the "start engines" signal. Don Hammond said this was the time when he started to worry about a mission. Many of the crew went into the ground crew tent and caught a bit of shuteye; others had a smoke or went out and relieved themselves before takeoff. Sgt. Ed Silverstone, ball turret gunner, reminded the crew of one very important rule to remember in case the bailout bell did not work or the intercom was shot out:

Maj Marvin "Red" Bowman, S-2 Intelligence Officer

Lt Glen Hudson, Bombardier/Navigator on *Our Gal Sal.*

"It is important, that if we bail out, I know about it! Because if I saw eight or nine chutes floating down to the earth below me and you didn't tell me about it, I'd figured I would have to help increase your velocity of decent."

On their arrival at the hardstand, Master Sergeant H. Wildrick, the Crew Chief, and his mechanics were already waiting around *Our Gal Sal* for Shoens and the rest of the crew to show up. The ground crew knew, based on the gasoline loaded into the B-17s' tanks, that the mission would be a deep penetration into Germany.

The ground crews were dedicated to the task of maintaining the aircraft in top condition. Mechanics had been working all night since the field order came down, preparing the planes for combat. They had long since double-checked everything because they knew men's lives and the success of a mission began and ended with their work. There can never be enough thanks and praise given to all the Ground Crews of the Mighty Eighth who worked in every form of inhospitable weather and conditions to make sure our fighting crews had the best chance to return from a mission. Their contribution and that of others on the ground helped make the difference between winning and losing the Air War over Europe. Men like Ken Lemmons, Dewey Christopher, Bill Carleton, Bob Spangler, Butch Rovegno, Bill Clift, Jack Herlihy, Don Blazer, "Bud" Frum, Ray Morton, Durio, Herrmann, Callihan, Roach, Sierminski, Rothman, Svendsen, Muszynski, Sokolsky, Ayers, and so many others whose names are seldom mentioned in history books, but whose contribution to victory ranks with the grand strategists, the Generals, for their efforts cannot and must not be forgotten nor minimized.

Even though *Our Gal Sal* was assigned to the Shoens crew, the ground crew "owned" it and considered it their "Baby." The "Baby" was an olive drab B-17G, but for Shoens and his gang she was more than a plane, she was the eleventh member of the crew. They got her new and Shoens asked his crew to each put a name in his hat. The one picked out was My Gal Sal from a song of the era. I said "it is not My Gal Sal, it is Our Gal Sal." Frank "Steve" Stevens painted the nose art on canvas and it was glued onto the

Colonel Neil B. 'Chick' Harding, 100th BG Commanding Officer.

Our Gal Sal Ground crew: Kneeling: Crew Chief H. Wildrick, and N. Davidson. Standing: H. Schluter, S. Nelson, and J. Sambrailo.

Elwood 'Bud' Frum from the 350th BS and Ray Morton, Crew Chief with the 349th BS.

nose section of the airplane. He painted their A2 flying jackets and stenciled the mission markers and fighter tally on the side of the ship.

Since the first B-17 mission by the 8th Air Force on August 17, 1942, to Rouen, France, crews had been painting their aircraft with catchy names and the "pin-up" girls of the day by Varga and Petty. Some fortresses would go on and achieve fame like *Memphis Belle*, *Hells Angels*, *Old Bill*, *Dry Martini and the Cocktail Kids*, *Pistol Packin Mama*, *Piccadilly Lily*, *Butcher Shop*, *Yankee Doodle*, *Ol'Gappy*, and *The Zoot Suiters*, to name but a few. Other names painted on the aircraft were dedicated to an unlucky flying buddy. Such was the case for *Nelson King*, Captain Frank Lauro's ship. T/Sgt. Nelson King was his original radio operator. Lauro lost him in November over Bremen. His hands were so severely frostbitten trying to save the life of a fellow crewmember that his fingers eventually had to be amputated. For his actions that day, T/Sgt King was awarded the Silver Star:

"Nelson R. King, 17064928, Technical Sergeant, Army Air Forces, United States Army. For Gallantry in action while serving as Radio Operator and Gunner of a B-17 airplane on a bombing mission over Germany 29 November 1943. While manning his gun, fighting off fierce attacks by enemy planes, Sergeant King noticed that the ball turret gunner had collapsed from lack of oxygen. As soon as there was a lull in the fighting, he rushed to the turret, removed his stricken comrade to the radio compartment and placed his own oxygen mask on his face. When the gunner regained consciousness, he was hysterical and immediately tore off the oxygen mask and began to hit Sergeant King. Still without a supply of oxygen for himself, Sergeant King tied the mask on his hysterical comrade and held him down until he had become quiet. A short time later, the copilot found Sergeant King unconscious from lack of oxygen and his hands badly frost-bitten as he had removed his gloves in order to tie the mask on the ball turret gunner. The gallantry, complete disregard for his own safety and devotion to duty displayed by Sergeant King undoubtedly saved the life of his comrade. His actions on this occasion reflect highest credit upon himself and the Armed Forces of the United States."

T/Sgt. Harry Greenfield replaced him as radio operator. Helmick's crew had given their aircraft the name *Our Mark* for the original ball turret gunner Henry Markowski, wounded "on loan" with the crew of Lt. Brannan.

Some crewmen had less personal feeling about their plane because they never had their "own" plane; they flew any aircraft assigned to them. Others simply never got the opportunity; they were shot down before they had a chance to name a plane. Still others had to fly a spare aircraft, as did copilot Harold Granger of the Massol Crew. Their regular plane, 238047 *Fever Beaver*, was grounded due to a bomb bay motor failure, so they flew the spare 232018 *Waticare*. As they were assigned to another plane, Granger did not feel so optimistic about their chances of getting to the target and back. His gut feeling would be prophetic today!

Lt. Montgomery's ship, a brand new B-17G, was out of commission, so his crew took *The Pride of the Century*; the oldest 'hack' on the field. After the success of their previous mission Lt. Robert Connaway, Montgomery's copilot, had a feeling they would make it back in good shape, in spite of whatever plane they were flying. Meanwhile, the gunners installed their weapons into their mounts. Each B-17G carried thirteen M2 50-calibre Browning machine guns each weighing 64 pounds with an average rate of fire of 750 rounds per minute with an effective range of 600 yards that was lethal to humans up to 4 miles!

On *Ronnie R*, S/Sgt. Kerwin got both waist guns out of the engineering shack near their hardstand and installed them in the waist. S/SgtCharles Allen had his own superstitions:

"Even though I knew Kerwin did a good job installing them, I reinstalled my gun each time just to make sure. You see, if that gun failed me, it was my life! The moment we stepped into that plane and shut the door, it was all business. No fooling around, no let up."

Frank "Steve" Stevens painting two swastikas on *Our Gal Sal*.

Above and left: 50 cal ammo loaded into waist and ball gunner positions.

Lt. Massol's Aircraft, 232018 *Waticare*.

The top turret was electrically powered and equipped by a very effective Sperry gun sight.

The ball turret hung under the fuselage and was also electrically powered. As he would have to spend the next hours curled up, the ball turret gunner would wait to enter the ball as long as possible. Furthermore, it was no place to be during take-off.

The radio operator manning the 50cal machine gun. This gun proved to be ineffective due to the limited field of fire.

Waist Gunner in full Flight Gear manning his 50cal machine gun.

The twin 50-cal tail position, nicknamed the "stinger," was where Staff Sergeant Don Blair would take up a kneeling position on a bicycle seat for long hours. His task was to scour the contrails looking for enemy fighters sneaking up from behind. A German fighter's first target when attacking from the rear was to take out the tail gunner first, then the engines.

At other hardstands around the base, final checks were being made as bombardiers or toggliers checked the bomb installations, aircrew armourers checked all the guns, and radio operators tested their equipment.

As Lt. Shoens and Lt. Shand did a final cockpit check, they unhesitantly trusted that M/Sgt. Wildrick and his ground crew had done everything humanly possible to insure the crew's safe return. Shoens had every reason to trust his ground crew; they would eventually be awarded the Legion of Merit for their maintenance work on four 351 BS aircraft, including *Our Gal Sal* (See Appendix B).

After the crew stowed their flight gear they gathered in the ground crew's tent or homemade shelter drinking black coffee and making small talk, anything to ease the nerves and tension waiting for the start engines signal. "Ok guys, time to go! Check your parachute harness." Each man looked at another's harness to see that it was not twisted or bunched tight. In the event of an emergency, a loose or twisted harness could cripple a man. Men in front of the plane pulled themselves up into the hatch or used the ground crew stepladder while the rest of the crew entered by way of the rear escape door.

As Shoens and Shand settled into their positions in the cockpit, they stored their parachutes and flak vests close by. The flak suit was so heavy and cumbersome that many crewmen preferred to put it on just before entering enemy territory. Some pilots had ground crews "midnight requisition" extra flak vests to sit on to protect the "family jewels." The pilots of *Our Gal Sal* had no such worry, as M/Sgt. Waldrick and company had put armor plates in the pilot seats to protect them.

As the crew settled in, Shoens looked towards the tower while the time ticked down. Ten, nine, eight (will the mission be postponed?), seven, six, five, (will the mission be scrubbed?),

Members of Capt. Cope's crew waiting for the signal to go!

2nd Lt Duncan Shand, copilot on *Our Gal Sal*.

four, three, two, one! A green flare arched up from the control tower: 0700 hours—start engines. Within minutes, the sound of 140 Wright Cyclone engines came to life on the hardstands surrounding the perimeter of the runway at Thorpe Abbotts. The ground vibrated throughout East Anglia with the sound of B-17 and B-24 engines turning over.

Onboard Ronnie R the radio operator, ball turret gunner, both waist gunners, and the tail gunner were in the radio compartment sitting against the bulkhead waiting for takeoff. This allowed the pilot a balanced aircraft at takeoff. Every man on the crew respected Lt. Radtke, the pilot. During training in Rapid City, South Dakota, Lt. Radtke made sure every man on the crew had at least 30 minutes at the controls of a B-17. This allowed him to inspect every station in the air and to see what is was like from their perspective, and they could get some flying time in case of emergency.

One by one, the ships started to taxi out of their hardstand to the perimeter track. For taxiing, the two inboard engines were set to idle and the outboard engines provided the power for maneuvers. Shoens and his crew watched for the tail number of the B-17 that they had to follow to take the correct place for take-off. They taxied *Our Gal Sal* behind 238044 *Spirit of 44*, Lt. Merrill Rish's plane. Pilots could not see ahead over the nose of the plane so they used the left edge of the taxiway as a guide. Lt. Shoens' top turret gunner and engineer, T/Sgt. Sergeant Bill Eresman, stood behind the pilot seats during taxi time. It took several minutes to reach the head of runway 28 west.

The crews taxiing in the thirty-five 100BG bombers represented a diverse cross section of combat experience. The Kendall, Barton, Chadwick, Harper, Gibbons, Thomas, and Wilson crews were newcomers, trying to get one more mission under their belts. Lt. Albert F. Amiero had a 'pick up' crew. His copilot, Flight Officer Howard L. Kilmer, had just joined the 100th. The radio operator, T/Sgt. Sergeant John J. Kovacs, was a 'spare' from the 'original' 100BG air echelon. The tail gunner, S/Sgt. Thomas D. Baer, was from Lt. Victor Reed's Crew. The left waist gunner, S/Sgt. Owen D. Stockton, was from the Lt. J. Brown crew, and the right waist

Lt Mark V. Wilson's crew in front of *SHILAYLEE*. Standing: John T. Johnson - NAV, Roth (not the regular CP), Mark V. Wilson - Pilot, Ralph A. Kroenke - BOM, and Cecil Davis - TG. Kneeling: John W. McAuliffe, Donald M. Rohasek, Eugene V. Sweeney, George B. Donahue, and William E. Moreland.

Lt. Morgan's aircraft *Horny*, 25957, on the March 6, 1944, Berlin mission.

gunner, S/Sgt. Hobart H. Spires, came from Capt. Sam Barr's original crew. In Leon Morgan's crew, Toggler S/Sgt. Sam LaFace took over Lt. Albert P. Rule's seat.

For Capt. Cope and his crew, it was mission number 23. Inside the radio room of 237807 *Alice from Dallas II* Cope's radio operator, T/Sgt. Sergeant John Eling, performed a strange ritual. Eling always placed on his radio table the orange and candy bar he got from the Red Cross. He would not eat them until they were at interrogation. For some unknown reason, Capt. Cope was not flying his usual aircraft that day, *Superstitious Aloysious*.

Captain David Miner had a very special reason for getting his crew through that mission without any problems. They were all flying their 25th and last combat mission; Twenty-four hard fought missions over Hitler's "Fortress Europe" with just one more to go.

In 230799 The Bigassbird II Lt Murray was taking a little ribbing. He was the old man of the crew at twenty-seven. They nicknamed him "the great whitefather," but the whole crew had great affection and respect for Murray. They thought him one of the best pilots a crew could have.

Captain Frank Lauro and his crew in 231306 *Nelson King* would be the lead aircraft of the B Group with Command Pilot Captain Jack Swartout flying in the right seat. Though Swartout was a fighter pilot at heart, he was regarded as one of the best "lead" pilots the 100BG had, or for that matter, the whole Third Bombardment Division. From October through December 1942, he was assigned to the Accelerated Test Branch at Wright-Patterson airfield in Dayton, Ohio, where he learned how far one could exceed an aircraft's limitations and get away with it. While at Thorpe Abbotts, he had made friends with several P-47 pilots from surrounding bases and never missed an opportunity to buzz their field. This never failed to stir up a couple of guys to come up and play: lots of fun and 'tactical' experience. He would get to use plenty of that 'tactical experience' today!

All the pilots were performing one final take-off check as the ships maneuvered towards the head of the runway. The distinct squeal of the B-17 breaks was heard around the perimeter as the cold morning air whipped through the officers on the control tower

Captain Frank Lauro's crew.

Lining up to take-off March 6, 1944.

The green take-off flare was fired from the tower and the first B-17 pilot released the brakes.

Superstitious Aloysious, Lt. Malooly's aircraft on the March 6, 1944, Berlin mission.

and the ground crews watching from the hardstands. Everyone was wondering, waiting, hoping, and praying for a successful take-off and return. The ships were overloaded with bombs and fuel. Even the slightest loss of power during the take-off run could result in a crash at the end of the runway or a stall just after lift-off. Everything had to be functioning properly. When it was your turn to take off, you pushed the throttles forward, stood on the brakes, and waited for the signal to go. You needed every bit of power you could muster from those engines to get you off that runway.

At 0754 hrs the green flare rose from the tower; 8th AF Mission 250 was underway for the 100BG. Lt Devore and Major Elton pushed the throttles forward, released the brakes, and began their take-off roll. When their plane lifted off, the controller flashed his Aldus lamp and another bomber began its take-off roll; one aircraft began its takeoff roll every 30 seconds until it was Shoens' turn. He pushed the throttle forward and released the brakes. The plane accelerated slowly down the runway, gathering precious air speed. They were always apprehensive about getting off the ground, especially with the load they were carrying. At 110 mph, Shoens eased back on the wheel and slowly *Our Gal Sal* lifted into the air. By 0826 hrs, the thirty-five planes of the 100 BG had all taken off.

Throughout East Anglia, a now-accustomed rumble shook windows, doors, and teacups. A total of 730 heavy bombers—B-17s and B-24s—took off from thirty airfields, carrying more than seven thousand men, five millions rounds .50 caliber ammunition, more than two million gallons of aviation fuel, and the bomb bays filled to capacity with incendiaries, high explosive, and general purpose ordnance.

On take-off, the top turret / engineer helped the pilots while the rest of the gunners gathered in the radio room, the safest place on a B-17 in the event of a takeoff crash. Once airborne, crewmen went back to their positions to watch for other aircraft getting too close. With all the traffic from the surrounding bases it was not uncommon for planes to stray into the neighboring airfields take-off pattern, especially if there was morning mist or fog to be dealt with. More often than any crew would like to consider, this situation invited a mid-air collision and a funeral pyre the next plane taking off had to fly over; a chilling, numbing effect on even the most seasoned crew.

To decrease the risk of mid-air collision, each pilot had a pre-set list of times, turns and climbing altitude in order to "corkscrew" his way up above the base and break out of cloud cover. Above and below, other planes were doing the same. A little too fast or a little too slow and you had another bomber in your face or chewing up your tail. All around East Anglia, hundreds of B-17s and B-24s climbed individually on course and assembled above the clouds into groups over their base. Shoens was flying through turbulence that was obviously prop wash; someone else had been there seconds before. The crew kept a constant vigil, scanning the sky for potential danger.

Once above the clouds, the B-17s maneuvered into their position in the formation as outlined at the briefing. Flying formation was a lot of tedious hard work on your arms, legs and nerves. One had to put the airplane in their assigned position and keep it there for hours on end. Some positions were more difficult to fly than others were, but none was easy. Formation flying was taxing both physically and mentally. Be caught out of position and you could present a good target for the Luftwaffe and leave your squadron vulnerable.

Lt John Harrison in front of *Liberty Belle*, SN#2107211. (Courtesy of Charleen Hill)

March 6, 1944, Berlin
13 B Wing After Assembly

100 A Group

	Lead Squadron	
	Devore – Elton 231981 LN E	
Chadwick 23413 LN V		**Granack** 239872 LN A
	Cope 237807 LN O	
Pearson 231074 LN Q		**Malooly** 231049 LN U

	Low Squadron	
	Wilkinson 239927 DI R	
Warren 239821 DI J		**Dower** 232089 DI W
	Sutters 231971 DI E	
Reich 238130 DI B		**Sterr** 231892 DI H

	High Squadron	
	Harrison 231710 XR P	
Murray 230799 XR J		**Amiero** 231731 XR M
	Cowan 231723 XR R	
Wilson 23534 XR N		**Morgan** 25957 XR D
	Lautenschlager 238197 LN T	
Gibbons 231968 LN D		**Harper** 232009 LN X

100 B Group

	Lead Squadron	
	Lauro-Swartout 231306 LD V	
Helmick 237936 EP M		**Handorf** 238011 EP P
	Brannan 231735 EP B	
Shoens 231767 EP E		**Rish** 238044 EP R

	Low Squadron	
	Massol 232018 EP L	
Ferbrache 23508 LD P		**Lacy** 231389 EP J
	Montgomery 230170 XR G	
Slot Not Filled		**Koper** 231051 EP K

	High Squadron	
	Miner 238059 LD A	
Kendall 230278 LD R		**Barton** 231800 LD U
	Gummersall 231895 LD Y	
Terry 297482 LD W		**Radtke** 297491 LD B
	Forsythe 238175 LD Q	
Thomas 26087 LD Z		**Barrick** 239994 LD D

Heading Out.

Lt. Forsythe crew in front of 230152 *Messie Bessie*.

The crews used to call the lowest, rearmost and most exposed flight 'Purple Heart Corner.' Lt. John Gibbons 231968 *Miss Irish*, flew opposite in 'tail end Charlie;' the last of nine aircraft in the high squadron, A group. Lt. Shoens was not sure that any position was any more dangerous than another was, as long as they had a good tight formation. Squadrons were rotated as to which one would fly lead, high, or low.

By 0833 hours, the 100 B group formation consisting of 20 planes led by Captain Swartout in Lauro's plane completed its assembly over the base. Two minutes later Major Elton, leading the 100 A Group, had assembled his 15 aircraft in formation (along with six aircraft sent over from the 390BG to fill in the Low Squadron) over Thorpe Abbotts. Devore's copilot, Lt. Jerry Felsenstein, took over the tail gun position as formation control officer. After both A and B groups had joined together, the 35 planes would continue to circle until it was time to depart, joining the 95BG and the 390BG to assemble the 13 A Wing and 13 B Wing. It was at this point that mechanical problems started taking their toll on aircraft, causing aborts. The crews would simply chalk it up to another SNAFU (Situation Normal All F—ked Up)

The Thomas Crew – B Group, High Squadron

At 0910 hours, the first aircraft turned back to base from 9,000 feet over Splasher 6. The pilot, Lt. William H. Thomas, and his copilot, Lt. J. J. Raring, were flying #9 position ('tail end Charlie') in the 100 B Group, High Squadron. They landed 26087 *Royal Flush* at Thorpe Abbotts at 1116 hours. This is the same *Royal Flush* that was the only aircraft in the 100BG to return from the Munster mission on October 10, 1943, with Lt. Robert 'Rosie' Rosenthal's crew.

The Forsythe Crew – B Group, High Squadron

S/Sgt. Percy J. Johnston, Lt. Wallace C. Forsythe's top turret - engineer, detected an oil leak, which forced the ship to turn back at 0924 hours while it was flying at 9,000 feet near Halstead. They were flying #7 position, third element lead, high squadron, B group; the same element that Thomas had vacated 15 minutes before. Aircraft 238175 landed at 1050 hours. Ground crew checked things out and determined everything was OK. The crew's diagnosis had been wrong!

Lt. Forsyth's B-17, 238175, back at Thorpe Abbotts.

S/Sgt Ed Silverstone (Stone) BTG on *Our Gal Sal.*

Fever Beaver (238047), Lt John Massol's regular A/C. He flew this B-17 on the two recalled Berlin Missions on 3 and 4 March 1944 and reached Berlin in *Fever Beaver* on March 8, 1944.

In *Our Gal Sal*, Staff Sergeant Ed Silverstone, like the other ball turret gunners in the formation, left the comparative comfort of the radio room and went back to enter his cramped quarters. Many people had the idea that a ball turret gunner had to be short. Stone, however, was 6 feet tall! There was not enough room inside to wear a chute, so it had to remain stored just outside the turret so he could get to it quick. The gunner knew that before he could vacate the ball he had to position the turret so that the guns pointed straight down and the escape hatch was inside the fuselage. He then had to unplug the oxygen and interphone connections, the heating suit, and the safety belt before climbing out of the Ball and into his chute.

Sergeant Bill Eresman went to remove the arming pins from the fuses of the ten 500 pound high explosive bombs. This would allow the arming vanes to turn when the bombs fell and fully arm them.

"Pilot to crew, 10,000 feet, oxygen on; repeat, oxygen on."

The oxygen mask was now glued to the face and connected to the oxygen system. The moisture from breathing could condense and freeze, plugging free passage of oxygen. At intervals, they needed to squeeze their mask to dislodge ice formations. At high altitude lack of oxygen rapidly induced unconsciousness, and 20 minutes later you were "cold meat." Since crews were on oxygen, the copilot Lt. Shand called each member of the crew for a regular check, by crew name position, starting with the tail and working forward. If someone did not acknowledge the closest man was dispatched to investigate. To walk around the plane or in case of emergency, the crew had to unplug their oxygen connection and fit it onto a walk-around oxygen bottle.

It was now 0956 hours. Just over two hours had passed since the first ship had lifted off from Thorpe Abbotts and when the 13 A Wing and 13 B Wing Combat Wing formed up at 10,000 feet over Splasher 7. Elements of the 4 Wing, 13 Wing, and 45 Wing gathered to make up the Third Bombardment Division before leaving the English coast. The coastline passed beneath the wings of *Our Gal Sal* and drifted away behind them; it was now 1019 hours. The A Group flew over Aldeburgh, 3 miles north of the briefed course. The aircraft started to climb to combat altitude. Each plane followed his leader and held formation even if he veered off from the briefed route. Nevertheless, a navigator never lost track of his position; his plane could develop a mechanical problem or battle damage and have to come home alone. It was essential for the navigator to know exactly where you were at all times. The gunners were charging their guns and scanning the sky as the gremlins once again struck!

The Massol Crew – B Group, Low Squadron

Lt. John Massol had his share of problems with the spare he took in place of 238047 *Fever Beaver*, his regular ship. There was a leak in the oxygen system that showed up after they had assembled at altitude. As they reached the North Sea, they had already lost half of its 400-pound pressure in the system. The mission was impossible to complete under those circumstances. This was the

Lt. John Massol's crew.

third time the Massol crew set out for Berlin, only to be turned back this time by mechanical failure. Flying as top turret-engineer was T/Sgt Sidney Cary. He had been with Lt. Arch 'Four Mile' Drummond's Crew on January 24, 1944, in 23307 *Skipper* when it crashed on take-off trying to avoid a collision with a B-24 that had strayed out of its flight pattern. Three men were injured and Lt Maurice Zetlan, the bombardier, killed. Since then, Cary had been in the spare gunner's pool and was a fill-in for Lt Massol's crew on all three of their attempts at Berlin. Sidney would have to wait until May 7, 1944, to finally complete a mission to Berlin; in fact, he went to Berlin four times that month with Lt Lucius Lacy's crew, who were fondly nicknamed "Lacy's Lushes." Cary's fourth mission that month to Berlin was May 24, 1944. Four days later the war was over for Sidney; he was shot down over Magdeburg and became a POW in *Stalag Luft* IV.

Lt Massol turned back at 1032 hours from 14,800 feet, 60 miles in front of Aldeburgh. They returned to base nearly 3 hours after takeoff at 1117 hours. The ground crew found and repaired the leak.[22] It was SOP (standard operating procedure) to maintain a balanced formation if possible. Therefore, with Massol's abort, Lt Montgomery took over lead of the low squadron and at 1100 hours Lt. Sam Barrick, flying #8 in the high squadron, B Group, had changed to low squadron to fill in for Massol. The formation and Wing could become a little loose while forming up and heading across the North Sea, but once the enemy coast was in sight, every group tightened up their formation. The pilots concentrated for hours, their eyes glued on their wingman, gunners watching the skies, tension mounting, heart pounding, and the enemy coast drawing near.

Over in *Our Gal Sal*, Shoens did most of the flying. From time to time Shoens let Shand fly formation and some landing time so that he would have the skills to do so. Since non-operational talking over the interphone was discouraged for the other members of the crew, assembly time was one of boredom. There was little to do but think, check the oxygen regulator, and try to keep warm. It was worse in the rear; more of a flying freezer than a flying fortress. The gunners depended on their electrically heated suits and heavy sheepskins for warmth. They wore silk gloves under their heating gloves because if they touched the metal with their bare hands, they would literally stick to it. Left waist gunner S/Sgt. Bill Wright was the youngest crewmember, just 18. At the right waist gun, S/Sgt. Virgil Warders was the "old man" at 30.

T/Sgt. Sidney A. Cary, Top Turret - Engineer on Lt Massol's crew.

100BG on the way to Berlin.

Sgt William Wright, waist gunner on *Our Gal Sal.*

"OK guys. Test-fire your guns."
"Watch where you are firing."

Each one of the 13 guns fired a short burst. Shoens ordered his engineer to pull the Tokyos. Sergeant Eresman went to open the valves that were located in the bomb bay on either side of the radio room door. The 18 self-sealing rubber cells contained 1,080 gallons of gas, adding 250 miles in range.[23]

The enemy coast was crossed at 1107 hours, 20,000 feet.

"OK. Flak suits."

The three Bombardment Divisions assembled in a tandem arrangement with 12-mile intervals between each combat wing. As the bomber stream was slogging along, the 'Little Friends,' the escort fighters, were 'essing' around providing top cover for their "Big Friends"

Even though the ceiling and visibility was unlimited (CAVU), the visual impressions of Lt. Joe Carty, Chadwick's bombardier, were reduced by the frosted B-17 nose due to a malfunction of the defroster. Carty tried to scrape the ice with an escape knife but the scraping turned out to be more Plexiglas than ice. On entering enemy territory, the gunners twisted and turned, peering in all directions, probing the sky for signs of enemy fighters. They called it the "Messerschmitt twist."

The Gummersall Crew – B Group, High Squadron
Lt. Mark G. Gummersall and Lt. Reginald C. Holliday turned back at 1132 hours from 20,000 feet, 16 miles before reaching the German border. They were the third aircraft to abort in the high squadron, B group, leaving only five planes where there had been nine. Gummersall's ship reached Thorpe Abbotts at 1231 hours.

* * *

Lt. Randall Chadwick's crew in front of 231537 *Randi Lou.*

Standing: Frank Roberts, Reginald Holliday, Ed Carr, and Mark Gummersall. Kneeling: John Gensel, Robert Braswell, James Penny, Mathew Boguminiski, James Daly, and Henry Bieze.

Capt. Joseph "Bubbles" Payne

Four planes of the 100BG had aborted form the "B" Group, resulting in 52 less .50 caliber machine guns to defend the formation. They would miss those additional guns today. Lt. Shoens recalled:

"It was a beautiful day. Western Europe lay below us, it looked like a road map. The sun was warm coming through the windows. It began to look too good."

But something was wrong, deadly wrong!

While over the North Sea, the gap between the Fourth A and B Combat Wings and the Thirteenth A and B Combat Wings had increased from the standard 12 miles to 20 miles. This would not have been a problem, except the 482nd BG pathfinder leading the First Bombardment Division suffered radar failure. The lead navigator did not adjust sufficiently for a 45 mph northeast wind, which took him off course to the south of the planned route. This created a deviation from the planned route, and the First Bombardment Division, along with the 4 A and B Combat Wings, were now drifting off course south of the planned route at a rate of approximately one mile for every two minutes of flying. As the 100BG crossed the Dutch coast, they were no longer in visual contact with the First Bombardment Division and the trailing element of the four A and B Combat Wings. The 100BG lead navigator Captain Joseph 'Bubbles' Payne had adjusted for the northeast 45mph winds and proceeded on the course as briefed. With radio silence in effect, Captain Payne presumed the bomber stream was up ahead and gave Major Elton and Lt. Devore the correct course. Colonel Ross Milton, leading the 8AF that day, unaware of the navigational error, presumed that the entire bomber stream was following the First Bombardment Division. Both presumptions created a huge gap between the bomber streams, and at noon the 100BG found themselves in the unenviable position of being "in the right place, at the wrong time"; right square in the front of the bomber stream with only eight P-47s for fighter support!

Lt. Bob Shoens realized that they had not seen their 'Little Friends' for several minutes; a relay had not caught up with the 13 A and B Wings. Somebody in the back of the plane said:

"Hey, there's no escort, has anyone seen our escort?"

They all perked up and scanned the skies. Shoens knew they were due to be relieved so he did not worry. Out in the distance, silhouettes could be seen heading towards the 100BG. Surely, this was the fighter escort relay catching up to them? Suddenly the intercom crackled to life:

"Nose to pilot, enemy fighters, 12 o'clock, level!"

It was 11.59 hrs, and all hell was about to break loose; *Our Gal Sal* and the 100BG were heading straight into the middle of it.

Our Gal Sal "Calm before the storm." 11:59 March 6, 1944.

100 B Group

11:59 AM March 6, 1944

Lead Squadron		
	Lauro-Swartout 231306 LD V	
Helmick 237936 EP M		**Handof** 238011 EP P
	Brannan 231735 EP B	
Shoens 231767 EP E		**Rish** 238044 EP R

Low Squadron		
	Montgomery 230170 XR G	
Ferbrache 23508 LD P		**Lacy** 231389 EP J
	Koper 231051 EP K	
		Barrick 239994 LD D

High Squadron		
	Miner 238059 LD A	
Kendall 230278 LD R		**Barton** 231800 LD U
	Radtke 297491 LD B	
Terry 297482 LD W		

III

High Noon!

"It looked like the whole damn *Luftwaffe* was headed for the front of the 13 A and B Wings!" As Lt. Shoens recalled:

"Fighters came at us like a cloud, I looked up and was startled and thought:

'Holy cow, look at that!'

They came in one big mass, a big ball of fire. My first hint that something was wrong was when the fighters went through us. Jack Swartout got that chunk taken out of his tail and he drifted off by himself, I thought he was a goner for sure. Then somebody said:

'Boy, look at the high squadron, it's all gone.'"

Lt. Hudson and T/Sgt. Eresman opened fire at about 1,000 yards with the chin and top turrets, and the recoil of their .50 calibers shook *Our Gal Sal*. A wisp of smoke and the smell of cordite passed through the flight deck. Shoens pulled into the tightest possible formation; they were now fighting for their lives. Ed Silverstone heard the call out for fighters and turned his twin 50s in the ball as close to the 3 o'clock level position as he could. He was hoping to track one of the fighters as it went past and get a shot. Silverstone recalled:

"It is funny what you remember in combat, as the guy came through, I could see his moustache and thought he needed a shave. These things happen so fast in battle that you don't have time to get scared!"

The German fighters were attacking the 100BG head on at a closing speed of 500 mph. The blinking flashes from the wings told the pilots and gunners that 20mm shells were coming their way. The gunners were firing off short sustained bursts at the fighters streaming past exceptionally close.

Lt Shoens' observation about the size of the German formation headed their way was not far off. The German fighter force, under the command of Rolf Hermichen from I/JG 11, had amassed one

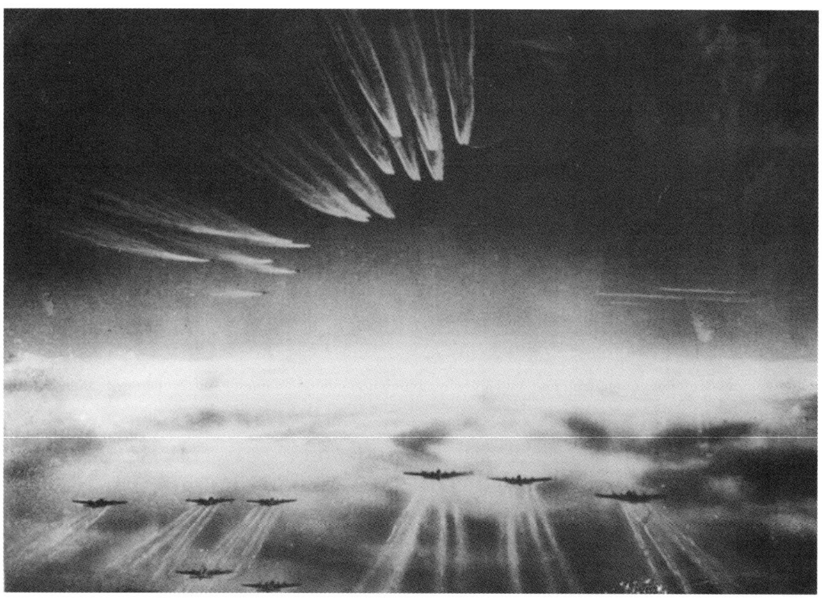

B-17s of the Mighty Eighth pressing into Germany.

T/Sgt William Eresman, TTE on *Our Gal Sal.*

of the largest *Luftwaffe* formations ever scrambled towards a bomber formation. In all, there were 107 Me 109s and FW 190s that comprised this lethal force. The composition of the German fighter force that attacked the 13 A and B Wings on March 6, 1944, was as follows:

Stab and I/JG 11 led by *Hauptmann* Hermichen – 4 Me 109s and 13 FW 190s
III/JG 54 led by *Hauptmann* Rudolf Sinner – 20 Me 109s
III/JG 11 led by *Hauptmann* Anton Hackl – 18 FW 190s
II/JG 11 led by Major Guenther Specht – 15 Me 109s
I/JG 1 led by Major Karl Schnoor – 16 FW 190s
II/JG 1 led by *Hauptmann* Hermann Segatz – 21 FW 190s

The *Luftwaffe* order of battle was such that I/JG 11 led by Hermichen attacked first, followed by III/JG 54. Rolf-Gunther

Rolf Gunter Hermichen: by all accounts he is responsible for shooting down either Lt Lohof or Lt Vollmer on March 3, 1944. He also has three B-17 confirmed kills on the March 6, 1944, Berlin mission, one of which was definately a 100th BG aircraft.

Hermichen shot down his first of three B-17s at noon over Haseluenne (there is no doubt this was a 100 BG aircraft). His next two victims were shot down at 12:06 and 12:12 respectively over S Delmenhorst.

Rudolf Sinner, leader of III/JG 54, followed I/JG 11 through the 13th Combat Wing. At 12:06 he is credited with shooting down a B-17 over the Essen-Vechta area, which is most likely one of the 100BG bombers. He did not escape unscathed from the air

Heinz Knoke was credited with shooting down one B-17 on March 6, 1944.

Major Heinz Bar was leading II/JG 1.

Ofw Heinz Stower of I/JG 11. Credited with shooting down a B-17 on March 6, 1944. Stower's luck would run out when he was KIA May 30, 1944. At that point in time he had 16 confirmed kills, eleven of which were B-17s. (Tim Calvert)

combat. During the battle his Me 109G was hit hard by .50 calibre fire during an attack on a B-17. He was badly wounded in the left thigh as his fighter's engine exploded into flames, causing it to spiral earthward and forcing him to bail out. Following closely behind Sinner in III/JG 54 was Freidrich Ungar, who had lined up a 100th BG fortress in his sites and was getting good hits. With a closing speed of approximately 500mph, and lining up the B-17 in your site, there was only enough time left for a short one second burst before you were forced to pull up. Waiting any longer invited a certain head on collision. Ungar left the stricken B-17 smoking and leaving formation, although he would only be credited with a "damaged" B-17.

It seemed like a procession of Me 109s and FW 190s were making their way through the 390th, 95th, and 100th Bomb Groups. Anton Hackl, Guenther Specht, Karl Schnoor, and Hermann Segatz were leading their Gruppens head on through the compromised formations, with flaming wrecks, parachutes, B-17s in all forms of distress and others hanging on for dear life.

Major Heinz Bar, flying in Hptm Segatz II/JG 1, claimed three B-17s on March 6, 1944. At 12 noon, over south Dinklage Germany, he shot down his first. Heinz Bar would become group commander of II/JG 1 just nine days later on March 15, 1944. Bar would go on to shoot down 220 allied aircraft. Sixteen of those victories would come in the Me 262A jet fighter.

As the German fighters made their way towards the 13th Combat Wing, the men in the Flying Fortresses had their own perspective of the events unfolding in front of them. Leading the 13th Combat Wing "A" Group was Lt Herb Devore, with Command Pilot Major Albert "Bucky" Elton.

The Devore-Elton Crew – A Group, Lead Squadron

As I/JG 11 and the rest of the *Luftwaffe* closed in on the Lead Squadron, 100 A Group, Lt Devore and Major "Bucky" Elton could not believe the amount of enemy fighters headed their way as the first passes by the Me 109s and FW 190s wreaked havoc on the formation. Captain Mark Cope was forced to leave the formation due to a damaged engine and oxygen system, while the crews of

Iron Cross First Class for downing 6-7 Allied Aircraft. (Tim Calvert)

Lt. Herb Devore's crew in front of 239934 *My Aching Back!* Standing from left: Jerry Felsenstein (Copilot), Herbert G. Devore (Pilot), Louis R. Jaebker (Bombardier), and Burton M. Joseph (Navigator, one of the 100th's greatest lead Navigators). Kneeling from left: Darrel Dickenson (Left Waist Gunner), Nicholas Delcimmuto (Ball Turret Gunner), Harry S. Lenk (Radio Operator), Harrison Longhi (Top Turret Engineer), John J. Barry (Right Waist Gunner), and Knute Knudson (Tail Gunner).

Lts Murray, Amiero, and Lautenschlager in the high squadron were fighting for their collective lives! As the Me109s and FW 190s pressed their attacks, Major Elton thought his navigator, Capt. "Bubbles" Payne, and bombardier, Capt. Robert Peel, were missing an excellent opportunity to shoot down enemy fighters. Elton got on the intercom to Peel "Get on em, Peel!," but Peel was quick to respond, "What the hell do you think I'm doing, playing checkers with Payne?"[24]

The Cope Crew – A Group, Lead Squadron

At 1205 hours, a damaged engine forced Captain Mark Cope to vacate the lead of the second element, lead squadron A group. The oxygen system was knocked out and the tail gunner, S/Sgt. Raymond Bryan, was wounded in both legs. Due to the lack of oxygen, Captain Cope ordered the bombs to be jettisoned and put *Alice from Dallas II* in a dive and leveled at about 6,000 feet. They would now be "stragglers," making their way back to England alone.

Captain Mark Cope's crew and Ground crew in front of 231049 *Superstitious Aloysious* before its name was painted on the nose.

The Malooly Crew – A Group, Lead Squadron

This was a new crew who were just assigned to the Group on February 21, 1944. They were flying *Superstitious Aloysious* in the #5 position of the lead Squadron, A group. This was Lt Frank Malooly's third mission to Berlin. They were recalled on 3 March, hit Berlin on 4 March with the composite group, and were now on their third mission to Berlin. This crew would have the distinction of going to Berlin a total of nine times (most of any crew with the 100th Bomb Group). Their last time would be on May 24, 1944, when they would be shot down and become POWs. Lt Malooly's copilot Robert Bailie describes the following action:

"March 6/44

Mission to Berlin again. All 8thAF, swell day, sunny and a few scattered clouds below us. We were at 23, 000 ft. about the coast of Germany, we picked up P-47's and 100 mi into Germany, they left us and another group was to pick us up. P-47's left us and a few minutes later about 50 FW's attacked us. Were were #2, second element, lead squadron. They came in between 10 and 2 o'clock, knocking down all but two of the high squadron also knocking Copes (Capt Mark Cope) ship in #1 causing him to drop out of the lead and we moved into his place taking over lead of the 2nd element, lead squadron. Tried to get fighter help but couldn't contact them. The FW's shot at us for about 30 min. We had no fighter escort from there to target and half way home."

The Gibbons Crew – A Group, High Squadron

Miss Irish was flying the #9 position "tail end Charlie" in the high squadron A Group. T/Sgt. John Craven, flying as Toggler, called out over the intercom:

"Fighters,12 o'clock high coming down."

Lt Francis J. Malooly's crew (left to right): Standing: Barrie (ROG), Bailie (CP), Mauvais (NAV), Malooly (P), and Guida (BOM). Kneeling: Miller (RWG), Pardee (BTG), Yeager (LWG), Perry (TTE), and Genovese (TG).

S/Sgt. Frank Buschmeier, looking out his left waist gunner position, estimated there to be approximately 30 FW 190s. This was Gibbons' crew's fourth mission since joining the 100BG in February 1944 and their fourth in a row flying as "tail end Charlie." They had been recalled on the 3 March Berlin mission, gone to Berlin with the composite group on 4 March, and were now on their third mission in a row to *Big B*. The law of averages had to be weighing heavily on their minds. As the fighters sliced through the Group, Buschmeier heard someone on the intercom:

"There goes Lauternschlager!
"There goes Amiero!"
"There goes Murray!"

Finally, someone asked:

"Who's left?"
"We're the only ones left!"
"Get us out of here John!"

As planes pulled out of formation in all forms of distress, the integrity of the formation was compromised, leaving very little defensive firepower to protect the high squadron. Sweat and cordite permeated the air around one as one tried one's best to survive. S/Sgt. Bushmeier recalled:

"If you were caught in a German fighter's gun site you were a goner. You just hoped he had the next guy in his site instead of you."

Gibbons' crew was not the only plane left in the 100A Group High Squadron, but after the first pass, the formation was so busted up it looked like they were the only ones left. Leading the 100 A Group High Squadron was Lt John Harrison. Tail gunner S/Sgt Bruce 'Curly' Alshouse remembers that first pass 63 years later:

"They beat the crap out of us! After the first pass, there were only 4 planes left in our formation! I saw parachutes and fighters all over the sky. . . .I filled the sky with lead with my twin 50's and used up a lot of ammo, don't know if I hit anything. . . .there were so many Forts going down, I kept asking our top turret gunner if the engines were all still running."

The parachutes were the remnants of the three Fortresses—Amiero, Murray, and Lauternschlager—the *Luftwaffe* had just shot down from the high squadron. They counted only 10 parachutes, leaving 20 friends, sons, and fathers MIA/KIA.

The Lautenschlager Crew – A Group, High Squadron

About a minute after the initial fighter attacks, the bomb bay of aircraft 238197 *Half and Half*, #7 in the High Squadron, A Group, ignited into an inferno. The radio operator, T/Sgt. John Stryjecki, bravely attempted to extinguish the flames but to no avail. Other shells had crippled the oxygen system and knocked the chin and ball turrets out. The bombs were immediately jettisoned and the crew prepared to bail out.

Pilot Lt. John Lautenschlager gave the order to abandon the bomber, then climbed out of his seat and held the aircraft straight to give his crew time to jump. Then he made his way to the nose escape hatch, where he found his top turret gunner, T/Sgt. Robert T. Bashaw, seemingly stuck in the exit. He pushed the man clear, then dove out the hatch after him. Lautenschlager was the last to leave the stricken aircraft, and as he cleared the tail, the plane flared up and exploded. The brave Stryjecki was killed when his parachute failed to open. The crew was on their 15th mission when *Half and Half* crashed at Halter, near Visbeck; nine men POW, one KIA.

The German interrogators thought Lt. Lautenschlager was a "plant" to test their procedures. The *Luftwaffe* did this from time to time to determine the accurateness of interrogators. They soon determined that Lautenschlager spoke flawless German and could not believe he was an Allied airman. It was the other members of

Lt. John '49 Missions' Gibbons' crew. Kneeling: Edward Walker, Jr., Bernard L. "Bernie" Spragg, Archie W. "Bugs" Bunting, and Frank W. Buschmeier. Standing: Ira L. Arnold, John P. Gibbons, Robert "Bob" Dykeman, Sterling B. Blakeman, Everett Max Johnson, and Myron J. "Ty" Ettus.

J. Lautenschlager (Pilot), W.J. Sugg (CP), D. Rolnick (BOM), L.C. Fink (NAV) C.W. Graham (WG), R.T. Bashaw (TTE), S. Wilenski (WG), J. Stryjeski (ROG), H. Fussell (TG), and H. Sheldon (BTG) of *Half & Half*.

Lt. Albert R. Amiero

the crew that changed their minds, since they, of course, did not know the Germans thought Lautenschlager was a *Luftwaffe* officer and soon inadvertently convinced the Germans Lautenschlager was their pilot!

The Amiero Crew – A Group High Squadron

Only S/Sgt. Owen D. Stockton, left waist gunner, survived by sheer luck and the Almighty from Lt. Amiero's 231731 before it broke apart. Toggler Sam LaFace, on the Morgan Crew, saw a B-17 leaving the first element, on fire and out of control. He shouted out "Jump! Jump!" and tried to see if any parachutes opened and how many. It is possible LaFace, along with the navigator Lt. Albert Rule, who had flown before with LaFace in the nose of Morgan's ship, witnessed the loss of the Amiero crew.

The Widow of Owen Stockton releated the following story to Craig L. Koontz, Colonel, USAF (relative of S/Sgt Virgil Summers, BTG), on the pick up Amiero crew, who in turn shared it with us:

"Owen Stockton was the left waist gunner on Capt Amerio's pick up crew. On the first encounter with German fighters, the tail gunner, 'Teddy' Baer was mortally wounded. Someone from the crew dragged him out of the tail and up on to the floor of the radio compartment. Apparently he was shot up pretty badly as the crew didn't think that they could help him other than to give him a morphine injection to ease his pain. It was Owen who went back and manned the tail gun since Baer absence left the guns silent and an open invitation to enemy fighters to attack from the rear. In any case, she didn't know if the aircraft blew apart, or spiralled down, but the stress on the fuselage caused the tail section to break off. Owen Stockton stayed with the tail section all the way down. He told his wife that he couldn't get out. (The G-forces of the tumbling tail section may have precluded his getting to and hooking up his parachute.) Apparently the tail section landed in some trees and cushioned the landing enough to spare his life but Owen Stockton's back was broken (in two places).

There was some initial confusion on the part of the Germans because there was some distance between where the tail "fluttered"

"Jump! Jump!" a B-17 starts its final plunge. (USAF)

Taken during stateside training, Lt. William Murray's crew near the tail section of 23447 *Stateside*. Standing: Mahlon Hall-TG, William Carr-BOM, Orrin Heinrich-NAV, William Kraft original CP, William Murray-Pilot, and Emory Brandt-TTE. Kneeling: Fred Schillinger-ROG, Jim Peace-BTG, Palmer Hanson-RWG, and Nick Hamalak-LWG.

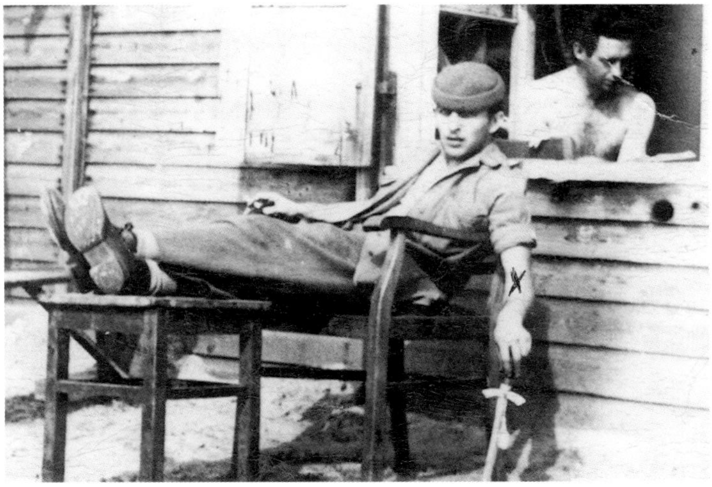

Lt William G. Carr, Bombardier for Lt Murray's crew at *Stalag Luft* 1, Barth, Germany, after liberation.

down and where the rest of the aircraft crashed with the remains of the crew. Mr. Stockton was immobile from his injuries and, once captured by the Germans, was taken to a hospital along with other POWs. He spent the better part of a year in the hospital before being transferred to Stalag Luft IV for the remainder of the war. She indicated that he had chronic back problems for the rest of his life and that he had significant psychological issues because he was the only one from his crew to have survived. Regardless, she told me that he lived with those demons for all his remaining life and that he rarely talked about the mission on March 6th."

The Murray Crew – A Group, High Squadron

Flying the # 3 position in the High Squadron of the 100 A Group, 230799 *The Bigassbird II* suddenly plunged out of formation with its tail afire. A 20mm shell had entered the cockpit and decapitated the pilot, Lt. William Murray. The tail gunner, S/Sgt. Mahlon Hall, was in the radio room having his head wound dressed by the radio

Staff Sgt. Fred C. Schillinger Jr.
... presumed dead

Schillinger, a senior radio operator-gunner, was on a mission over Berlin when, according to War Department reports received by his parents, his plane was shot down in flames. Seven members of the crew have ben heard from but no information has been received from three, one of which is the Scranton flier.

Schillinger enlisted in the Army Air Forces Nov. 11, 1942, and was called to active duty five days later. He trained at Sioux Falls, S. D.; Las Vegas, Nev.; Moses Lake, Wash., and Rapid City S. D. A graduate of Central High School, he was employed by the Dollar Dry Cleaning Company before entering service. He left for overseas duty in November, 1943. Schillinger was on his 11th mission when his plane was shot down. He has been awarded the Air Medal with Oak Leaf Cluster.

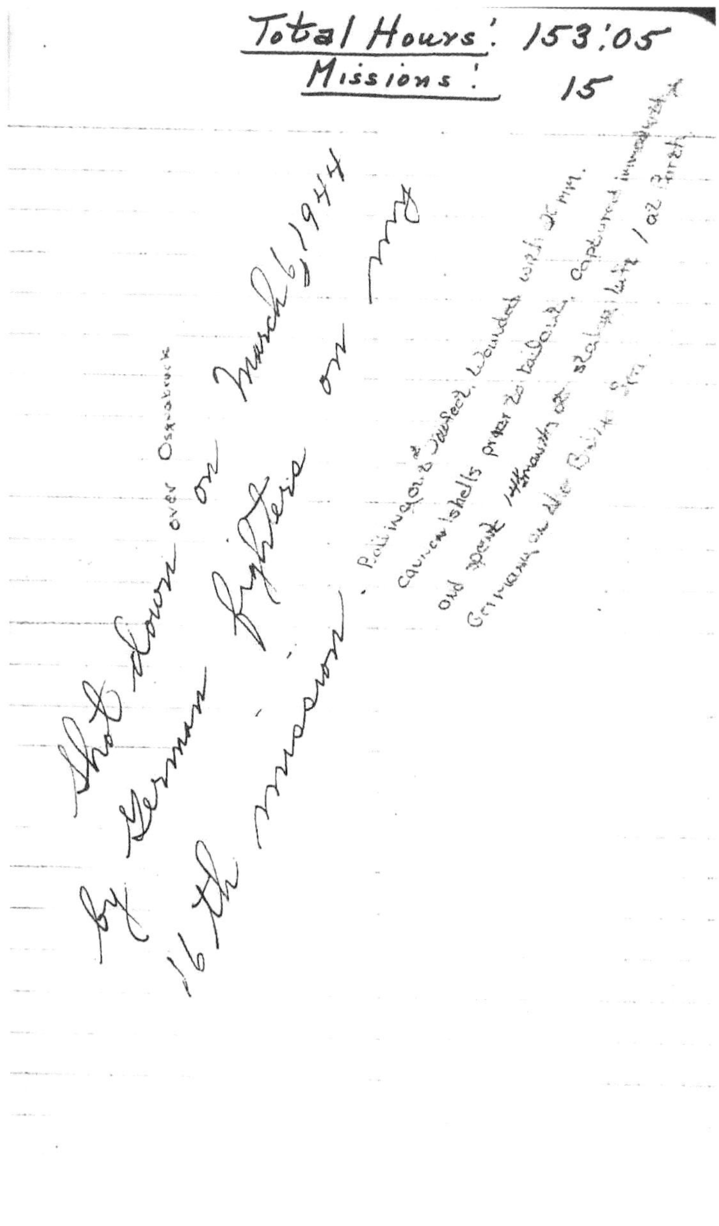

Orrin Heinrich's diary and S/Sgt Schillinger Jr's MIA notice.

operator, S/Sgt. Fred Schillinger, when the plane went into a dive. The centrifugal force pinned them inside the plane and they both died in the crash.

An article in the *Antigo Daily Journal*, Antigo, Wisconsin, describes Lt. Orrin Heinrich's experience over Germany on March 6, 1944. This was his 16th mission after flying 153 total hours:

"Heinrich's story began March 6, 1944, when his B-17 bomber with a ten-member crew was shot down by German ME-109 fighters over the Diepholz swamp in Vechta County. The 28 year old lieutenant and flight navigator was one of seven who survived [three did not]. He and another crewman parachuted to earth somewhere in the southern part of the county. Heinrich says he remembers landing near a barn and farmhouse, located at a crossroads. A fish pond was nearby. The downed airmen, both wounded, were treated well by a tall pipe-smoking farmer and his 14-year old son who spoke English. They didn't bother us at all. They wanted us to walk the four or five miles to town. 'I was wounded and my companion was wounded and I didn't think we'd make it', Heinrich says. 'I got him to hitch up the horse and wagon and take the two of us to town.'

The casualty report read:

"First pass by fighters damaged the plane, second pass injured Lt. Murray…third pass killed Lt. Murray and seriously damaged *The Bigassbird II*. Lt. Murray's Crew was shot down by German fighters in the vicinity of Haseluenne and Holdorf, in Vechta County, Germany [about 80 miles south of Bremerhaven on the north coast of Germany]."

On March 10, 1944, Lt Orrin Heinrich was registered as a POW at *Dulag-Luft*. *Dulag-Luft* was a central German Air Force Interrogation Center near Frankfurt. His identification number (KGF) was 3377. Orrin spent 14 ½ months as a prisoner of war at *Stalag Luft* I as a "guest of Germany." What Orrin found particularly hard was the loss of T/Sgt Freddy Schillinger. He was a close friend.

Here is Lt. Orrin Heinrich's personal log he had for March 6, 1944:

"Shot Down over Osnabruck on March 6, 1944 by German Fighters on my 16th mission. Bailing out at 2000 feet. Wounded by 20mm cannon shells prior to bailing out. Captured immediately and spent 14 ½ months at Stalag Luft 1 at Barth, Germany on the Baltic Sea."

From his radio hatch on *Our Gal Sal*, Don Hammond saw a B-17 from the 100 BG falling down in flames and hollered into the intercom for Shoens:

"We gotta move, there's a plane on fire."

Shoens replied:

"I can't move, we're in formation. If we move, we'll all be down."

Then the blazing plane came lower, gradually sinking back and below them. Under these extremely scary attacks, Hammond was starting to feel as if they were not going to finish the mission. He thought of his mother and wished he could see her now.

The Harper Crew – A Group, High Squadron

Lt. Celesta B. 'Red' Harper with copilot Lt. Robert S. Flannigan were flying #8 in the High Squadron, A Group, trailing in the third and last element along with Lt. Gibbons. They and their B-17G 232009 *Black Cat 13* faced the onslaught of the German fighters. On the second pass by fighters of *Jagdgeschwader* 54 led by Rudolph Sinner, Harper's Toggler, Sgt. Walters, shot down two Me 109s. "Red" Harper describes the action:

230799 *The Bigassbird II*, A/C Lt Murray flew on March 6, 1944.

Left to Right: A. James (ROG), A. Frank (TG), W. Dobbs (LWG, J. Bowers (RWG), A. Curlee (BTG), and C. Luquet (TTE). Kneeling: C.B. "Red" Harper (P) and A. Cox (BOM).

"They were throwing everything they had at us. A rocket hit us in the waist section after damaging the right horizontal stabilizer. Our oxygen tanks in the rear were damaged and the electrical cables had been severed."

During debriefing the top turret engineer, T/Sgt. Luquet, reported:

"A 20mm shell entered the flight cabin just behind the pilot and exploded. Among the equipment destroyed by shrapnel was my two canvas spent cartridge bags, my electrically heated flying suit and boots. Another shell had penetrated the cabin behind the pilot and exited behind the copilot after destroying the cockpit oxygen tanks."

'Red' faced a life or death situation. To save the crew from anoxia, due to the destroyed oxygen system, the pilots put the plane in a dive from 21,000 to 5,000 feet and headed for England. Lt Harper and Capt. Cope were now stragglers heading for home over enemy occupied territory…alone!

The Gibbons Crew – A Group, High Squadron

During the relentless fighter attacks, four bombers from the 100 A Group High Squadron—Murray, Amiero, Lautenschlager, and Harper—had either been shot down or badly damaged. This left Gibbons with a big gap between himself and the remainder of the squadron. Lt. Gibbons' tail gunner, S/Sgt. Archie 'Bugs' Bunting, yelled to his pilot to do something quick, as the German fighters were turning and coming back. Lt. John '49 Missions' Gibbons very calmly replied to take it easy, as they were going to tack onto the lead squadron. John moved his plane down to the #5 position in the lead squadron. This offered him the defensive protection he needed, at least for the moment. Right after "Bombs Away" Lt. Granack, flying in 239872 *Rubber Check*, would be hit by flak and start to fall behind. His position in the lead squadron, just off Major "Bucky" Elton's right wing, would be taken over by Lt. Gibbons. Maybe now Johns' crew could feel a little bit safer.

If the Gibbons Crew was feeling a little bit safer, nobody in the 100th B Group felt like they would be coming out of this alive. The concentrated attacks by over 100 Me109 and FW 190 fighters were focused on the 13th Combat Wing, and in particular, the 100th A and B Groups. The sky was ablaze with burning wrecks on both sides of battle, and parachutes were strewn across the sky; there was not even time to count them all. In a matter of minutes, almost the whole B Group would be wiped out of the sky. There was not even time to say a prayer.

The Helmick Crew – B Group, Lead Squadron

Down in the 100 B Group Lead Squadron, T/Sgt George Madden, top turret gunner in 237936 *Our Mark*, saw a group of FW 190s coming in. One attacked *Our Mark*, but pulled up too soon. Out of the side of his right eye, Madden saw a FW 190 attacking Captain Swartout's lead bomber 231306 *Nelson King*.

T/Sgt. George Madden turned the turret at full speed to 12 o'clock level. Unfortunately, the reticule of his Sperry computing gun sight could not handle that situation.

As soon as the gun barrels pointed ahead he pulled the triggers. The bursting 20mm cannon projectiles were closing fast. The German fighter pilot started pulling down and went under Helmick's plane. By this time his gun sight had stabilized. T/Sgt. Madden set the vertical reticules on the wing tips of a 109 and pulled the triggers. The Me 109 started firing, did a half roll, wingtips and nose blinking as 7.92mm and 20mm shells poured in towards *Our Mark*. Then he pulled down to slide under the B-17. Another Me 109 came in and started firing, rolled over, and went under Helmick's ship as well. It was like shooting fish in a barrel, and Helmick's crew were the fish!

After another short burst from his guns both stopped. To reload as fast as possible, Madden dropped his shoulders down below the control motors so he could get both hands on the recharge handles at the same time. He recharged his twin 50s and came back up ready for another fight. The attack from the front seemed to be over. He looked back over at *Nelson King* and he was horrified to see the mess she was in. There was just enough vertical stabilizer

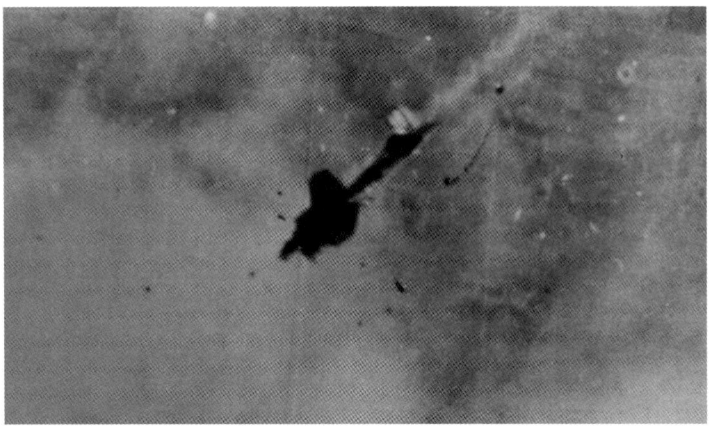

Fortress going down. (USAF)

Lt. Helmick's crew in front of 231412 *Mason and Dixon*.

left to hold the rudder that was going from side to side. Captain Lauro moved his bomber off to the right where he had plenty of room. T/Sgt. Madden turned around to the rear to see how many fighters were coming back. At this point, he realized formation flying was no longer a problem: there was no formation left.

One bomber was falling behind on fire. The crew was bailing out. Somebody sat down in the rear door and the slipstream blew a boot off. There was one other bomber in trouble a little lower at about 7 o'clock. As one fighter was turning to come back, Madden started firing at it. He thought it was going to attack the lone bomber at 7 o'clock. The engineer rotated forward to discover they were flying alone. He did not hear any talk on the intercom and had a weak feeling that maybe his aircraft had been hit. He discovered that in his violent gun recharging maneuver he had jerked his head set cord loose. He plugged it in. To his relief he could hear voices. Lt. Helmick was trying to tack *Our Mark* on to the 100 A Group, which was the high lead group.

Damage to 231306 *Nelson King* from FW 190 collision.

The Lauro Crew – B Group, Lead Squadron

The gunners were so busy firing their guns that they had not seen the FW 190 collide with their vertical stabilizer, taking a large piece out of it and damaging the cables. It is not known whether the German pilot was dead from the hail of lead from the bombers or simply miscalculated his closure rate. Immediately *Nelson King* was knocked out of formation. When Lauro and Swartout brought the ship under control they had lost considerable altitude. At 1210 hours they salvoed the bombs near Lohne/Dinklage and continued with the mission. Behind *Nelson King*, the first pass had taken its toll on the lead squadron. The B-17s of Lts Brannan and Merrill Rish were both severely damaged and going down.

The Rish Crew – B Group, Lead Squadron

Lt. Rish's B-17—Brannan's right wingman—was severely damaged by several Me 109s from III/JG 54 making head-on attacks. Rish's aircraft received numerous hits from 20mm shells and fire was visible around the #3 engine, causing the plane to immediately go into a tight spin. Centrifugal force prevented bombardier Lt. Don Kehm from releasing the escape hatch and the ship's interphone was inoperable. At about 3,000 feet, the tail broke off of the aircraft and the ship then began to nose up, as the bombardier could see all the objects coming toward him. T/Sgt. George F. Danehower, radio operator, and S/Sgt. Armand C. Burt, right waist gunner, had time to bail out just before the plane exploded, killing both pilots, Lt. Merril T. Rish and Lt. Frank A. Smith.

The blast had also blown out bombardier Don 'Heinie' Kehm, left waist gunner Estil V. McGuffee, top turret engineer gunner Howard T. Skaggs, and navigator Royal W. Lingenfelter. Don Kehm awoke on the ground with two German soldiers approaching him. For Kehm, McGuffee, Skaggs, and Lingenfelter, the familiar phrase "for you the war is over" rang in their ears. Barbed wire, Goon towers, bad food, and bad memories were in their future at POW camps *Stalag Luft* I and IV. The tail gunner, S/Sgt. Angus Alsup, was killed, as was the ball turret gunner, Sgt. Dewey Essary. Both men were still inside 238044 *Spirit of 44* when the bomber crashed and burned at Aschenbehl Berg.

"Fortress Engaged" by Keith Ferris depicts the aerial combat in the 351st Bomb Squadron as III./JG 54 Messerschmitt 109 pilots *Feldwebel* Friedrich Unger in "6" and *Unteroffizier* Erwin Muller in "4" pass Lt. Richard Hemlmick's undamaged B-17, 237936 *Our Mark* EP-M, and the mortally wounded B-17s Lt. George Brannan's 231735 *Lucky Lee* and Lt. Merril Rish's 238044 *Spirit of 44* EP-R. Both Rish and Brannan's B-17s were lost in the action. The two Messerschmitts were hit by the bomber formation's gunners and had to make forced landings. ((c)1985 Keith Ferris, United States Air Force Art Collection)

Lt. Merril Rish's crew. Standing: Estil McGuffee (Left Waist Gunner), Donald Kehm (Bombardier), Royal Lingenfelter (Navigator), Frank Smith (Copilot), and Merril Rish (Pilot). Kneeling: Armand Burt (Right Waist Gunner), George Danehower (Radio Operator), Angus Alsup (Tail Gunner), Harold Skaggs (Top Turret - Engineer), and Mike Kosh (grounded and replaced by Chester L. Powell).

Lt Shoens looked over at his wingman and roommate's plane (Lt Rish), and the whole wing was a sheet of flame. He would later report: "Saw '044,' number 2 in our element shot down by fighters. Saw 4 chutes." No sooner had Lt Rish gone down than Lt Shoens witnessed the enemy fighters shred another crew from the 351 Squadron. Flying in the #4 position in the 100 B Group, lead squadron, Lt George Brannan's plane *Lucky Lee* was under attack.

The Brannan Crew – B Group, Lead Squadron

The German fighters knocked out the two right engines of 231735 *Lucky Lee*, leading the second element in the lead squadron, B group. The regular ball turret gunner, S/Sgt. Charles Elliott, flew in the waist. S/Sgt. Robyn Fulton, who had taken over his place, was having his share of problems. With his ball turret damaged, the intercom inoperative, and injured in his right arm and leg, Fulton rolled the guns down and exited into the waist section. As he pulled himself from his turret, he glanced towards the bomb bay; a great stream of gasoline was pouring out of the right wing. It was quite evident it would only be a matter of seconds before the plane blew up. He put his chute on and tried to leave through the waist exit, but it was jammed and would not open. Like breaking down a door, Elliot shouldered the hatch several times before the hatch and Elliott were whisked away by the slipstream.

Lt. George W. Brannan ordered the crew to bail out. A few moments later the ship exploded, killing copilot Lt. Thomas Leslie and navigator Lt. Clyde F. Dale. The rest of the crew, including Lt Brannan, bailed out successfully and ended up POWs. T/Sgt. Teaff bailed out successfully and was taken prisoner, but died from diphtheria on July 10, 1944, while at *Stalag Luft* VI. According to Charles F. Elliott:

"On 6 March '44 near Stettin, in East Prussia, the plane was hit amid ship by ground fire. Two crewmembers were killed immediately, the co-pilot died in the fall, the pilot and navigator made it out of the plane, but a German fighter killed the latter in his chute."

Sgt. Elliott was snagged in the hatch and was pushed out by another crewman; he bumped the horizontal stabilizer, but successfully opened his chute around 6,000 feet and then drifted slowly to the ground. He was immediately found by Polish peasants, but German soldiers commandeered him. He spent the rest of the 16 months of the war mostly in *Stalag Luft* IV, until his camp was liberated by Russian troops. After that, he spent months in a Veterans Administration hospital recovering from a back injury courtesy of a German guard's rifle butt. *Lucky Lee* crashed near Hausstette.

* * *

The lead squadron of the 100 B Group had been bloodied with the loss of 2 aircraft, but the high squadron was decimated. Three crews—Lt Gummersall, Lt Forsythe, and Lt Thomas—had already returned early, and Lt Barrick had moved down to the low squadron to fill in for Lt Massol's abort. This left the high squadron with only 5 of the original 9 bombers that left Thorpe Abbotts that morning. By 1204 hours all 5 of the remaining planes in the high squadron would fall to the *Luftwaffe*.

"First Strike on Berlin" by Nicolas Trudgian portrays the fierce aerial combat on March 6, 1944, as B-17 Flying Fortresses of the 100th Bomb Group are attacked enroute to Berlin. Fw190s of II./JG I based at Stormede attack head on into the bomber stream while eight P-47s from Hub Zemke's 56th Fighter Group (Zemke's Wolfpack) try to break up the onslaught. Lt Brannan's crew in *Lucky Lee* survives the first pass, but her luck will run out soon. Lt Robert Shoens' crew in *Our Girl Sal* (to the right of the picture) will survive the mission unscathed. Chalk it up to "luck of the draw." (Courtesy of Nicholas Trudgian, www.nicolastrudgian.com)

Lt. George Brannan's crew and 231735 *Lucky Lee*. Kneeling: Thomas Leslie (Copilot), Clyde F. Dale (Navigator), George W. Brannan (Pilot), and Louis J. Denisco (Bombardier). Standing: Walter Austin (Top Turret - Engineer), William F. Teaff (Radio Operator), Charles F. Elliott (Waist Gunner), Howard T. Larimore (Waist Gunner), and Robert L. Greenleaf (Tail Gunner).

Captain David Miner's crew.

* * *

The Miner Crew – B Group, High Squadron

Captain David Miner had a very special reason for getting his crew through this mission without any problems. They were all flying their 25th and last combat mission, except Lieutenant George Kinsella (from Lt Reilly Crew) and Lieutenant Earl Richardson (from Lt Flanigan Crew), filling in as copilot and navigator, respectively. If the Rish crew completed this mission, they would finish their tour and be rotated back to the States for reassignment. They had survived twenty-four missions in the "Big Leagues" of aerial warfare. All that was left was to find some way to complete this mission, but the grim reaper had stacked the deck against them this time!

Some fighters split off and attacked the high squadron B group. Cannon fire raked the front portion of the lead aircraft, literally wiping out the cockpit of 238059 and killing pilot Captain David L. Miner and copilot Lt. George E. Kinsella. The navigator, Lt. Earl Richardson, heard an explosion just above his head and saw a lot of smoke. Unlocking his flak suit, Richardson said to bombardier George Jones:

"Let's get the hell out of here!"

Jones said Captain Miner would let them know when, so both kept on firing the guns. Then Earl Richardson passed out from lack of oxygen. The plane went out of control, heading towards high squadron, A Group. Lt. John A. Harrison maneuvered 231710 *The Savage* to avoid a mid-air collision. Again the doomed, pilotless bomber approached, and again aircraft of the high squadron maneuvered to avoid a mid-air collision. This time the stricken Fortress stalled, went up on its tail, then slid down. Waist gunners S/Sgt. Sam Pry and S/Sgt. Leonard Malcuit escaped through the waist door, only to find themselves engulfed in flames trailing from the blazing right inboard engine. In the nose, Earl Richardson regained consciousness just in time. The B-17 had already gone into a dive with the Plexiglas nose gone and minus the tail section. Bombardier Lt. George Jones was nowhere in sight; maybe he had already bailed out. Richardson wasted no time, snapped on the chest pack, and crawled out of the nose. His parachute popped open just as the B-17 hit the ground. He felt the heat of the fire as he landed about 30 yards from the plane, near Quakenbrück. Unhooking his parachute, he ran for a ditch but the bombs never detonated. The whites of his eyes were cherry red from the blasting wind that had come through the shattered nose of the stricken B-17.

The bombardier, Lt. George Jones, had indeed left the mortally wounded aircraft, but was found dead on the ground. It appears that he had been blown out of the nose without his chute. He, like many others that day, died flying his 25th and last mission. Eyewitness Report:

"Four parachutes were observed to come from lead ship, low squadron, believed to be #059, after enemy fighter attack at 1213 hours, north of Hanover."

Lt Chadwick (from Lt Chadwick's position in the A group, this would have appeared to be the lead for the low squadron, but Lt Miner was in fact leading the B Group High Squadron...MPF)

Exerpts from *My Twenty-Fourth Mission With The Hundredth Bomb Group* by Earl L. Richardson, Major USAF Retired:

"Here we go again March 6, 1944. Talk about Blue Monday. Over eight hundred bombers of the Eighth Air Force formed over England. The flight plan was a straight line to 'Big B' and back—maybe. Bucky Elton was leading the Hundredth's 'A' Group consisting of twenty-one planes. Swartout was leading the 'B' group of 21 planes. I was replacing the navigator on Dave Miner's crew, leading the high squadron of the 'B' Group. Miner's crew and Flanigan's crew lived together and this mission would finish our tour of duty.

We were fifty miles into German territory and somehow missed the fighter escort. The time was high noon and the area south of Bremen near Dummer Lake was a major checkpoint. The fighters hit the lead and low squadron from eleven o'clock. They were sufficient to completely wipe out or scatter the two lower squadrons. They charged in twelve at a time, over forty of them. Jones (Miner's Bombardier) and I had a box seat while shooting at the enemy: fires, explosions, and gyration of the planes being shot down and thinking how lucky we were to be high and dry.

One amazing thing stays in my mind about Swartout's plane. Its vertical fin collided into a German Fighter, but somehow he managed to make his back to England. Out of the 'B' group.

The first enemy fighter I saw shooting at us was coming in on the high squadron less than five hundred yards straight out. I remember wishing I had Royal Flush's manual nose guns because this plane was fitted with slow moving electric operated sights, which never had time to catch up with the target. As it turned out, this could have saved my life. By hitting the FW190 with rounds from our nose guns, we may have had a head-on collision. I am sure it was this first pass that killed Miner and copilot Kinsella. The FW held level and split off at less than fifty yards. The twenty-millimeter shells went into the windshield. We couldn't hear a thing on the intercom after several loud explosions.

Several following passes came in higher, out of the sun, at one o'clock and further out, it seemed like they never stopped coming at us. Our right engines were on fire, I called this to Jones' attention and said we had better get the hell out while stripping off my flak suit and looking for my chest-pack parachute. Jones answered that he had all the confidence in his pilot and crew, so we went back to firing the fifty-caliber machine guns. The last I remember (no oxygen) was the plane going into a sharp turning climb. Luckily, I regained consciousness just above lightly scattered clouds, we were briefed that scattered clouds would be at approximately four thousand feet.

Out of the clouds the B-17 was heading earthward in a straight gliding dive. Everything had occurred so rapidly that the natural fear one has approaching death hadn't been felt. Time slowed down. The one thought which absorbed my mind was to find and get my parachute pack attached to my harness. I attached one hook, which proved sufficient. I could see the earth moving at a blurring speed. I dove out through the nose as the plastic cone had been completely shot out, pulled the ripcord, and the chute made a loud pop and at the same time the B-17 hit the ground with a thunderous explosion (over two thousand gallons of fuel on board). I was sure to go back to 25,000 feet when the bombs went off.

I landed less than a hundred yards of the burning plane. I could feel the tremendous heat, unhooked the chute, and ran for a ditch and hedgerow. I hit the ground several times, thinking that I was being shot at—turned out to be my ears clearing from the altitude. A FW190 hovered overhead while I was in the ditch taking off my shredded flying suit. The suit was denim and new for this mission but now it was a bundle of rags. Miraculously, I hardly had a scratch. The FW left the area and the B-17s bombs never exploded.

With my escape map, candy bar, etc. I started walking down the hedgerow toward a timber growth. The home guard was coming across the field, so I just kept on walking. They called 'Hite.' I waved at them and kept on walking. Their second shout brought rifles to the shoulders of two soldiers and my hands to high heaven. While I was being searched I looked up and could maybe eighty or ninety parachutes floating down. The soldiers kept the civilians at bay for they were mostly from bombed-out Bremen and were carrying pitchforks, clubs, etc. They paraded me up a little one-way street of a village named Addrup.

I was glad I wasn't wearing my Royal Flush flight jacket with the picture of Hitler, Tito, and Mussolini in a toilet bowl being flushed. The number of Germans that spoke English surprised me, and most all had the same question: why did America want to bomb Germany? I would say, 'Democracy' and they would yell 'Jew-lover' and spit in my face. Two soldiers put me in a wire closure. Later, at dark about fifteen Russians showed up, they were working as forced labor in the farm fields. The Russians would say, 'You Roosevelt, me Stalin.' Later, a truck took me to an airfield where in a gymnasium there were well over a hundred US Airmen. We were put on a train to Frankfurt.

How did I bale out of the nose section of a fortress in a dive? Easy. The plexiglass nose cone was gone and all I had to do was miss the vertical fin, wings, props, stabilizers, etc. What happened to Jones the bombardier? I later discovered the German's found his body without a parachute. The side fuselage door was the other escape exit being used. Gas and fire had been flowing past it and the first and third gunners were burned, but survived. I later saw them at La Havre, France on our way home.

At Frankfurt I was stripped and searched. My clothes were returned to me minus my shoes. I was led to a 3X6 foot cell with a wood platform for a bunk and no covers, but at least the room was warm. During the night they tuned the heat off and I woke up freezing. I began pounding on the door and the guard who spoke some English opened it. I was delighted to see my shoes by the side of my door. I asked him about the heat and he showed me a thermostat and instructed me not to pound on the door for attention but to pull a rope and a wooden arm would rise just above my shoes in the hallway.

After four days of this, plus a bowl of cabbage and potato soup each day, a soldier took me to be interviewed. There I received my first demonstration of a 'Heil Hitler Salute' and heel clicking. This German officer acted like he was overjoyed to meet me. He offered me chocolates, cigarettes, his version of 'real' friendship. Almost starved, I popped those chocolates as fast as I could. He showed me pictures of B-17s on the ground in England. He knew our squadron leader Blakely just made Major, but what he wanted to know from me was why I was flying with Miner's crew on their last mission, and what was the target. They were very well informed; he showed me a file that included information on most members of Flanigan's crew.

He kept asking me again about the target so I pointed to a section of Berlin. He blew his top and yelled for the soldiers to take me back to my holding area. The next day brought the same routine without the goodies. I stuck with my story and he yelled that this area couldn't possible be our target because it was a residential area and was where his family lived. Out again I went, only to have him come to my cell to inform me that I had been telling the truth. He was just informed that he lost his family in one of the raids. Our target on March 6th was a factory about ten miles outside of Berlin.

On the eighth day they released me to the compound. I had my first cold shower and shave. In the mirror, I realized why everyone noticed me. The whites of my eyes were fire red from broken blood veins from the wind rushing through the open nose section. It took almost nine months for my eyes to clear up.

We rode crowded boxcars from Frankfurt to Barth and Stalagluft I. This was on the Baltic Sea, it was freezing cold and snow on the ground. Small world, I was greeted at the barbwire gate by a fellow from my hometown, Washington, Iowa and my ole sidekick Scottie who had been with me off and on since Santa Ana, California. At prison camp I was issued two blankets, a GI overcoat, a mattress cover to be filled with straw, the top bed on a double bunk with boards for springs, and fifteen more roommates in a 12X14 room. The blankets, coat, straw, and I were pretty thin fifteen months later when the Russians liberated us during May, 1945. It was like a dream come true when B-17s arrived to fly us to Reims, France for our first good meal and freedom, although our stomachs could only hold about 4-ounces of food.

My crew began flying the Royal Flush in early September of 1943. The Flush was shot down on its seventy-fifth mission, while flying with its third crew."

One pilot in a badly damaged B-17 begged for fighter support on the VHF radio frequency but there was only silence.[25] There would be no reprieve, and the pilot's voice was silenced forever. In combat, some sights and sounds are harder to forget than others. Lt Sam Barrick had moved his B-17 *Snort Stuff* from the High Squadron B Group down to the Low Squadron, B Group, when Lt Massol aborted the mission and returned to base. While holding formation and watching out for enemy fighters, Barrick looked up at his previous residence in the High squadron. In a split second, he saw just how fast life could be stolen away from you.

Sly Fox, Lt Kendall's ill fated A/C on March 6, 1944.

The Kendall Crew – B Group, High Squadron

Pilot Sam Barrick glanced up to his right at the high squadron and watched Lt. Zeb Kendall's 230278 *Sly Fox* disappear in a large ball of fire and smoke. There were no survivors, just four engines trailing fire and falling debris. The official report reads: "Aircraft '278' was not seen after the first enemy fighter attacks at 1200 hrs." Kendall, Loughran, Gowen, Thorpe, Hickman, Tutor, Aguila, Bridges, Aven, and Stoffregen, all gone in the blink of an eye!

There is a feeling very rarely talked about or spoken about between combat fighting men—guilt. The uncomfortable feeling associated with the thought "better him than me" when a bomber explodes into thousands of bits and pieces, or is simply missing in action. Many may have experienced it, thought it, but very rarely will they speak about it. It is buried deep, never to surface; it is a kind of survivor's guilt that carries an obligation to speak for those who cannot. Such moments linger only as long as there is a lull in combat; for Lt Barrick and his crew the fighters were coming through again! The inter phone was crackling with the anxious chatter of his crew calling out the "bandits" while they were counting on their pilot to get them out of this mess alive!

Lt. Zeb Kendal's headstone in the Ardennes Cemetery.

Below: Lt William Thorpe Jr., Lt Clifford Gowen, and T/Sgt Leman Tutor from Kendal's crew.

S/Sgt Raymond Bridges and S/Sgt Aguila from Kendall's crew.

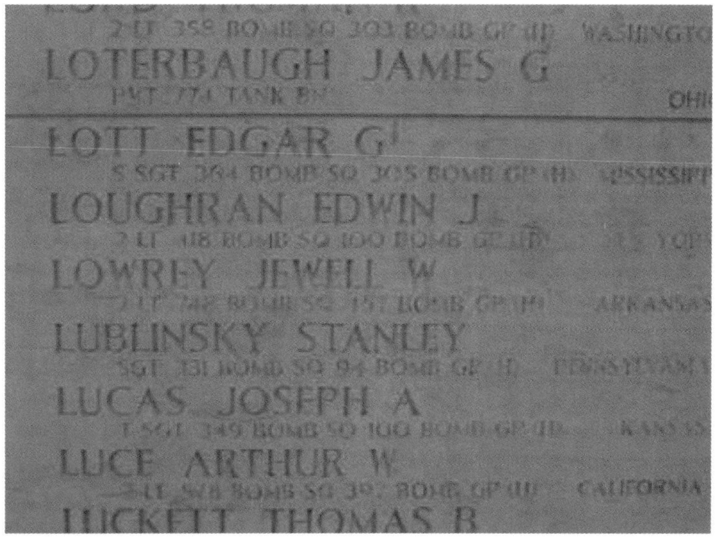

2nd Lt Edwin Loughran, CP on Lt Zeb Kendal 's crew, his Purple Heart, and his name on the Wall of the Missing in Netherlands American Cemetery at Margraten (Photos from Rick Rock's Collection taken by Joe O'Leary)

The Barton Crew – B Group High Squadron

Lost to enemy fighters south of Oldenburg, Germany, in the wide-ranging air battle at Haseluenne. Pilot Lt. Sherwin L. Barton and his crew successfully bailed out of the plane, putting an end to their two weeks in the ETO. This crew was on its fourth mission, having arrived at Thorpe Abbotts in February 1944. Until recently, we only knew that Lt Barton was briefly a prisoner of war at *Dulag Luft* in Frankfurt am Main, Germany, before being transferred to North Compound 1 at *Stalag Luft* I in Barth, Germany.

The following is a transcription of Lt Sherwin Barton's diary kept while in *Stalag Luft* I:

"This will start out as all stories do, with the date and time of arrival in Germany via parachute. We, Combat Crew 32, 418th Sqdrn, 100th Grp, 8th Air Force were shot down in flames near Oldenburg Germany, March 6, 1944. Four men were wounded, but all arrived alive. Sgt Taylor [Ball Turret] was hit in both legs above and below the knees with 20mm fragments, T/Sgt Moore [Top Turret - Engineer] was hit in the leg with .303 slugs, Sgt Morris [Waist Gunner] was hit in the legs with fragments and Second Lieutenant Burtch [Navigator] was hit in the left wrist with 20 mm fragments.

We started out for our third try in a row for Berlin. We all felt that we'd succeed this time, we did succeed, via a '40 and 8' box car.

As usual my insides were tight and I couldn't seem to check our ship enough. Oxygen, ammunition, flak suits, guns, spare chutes and spare oxygen masks were all O. K. but I still checked and rechecked until time to start engines. I apparently had a premonition of what was to follow, because I changed our bail out signals to , if you hear the warning bell and there are no planes within 1,000 feet, jump!

We were flying a borrowed ship 'Harpers Ferry'[26], as the 'Susan B' was laid up for repairs from our pervious mission. Our position in the group was as good as could be expected, but flak is no respecter of position.

We assembled and gain altitude as we crossed the North Sea, heading for the coast of Holland. We arrived, naturally, and Jerry sent up his greeting in flak-mean stuff and rather sudden in its appearance. We threaded our way through the first flak belt and prepared to go through some heavy stuff. One of our ships had been hit going in and had "aborted" with No. 3 Engine feathered. We could see the next flak barrage ahead, it was slowly getting the altitude and I could see we were going to get some hits. Our fighter escort left us at this point and I could see, high above us and to the left, contrails being made by approaching enemy fighters. I had just settled down to do some conscientious formation flying when we flew into the flak. About this time enemy fighters attacked from head on, and their first past sent our Squadron leader down in flames [Lt Miner's crew in 238059]. His left wing man was knocked out and set on fire in the same pass [Lt Kendal in 230278 *Sly Fox*]. The both went down and to the right. We were hit but still under control. I slipped the ship down and to the left to close the gap left by the first pass. Before I could close the gap, we were hit again. Folke Wulfe 190's were going through our formation like wind through a picket fence, ten and fifteen at a time. I looked ahead and saw two 'Forts' going down from the group ahead of us. Chutes were all over the sky. We were catching hell for sure. I'd had the dubious pleasure on my first mission of seeing another group under fighter attack. Now I was on the receiving end, and 'It aint funny McGee.'

We were hit for the third time just as I got into position and my rudder controls went slack. I knew we were getting hit in the tail but didn't know how badly. I pulled No.3 and 4 throttles back and just barely missed side swiping the ship on my left. My rudder was gone, and I was using my throttles to give me lateral control of the ship.

I had just got back into position again when a '190' got direct hits in the leading edge of the right wing just outboard of No.4 engine. He was using 20mm explosives, and as luck would have it, the wind got under the frayed edges of the wing 'skin' and ripped off a strip that was about six feet wide; it ran all the way back to the trailing edge of the wing. The ship immediately went into a violent turn to the right and it was all my Copilot and I could do to keep the ship from going over on her back. I said a prayer then and there and thanked God it hadn't been my left wing, because we'd have ploughed into the ship on our left, and I probably wouldn't be alive to tell of it.

Even when things were rough, a lopsided sort of luck was on our side. Our left wing tip was shot away which helped balance the loss of so much skin from our right wing. Even then, with our entire aileron to the left, we were in a bank of 5 or 6 degrees to the right. Something was wrong with the tail, and we had to keep the stick full forward to stay on a level keel.

You have read stories of wolves gathering around a campfire waiting for a victim. Picture yourself in that predicament, and walk away from the fire; then you'll know how I felt when I saw our group drifting away to the left. The '190's' were building a traffic pattern around us and were moving in for the kill. Suddenly, the controls went slack! It took me three weeks to get my heart out of my throat. I flipped on the automatic pilot, and I did some frantic knob-twisting. The only control that worked was the aileron. I threw it full left and glanced up at the instrument panel. My airspeed was dropping fast and if she stalled, we were 'gone geese'. I tried my last resort and spun the elevator trim tab full forward. Thank God it worked but even with it full forward the ship just barely flew level. I had wanted to 'hit the deck' but no chance now. I was hoping we could pick up some fighter escort and fly a huge circle until we were over England. Just then the ship jerked, we had been hit by flak. A shell had gone through the leading edge of the left wing between No.1 and 2 engines, and had exploded about fifty feet above the wing. I took a good look and part of No.1's oil cooler was sticking up like a finger of fate. About this time, the interphone was shot out and I was beginning to wonder what the hell I was doing in the Air Corps. My Copilot started pointing at No.3 engine. I looked over and we had a nice fire in No.3 nacelle. The blaze was 'behind the firewall'. I motioned for my Copilot to get his chute on, but he couldn't seem to understand me. I took off my oxygen mask off and hollered at him twice. Still he could not seem to understand. When I ripped off my flak suit and reached for my chute, he didn't waste any time getting his own.

I flipped the warning bell on and did something I'd wanted to do ever since I'd flown 'Forts,' I salvoed the bombs from the cockpit. There were ten 500 lb demolition bombs and I often wonder whose turnip patch I ploughed up. I pulled the engineer out of the top turret and his only comment was 'That right wing sure looks like hell'. He picked up his chute and started back through the bomb bay. I went down into the nose and pulled my navigator away from his side nose gun. We were still under attack. When he turned around, he looked as though he was wondering 'What the hell are you doing down here at a time like this.'

He saw what was wrong, and I motioned at my bombardier. The navigator pulled him around and I saw there he knew what was up. I had planned on going back up into the cockpit and on through the ship to make certain the crew were aware of our danger. However, when I turned around to go, my Copilot was standing in the catwalk opening, and he yelled 'For Gods sake Bart, get out, she's going to blow.' I ripped off the navigators escape hatch and the Copilot assisted my exit with a shove. He followed immediately.

My first sensation wasn't one of falling but of the quietness all around me. I tumbled and flopped around trying to see the ground but every time I'd twist, I'd start spinning around. I finally settled down on my back and looked at the plane. I could see several chutes but not nine. I checked and adjusted my harness, then I pulled the rip-cord and received a stiff jolt when the chute popped open. I rechecked on the chutes and a couple more came out of the plane while I was watching. I could see seven chutes. That left two more in the ship-when suddenly she blew up! Right then and there I said my prayers. I thanked God for getting out as many as he had before she blew.

I found out later that two of my enlisted men had trouble getting their chutes open and were far below me when I was looking for them. We had bailed out at approximately 21,000 feet and my ride down took quite some time. I was full of escape details of which S-2 had pumped me full, but alack and alas, Jerry's S-2 was full of 'nix' escape details. I was greeted soon after landing by a party of civic-minded citizens from the small village near which I landed. Three were led by a Gallant Corporal from 'Der Luftwaffe' and thanks to him, I am alive today. I was slugged by some eager Dutchman and would have been killed if it hadn't been for my man Friday.

All of this action, from the time of attack until 'Harpers Ferry' went up in a 'burst of glory' lasted approximately 15 minutes. We left our ship when the Jerries were making their ninth pass and 8 of

Lt. Barton's crew in front of 25967 Royal Flush.

them went down with us. Our career was ended on my 4th mission and 3rd mission for the rest of the crew.

We did all we could and I know that each one of us regrets not being able to do more. In the same breath we thank God for our life."

In the back of the plane, T/Sgt Jack Robins, ROG on Lt Barton's crew, remembers the events:

"We made our way towards Berlin through more flak then I have ever been through along with the fighter attacks and yet, being scared to death seems to make you a more alert gunner. As we neared Hanover, two engines were on fire from the flak and the plane dropped out of formation. I looked to the rear and saw a German fighter off our left horizontal stabilizer pumping lead into #2 engine. I was frustrated because I could not bring my 50 cal to bear on the enemy[27]. At that moment the bail out bell rang and I signalled the guys in the back with thumbs down, connected my walk around oxygen bottle and opened the door to the bomb bay. Finding the bomb bay doors open, I crawled along the catwalk and saw the flight deck empty so I headed for the back of the plane. I had an obligation to get the BTG out of his position so with the assistance of one of the waist gunners, we were able to pull the injured ball turret gunner out. He had been severly wounded in both legs by 20mm fragments so we put his parachute on him and the waist gunner and I shoved him out the side door. I went back to the radio room, put on my chest chute and headed back to the bomb bay. As I left the radio room, bullets came up through the floor so I knelt on the catwalk and tumbled out through the bomb bay. When I pulled the rip chord, the chute did not open, so worked frantically to tear it open, succeeding after free falling over 15,000 feet. As I floated down the last five thousand feet, it felt like an almost out of body experience. It was the most ethereal feeling I ever had. Landing in a plowed field and had just gotten off my chute when rifle shots rang out and a farmer and family captured me. I was given some sausage and bread to eat and an hour later a German soldier in a black leather jacket arrived on a motorcycle with a side car and drove me away to be interrogated. Bring Jewish, I was suppose to wear my fake dog tags on missions but had forgotten to switch them out today and now my interrogators had them. In a scene right out of a Hollywood movie, this tall blonde blue eyed officer speaking perfect English came in and tossed my dog tags on the table in front of me and said 'Ahh, Judah'. Naturally I was quite concerned, but that was the last time I heard of it."

The battle continued to rage across the sky. Burning wrecks of German and American aircraft littered the air and ground with debris and bodies alike. It was a horror show unsurpassed in the annals of aerial warfare. Witnesses to this unfolding spectacle kept pushing the nightmare images into the deep recesses of their minds while dodging a sky full of cannon and machine gun fire. They all saw the carnage and knew the clock was ticking down on their chances for survival. From every station on the Flying Fortresses men wondered when it would be "their turn." For the crew of Lt Terry, the clock had struck 12 and their wait was over!

The Terry Crew – B Group, High Squadron

Just after Miner's ship left formation out of control, Lt. William A. Terry's 297482 *Terry and the Pirates* was hit hard by 20mm cannon shells and the main control cables to the tail were severed. The B-17 nosed over and went into a spin. Navigator Lt. Robert Schremser was hit in the face and arm by fragments of one of the exploding 20mm shells. The centrifugal force of the spin had pinned him on top of his chute. He finally managed to clip it on as a hole broke in the Plexiglas nose. The bombardier, Lt. Ralph Cotter, sat there motionless but evidently not hit. He had not put his chute on. The night before this mission, Lt. Cotter wrote home to his mother:[28]

"Well today is Sunday and I am sitting in the club. We did not have a raid today, but it was such a nice day we went up and practiced bombing all afternoon. I had a very good day. I guess that is why I feel so well. Oh, Mom, I want you to look carefully in the Gazette, and the Boston papers because they gave our crew a write-up about Lieutenant William Terry, my pilot, and all our names are mentioned. Enclosed you will find a clipping on my 16th raid. Just think only 9 more raids and then I will be home. It will take about a month or more after I finish my 25 missions, but there is nothing to worry about. Well Mom, everything is fine, and I will say goodnight until tomorrow.

Love
Ralph"

There would be no more tomorrows for Lt. Cotter. The next letter his Mother would receive would be from the Secretary of War reporting her son Missing In Action.

S/Sgt. James Bain, in the ball turret, never realized anything was wrong until the aircraft started to dive and spiral out of control. Fortunately, his turret still had power and he was able to

Lt William Terry's crew. Top Row: Lt Schremser (Navigator), T/Sgt Aiken (Top Turret - Engineer), S/Sgt Bain (Ball Turret Gunner), and Lt Cotter (Bombardier). Bottom Row: S/Sgt Horn (Right Waist Gunner), T/Sgt Howell (Radio Operator), Lt Peterson (Copilot), and Lt. William Terry (Pilot).

rotate it down so that he could get back into the aircraft. There were two large holes in the fuselage. The main control cables to the tail were snapped and hung loose from the overhead structure. Bain managed to snap on his chest pack parachute and left through the gaping hole in the side of the ship. After thousands of feet, *Terry and the Pirates*' wings separated from the fuselage and the three major sections of the B-17 twirled the rest of the way down. The centrifugal force let up just enough for navigator Lt. Robert Schremser to head for the hole in the nose and dive out. S/Sgt. Bain floated peacefully to the ground and was picked up immediately by some *Luftwaffe* guards and loaded in an open bed truck.

Lt. Schremser was already in the back of the truck, as was the severely wounded top turret gunner / engineer, Sgt. Aitken.

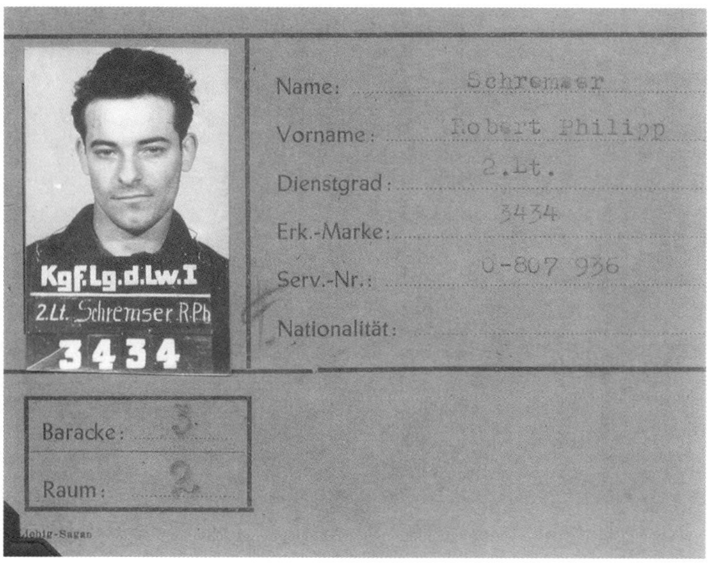

Kgf.Lg.d.Lw.I
2.Lt. Schremser R.Ph
3434

Name: Schremser
Vorname: Robert Philipp
Dienstgrad: 2.Lt.
Erk.-Marke: 3434
Serv.-Nr.: 0-807 936
Nationalität:

Baracke: 3
Raum: 2

POW card.

Except for small shrapnel wounds to his arm Bain was okay. Lt. Schremser was not as lucky, as he was bleeding quite badly from his face and arm wound, but was conscious and able to walk. Sgt. Aitken had lost his right leg, below the calf, to a 20mm shell. He seemed to have been thrown out by the pilots and the bombardier just before the plane crashed. The other seven crewmembers did not manage to get out. Schremser, Aitken, and Bain ended up at *Stalag Luft* I POW camp until the end of the war. The front section crashed and exploded at Brokstreek, near Quakenbrück. The tail section of *Terry and the Pirates* came to rest still containing tail gunner S/Sgt. Carl Hampton. This was the crews' 17th mission.

The Radtke Crew – B Group, High Squadron

With two engines knocked out, the Radtke crew flying in 297491 *Ronnie R* became a straggler. A German pilot pulled his Me 109 in behind the lone B-17 and poured more cannon shells into the bomber. Those rounds started a fire in the fuselage that soon reached the rack containing recognition flares. There were reds and greens shooting off, hurtling down the fuselage and bouncing off the walls. The only escape for radio operator T/Sgt. Bob Ray was through the bomb bay, where the bombs were still in the racks. Ray jumped off the catwalk onto the bomb doors that stayed desperately closed. As he was trying to climb back onto the catwalk somebody salvoed the bombs; one radio operator and his unfriendly escort were falling down to terra firma.

T/Sgt. Van Pinner came out of the top turret, put on his chest pack, and left through the bomb bay. The ball turret took a direct hit and the ball turret gunner, S/Sgt. Joseph Krusienski, became deathly silent. A 20mm had exploded on top of his ball turret, which never moved again. Oxygen bottles and lines were feeding the fires that started, filling the fuselage with smoke. Both waist gunners, S/Sgt. Charles F. Allen and Richard Kerwin, could not even get close to the ball turret to get Krusienski up into the ship. The intercom was knocked out. Kerwin kicked the escape door out and bailed out, and Allen followed a few seconds later.

This is how S/Sgt. Charles Allen remembers the events of that day:

"On March 6, 1944, we were flying *Ronnie R*, which was named after his newly born son Ronald R. Radtke. Take-off and assembly went off without a hitch. We were on our way to Berlin! It was a beautiful day and I kept scouring the skies for our little friends and enemy fighters. It had seemed like a long time since I had last seen our fighter protection. Radtke always kept me informed of the outside temperature, just as he said; it was 60 degrees below zero outside, and the first wave of fighters came barreling in head on. We never knew what hit us in the back of the plane; 20mm shells were exploding everywhere! As one of the FW 190s went by, I could see the pilots face, now that's too close. There was fire and smoke, communications were shot out, Oxygen was out, one 20mm exploded on top of the ball turret and his position went silent. We could not get to S/Sgt. Krusienski, I believe he was killed instantly. During the attack I had been hit by shrapnel on the right side of my face and eye, the plane was on fire, control cables shot out, we'd had it! It was 'every man for himself.' T/Sgt. Ray, our radio operator went out the bomb bay, along with bomb load, which just happened to be jettisoned at the same time. He told me later, 'As I was falling I was shouting for the bombs to 'get away from me!" I could not see the tail gunner but found our later he made it out but had lost a big toe from enemy fire. It was time to go, I pulled the release on my flak vest, clipped on my parachute, Sgt. Kerwin kicked out the escape hatch and I followed him out. When I landed I was captured by the German Army. I was thankful because there had been reports of American fliers being captured by civilians and being lynched or pitch forked to death. I had my G.I. issued .45 cal. Revolver on me just in case. We had been taught to shoot first, killed or be killed. I didn't plan on surviving a bail out only to end up on the end of a pitch fork! Instead, I was a guest of the Germans in Stalag Luft IV and Stalag Luft VI."

Lt. Dean Radtke Crew in front of 230091 *Blivit.*

Ronnie R crashed into a small wood just west of Bassum, at Binghausen. All indications point to *Ronnie R* being shot down by *Oberfeldwebel* Reinthaler of II/JG11. Reinthaler himself became a victim when three P-47 Thunderbolts of the 78th Fighter Group (stationed at Duxford) jumped him. After being hit by the eight 50 cal machine guns of Lt Robert Wise, the severely injured Reinthaler bailed out of his stricken Me 109. This would be his last combat. One of Lt Wise's rounds shattered his left elbow so badly; his arm had to be amputated above the elbow.

S/Sgt William Sapp (waist gunner), on Lt Barrick's crew, recalls their luck:

"We were shot down on 6 March 1944 on our way to Berlin on the first big Berlin raid. We had been to Berlin two days earlier when only 31 of us got there the rest of the Air Force had been recalled but we missed the recall. I was on my 13th mission when we were shot down. However, we were lucky in several ways. We had been flying in the high squadron until, at 11 o'clock, we switched to the low squadron to replace planes that had aborted. When the fighters hit us at noon, I saw the whole high squadron go down before I saw an enemy fighter. We had two engines hit in the initial attack and would not have been able to keep up with the formation except that there was no formation to keep up with we had lost 14 planes and, including our plane, this left seven planes flying."

In the low squadron, 100 B Group, Lt Montgomery moved into the lead position when Lt Massol aborted the mission due to oxygen malfunctions. There were 5 aircraft in the low squadron, including Lt Barrick's addition for the high squadron. There was no escape from the swarm of Me 109s and FW 190s that just poured through the remnants of the formation.

The Montgomery Crew – B Group, Low Squadron

After returning from Berlin on 4 March with battle damage and 3 good engines (231429 XR-L *Miss Carriage*), Montgomery was forced to take war weary B-17F model 230170 *Pride of the Century* back to Berlin. Enemy fighters are believed to be the cause of their loss. The plane crashed at Colnrade, killing its pilot, Lt. Coy I. Montgomery. The rest of the crew successfully bailed out. According to Lt. Connaway, "the pilot ordered the bombs salvoed and everyone to abandon ship." Just as he was leaving the stricken plane Connaway was knocked unconscious, most likely by the aircraft exploding.

Lt. Chadwick provided this eyewitness account:

"At 1215 hours just north of Hanover an A/C believed to be #170 was attacked by enemy fighters & was shot down. Four or five chutes were seen. I.D. of this aircraft is not positive; it may have been #051." (Lt Koper's aircraft)

Coy I. Montgomery.

(Courtesy of Kurt A. Stauffer)

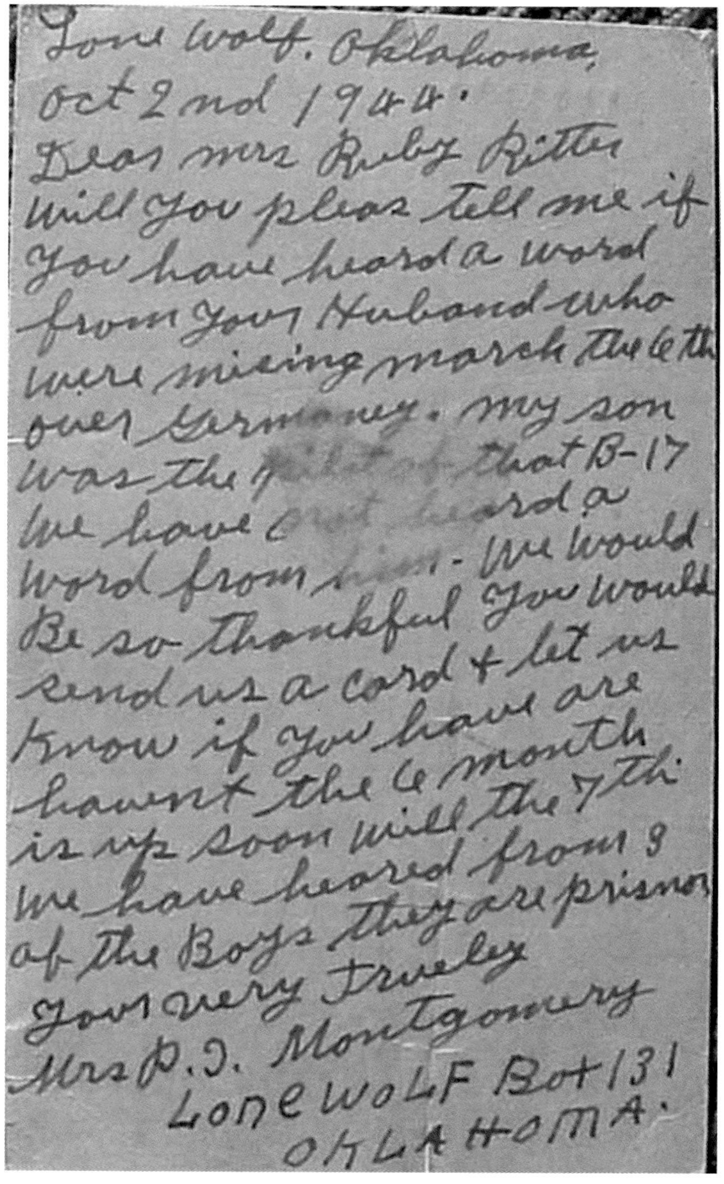
Lone Wolf, Oklahoma,
Oct 2nd 1944.
Dear mrs Ruby Ritter
will you pleas tell me if
you have heard a word
from your Huband who
were missing march the 6th
over Germany. my son
was the pilot of that B-17
we have not heard a
word from him. We would
Be so thankful you would
send us a card & let us
know if you have are
havent the 6 month
is up soon will the 7th
we have heared from 3
of the Boys they are prisnor
Your very truely
Mrs R.J. Montgomery
Lone Wolf Box 131
OKLAHOMA.

(Courtesy of Kurt A. Stauffer)

The Germans buried Lt. Coy I. Montgomery on March 10, 1944, noting the cause of death as associated injuries sustained from the crash and ensuing fire. Lt Montgomery had stayed at the controls in order to give his crew the time needed to bail out. The crew was on its tenth mission.

Tail Gunner S/Sgt Earl W. Ritter would end up in *Stalag Luft* 4, while at home all the families of the Montgomery Crew could do was wait and hope for news. For some time all they received was the Western Union Telegram saying your son was MIA, and returned letters.

In the case of Lt Montgomery's family, they would not find out for some time that their son had kept his plane in the air just long enough for his crew to bail out, sacrificing his life in the process. Here is a letter from Montgomery's mother to the wife of S/Sgt Ritter:

The Koper Crew – B Group, Low Squadron

Lt. Robert G. Koper and his crew ended their fifth mission with *Goin Jessies* going down on fire; only 3 men were able to bail out before the ship exploded: copilot Lt. Gordon C. Lien, bombardier Lt. Thomas O. Drinkwater, and top turret gunner T/Sgt. Charles P. Corea. According to John Nilsson's *The Story of the Century*, Bob Koper ordered his crew to "bail" and was alone in his ship when it blew up:

"I've spoken with and corresponded with Weston Rodkey [radio operator] (who was grounded that day with an ear infection] and Charles Corea [top turret engineer] who bailed out some 60 miles west of Berlin, along with the bombardier and navigator. I now know what happened that day, even if I'm not sure how or why.

Corea was the last of the only 3 survivors to exit the AC that day, and he and 2Lt. Gordon Lien [navigator] landed near each other in a farm field [Drinkwater was the 1st one out of the AC and landed about 10 miles west of the crash site]; as Corea attended to Lien's injured leg, *Goin Jessies* crashed about 200 yards or so from their position. The AC fuel load caught fire, and then the bomb load exploded.

Corea, Lien, and 2Lt. Tom Drinkwater [bombardier] stated in their post-war debriefing in the MACR that they last saw my Dad [Lt. Koper] standing between the Pilot and Copilot seats, asking where his parachute was. Lien and Drinkwater, at different times, told him it was near the escape hatch and even pointed to it.

Why he did not exit the AC before it crashed. . . I don't know. He was the last one on board. His chute may have been damaged, it may have fallen out of the AC before he could grab it, he may have been injured after the others left the AC, or he may have just run out of time. The sadness of this story, for me, is somewhat offset by the simple satisfaction of knowing.

Bob Koper Jr.
Son of Lt. Robert G. Koper, KIA March 6, 1944"

Lt. Robert Koper's B-17G 231051 *Goin Jessies* on March 6, 1944.

According to Lt Lien's casualty report:

"Lt Wing (Nav) was hit by 20mm and last seen by Lt Drinkwater (Bomb), our plane crashed in a farm field close to a Hitler Youth Training Camp."

Lt Drinkwater's report went on to state that "Lt Wing was mortally wounded in the throat or upper chest and slumped over his navigational desk, when I left the aircraft." The rest of the crew—Tanowigch, Luquette, Fankel, Zarzecki, and Sundin—never made it out of the back of the aircraft and were killed in the crash.

The Barrick Crew – B Group, High Squadron (moved down to B Group, Low Squadron when Lt Massol returned early)

In the fuselage of 239994 *Snort Stuff* right waist gunner S/Sgt. William D. Sapp had been stunned by the gruesome sights filling his waist window:

"I saw no fighters - theirs or ours. I could see nothing ahead of us because, from the right waist window, I could see only from about 1 o'clock to about 6 o'clock

Where we had been an hour earlier in the high squadron was now a plethora of bright flashes and falling debris.

There was no longer a high squadron. None at all, it was gone!

There were planes going down everywhere, vertical dives, slow rolls, spin upside down and right side up. Flames were seen coming from engines, cockpits and the mangled fuselages but most of all, there was junk, junk, junk! Little pieces floating down like confetti and in one case what was either an outer wing panel or a horizontal stabilizer went by turning over and over around its longitudinal axis.

Sgt. Rodkey, Lt. Koper, and T/Sgt. Corea.

Worst of all, among all this flying junk, there was a fellow in a parachute hanging up there. He had either been thrown out of his plane by his crew to save him or had jumped and pulled the ripcord as soon as he jumped.

About this time, the German fighters began to flash by. Because there were no longer any of our planes on my side of the ship, I could take a chance on hitting one of the fighters but I really could not swing the gun fast enough to track them before they were past.

The copilot called out:

'One coming in at 2 o'clock high'

In addition, I was able to fire at him in reasonable order. Even then, I remember thinking to myself:

'Don't get down in the prop arcs!'

Because he was coming down, I had to aim below him and could, therefore only get one burst of three or four rounds off.

Meanwhile the ball turret gunner was calling planes coming from below and the tail gunner was calling 3 planes coming in at about 5 o'clock. I could not depress my gun muzzle sufficiently to do anything about the planes coming in from below and so I swung around to the planes in the rear and fired at them."

After the demise of Lt. Koper's and Lt. Montgomery's planes in the 100 B Group Low Squadron, Barrick moved into the lead group. The fighters came back, leaving *Snort Stuff* with the #4 engine on fire and the #1 smoking and losing oil. The #4 engine fire was extinguished and was still pulling power. Barrick told his copilot, Lt. Ira A. Munn, to feather it at first sign of oil pressure drop. When the time came to feather #4, Munn was unable to do so and the propeller started to windmill. Barrick salvoed the bombs, but the aircraft was still losing airspeed and started to trail the formation. The #4 engine seized, and the propeller almost stopped and then broke loose. Evidently, the crankshaft had sheared and the prop began spinning again. Right waist gunner S/Sgt. William D. Sapp heard his pilot calling for a check: "Everybody responded. By this time we were all alone, losing fuel."

As Lt Samuel Barrick wrote in his diary:

"6 Mar 1944 6:00 994 Briefed target - Berlin, Germany.

At about 1200 hours near Dummer Lake, fifty - sixty FW-190s and Me-109s attacked us from head on. No fighter escorts at this time. I had changed from high sqdn to low sqdn at 1100 hrs to fill in for an abort. Fighters in first pass took out all of high sqdn and lead sqdn, left two of us in the low sqdn. Our formation was lost, dropped into lead group. Fighters same tactics on lead group. No 4 engine was on fire, No 1 smoking and losing oil. No 4 fire went out, still pulling power. Told Munn [co-pilot] to feather at first sign of oil pressure drop. No 1 pulling only half power, when No 4 went dead; Munn failed to feather it, engine [propeller] started wind milling. Had to salvo bombs, kept losing airspeed and trailing formations. No 4 engine seized, the prop almost stopped, and then broke loose, evidently the crankshaft had sheared, the prop was spinning again. At 1255 decided to go home, crew said we were losing fuel. Due to fuel loss Guerrini said only enough fuel to reach German coast, then decided on Sweden. Hit light flak from ship on the Baltic, flak on the Swedish coast. Landed at 1445 hours. Damage was heavy, the Swedes counted over 13 20mm holes in front and about fifty flak holes. No wounded but everyone scared stiff.

Note: Some other things happened that I will never forget. During the attack there were parts falling off airplanes, airplanes on fire going down, and some airplanes just blew up. The fighters came so close passing by, that I could see the pilot. The whole thing may have lasted two or perhaps three minutes. Very few parachutes were seen. As we were heading towards home, looking upward I could see formations of B-17s continuing on to the target. I had the very distinct feeling that regardless of what happens; the 8th Air Force could not be stopped or turned back.

A recollection of our predicament after the attack follows: In an effort to stay with the formations, I had been running No 2 and 3 engines at full power for over 45 minutes; No 4 propeller was wind milling, No 1 was slowly losing power, we could no longer maintain altitude, and had lost the remaining fuel in two tanks when we made the decision to go to Sweden. Maintaining altitude was no longer important, if we could save the engines and reduce fuel consumption. We reduced to climb power, and started losing altitude. Some minutes after the No 4 engine had seized and broke loose the first time, the engine seized once more, almost stopped, and broke loose again. The reduction gearing had failed, with the prop turning free. The only thing holding the prop to the engine was air drag. As time went on the prop shifted so that it was slanted inboard toward the No 3 engine. It actually wore off about six inches of engine cowling at the inboard side. If the prop came off it would surely damage No 3 engine nacelle. We continued to lose altitude as we approached the Baltic coast of Germany. Near the coast we passed over an airfield with a number of fighter type aircraft. They remained in position, none took off. Probably dummies.

We continued to lose altitude, and by jettisoning the removable guns, ammunition, flak suits, and other loose equipment we could maintain altitude at about 5,000 feet and 110 mph IAS. We had been briefed to land at Ystad, Sweden if we had to, so we headed there. However there was a low overcast in that area, and after letting down to 500' we couldn't get under it. We were looking for a place to belly land in the snow when two Swedish fighter airplanes arrived. These were Italian made Reggiane 2000 models, similar to our Republic P-35. One of them lowered his landing gear and flaps and flew off my left wing, giving me hand signals when to turn. The other fighter was having a good time diving on us and pulling up just ahead so we would fly through his prop wash. Each time the No 4 prop would move into the cowling, and our left wing would sort of flap. I motioned to the guy on our left for him to get the other one away. He just grinned back, he too was enjoying the fun. I told Johnson to turn the top turret toward the fighter. They got the message and escorted us to a small airfield at Malmo. We lowered the landing gear, and I told everyone to get into the radio room in ditching positions until the airplane stopped, then get out immediately and form a rank at the rear entrance door.

I made the smoothest landing that I ever made on the grass turf and parked the airplane. The crew scrambled out, and as I shut down the engines, a voice said in my ear 'Valcome to Shveden'. I turned, he had a pistol pointed toward me. I put up my hands, he grinned at me, put the pistol away, and he shook my hand. We were in a friendly country after all!

We marched, very military, under guard, to a building where there were a number of Officers and we were given coffee with cream, fresh milk, and delicious items of pastry. They asked us questions, we stuck to our briefed instructions of giving name, rank, and serial number; and that we had become lost while on a navigation training mission. This was supposed to have us immediately released from internment. For some reason they didn't believe us.

Then there was some excitement. Everybody went outside, our crew as well, and watched a B-24 [129191 *Hello Natural* of the 448BG 712 BS] land. It was flown by a Lt. [Charles C.] York, on his first combat mission. He told everyone that he had bombed Berlin. Of course the Swedes already knew the target, having listened to German radio. So our story was pretty weak.

We had a quick look at the airplane while we were outside. The No 4 prop was laying on the ground. A curious guard had shaken it, and it fell off. There were numerous holes in both wings, one hole through a No 3 prop blade, and No 1 engine had a large hole in the cowling. The airplanes fuselage had not been hit; someone had been looking out for us."

While heading for Sweden, right waist gunner S/Sgt. William D. Sapp slowly shook his head and thought: "Those poor damned dumb Germans don't have any idea of what they started and how it is going to hurt."

"Over the sea, our ship continued to lose altitude. The pilot ordered the crew to jettison guns, ammunition, flak suits, and other removable equipment to lighten the weight so they could fly at 110 mph at 500 feet. In the rear, there was no ammunition left so the crew did not have to throw that out but the guns went, the flak vests went, the spent brass casings went, the relief cans went. While looking for something else to throw out, I realized I had been using my tin lid helmet to scoop out the brass, out it went - and made one heluva splash when it hit."

The Ferbrache Crew – B Group, Low Squadron

The old B-17-G model 23508 *Bastard's Bungalow* was pretty well shot up on this, Ferbrache's third mission. In the radio room, Luc Lucarelli found his 50cal useless as the fighters flashed by. He charged the gun and it would not work, so he took his frustration our on his chair with a few kicks. Up in the top turret, T/Sgt. Harold Patterson was firing his twin 50s at a Me 109 that was going through the group. He was so fixated on the target he had not seen the carnage taking place in the high squadron. As he tracked the fighter with his lethal spray of tracer and incendiary ammo, he witnessed a B-17 go down. This shook Patterson to the core, because he thought that his bullets had in some way attributed to the demise of that B-17. 'Luc' Lucarelli remembered:

"Harold swore he shot down a B-17 but we knew that was not the case. We knew it was due to the enemies' concentrated attacks on the group. But we could never convince Harold otherwise, what a terrible memory to live with."

In the tail, Sgt Howard Williams saw two Me109s making a turn and heading back towards their plane and the low squadron. He picked one out, trained his twin 50s, and started firing:

"You were trained to fire short bursts but I let the German fighter have one long burst and watched it smoke and go down. I called to Bill Behr in the ball turret to confirm the kill but Bill had

Lt Elmer Ferbrache's crew.

The Green crew in front of 23508 *Bastard's Bungalow*, which was flown by the Ferbrache crew on March 6, 1944.

rotated the turret to the front, yelling over the intercom 'three 109's coming in head on, twelve o'clock low.'"

Despite the battle damage, Lt. Elmer E. Ferbrache and Lt. Anthony D. Slatinsky maintained their position and stayed with the group. There was no way they wanted to be separated from the rest of the Group. They knew life was often short and brutal for stragglers isolated deep over enemy territory.

Bastard's Bungalow and Lt. Lucius Lacy's ship *Lucious Lucy* were the only two survivors of B Group, Low Squadron. John Lucarelli remembered: "You felt like you were all alone out there, we looked around and everyone was gone except for us and Lacy."

Sixty-three years later old memories start to come back. The compartmentalized horrors you thought you had permanently buried away in the deep recesses of your mind had returned to haunt you. Lt. Bob Shoens knew this all too well. Reliving this mission in his mind, he had put himself back into that intense air battle unfolding all around him:

"While we were under attack, I believe during the Luftwaffe's second pass at us, I looked out the corner of my right eye and saw the entire wing of a B17 burst into flames from one end to the other. Then in a few seconds 'bahlooey' and there was nothing but a big ball of fire and smoke with bits and pieces falling away. You don't think about it otherwise you're not going to fly again. A battle with things like that going on is hard to put into words and make it seem real."

Don Hammond, "keeping small under his helmet" in the radio compartment of *Our Gal Sal*, remembers:

"I heard something like 40 fighters had gone through us on the first pass and we lost the whole high squadron. Then they came around again and got a few more of us. We heard Bob say 'This next time will be our turn; you better put on your chutes on.'

So we put our chutes on but for some reason the fighters didn't come back. We survived!"

There were only a few planes still flying in any semblance of a formation, and he believed that the German fighters would come back to finish off the rest of the Group. The pilot glanced at his chest pack chute, looking to see if it was still under his seat. Luckily, the fatal blow failed to materialize; the German fighters were now departing to land, refuel, and rearm.

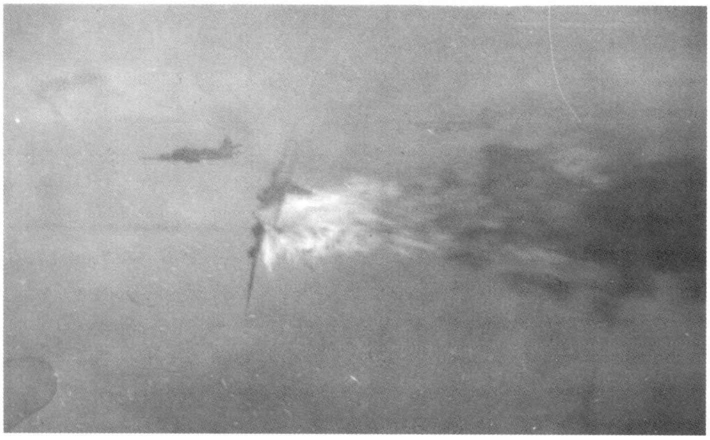

This dramatic photograph is of Lt. Rish's 238044 *Spirit of '44*, shortly after the first wave of German fighters struck at Haseluenne. The B-17 in the background is probably the Handof crews' 238011 *Kind-a-Ruff* before it was shot down.

Sgt Donald Hammond, ROG in *Our Gal Sal*.

IV

They Can't Stop the Mighty Eighth

From 1200 hours, when the first 100BG B-17 slammed into the ground until the last B-17 crashed, the 100 B Group had lost two-thirds of its number. Nine of its 17 remaining B-17s had fallen to the enemy. The high squadron was decimated. In addition, 2 planes from the lead squadron and 2 from the low squadron suffered the same fate. The 100BG A group had lost 5 planes: 3 went down, and the Cope and Harper ships were now limping back to England alone, stragglers and easy prey for German fighters. From start to finish, the *Luftwaffe* attack at Haseleune and eastward lasted 25 minutes. To the crews of the 100th Bomb Group, it felt more like 25 years!

Half of the 100BG ships that had crossed the German border had been shot down or were trying to reach home. The sky was filled with parachutes from both sides. No semblance of the formation that assembled that morning existed. *Our Gal Sal* and the Shoens crew were alone. Despite the ferocious German fighter attacks, the aircraft had managed to avoid any battle damage. In comparison to what had already occurred to their comrades in the other bombers, the Shoens crew had experienced a much better day of it.

Contrails to Berlin.

"Clash at Haseleunne" by Robert Bailey: Noon on March 6, 1944, Lt Robert Shoens in *Our Gal Sal* fights off fighter attacks with the help of Lt Robert Johnson in his P-47 "Lucky."

According to Lt. Shoens:

"During the attack, the only escort near us were eight P-47s led by Lt. Robert Johnson from Colonel 'Hub' Zemke's 56th Fighter Group. On the Lufftwaffe's second pass, Johnson went through the formation along with the Germans. Later at debriefing some of the gunners accused the Germans of carrying US markings, but it was actually Lt. Johnson. He also alerted the rest of 'Zemke's Wolfpack' and the nearest one was 'Hub' himself."

Lt Robert Johnson, 56th Fighter Group:

"The mission on March 6, 1944 is as clear in my mind as it was yesterday. Eight P-47's against 3 gaggles of German Fighters. We were so few; they ignored us and went straight for the bombers."

Col Hub.Zemke, C.O. 56th Fighter Group:[29]

"Our ground control officer gave me the warning that a large formation of enemy aircraft were north and ahead of us heading for the Bombers. I was leading the 63rd Fighter Squadron protecting the lead box of the 1st Air Division when the call came in from Major Jim Stewart saying he was engaging approximately 100 German fighters. He was leading the 61st Fighter Squadron which was northwest of our position so we headed back towards the fight. While at maximum throttle we could hear in our radios that the battle was already in full swing. We searched the sky looking for signs of combat but within minutes the radios went silent, the battle was over. By the time we got there, all we saw were burning aircraft and parachutes; we had arrived too late."

Harold Stearns, top turret gunner on the Granack crew, experienced this dangerous cat and mouse game first hand:

"I had the top turret in *Rubber Check* and had just turned around when I saw Lautenschlager's plane [*Half and Half*] burst into flames and go down. A Me 109 cut in front of us with a P-47 right on his tail. He looked like he was headed right for our cockpit and this P-47 was firing his guns and I could see the bullets hitting the 109 and she just went down."

Oberlentnant Wolfgang Kretschmer of 2 *Staffel*, 3/JG 1 was flying his first mission on the Western Front in an FW 190. He had lost track of his wingman after a "head on attack" on the 100BG and was coming back around to attack the remnants of the formation from the rear. Unbeknownst to the German pilot, it was at this point that Hub Zemke arrived on the scene with 8 more P-47s from "Zemke's Wolfpack" and lined Kretschmer up in his sites. As he squeezed the trigger, the plane shuddered as the eight .50 calibre machine guns opened up and bullets tore into the FW 190, sending it screaming towards the ground in flames. Kretschemer was severely burned while bailing out of his plane and spent months in a hospital recuperating. 'Hub,' on the other hand, went searching for more bandits and got his second kill of the day, a Me 109 flown by *Uffz* P. Reinhardt of 11 *Staffel*, 2/JG 11 .

Several years later Stearns, Shoens, Zemke, and Kretschmer would be brought together by famed aviation artist William Phillips for his painting "The Hunter Becomes the Hunted," depicting the events of that day. Shoens talked with Hub about the raid during this gathering, and he said "by the time he [Zemke] got back to try and help us all he could see was a smoke filled sky and fires all over the ground."[30]

Me 109. (courtesy of Mark Copeland)

William Phillips, Wolfgang Kretschmere, Robert Shoens, Harold Stearns, and Hub Zemke, July 1990. (Photo: Robert Shoens)

"The Hunter Becomes The Hunted," copyright 2008 William S. Phillips. (Courtesy The Greenwich Workshop, Inc.)

Robert Johnson and *"Lucky"* give the "we're # 1" sign. (USAF)

Above: Hub Zemke. (USAF) Right: Robert Johnson, Hub Zemke, and Bud Mahurin. (USAF)

Hub Zemke. (USAF)

The Malooly Crew– A Group, Lead Squadron

"During the end of the fighter attack we ran into heavy and very accurate flak. Serverl planes hit. Some (2) blew up and 1 caught fire. Saw 8 men bail out of one ship and 6 out of another. Went on to target and ran into flak all along the way. Over the city we saw the Bowl the 1936 Olympics were held in and many other points of interst. On bombs away our bombs would not release. Finally, we were able to drop them on the outskirts of Berlin. It was a beautiful day and you could see everything. It reminded me of the times I use to go on drives in the summer time. It was only -30 degrees. I changed my mind however before we ever reached the target. Turning back for home our bomb bay doors would not close causing the ball (turret guns) to be very ineffective against the fighters that started attacking us and continued until we were about 150 mi. from the coast, where we met our excort. We were hit in the wing and in the nose by flak, one piece coming through and hitting Ralph (Guida-Bomardier) on the flak vest and going off to the compass, denting the cover. (Lost Mailman from the 95th BG and Koper and Barton from here too). Another B-17 caught fire and 8 got out. Several FW's were shot down. Our Ball possibly hitting one which blew up and another, the pilot bailed out. A B-17 was hit in the tail cutting it in half. We had heavy flak in some spots." Lt Robert Bailie, co-pilot.

In the rear of *Our Gal Sal*, the gunners were shoving out machine gun belt links and spent casings that covered the floor. The tail gunner, S/Sgt. Don Blair, and the left waist gunner, Sgt. Bill Wright, had each dispatched one enemy fighter. Lieutenant Shoens had been playing "catch up" since the demise of the B Group. It would be safer to attach themselves to another group. He saw one some distance ahead at the same altitude. When he caught up with them he flew to the left of their high squadron. They were about to join the 95BG "Square B" on the tail from the 13 A Wing. There was a glitch to this effort. Heavy bomber gunners had been

100 A Group
Over Target[31]

Lead Squadron		
	Devore - Elton 231981 LN E	
Chadwick 23413 LN V		**Granack** 239872 LN A
	Malooly 231049 LN U	
Pearson 231074 LN Q		**Gibbons** 231968 LN D

Low Squadron		
	Wilkinson 239927 DI R	
Warren 239821 DI J		**Dower** 232089 DI W
	Sutters 231971 DI E	
Reich 238130 DI B		**Sterr** 231892 DI H

High Squadron		
	Harrison 231710 XR P	
Wilson 23534 XR N		**Morgan** 25957 XR D
	Cowan 231723 XR R	

FW 190 A. (courtesy of Mark Copeland)

Our Gal Sal all alone.

warned on more than one occasion to watch out for Germans flying captured aircraft attempting to join the formation. *Our Gal Sal* took it easy, as Shoens stayed slightly in trail and decided to make the bomb run with them. It does not appear than any of the 95BG gunners shot at the Shoens crew.

Although the 13th Combat Wing had suffered a terrible mauling, the other Wings had also encountered enemy fighters and suffered losses as the endless procession of bombers continued towards Berlin. By the time the 100 B Group reached the Initial Point, the formation was decimated and scattered. Three aircraft were left from the lead Squadron and one of them, Lauro/Swartout's *Nelson King*, was still taking fighter attacks to go with their vertical stabilizer damage. How *Nelson King* stayed in the air is a tribute to the durability of the B-17, and astounded those who witnessed the fighter attacks and the collision with the FW 190 that caused the tail damage. Captain Jack Swartout gave this description of his ordeal:

"After we were hit and fell out of formation, Captain Lauro and I had almost three hours alone fighting 3-4 fighters at a time. One engine out, one engine with no control, no hydraulics, fire in the cockpit, myself and a gunner wounded, instruments blown out, 3 large flak holes in the wings, ball turret out."

Down in the Low Squadron, only three aircraft had survived. The entire High Squadron was gone due to mechanical aborts or had been shot down in the clash over Haseluenne. What was left of the 100BG B Group maneuvered for the protection of other bomb groups.

Lt. Clement Cowan's crew photographed in the States. Kneeling: Clement H. Cowan (Pilot), Hank A. Dibbem (Copilot), Fred W. Robertson (Navigator), and Harold L. Heyneman (Bombardier). Standing: Murray W. Holditch (Top Turret - Engineer), William A. Geigle (Ball Turret Gunner), Sherwyn W. "Sparky" Meyers (Radio Operator-Gunner), Adam C. Stoppel (Left Waist Gunner), Robert Patrick (Right Waist Gunner), and Horace R. Kemble (Tail Gunner).

Lt Clement Cowan's A/C on the 3, 4, and 6 March 1944 missions to Berlin.

March 6, 1944, Berlin
13 B Wing
100 B Group
Over Target

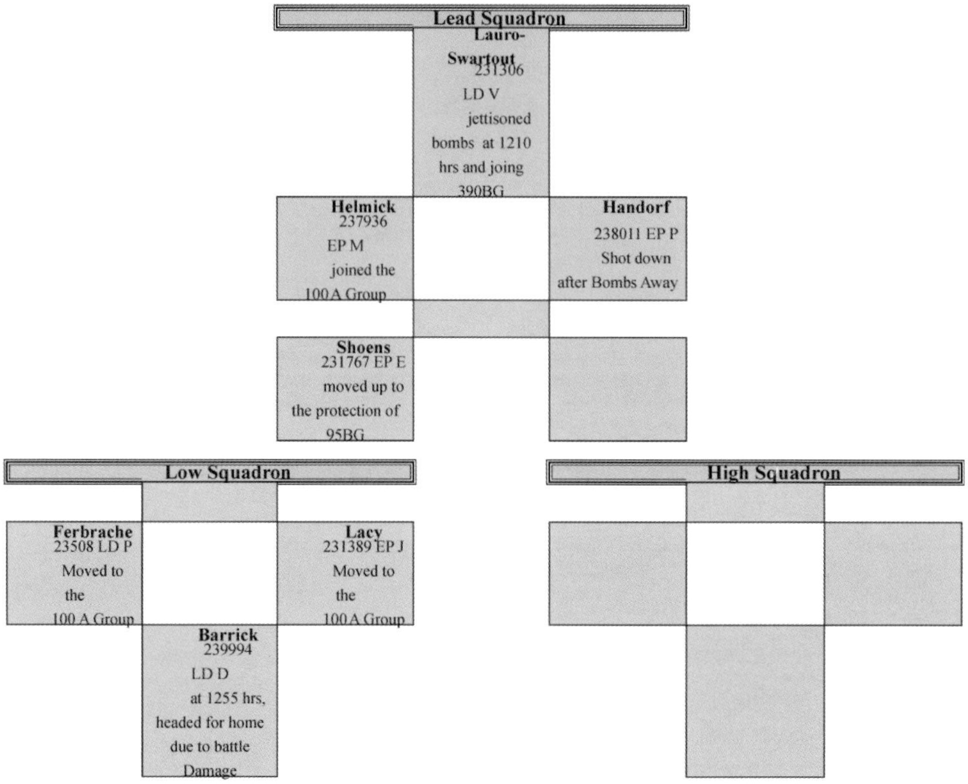

The Lauro Crew – B Group, Lead Squadron

Captain Swartout had decided it would be suicide to turn back, so they elected to try to follow the wings above and join them. All of a sudden all hell broke loose again. A solitary Me 109 showed up from out of nowhere and hammered several 20mm shells into *Nelson King*. One of them penetrated the right side of the cockpit.

Capt. Jack Swartourt, Lead Pilot 100th "B" Group. (courtesy of Jack O'Leary)

The shell exploded, wiping out the instruments and spraying the Command Pilot's left ankle with fragments. The butt of the shell punched him just below the sternum, completely knocking his breath away.

This explosion rendered the hydraulic system useless and started a fire to the right of the control quadrant. The engineer, T/Sgt. Dewey Thompson, came down from the top turret to assess the damage. The pilot, Captain Frank Lauro, was okay and was concentrating on flying. When Thompson saw all the red hydraulic fluid on the floor, he thought it was Captain Swartout's blood. He wanted to put him in a tourniquet, but a sign language ended Thompson's efforts.

The chest chute under the copilot seat was a disaster from fire and hydraulic fluid. The ship had taken serious hits in two engines. A 20mm shell had pierced the number three engine gas tank, damaging the oil cooler line. Large spouts of oil were thrown back over the ball turret, thus rendering it inoperative. A second 20mm shell had shredded the cables of the #4 engine controls to such an extent that no response could be obtained. The number four fuel shut off switch and booster pump system were inoperative, and all interphone radio communication on the copilot side was smashed. The command transmitter and receiver were non-operational, and the feathering motor on the number four engine was blasted away. The pilots also discovered they could not exceed 140 mph without serious vibration from the tail. They had a survival problem, which made them a sitting duck for the German fighters.

Members of the Lucius G. Lacy crew. Seated from left: Raymond J. Mitchell - WG, Chester J. Carknard - TTE, and Clarence H. Wood - ROG. Standing from left: Joseph A. Howell - TG, Joe Folsom - WG, and Jerman H. Hillburn - WG.

The LACY Crew – B Group, Low Squadron

Lt Lucius G. Lacy in 232018 *Luscious Lucy* watched as the B Group disintegrated around him. The Lead Squadron had three planes left and they were seeking the safety of other groups. By the third pass of the *Luftwaffe* the high squadron had been decimated. Down in the Low Squadron, Lt Massol had returned early, and Lts Montgomery and Koper were shot down. Lt Barrick was falling behind due to battle damage and Lt Ferbrache has sustained damage but kept formation. That is, what was left of a formation?

S/Sgt Raymond Mitchell, left waist gunner, remembers the day "German fighters just kept pushing their attacks. They were so relentless that they even hit us through their own flak."

S/Sgt Ray Mitchell had bestowed the dubious nickname "Lacy's Lushes" on his crew. At the end of each mission, the Doctor prescribed a shot of scotch or whiskey to each man to calm the nerves. Well, not all the crewmembers on Lacy's crew fancied a drink, so S/Sgt Mitchell could not see all that fine alcohol go to waste; he drank *all* the crew shots!

The Lauro Crew – B Group, Lead Squadron

Me 109s and FW 190s in singles and pairs tried to finish them off. Since they had no intercom between them, Captain Jack Swartout looked at Lauro, ripped off his mask, and yelled to Lauro that he would take over the controls while Lauro told the rest of the crew to hang on. With all the experience and strength he could muster, Swartout used every available maneuver he knew to evade the onslaught of head-on passes by the fighters. To do nothing meant being chopped to pieces by the 20mms. With a stricken aircraft, Jack relied on his flaps to turn inside the fighter attacks and dodge the hail of lead coming his way.

The three Bombardment Divisions reached their turning point at Celle and then began to split up, each one making its way independently to its own initial point. The combat wings began to dispatch their individual groups to make their bomb runs.

The sky over Berlin had a cloud of its own over it. Flak! A dark, puffy veil covered the city. It was the heaviest flak Shoens had ever seen, a real flak field, "so thick you could walk on it."

The leading planes found their primary targets blanketed by cloud banks. A visual bomb run was impossible and the target was too small for attack using radar, and it was too late to realign the force for a radar bomb run on the Friedrischstrasse railway station. The Group leaders ordered to attack any target of opportunity found in the Berlin area.

Sgt. Don Hammond, Shoens' radio operator, started to push out bundles of chaff or windows (thin aluminum strips that saturated the screens of the enemy's gun-laying radar). The fighter attacks stopped temporarily as the flak batteries took over. Four miles below, the Germans were pumping 88mm, 105mm, and 128mm shells towards the heavies. Flak was a worse fear than fighters for many combat crewmen; at least you could shoot back at the fighters. With flak, you had to sit there and take it, and hope your luck had not run out.

John C. 'Red' Morgan

Lead ships opened their bomb doors and fired flares. The bombardier, through the Norden bombsight, now controlled the aircraft. The bomb run had begun. Until the call from the bombardier "Bombs Away," and returned control of the bomber to the pilots, the course or altitude could not be altered. The bombers had to fly straight and level. They had no choice but to ride through the gauntlet of flak, hoping a piece of shrapnel would not hit a vital part of the plane. Shoens' copilot, Lt. Shand, watched nothing but the control panel, waiting for that telltale sign on some instrument that would indicate a potential problem. This also helped ease the stress of the flak barrage going on outside his window. In the nose, bombardier Lt. Hudson flipped up the safety cover on the bomb release switch and kept his finger ready while he watched the open bomb doors of the lead plane. Sitting in his fishbowl he felt terribly exposed; the Plexiglas nose did not stop anything but flies.

In the lead Third Bombardment Division 482BG pathfinder 23491 was the Command Pilot Brigadier General Russell A. Wilson, Commanding Officer of the 4th Combat Wing. This crew drew the dead man's hand aces and eights! On the bomb run 23491 received severe flak damage. The pilot, Major Fred A. Rabo, and copilot, John C. 'Red' Morgan, kept the plane level and made the bomb run before hitting the bailout alarm. It appears no one bailed out prior to the aircraft exploding. Rabo, Morgan, ball turret gunner William H. Wescott, and the left waist gunner survived when the B-17 exploded shortly after this photograph was taken. The rest of the crew perished. Of note, on December 18, 1943, Morgan received the Congressional Medal of Honor (MOH) for "conspicuous gallantry and intrepidity above and beyond the call of duty" during a July 26, 1943, mission to Hannover, Germany. "Red" Morgan became the only MOH recipient to become a POW after receiving the medal. He ended up in Stalag Luft I, Barth, Germany. (Photos: USAF)

A view of a German crew firing an 88mm anti-aircraft "flak" gun. (USAF)

On the bomb run. (Photo: USAF)

The burst of the exploding shells was more intense than top turret gunner Sgt. George Madden had ever experienced on previous missions. He could see a dark red flash when it burst close and then a black splash of smoke. Suddenly he felt a rush of air in his face. At first, he thought 237936 *Our Mark* had taken a hit and slipstream air was pouring into her. He realized soon that it was under his oxygen mask. It was running away and the regulator was out. He thought they were losing their oxygen supply. Shells kept on bursting, and he realized that this could have upset his oxygen regulator. He tried puffing back into his oxygen regulator mask. This set the diaphragm back into place and returned it to normal. Madden had sunk into his top turret, well below the metal ring traveling on top of the bomber, surrounded by the motors, the sight, guns, and ammunition cans. The hole formed a little protection for the upper part of his body, giving him a secure feeling. He knew, though, that the aluminum skin was no match for a direct flak hit or those 20mm shells the fighters were tossing their way. The close bursts of flak peppered the ships with shrapnel. Madden heard them hitting the bomber above the roar of the engines. All the Bombardiers and Togglers in the group had their hands on the

Big B – Berlin.

bomb release switch, waiting for the signal to release their lethal payload. As the flak crept closer and your chances got slimmer, you'd pray, plead, and swear for that signal. Finally, it happened; a smoke marker and a string of bombs fell out of the lead ship: "Bombs Away!"

Bombs Away!

The lead plane and what was left of the 100BG, still tagged low on the 95BG, dropped their bombs at 1323 hours on a target of opportunity—a factory district near Berlin. Simultaneously, *Our Gal Sal* jumped upwards, relieved of its explosive load. Over the interphone, Hudson said "Bombs Away" and flipped the toggle switch to close the bomb bay doors. With a sigh of relief they could start home. Eresman checked that all bombs had gone. If a bomb had hung up, he would have to work on the narrow catwalk without a chute and with nothing between him and Berlin but four miles of air. The 95BG turned off the target towards a heavy flak area. Since Shoens was not part of this group, he decided to turn right and got out of the flak. Once again, they found themselves alone over the Third Reich. The *Luftwaffe* was out in force, so they had to join another group for the trip home. Speed increased now to 225mph. Suddenly the lonely *Our Gal Sal* felt the heat from the flak batteries again. She was taken under fire by four 88mm flak guns that got off 40 rounds before flying out of range. The smell of gun propellant filtered through the oxygen regulator. Blasts shook the plane but caused no further serious damage. Not all were as fortunate. For ten agonizing seconds after bombs away, the 100th BG formation flew without evasive action as flak batteries sent lethal shells hurling skyward. Exploding shells sent fragments through the sky with deadly results. Lt Granacks' #4 engine was hit by flak, causing them to leave formation.

The Granack Crew – A Group, Lead Squadron

Lt. Murray Geisler, Granack's navigator, informed the pilot that he would give him a bearing for Sweden, but was interrupted: "Fighters at 3 o'clock" crackled over the intercom from radio operator Grant 'Scotty' Scott. Me 109s and FW 190s were also attacking from the 6 o'clock and 3 o'clock low directions and a fierce running battle ensued. Unlike S/Sgt. Glenn 'Brownie' Brown, the right waist gunner, who was firing constantly, Ed Harrell, the left waist gunner, had to retain his fire until the fighters passed over his position due to the closeness of the Malooly and Chadwick B-17s. Many a B-17 had their tails "stitched" by overzealous gunners with target fixation, and Ed did not want to join the club.

During one of the attacks his right leg went numb. He looked down and saw a hole in the top of his boot but no hole at the other side; the projectile was still in his leg. At approximately the same time 'Brownie' went down against him. Harrell could not detect any pulse or sign of life so he got back on his gun and continued firing. The return fire hit several enemy fighters. T/Sgt. Harold Stearns was sure he got one with his top turret guns.[32] Stearns picks up the story:

> "I turned my guns to 3 o'clock just as 'Scotty' got it right in the neck, he died just like that!"

The fighters inflicted considerable damage on Granack's ship. The #2 engine was having problems and #3 was out of commission. Both #3 and #4 engines were now smoking and fire was a serious threat. About this time the enemy fighter attack slackened. Granack had to ease up on his good engine (#1) when it appeared to be developing trouble. They were now losing altitude rapidly to maintain air speed. Cockpit adjustments to maintain control were steadily getting more difficult.

Their position was getting more perilous by the moment, and to preclude the possibility of a total disaster, Granack decided to order "abandon ship." The intercom was out, so he instructed his copilot, Lt. Dunham, to go through the plane and see that each surviving crewmember was aware of the order to "bail out immediately." The copilot was also to provide assistance to anyone who needed it and to report back to Granack. Knowing the urgency of the situation, Dunham left quickly to carry out the order.

Harrell, the left waist gunner, was still firing away when he felt something hit him in the back. He turned and saw Lt. Dunham standing on the catwalk in the bomb bay, pointing down. He went back to the escape door to release it, but the door was jammed and would not release. Dunham meanwhile returned to the cockpit and told Granack he had carried out the order. The pilot thanked him and ordered him to bail out with the crew. They shouted a few brief words of farewell as Dunham took off for the bomb bay.

Harrell thought of S/Sgt. George Christian in the tail. He threw some spent brass around the tail, got his attention, and pointed down. Then he made his way up to the radio compartment and found the radio operator, T/Sgt. Grant Scott, lying face down on the floor, dead. He realized that the ball turret gunner, Staff Sergeant Lloyd Rogers, might not know what was happening. Harrell took the hand crank and rotated the turret until the escape door was inside the aircraft and helped get Rogers out, and they both went out through the bomb bay. After free falling a few thousand feet, Harrell started tumbling and was not able to estimate his altitude,

Lt Frank Granack's crew. Standing: Joseph F. Kawiecki (Bombardier), Murray Geisler (Navigator), Robert L. Dunham (Copilot), and Franklin A. Granack (Pilot). Kneeling: Grant H. Scott (Radio Operator, KIA Mar 6, 1944, Berlin), Edward T. Harrell (Waist Gunner), George C. Christia (Tail Gunner), Harold Stearns (Top Turret - Engineer), Lloyd H. Rodgers (Ball Turret Gunner), and Glen D. Brown (Waist Gunner, KIA March 6, 1944, Berlin).

so he deployed his chute. He knew he would not be able to escape so he tossed his Colt .45 away and passed out due to the loss of blood. When Harrell regained consciousness he was lying in the backyard of a German home. One German soldier was swinging a submachine gun around to keep a crowd of German civilians away.

From the cockpit Granack looked back towards the bomb bay and watched as crewmen tumbled out one after the other, until they were all gone. *Rubber Check* was virtually without power: the #3 and #4 engines were smoking, and another was making death sounds. Granack turned the trim tabs to put the plane into a steeper glide, hoping to reduce the chances of a stall while he was trying to get out. He then slipped out of his pilot's seat and held control as long as he could. He let go, hurriedly making his way to the passageway in the bomb bay where he made a head first dive into space. As he cleared the plane Granack pulled the ripcord. He was twisted and wrenched as the parachute billowed open: a welcome sight.

"Following is my best shot of what happened when we went down on March 6, 1944," by Lt Frank Granack:

"Shortly after Lt. Joe Kawiecki, our bombardier, announced 'Bombs away' over the Berlin target area, we were hit by heavy flak. 'Rubber Check' was rocked by a shell exploding very close to our right wing. The plane was damaged and the No. 4 engine knocked out of commission; it was smoking and a few licks of flame appeared but they quickly dissipated. We were momentarily knocked out of formation and we were busy making adjustments in the cockpit controls as I struggled to regain our position in the flight. At that altitude, because of the flak damage, I found it impossible to catch the faster moving formation. I informed flight leader Major Bucky Elton that if his air speed was reduced about 5 MPH, I might be able to get back into the protection of the group. He said that would be impossible, but he wished us 'Good Luck.' Gradually, we fell further and further behind, and below the formation until we were all alone. I still had basic control of the aircraft although we had to lose some altitude to maintain safe air speed. Meanwhile, we were trying to assess the extent of the flak damage. Lt. Bob Dunham, my co-pilot, and I carefully monitored the cockpit controls and panel for any signs of additional problems.

The entire crew became extra alert because we were now easier prey and more vulnerable to enemy fighter attacks; we knew there were many bandits in the area. About this time, Lt. Murray Geisler our navigator, informed me that he would give me a bearing for Sweden any time it became necessary to head in that direction.

We weren't alone for long! 'Fighters at 3 o'clock' crackled over the intercom. Me 109s and FW 190s were attacking from several different directions and we were raked the length of our plane with heavy gunfire; a fierce running battle ensued. All the gunners in our valiant crew fought back with all the .50 calibre fire power they could muster. Several enemy fighters were hit; two or three may have been downed; Sgt. Harold Stearns was sure he got one with his top turret guns. However, the additional damage inflicted on our plane was considerable. Our No. 2 engine was having problems and No. 3 was damaged and out of commission (both 3 and 4 were now smoking and fire was a serious threat); our intercom was shot out, therefore, it was impossible to get a rapid assessment of the extent of our damage and casualties. However, it turned out that our greatest and most painful losses were in the crew. Sgt. Grant Scott, radio operator and Sgt. Glenn Brown, waist gunner were both killed by the fighters; Sgt. Ed Harrell, the other waist gunner was wounded in the leg.

About this time the enemy fighter attacks slackened, at least for the moment. We had to ease up on our good engine, No. 1, when it appeared to be developing trouble. We were now losing altitude rapidly to maintain sufficient air speed to keep basic control of the plane. Cockpit adjustments to maintain control were steadily getting more difficult. Our position was getting more perilous by the moment and to preclude the possibility of a total disaster, I decided to order the plane abandoned. Because our intercom was out, I instructed co-pilot Dunham to go through the plane and see that each surviving crew member was aware of my orders to 'bail out immediately.' He was to provide assistance to anyone who needed it; Sgt. Lloyd Rogers, ball turret gunner and Sgt. George Christian, tail gunner were to be free of their confining positions as soon as possible to prevent being trapped in case of a sudden control emergency. Lt. Dunham was to report to back to me; knowing the urgency of the situation, he left quickly to carry out the orders. Meanwhile, the bomb bay doors (an important exit) would not open; fortunately, later they suddenly dropped open. Lt. Dunham returned shortly and told me he had carried out all my orders. He had done a fine job; I thanked him and ordered him to bail out with the crew. We shouted a few brief words of farewell as he took off for the bomb bay. From the cockpit I looked back toward the bomb bay and watched as crewmen tumbled out one after the other, until they were all gone.

'Rubber Check' was virtually without power; the #3 and #4 engines were smoking, another was making death sounds. I turned the trim tabs to put the plane into a steeper glide to reduce the chances of a stall or other sudden negative, violent movement by the plane as I was trying to get out. I then slipped out of my pilot's seat and held control of the plane as long as I could; I let go and ran down the passageway to the bomb bay where I made a running, head first dive into space as I bailed out. All the remaining eight crew members had bailed out successfully and were taken Prisoners-of-War."

As the pilot floated down he heard the sputtering death throes of *Rubber Check* and the distant drone of fighters. Then silence. The earth was coming up rapidly, and he tried to guide his chute away from small trees. The result was almost fatal, as the chute nearly collapsed. Then he landed on a small tree. He unbuckled his harness and dropped to the ground. Granack could see military vehicles and armed soldiers fast approaching. Also, many civilians armed with rifles and shotguns were surrounding him—there was no escape.

If there was any consolation for Granack, it was from Lt Jerry Felsenstein. Flying as formation officer in the tail of Lt Devore's

P-47 of the 56th Fighter Group providing escort.

aircraft, he had witnessed the fighter attack and unleashed a lethal barrage of fire from his twin 50s and scored a kill on the FW190 that had doomed *Rubber Check*.

After reaching their rally point, the three Bombardment Divisions flew in line abreast with the First Bombardment Division in the north, the Third Bombardment Division in the middle, and the Second Bombardment Division in the south. This huge mass was much easier to escort. The 100BG planes were heading now to a place where they should meet their "Little Friends."

The Berlin raiders were on their way home after running the fighter and flak gauntlet to their targets. However, while the bombers were plowing through the thick corridor of flak over Berlin the German *Luftwaffe* had time to land, rearm, and refuel their aircraft and get airborne to attack the 8th Air Force bomber formations as they left the target and headed back to England. They were looking for the stragglers, the unprotected, and the easy prey. Damaged aircraft with engines trailing smoke and propellers not moving were falling behind the formation and frantically searching for their fighter support.

Lt Robert Shoens' crew was still playing a game of cat-and-mouse over the Third Reich. Luckily, the pilot saw another group above and behind them heading west. *Our Gal Sal* was still heading east, so Shoens had to gain altitude, avoid flak, turn back west, and catch up with them. And hope no German fighters caught them all alone, stragglers! As Lt. Shoens maneuvered his plane as fast as he could west toward the formation, he recognized the group ahead. The group ahead bore a "Square J"; it was the 390BG, part of their own 13th Combat Wing.

The Helmick Crew – B Group, Lead Squadron

The sun was getting low, and the German fighters came back on the 100BG. George Madden, Helmick's top turret gunner, saw a lone FW 190 coming down the left side of the bomber stream. He floated his guns toward him, framed him, and started firing. The wing root tore open and the left landing gear fell down. The left waist gunner, S/Sgt. Jack Shope, confirmed the kill.

Madden heard their tail gunner, S/Sgt. Chester Coulam, call for help as three German fighters attacked from the rear. Madden turned left and saw three Me 109s closing with them. The center one was firing and Coulam was returning the fire. He stopped the top turret and fired on the one in the 7 o'clock position. He winged over and broke off the attack. Madden switched to the Me 109 at the 5 o'clock position. He opened fire and the German pilot shoved his plane down into a violent dive. By that time, the center Me 109 had broken off his attack. Off to his right side, the top turret gunner realized there was a fighter closing at about 8 o'clock. He came up firing and then quit, as it was a P-47. He saw a couple of bullet holes in the left wing tip. Hopefully for the P-47 Madden's guns had outrun the sight. He jerked his guns straight up to express his apologies as the "Jug" rolled on out of the bomber formation and went to find friendlier company.

"From Somewhere in England[33]

By golly, I've really been in combat and I don't mean maybe. You ought to see a big air battle. Mom would be plenty worried if she could see me now so I didn't write to her. Velma, I got up at 3 O'Clock in the morning and ate breakfast, never showed up for dinner and finally got back by night, so you can see what a fellow goes through. Well, people don't understand what we face so it isn't much use to explain it. Ginny probably thinks I am having a good time with the English girls but it just so happens that I don't go out. I'm so damn tired that I hit the bed and never wake up till I'm ready to fly again. Are your eyes okay, I've been thinking about you quite a bit because I sure realize how good you were to me.

Goodbye Sis
Norman"
(Lt Norman Rasmussen, Bom on Handorf Crew)

Lt. Handorf's crew.

238011 *Kind-a-Ruff*, Lt Handorf's B-17 on the Berlin mission.

The Handorf Crew – B Group, Lead Squadron

At 1420 hours, near Diepholz, Lt. Edward Handorf's luck ran out when he met a Me 109. According to S/Sgt. Willsey on March 6, 1944:

"This crew was flying as Deputy Group lead [100 B Group] and had assumed the lead position when Lauro/Swartout were shot out of formation. Lt Handorf was headed home after unloading on Berlin, when a ME 109 came in at 1 o'clock low and sprayed the front of *Kind-a-Ruff* with 20mm, causing the wing tanks to erupt into flames!" Willsey says he "pulled the emergency bomb bay door release and snapped on his parachute." He moved forward to the flight deck, and tapped Lt. Handorf on the shoulder as Handorf and the co pilot, Lt. Spence, were getting ready to bail out.

"I stepped through the open bomb bay doors and, while still in the prop wash, the aircraft blew up blowing the Tail Gunner Staff Sergeant Lawrence C. Fair clear. I delayed opening my chute until I was going through the last layer of clouds at about 10,000 feet. The TG & I landed about 60 yards apart. Lawrence had his leg broken and told me to try to escape and leave him alone. About 3 hours later, I was captured by some German civilians with shot guns."

This was Willsey's ninth mission. The remaining eight crew members were killed in the explosion of *Kind-a-Ruff*. This was the 15th and last 100BG crew shot down that day by the *Luftwaffe*. The broken remnants of the plane came down near Neubruchhausen.

The Lauro Crew – B Group, Lead Squadron

Although the rear oxygen system was damaged and not functioning, the gunners had faithfully stuck to their guns. They warded off numerous fighter attacks by passing around emergency oxygen bottles, stopping only long enough to enable them to remain conscious. Despite the damage sustained and the intense fighter attacks, Swartout's passion for dog fighting and his determined crew had brought *Nelson King* into the Berlin area. They turned to the left to skirt the flak and turned inside the out-coming groups, looking for company. As they were at a lower altitude below the flak bursts, three shells went through the wings and exploded above. Their move brought them in the vicinity of the outgoing 13th A Wing 390BG. Lauro and Swartout went redline again to get close for preservation.

The bandits found a new opportunity to finish them off and came back to peck at them. Swartout yelled to Lauro to go under their wing-mate's high squadron and up to the other side, depending of the angle of the bandits' passes. *Nelson King* played this seesaw game for a long time; the pilots took turns flying, depending on the side of the attack. All this evasive action brought attention on them. Swartout had his transmitter and intercom out, but he could receive.

In the last element of the 390BG High Squadron a guy kept calling the 390BG leader to tell him a weird B-17 was out there leading bandits to them. The leader told him to keep an eye on him, and if he attempted to turn away, to shoot him down! When the Germans departed the scene, Lauro and Swartout maneuvered closer on the left wing of his cautious wingman and slightly under. A P-38 flying on one engine and apparently out of ammo tucked under *Nelson King's* left wing for protection. He thought the 390BG was a sanctuary too when suddenly Swartout heard:

"Fighters at 10 o'clock high!"

Gunners on *Nelson King* braced for another *Luftwaffe* attack, but luck finally showed up, as the fighters were P-47s. What a beautiful sight they made as they swept over, dipping their wings. What a terrific sense of relief it was. Soon P-47s and P-51s were all over the place, but too little too late.

The Barrick Crew – B Group, High Squadron

Snort Stuff had tasted the flak from German ships on the Baltic Sea, and now it was the turn of the Swedish flak to take over as she cleared the coast. They had been briefed to land at Ystad, Sweden, if they had to. However, there was a low overcast in that area, and after letting down to 500 feet they could not get under it. They were looking for a place to belly land in the snow when two Swedish fighter planes arrived. One of them lowered his landing gear and flaps and flew off *Snort Stuff's* left wing, giving him hand signals when to turn. The other fighter was having a good time diving on the Americans and pulling up just ahead so they had to fly through his prop wash. Each time the #4 propeller moved into the cowling and the left wing flapped. Barrick motioned to the guy on his left

Crew at lunch in Sweden (start at lower left and go around the table): Hugh Fantone (tail gunner), James Brady (togglier), Frederick Thorpe (left waist gunner), Walfred Johnson (engineer/tte), Samuel Barrick (pilot), Ira Munn (copilot), Edward Marlen (ball turret gunner), James Guerrini (navigator), and Clifton Barton (radio operator). (Courtesy of William Sapp Dixon)

Left: William D. Sapp in Sweden. (Courtesy of William Sapp Dixon) Right: Lt. Sam Barrick in Sweden.

for him to get the other plane away. He just grinned back; he too was enjoying the fun.

The pilot told T/Sgt. Walfred J. Johnson to turn the top turret toward the fighter. They got the message and escorted the plane to a small airfield at Malmö. They lowered the landing gear, and Barrick told everyone to get into the radio room in crash landing positions until the plane stopped, then get out immediately and form a rank at the rear entrance door.

At 1445 hours, Barrick made the smoothest landing that he had ever made on the grass turf and parked the airplane. The crew scrambled out as Barrick shut down the engines. Flight School in Roswell, New Mexico, with classmate Bob Shoens was nothing like this! Sam had little time to wonder what happened to his classmate, as a voice rang in his ear "Valcome to Shveden."

Lt Robert Shoens and Sam Barrack went through Kearney Neb. together in final Phase Training:

"We came to Thorpe Abbotts together, along with Stan Seaton and some others. While at Kearney both our wives were with us and they were both pregnant, and they would commiserate together over the early stages of their condition. Sam ended up in a different squadron than me, and I lost track of him. After the Berlin Raid I found out he was in Sweden and wired my wife that he was ok and my wife relayed that to his wife. She hadn't heard anything at that time except that he was MIA."

The Ferbrache Crew – B Group, Low Squadron

During the bomb run both waist gunners (Sgt. Clifford H. Leming and Sgt. Benjamin J. Devine) were wounded. According to S/Sgt. John Lucarelli, the radio operator, Lemming came up to him and said that the elastic in the back of his helmet was irritating him; turned out it was a flak wound. Devine had also suffered a small flak wound in the back of the head:

"We had a flak hole in our ship the size of a door but we were still in the air. At 'bombs away' we had six bombs hung up in the bomb bay so Devine strattled the catwalk to jettison the bombs. To make matters worse, the bomb bay doors would not shut either so we had to crank them back up."

Tail Gunner Sgt Howard Williams remembers:

"We encountered a lot of flak on the way into and over the target. It felt like every flak gun in Germany was aimed at us. The only reason we got back was because of Lt Ferbrache, he was one hell of a good pilot."

239994 *Snort Stuff* in Sweden.

V

Stragglers "Home Alone!" Homeward Bound and the Morning After

Gamblers and pragmatists alike react unfavourably to the odds of a heavy bomber crew flying alone deep in enemy territory in a damaged aircraft ever returning to home base. Being a straggler is akin to playing Russian roulette! If "Lady Luck" did not abandon the crew because of damage to the aircraft, they still faced the prospect of flak and/or fighters dashing away any hope of seeing England again to enjoy a pint with the mates. Navigators were briefed as to the known locations of flak batteries and German airfields. Flak and fighters were formidable challenges, but when you were flying home on a proverbial "wing and a prayer" in a battle damaged heavy bomber with the possibility of wounded, if not dead men aboard, then flying as the crow flies seemed reasonable, if not a risky decision.

Even if flak and fighters did not bring into question a crew member's belief in his talisman, there still existed the challenge before setting sights on the Cliffs of Dover—traversing the English Channel. As the notion of returning to England seemed a possibility, reality in the guise of the boogie man could arrive to

232009 *Black Cat 13*, 'Red' Harper's B-17 on the March 6, 1944, Berlin mission.

Touching down at Thorpe Abbotts, March 6, 1944.

strike fear, if not terror. Lt Handorf's crew had learned that lesson the hard way over Diepholz, so everyone scanned the skies for fighters.

The Harper Crew – A Group, High Squadron

Moments after tail gunner Sgt. Ross Frank called over the intercom "Fighters!" fifteen Me 109s attacked Lt. C. B. 'Red' Harper's *Black Cat 13*. He had been forced down to 5,000 feet when a rocket exploding in the waist section damaged the rear oxygen system. To the fighters Harper's plane was "meat on the table," and the wolves were hungry. Harper jettisoned his bombs and ducked into the nearest cloud cover while calling for his "Little Friends." 'Red' did not plan to stick around for the fighter support to arrive. Later he learned that the P-51s heard his call and came down and shot down ten of those fighters. For the moment, the only thing on his mind was "running like hell" to get his aircraft and crew home safe.

As they came to the coast the navigator gave Harper a new course, which took them parallel to the coast. When they saw flak coming up over Dunkirk it gave Lt. Harper the bearing he and his navigator were looking for, and he turned the damaged B-17 out into the English Channel. *Black Cat 13* was anything but what other black cats bring—bad luck. When they landed at Thorpe Abbotts, Harper's ground crew could not believe everyone walked away with only a few scratches. *Black Cat 13* was full of holes and some stretched skin from the 300 mph dive and pull out with a full bomb load!

The Cope Crew – A Group, Lead Squadron

In the cockpit, the battle was on to keep the plane in the air; the bombs were jettisoned, and Captain Cope put the plane in a dive heading for cloud cover and air to breathe. They had a damaged engine, oxygen loss, and severe battle damage, and Cope knew they were "easy pickings" as fighters swarmed in. In the back of the aircraft, all hell was breaking loose! S/Sgt. Ray Bryan had staved off one attacker in his tail position, but with both his legs wounded he needed medical attention fast. He was pulled from his position by S/Sgt. James Morrison and propped up by the tail wheel. Morrison gave medical attention from his first aid kit (morphine).

Capt Mark Cope's 237607 *Alice From Dallas II's* battle damage March 6, 1944.

While this was happening Me 109s continued to attack 237607 *Alice From Dallas II*. Waist gunner S/Sgt. James E. Morrison took Ray's place in the tail and waist gunner S/Sgt. Donald Walker went above and beyond the call of duty.

With fighters attacking from all sides he alternated between both waist guns, keeping the wolves at bay, firing short bursts at the attackers. During the battle, a 20mm shell exploded in his face opening up a gash under his left eye. T/Sgt. John Eling, operating his .50 caliber in the radio room, peered out towards the waist area and could not believe what he was seeing: Walker looked like death warmed over, moving from one waist gun to the other, his face a bloody mess. T/Sgt. John Verbovski, in the top turret, shot down 3 fighters in the melee, including the one that had hit Walker, while James Morrison, Arthur Cox, and Richard Donnelly each got credit for a fighter each. Copilot Lt. Martin Tashjian helped Captain Cope bring their damaged plane back to Thorpe Abbotts, firing multiple red flares to indicate wounded on board. For his actions that day, Donald Walker was awarded the Silver Star and the Purple Heart.

'Take the Atlantic to put fires out'

Express Staff Reporter: U.S. Bomber Base, Monday

HERE at this American bomber base tonight men of the Forts and Liberators told of their day blasting of Berlin.

This is what they had to say:—

The hero-gunner, told by 1st Lieutenant Mark Cope:—

Our waist gunner saved all our lives.

We were within shot of the target, but we were hit, and dropped to 5,000 feet. All the while Jerry fighters attacked.

Our tail gunner was hit in both legs, but the waist gunner patched him up. The waist gunner then manned both waist guns and continued to man them after being hit in the face by a 20-mm. shell.

He kept off the fighters and put out a fire that another shell had started in the plane. The navigator and the bombardier dealt with another fire in the nose.

While the fires were raging we were being continually attacked by fighters all the way to the French coast, but the sergeant kept them off and we flew back on instruments."

"A hell of a way to make a living."

Staff Sergeant Knudson, who shot down two Me. 109s, said: "They jumped on us about 150 miles inside the coast. The first one made a pass at us and after he had come through my bullets he was on fire from wing to rudder.

"The second one attacked us on the way back and I sent him down in flames." With a smile, Knudson added: "This is a hell of a way to make a living."

Five Forts were sent down at one pass.

By Tactical Sergeant Harry. S. Lenk: "I did not have time to notice what we hit with our bombs. The Luftwaffe really went to town tonight. A flock of F.W.190s jumped our top squadron and knocked five Forts down at one pass.

An ocean to put out the Berlin fires.

Staff Sergeant J. G. Brown, speaking of the fires raging in the city: "It will take the Atlantic Ocean to put those fires out." Staff Sergeant M. D. Benefield said he saw at least 16 German fighters shot down by the Forts' escort."

Lieut.-Colonel G. Thorup, who led a wing: "We bombed the target and we did not miss it.

Strip of flak was two miles long.

Staff-Sergeant Chester said they could see flames when they were 100 miles away on the return journey. He described the flak as terrific, and said there was "one strip of flak two miles long and 1,000 feet thick over the target area.

Fighters attacked for nearly five hours.

Lieut.-Colonel Robert Kuttle, a wing leader, said: "We were under fighter attack for nearly five hours. The assaults were bold and vicious, coming from every conceivable position. Single-engined fighters attacked in groups of ten,

Lt Mark Cope press clipping after Berlin Mission March 6, 1944.

Lt Francis Malooly

The Malooly Crew– A Group, Lead Squadron

"Landing at the field with our bomb bay doors open and having to crank our flaps down. Cope's ship off the side of the runway all shot to hell. Wing tip shot off, all around waist windows and all over. Quite a few men wounded. One waist gunner kept both waist guns going while he gave first aid to another gunner. 16 planes failed to return from this field and 20 more from another group. I know of 2 crews lost from my squadron. This mission is one of the roughest they have had at this field. I hope we will never have to go on another to Berlin. If only we had fighter escort all the way it wouldn't have been so bad. Most of the ships that got back were shot up in some way. The whole mission was on long nightmare of burning planes and heavy flak, guns firing and fighters attacking, bailouts, etc. Time; 10 ½ hours and alert is on for tomorrow."

Lt Robert W. Bailie, copilot

During the return trip, fighter escort was making this a better world. The formation altitude was down to 20,000 feet. Everyone had set up for the long glide down across the North Sea to England. Into the West they flew, while the minutes turned to hours and the miles clocked beneath them in endless and fatiguing procession, the ground moving "homesick" slow. The sun swung low, streaming through the windshield in a bright but eerie light.

Sam Barrick's classmate in *Our Gal Sal* began to wonder what had happened to their group. It could not be that they were the only survivors from the 351st Bomb Squadron. There was very little conversation. They were too tired, too emotionally drained and overwhelmed with the thought that they had survived that gauntlet.

Devore and Elton led the remnants of the battered 100BG, leaving the coast of occupied Europe at 1510 hours at 16,000 feet. Everyone had a brief sense of relief, but they still had to be on guard in case the *Luftwaffe* had one more surprise for them; fortunately, it never materialized. At 10,000 feet, Lt Shoens to crew:

"Ok guys, you can go off oxygen!"

Lt. Devore and Major Elton's aircraft following a May 15, 1944, crash landing at Honington. Note the backwards N in the squadron code.

The damn masks felt now more like muzzles than a life-sustaining aid. Down in the ball turret in *Our Gal Sal*, Sgt. Silverstone was relaxing. Silverstone began smoking cigars at the age of 16, and his idea of relaxing after a mission was to take off his oxygen mask, making sure the flow of oxygen was shut off, and then fire up a nice fat cigar! Winston Churchill would have been proud.

The formation began to spread out. It made it easier for pilots, and there was not the risk of getting into the prop wash of an aircraft ahead. Nevertheless, there was still need for vigilance. Crews were tired and less cautious. As they neared the coast, they could see the British air sea rescue boats coming to pick anyone up who could not make it. *Nelson King* kept losing altitude, so the Lauro crew threw out any excess weight they could find to lighten the ship and make it across the North Sea.

Bastard's Bungalow, with the Ferbrache crew, had made it back to England. Both the crew and plane were pretty beat up: flak damage, the brakes shot out, and two crewmen slightly wounded. Lts. Elmer E. Ferbrache and Anthony D. Slatinsky managed to set 23508 down but with no brakes, and brought the plane to a stop after running off the end of the runway. Sgt. Clifford Leming could not wait to get out of the plane. He opened the rear door, jumped out, and fell to his knees kissing the ground. They had survived Berlin, even if just barely. Leming would go on to complete 30 more missions. Lt. Ferbrache would sign up for a second tour and return to the Group as a Major.

The English coast passed under the wings of *Our Gal Sal* well behind the rest of Group. They had flown over Great Yarmouth at 1537 hours. The gunners started removing the ammunition from their guns while the ball turret and tail gunners came out, stretched their arms and legs, and relaxed in the Radio Room. Where did that cigar smell come from?

Wings peeled off; Groups were heading for home to lick their wounds. Lt. Shoens relates what happened next:

"We left the 390th and started our own descent toward Thorpe Abbotts. Then I began to wonder whether anyone would believe we were actually involved in the battle that had gone on. Here we were a lone survivor as far as we knew no injuries and no damage. We could have dropped our bombs anywhere. That question never arose. Later I learned that both the 95th and the 390th had confirmed our presence."

As Lt. Shoens approached Thorpe Abbotts, the control tower gave *Our Gal Sal* clearance for landing. They circled the airfield alone and saw many empty hardstands. Shoens' crew could only imagine the shock of the ground crews scanning the empty sky in disbelief. The returning heavily damaged B-17s began to tell a story. M/Sgt. Wildrick and the rest of the ground crew for *Our Gal Sal* had been "sweating them in" all day around the hardstand, waiting, hoping, and praying for their plane to return. They were stunned by the losses and the damage they had already witnessed. Now they saw "their Baby" on final approach and relief set in.

Our Gal Sal landed and taxied to her hardstand. They were back home after 8 hours and 5 minutes in the air. All day long, the Shoens crew had cheated death. As they got out of the plane, they looked up and saw Captain Lauro's crippled aircraft, *Nelson King*, fly past the tower to get a damage report. The decision was to take their "flying junk pile" to the main aircraft repair depot at Honington. Lauro and his crew eventually reached Honington and Captain Swartout made a successful landing, even with the landing gear mechanism destroyed, brakes completely wiped out, and without the aid of flaps! The Lauro crew gave Swartout credit for getting them back alive. For his actions this day, Captain Jack Swartout was awarded the Silver Star (See Appendices B). *Nelson King* would not be alone at Honington. A few days later *Alice From Dallas II*, which had been flown by the Copes crew, would be sent there for extensive repairs.

Soon after landing, Lt. Colonel Ollie Turner, 351 CO, arrived in his jeep and asked Lt. Shoens through his tears "What happened?"

Landing gear down, tail wheel locked, flaps....

On final approach to Thorpe Abbotts. Just keep her in the air just a few seconds more.

231306 *Nelson King* at Honington on March 6, 1944.

"What do you say? What do you do when your Squadron CO is crying and wants to know what had happened? You did the same."

By this time, John Massol and Harold Granger had returned to Thorpe Abbotts after their test flight, and they were shocked to learn of the losses: 15 planes and crews! This is especially so because five of the missing crews were their friends. These were men they had trained with in the states and traveled with overseas; now they were among the lost—Sam Barrick, George Brannan, Bill Murray, Merril Rish, and William Terry. The Massol crew radio operator, Asa Spengler, was happy to see *Our Gal Sal* return; his good friend, roommate, and pocketbook watcher Don Hammond had returned. Both men would spend many more missions watching over each other's pocketbooks until completing their tour of duty. What was left of the 100BG was back home just after 1602 hours.

The gunners took their guns out, cleaned them, and placed their flying gear and parachutes into bags to store at the flying equipment room lockers. It did not take the trucks long to move the crews to the debriefing room. When they went into the room, it was full of curious base personnel. Some picked up a cup of coffee that the Red Cross members were serving while others reached for the shot of whiskey the 'Doc' had waiting to calm the nerves. Some men drank it while others did not. Shoens had no trouble downing his. A photographer flashed a picture some place in the room. T/Sgt George Madden, Helmick's top turret gunner, had all he could do to restrain himself from throwing his cup of coffee at the photographer. He had seen enough flashes for one day. Sgt Howard Williams, tail gunner on the Ferbrache crew, claimed one fighter shot down, but with no one to confirm it and the loss of fifteen crews he did not feel much like pushing the issue.

The Gibbons crew had beat the odds and made it home with flak damage to the wing and stabilizer. They had hoped they had seen the last of Berlin for a while, but they were wrong! Gibbons and his crew would go back to *Big B* five times in the course of their tour of duty. Acting Commanding Officer Lt. Colonel John Bennett awarded the Gibbons crew a commendation for their action and bravery during their first 5 missions.[34] Many years later retired Air Force Colonel John P. Gibbons would be asked what his most vivid memories of March 6, 1944 were:

"Burning airplanes, buddies going down, a catastrophe, getting back to base and finding empty barracks, you worried how you were going make it."

A review of the debriefing notes revealed that the *Luftwaffe* had a new tactic. Massive head-on attacks by the *Luftwaffe* were designed to absorb the concentrated bombers' firepower. There were many empty tables at debriefing. Some of the crews had their shot of whiskey to settle the nerves while others grabbed a sandwich. Lt. Gibbons was not a drinker:

John P. Gibbons' crew (left to right) at Thorpe Abbotts. Standing: Sterling B. Blakeman, John P. Gibbons, E. Max Johnson, and Robert Dykeman. Kneeling: Ira L. Arnold, Carmine V. Roberto, Myron J. Ettus, Bernard L. Spragg, Archie W. Bunting, and Frank W. Buschmeier.

Three views of the damage to 231968 *Miss Irish* on March 19, 1944, after an 88mm hit the radio compartment (see the full story in Appendix E).

"I was a prohibitionist when I joined the Army Air Force, but after my sixth mission [when an 88mm shell went off in the radio room, killing the radio operator and almost cutting the B-17 in two] I learned rapidly the finer points of drinking."

Interrogation officers were in disbelief. There were not that many returning crews to interview. They gathered around the Shoens Crew and listened to what had happened. The returning gunners claimed twenty-six enemy fighters; Don Blair and Bill Wright, from the Shoens crew, were credited for two of them. Many questioned the pre-mission predictions that the "heavies" were going to annihilate the *Luftwaffe*. Some wondered, "who was going to annihilate whom?"

Major Marvin Bowman, S-2 Intelligence Officer, jotted down the following in his diary:

"Mar 6, The 100th dispatched 36 planes led by Major 'Bucky' Elton flying with the superb lead crew of Herb Devore's, with one of the 100th's best Navigators, Burton Joseph as lead navigator. The 100th was to lose 15 aircraft, most of then on the huge air battle over Haseluenne at almost exactly noon on the 6th of March 1944."[35]

The crews finished debriefing and went to the mess hall. For those interested in food, there was no problem finding a seat. Many personnel had upset stomachs. Others went to the barracks area, but they could not hide from the pal of death that hung heavy in the air. All around the base, supply was already there, picking up clothes and personal effects from those who had failed to return. Shoens' hut was vacant; the officers of Lt Rish's crew were his bunkmates, but they were now somewhere in Germany, hopefully? They used to kid each other about what they wanted if the other went down, and both crews had fun razzing Rish's bombardier Lt. Kehm. They nicknamed him "Heinie" because of his strong German features. Now all Bob could hope for was that Merril and "Heinie" had been in one of those four parachutes he had seen.

Few men wanted to talk, and if they did, it was in a low tone, or in a whisper. Some wanted to be on their own, while others remained quiet. That evening many drank more than usual.

Some cursed the Generals that sent the 8AF back to Berlin when it was obvious the Germans knew they were coming. Meanwhile, the many heartbroken ground crews, whose ships had not showed up yet, continued to hang around their hardstands listening for any faint sound that might be a returning B-17. As the events of the day unfolded, it was becoming clear the 100BG had suffered a catastrophe.

Fifteen planes and 150 men were missing in action!

Squadron Adjutants and Chaplains started the unwelcomed task of writing letters to the next of kin. There was no comfort to learn eventually that of the 150 missing in action, 59 were killed in action, 81 became prisoners of war, and 10 were interned in Sweden.

That night sleep would come at a premium, hard to find, if at all. This was especially true when the whole side of your hut was vacant. The silence was deafening.

S/Sgt John A. Miller

S/Sgt John A. Miller flew the first 100BG mission to Berlin on March 3, 1944, but the mission was recalled. After the 6 March mission to Berlin, Miller recalled there was only a Sgt Lovin and himself left in the spare gunner's hut. Lovin eventually was rotated home. All alone in the hut was getting on John's nerves, so the squadron CO gave him a 48 hour pass to London to take the edge off. When he returned to Thorpe Abbotts he discovered he was scheduled to fly. He had just enough time to change and make it to the hardstand. Since he did not attend briefing, he asked what the target was for today. The answer came back loud and clear, "Big B," Berlin! John Miller felt sick.

Waist Gunner S/Sgt. John A. Miller would complete 35 missions and hit "Big B" six times, 5 with Lt Lawrence Townsend's crew. He was credited with shooting down a Me 410, and was awarded the Distinguished Flying Cross and Air Medal with clusters, and he was still only 17 years old "going on forty." He falsified his age when he enlisted in Indiana in October 1942. He celebrated his 18th birthday on July 22, 1944, five days after completing his final mission.[36]

The actual total that day was 69 Heavies lost, fifteen from the 100BG alone, amounting to 25% of the losses of the entire 8th Air Force for the day. It was a fearful price to pay in the quest for air supremacy, particularly as the majority of the bombs fell on the suburbs without even scratching the primary targets. In the following days, all over the States, families would receive telegrams and learn the fate of a son, father, brother, or husband:

The Secretary of War desires me to express his deep regret that your ... has been reported missing in action.

"New York Times
March 7, 1944

Drew Middleton

800 US BOMBERS SMASH AT BERLIN BY DAY
68 LOST IN BATTLES
123 OF FOE SHOT DOWN

Air War at Peak
Fortresses and Liberators, Loose 2,000 Tons on German Capital

Fighters Swarm on Nazis
Three-Hour Combat Over the Reich Gives Major Victory Against *Luftwaffe*

The war in the air reached a new and perhaps decisive phase yesterday when about 800 American heavy bombers fought their way through the massed strength of the Germans' metropolitan air force to blast factories, airfields and other military installations in the Berlin area.

The air battles that raged around and within the tight wedge-shaped formations of Flying Fortress and Liberators were the greatest in history, with American fighters, hundreds of which accompanied the bombers, and the 'heavies' engaged throughout the mission.

...

American losses in the big blow at the Nazi capital were serious. Sixty-eight heavy bombers and eleven fighters were missing – representing a loss of nearly 700 trained airmen."

When the subject of the 6 March Berlin mission came up between Jack Swartout and Bob Shoens years later, Bob asked Jack what it was like being alone out there:

"After we were hit and fell out of formation, we had almost 3 hours alone! Fighting 3-4 fighters at a time, one engine out, one with no control, no hydraulics, fire in the cockpit, myself and a gunner wounded, instruments blown out, ball turret out, and three large flak holes in the wings. Imagine the above my friend, that was *all alone*!"

Eighth Air Force Combat Chronology
MONDAY, 6 MARCH 1944

STRATEGIC OPERATIONS (Eighth Air Force): Mission 250: 504 B-17s and 226 B-24s are dispatched to hit industrial areas in the suburbs of Berlin; fierce fighter opposition claims 69 bombers (the highest number lost by the Eighth Air Force in a single day) and 11 fighters; the bombers claim 97-28-60 *Luftwaffe* fighters; details are:

1. 248 B-17s hit secondary targets in the Berlin area; 18 B-17s are lost, 2 damaged beyond repair and 172 damaged; casualties are 2 KIA, 8 WIA and 184 MIA.
2. 226 B-17s hit targets of opportunity at Templin, Verden, Kalkeberge, Potsdam, Oranienburg and Wittenberg; 35 B-17s are lost, 3 damaged beyond repair and 121 damaged; casualties are 15 WIA and 354 MIA.
3. 198 B-24s hit the primary target (Genshagen industrial area), secondary targets in the Berlin area and targets of opportunity at Potsdam; 16 B-24s are lost, 1 damaged beyond repair and 54 damaged; casualties are 15 KIA, 8 WIA and 148 MIA.

Escort is provided by 86 P-38s, 615 Eighth and Ninth Air Force P-47s and 100 Eighth and Ninth Air Force P-51s; results are:

1. P-38s claim 3-0-1 *Luftwaffe* aircraft; 1 P-38 is lost, the pilot is MIA.
2. P-47s claim 36-7-12 *Luftwaffe* aircraft; 5 P-47s are lost, 3 damaged beyond repair and 4 damaged; casualties are 2 WIA and 5 MIA.
3. P-51s claim 43-1-20 *Luftwaffe* aircraft; 5 P-51s are lost and 2 damaged; casualties are 5 MIA.

The fighters also claim 1-0-12 *Luftwaffe* aircraft on the ground. Mission 251: 5 of 5 B-17s drop 250 bundles of leaflets on Nantes, Cambrai, Lille, Chateauroux, and Lorient, France, at 2029-2130 hours without loss. CARPETBAGGER missions are also flown.

If it had not already, reality began to set in for the survivors of March 6, 1944. Similar in response to any difficult human endeavor, doubt surfaced to the ease of completing a tour of duty and becoming a member of the *Lucky Bastard Club*, whose membership rules required the completion of a combat tour of duty. Some must have thought that the only Lucky Bastard was the crewman not scheduled to fly to Berlin on March 6, 1944. The S-2 officer wrote in his diary:

"Mar 7, 1944 the 100th mercifully stood down due to weather."

As it had so many times before, the teletype chattered to life again early in the evening of March 7, 1944. Everyone thought, there is no way that the top brass at PINETREE would send us

Berlin Gets 1st Big Day Bombing

Fierce Battles Rage As Huge U.S. Force Dumps Tons on City

No. 17 3-6-44

One Fort Division Fights Way In and Out; Other Forts, Libs Meet Few Fighters; Flak Heavy; Weather Better

By Bud Hutton
Stars and Stripes Staff Writer

American heavy bombers attacked Berlin in force yesterday.

With Saturday's attack by a single formation, it was the second U.S. blow in three days on the German capital, and the city's first major daylight assault.

Flanked and covered by relays of Eighth and Ninth Air Force long-range fighters, the Liberators and Fortresses heaped high explosives and incendiaries on their Berlin targets with both visual and "cloud" technique bombing to smash the Nazis' last lingering hopes that any defense could stop the daylight bombers from destroying any objective in the whole Reich.

One division of Fortresses had to slug its way with heavy losses almost every bit of the 600-mile route in to the city, while other divisions reported moderate to almost negligible fighter opposition. Virtually every bomber crew, however, told of intense walls of flak ringing the capital.

There was no official announcement up to last midnight of American losses or claims, but it was expected that the number of bombers reported missing from the day's operations might be among the highest in Eighth Air Force history.

A new record of enemy aircraft destroyed by the escorting fighters also was expected as intelligence officers checked claims and camera gun films. Mustangs, Thunderbolts and Lightnings, on preliminary reports, probably had outscored the Nazis in the ratio of eight to one and had gone well over the previous single day's score of 61, established on Feb. 22.

While the heavies and their escorts were completing their seventh attack in eight days, a record force of nearly 300 Marauder mediums of the Ninth Air Force carried out heavy attacks on the Nazi airdrome at Beauvais-Tille and military objectives in the Pas de Calais area, all without loss. Sunday night, RAF Mosquitoes had kept the Nazi defenses strained by attacks on western Germany.

With weather conditions obviously much improved over Saturday's when Fortresses dropped the first U.S. bombs on Berlin through almost solid six-mile cloud, Eighth Bomber Command ordered a major, although not record, force to go right back to the same target.

It was scarcely noon when German radio stations began to describe "a gigantic air battle" raging over the Reich from the Zuyder Zee to the capital. Just before 1 PM the sirens began to sound in Berlin.

Stars and Stripes

back to Berlin so soon after this mission. They would at least let us lick our wounds and replenish the lost planes and crews? Maybe get a few milk runs to a "no ball" target [V-1 rocket instillation] in France to "bloody" the new crews before they sent us back to that hell. If we were lucky, the weather would turn bad and we would be stood down for a couple of days.

Lt. Colonel 'Jack' Kidd, Group Operations Officer, sat in his chair and read the field order. Kidd was livid:

"What are those fools trying to do, kill all of us?"

Then he diligently began preparations for the mission the following day. Target: the Erkner ball bearing factory in BERLIN!

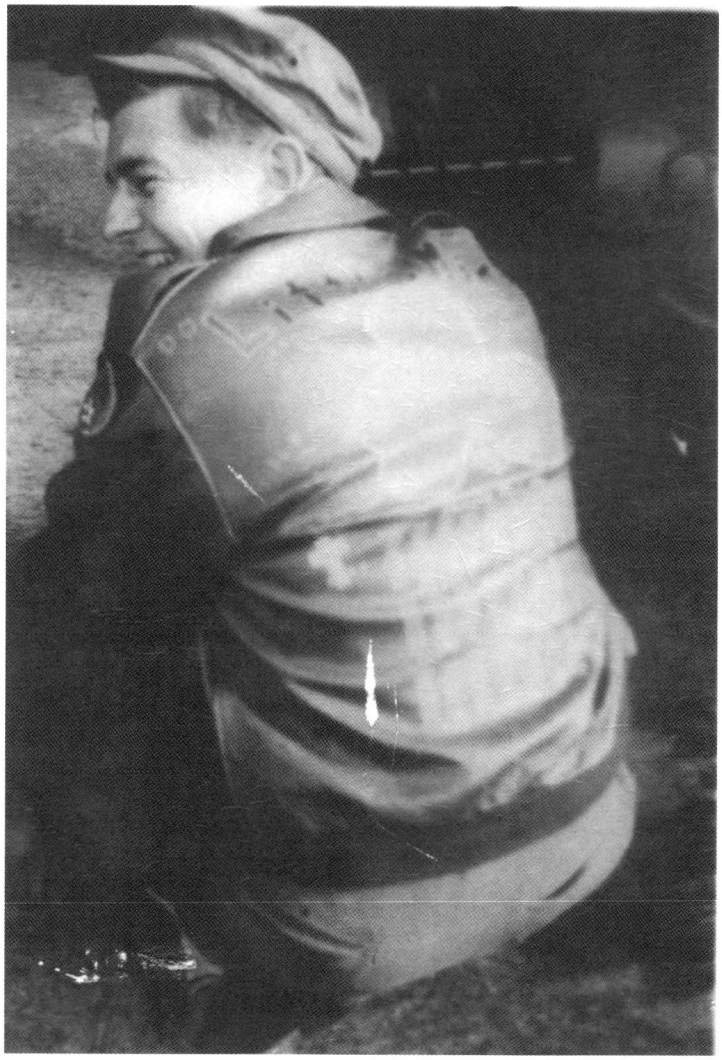

Waist Gunner on Lt John Gibbons' crew.

VI

Not Again!

Lt Robert Shoens and his crew would once again go to Berlin on March 8, 1944. The route was the same as two days before, but the outcome would be very different. Even though it was not their turn to lead the Wing, Lt. Colonel John M. Bennett Jr. knew that morale at Thorpe Abbots was extremely low due to the losses suffered on 6 March. He called 13 Combat Wing Headquarters at Horham and, upon explaining the conditions, he requested permission for the 100BG to lead the Wing with him in Command. His request was granted. At briefing the next morning, when the curtain was pulled back and Berlin was announced as the target, there was not a sound. Bennett remembers "I was petrified; this was a definite sign of very low morale." The prospect of massive aborts due to mechanical and personal failure could not be denied as the S-2 Officer showed photos of the Erkner ball bearing plant and Lt. Colonel 'Jack' Kidd outlined the order of battle. The 45 Combat Wing was to lead the 8AF followed by the 13 Combat Wing, which was to be led by the 100BG.

The 100BG mustered only fifteen B-17s for the 8 March mission. Lt. Colonel Bennett would be flying in the Lead Aircraft PFF, a radar equipped B-17, with Capt. Leonard Bull as lead navigator and Lt Charlie Stapleton flying as formation officer in the tail gunner's position. Stapleton's job was to be Bennett's "eyes" on the Group and Wing. Take-off and forming up went without a hitch, and as the 13 Combat Wing took their position echeloned to the right of the 45 Combat Wing, Bennett called back to Lt Stapelton on the intercom to check up on the Group. He was sure there had to have been some aborts and was afraid of the answer. What he got back both shocked and pleased the Colonel; there were no aborts, all 15 aircraft were still in formation.

"We had picked up our P-47 fighter escort over Holland and they stayed with us until just before Dummer Lake. Now we scanned the skies looking for our P-51 escort that was due to rendezvous with us. This was where the Luftwaffe bushwhacked

Back to Berlin.

the 100th two days earlier and there were many nervous stomachs in the Group. Just after passing Dummer Lake we spotted fighters off to our right and above heading towards the 45th CBW up ahead. We all let out a silent sigh of relief.

This relief was short lived.

We were admiring the fighter formation when all of sudden they peeled off and dove on the 45th CBW guns and cannons blazing. We had been duped; the Luftwaffe had mimicked our fighter tactics and hit the Wing with 150 fighters. FW 190s and Me 109s streaked in fifteen abreast."

The carnage that ensued is detailed below. Lt. Colonel Bennett had a front row seat as the 45th CBW was raked over by E/A machine gun and cannon fire:

"At 1251 hours, near 5228N - 0855E one B-17 pulled out of the lead group of the 45th CBW firing green flares. It went down in a nosedive and started to fall apart before it crashed. 4 chutes were seen.

Lt Col John Bennett in flight gear.

At 1300 hours, North of Hanover, 4 B-17s from the 45th CBW were knocked out of formation. They turned back toward England with engines smoking but were jumped by more E/A and all were believed to have been shot down. No chutes were seen.

At 1304 hours two more B-17s were seen to be knocked out of the 45th CBW by E/A. No. #1 engine was on fire and parts of the tail were shot away on one. Six chutes were seen from this one aircraft. The other went straight down and crashed. 1 chute was seen.

At 1310 hours, near 5236N - 1014E, a B-17 fell out of the 45th CBW and pulled away with its wheels down. It was last seen in level flight with E/A circling around it. No chutes were seen.

At 1327 hours, near 5229N - 1121E, two B-17s were knocked out of the 45th CBW by E/A. Both went down smoking but apparently under control. Three chutes were seen.

At 1337 hours, in the vicinity of Magdeburg, a B-17 from the Lead Squadron of 45th CBW was apparently hit by flak and fell out of formation with fire in No #4 engine. As it fell away from its formation, it broke in half at the Ball. 9 chutes were seen.

At 1338 hours, near Magdeburg two B-17s were knocked out of the Wing ahead of us and went down under control but flaming. 4 chutes were seen from one and 3 from the other."

In a little less than 90 minutes, thirteen B-17s had been either shot down or knocked out of formation. The lead plane in the 45 Combat Wing was one of those thirteen. The bomber stream was now 50 miles south of Berlin, and the Deputy lead in the 45 Combat Wing missed the turn at the Initial Point. After checking with his navigator Capt Leonard Bull to verify this miscue, Lt. Colonel Bennett made the command decision to turn the 13 Combat Wing north towards Berlin and was now leading the 8AF. He had not made this decision lightly, knowing the circumstances of a few days earlier and the fact the *Luftwaffe's* new tactic was to concentrate fire on the Lead Group. The 100BG was now in the lead and faced the brunt of the German fighter attacks. Miraculously, only one 100BG aircraft was seriously damaged, that of Lt Norman Chapman, during these ferocious E/A attacks. Lt Chapman's 240056, known as *Holy Terror III* and *Katie's Boys*, was still airborne and heading for Berlin. As he headed towards Berlin, Lt. Colonel Bennett had this thought:

"A man is a damn fool to sit in a big tin can with three tons of TNT and two thousand gallons of high octane gasoline and let somebody else throw firecrackers at him. There's no future in it."[37]

The skies over Berlin were clear, and bombing would be visual instead of radar. Flak was surprisingly light by Bennett's account, and all fifteen planes of the 100BG made it to Berlin. Bombing results would later show that the group hit the target with good

Lt. Norman Chapman's crew. Standing: Rex M. Ellis (Copilot), Norman L. Chapman (Pilot), George F. Dobbs (Tail Gunner), Wilson D. Clark (Bombardier), and Glenn G. Lindbom (Navigator). Kneeling: George B. Silverman (Top Turret - Engineer), Frank A. Yzenas (Right Waist Gunner), Leon E. Hill (Left Waist Gunner), Milton Scharf (Radio Operator), and Durward E. Hutchings (Ball Turret). This crew was scratched before take off on March 6, 1944. They would be shot down two days later on the March 8, 1944, mission to Berlin. This photograph is of the crew during stateside training in front of 23479 *Blackhills Ltd.*

results with the loss of only one aircraft. That one loss would be the damaged aircraft of Lt Norman Chapman's crew. The Mission Report states:

"One of our A/C is missing: A/C No. [240]056 was seen to have trouble with No. 1 engine in the Dummer Lake area on route to the target. An attempt to feather this engine was unsuccessful and the A/C fell out of its position in the formation. It is believed that this A/C flew with the Low Squadron of our group until we were near the I.P. where it was seen to lag behind and receive attacks from three E/A. Escort fighters came to its rescue and it was last seen some distance behind still in level flight. No chutes were seen."

The events of this crew and its final shoot down have been thoroughly investigated by researcher Andreas Trotz in Germany. He has confirmed without a doubt that the crash site near his farmhouse is that of *Holy Terror III/Katie's Boys*. Here are the events surrounding the loss of the Chapman crew along with additional information:

"On the morning of March 8, 1944, pilot Norman Chapman was on 8th Air Force mission number 252, which was to take him and his crew to the Erkner [located near Berlin] ball bearing plant factory. Since their usual aircraft, a 4-engined B-17 named *Katie* [239983] was under repair they were forced to fly a replacement plane named *Holy Terror III* [240056]. Lt Chapman wife's name was Katie, and Chapman quickly renamed the new plane [240056] *Katie's Boys*. Due to E/A attacks on the way to the target, one of the plane's engines was damaged. In spite of this, the crew was able to make the bomb run on the target but the airplane was still straggling. After turning away from the target, their engine continued having problems, which slowed them down. They were forced to leave the formation making them an easy target for the waiting German fighter planes.

Near the town of Jüterbog, another enemy fighter attack on the plane occurred. The German Sergeant Pilot Werner Rubel attacked the plane in his Messerschmitt 109-G, approximately 6 miles east of Jüterbog. One of the engines on the B-17 caught fire. Since staying any longer in the aircraft would have been dangerous, Lt Chapman hit the bailout bell, the order for the crew to abandon ship. Rubel, who was stationed in Jüterbog at this time with the 53. Jagdgeschwader [II. Group 6./JG53 - Pik As] got a confirmed kill. He noted that this attack happened at 2:17 p.m German time that afternoon. All ten crewmembers bailed out and landed safely in the fields between the villages of Hohengörsdorf, Fröhden and Markendorf. As seen by eyewitness G. Hannemann, the B-17 continued on its course but in a big spiral, with the engine No. 3 ablaze, near the village of Riesdorf. Approximately 1.2 miles from Riesdorf in the northern part of Sernower Heide, the B-17 crashed into the woods and airplane fragments scattered over the ground. Copilot, Lt Rex Ellis, landed in a field north of the village of Hohengörsdorf. He remembers the villagers coming after him with shovels and pitchforks ready to fight. There were only two members of the Wehrmacht present to stop the villagers and take Ellis into custody. The other nine crewmembers landed near the same area and were also captured and taken as prisoners of war. The officers, Chapman, Ellis, Lindbom and Clark, were sent to the POW camp in Barth/Ostsee (Stalag Luft I). The flight engineer, T/Sgt Silverman, and the radio operator, T/Sgt Scharf, were sent

Pieces from *Holy Terror / Katie's Boys* courtesy of Andreas Trotz.

Holy Terror III / Katie's Boys. Aircraft Lt Norman Chapman's crew was shot down in on March 8, 1944.

C A S U A L T Y   R E P O R T   Air Forces

Date : 8 March 1944
Time : 1345h   8th AF.
Type aircraft: B-17G   42 - 40056   ' HOLY TERROR III '
Codes : EP - F
Crashed at : 9½ km ESE of Jüterbog in the Sernower Heath, 1 km S. of the fieldpath Froebden-Schlenza, Germany. Is 50 km S. of Berlin.
Due to : crippled by fighters but proceeded to the target, bombed and later the crew abandoned the B-17.
Group/Squadron: 100 BG -H- 351 BS Thirpe Abbotts, Norfolk
Target : Germany. Berlin.

The aircraft was completely destroyed on impact in the woods.

P.O.W. :

P	:	CHAPMAN Norman L., 1/Lt.	0-746292
CP	:	ELLIS Rex M., 2/Lt.	0-752187
N	:	LINDBOM Glenn G., 2/Lt.	0-809659
B	:	CLARK Wilson D., 2/Lt.	0-750274
RO	:	SCHARF Milton, T/Sgt.	12188872
E	:	SILVERMAN George B., T/Sgt.	31153017
BTG	:	HUTCHINGS Durward E., S/Sgt.	12171577
RWG	:	YZENAS Frank A., S/Sgt.	12161945
LWG	:	HILL Leon E., S/Sgt.	38273822
TG	:	DOBBS George E., S/Sgt.	39406131

Lt Chapman's crew Casualty Report.

to Stalag Luft IV, a prison camp in East Prussia. The rest of the enlisted crewmembers were sent to different POW camps."

To this day, Andreas Trotz can still go out to that crash site near his farmhouse and find remnants of 240056 *Holy Terror III/ Katie's Boys*.

The group touched down at Thorpe Abbotts after 9 hours and 30 minutes in the air. The crews were exhausted but relieved to be back. One crew in particular was elated, since this mission to Berlin was their 25th and final mission, and they wanted to celebrate. They urged their pilot to buzz the control tower, a practice that was frowned upon by the brass. The young Captain, although reluctant, gave into the request and was determined to give the base a buzz job they would not soon forget. As he came in, the Captain's pass was so low that all the Officers gathered on the Control Tower "hit the deck" in their Class A uniforms. When he had landed and exited 231504 *Rosie's Riveters*, the young airplane commander was informed that the 13th Combat Wing Commander Colonel Alfred Kessler was on the tower when he buzzed it and had hit the deck with the rest. This was not good! Later, when Colonel Kessler approached the young pilot, he feared the worst. Instead, he reached out, shook his hand, and said "hell of a buzz job Rosie!" Captain Robert "Rosie" Rosenthal would go on to fly 52 missions (tops in the 100BG), reach the rank of a Lt. Colonel, be shot down twice, assigned as commanding officer of two squadrons (350 and 418), and finish the war as one of the most decorated officers in the 8th Air Force. A lawyer by trade before the war, he would serve as part of the Army legal team at the Nurnburg War Crimes trial after the war.

Major Red Bowman was relieved to enter this into his S-2 Diary:

"Mar 8, 1944 The 100th, led by Lt. Colonel John Bennett again went to Berlin, this time they could put up only 15 planes and in spite of the previous loses there were no abortions from the 100th, a fact said to have moved Colonel Bennett close to tears.

Capt Robert "Rosie"Rosenthal Crew. Back row is Lt J.A. Busalacchi-Nav, Lt C.J. Milburn-Bom, Capt. Robert Rosenthal-Pilot, Lt Winfrey "Pappy" Lewis-CP, and S/Sgt James Mack. Bottom Row: T/Sgt. C.C. Hall-TTE, S/Sgt Marion Sheldon-WG, S/Sgt William DeBlasio-TG, T/Sgt Mike Bocussi-ROG, and S/Sgt Ray Robinson-BTG. Photo taken on 8 Mar 44 at Thorpe Abbotts after Berlin mission. That completed 25 missions for the Crew. Rosie went on to fly 27 more missions and lead all 100th pilots in missions flown.

Mason and Dixon, Lt Helmick's A/C on the 8 March mission to Berlin. (Mark Brown, USAF)

Enlisted men of *Our Gal Sal*. L-R: William Eresman (top turret gunner), Ed Silverstone (ball turret gunner), Don Blair (tail gunner), William Wright (waist gunner), Virgil Warders (waist gunner), and Don Hammond (radio man).

The Group returned with the loss of only one plane, that flown by Lt. Norman Chapman. (The entire crew bailed out safely and all became POWs. Bombing results were good."

A new medical policy of a double shot of Scotch for returning crews had an immediate uplifting effect on the men, but it would take more than that to numb the effects of Berlin.

For Lt Robert Shoens, there would be no celebrations. This was only his 18th mission, and he would still face one more mission to Berlin before completing his tour of duty on May 1, 1944. Upon completion of the March 8, 1944, mission to Berlin, Ed Silverstone, ball turret gunner on the Shoens crew, joined the Lucky Bastard Club. After finishing his 25th and last mission, Ed got out of the B-17, kneeled down, and kissed the ground. This was immediately followed by getting sick. Ed recalled:

"I never get sick, but I went back to the barracks and was lying on the lawn in front of the Quonset hut and heaved up for 15 minutes, after that I was fine! The tension built up from 25 missions all came up at once, literally!"

On March 13, 1944, General Doolittle presented to Lt. Colonel John Bennett the Silver Star for his "superb judgment and gallantry" on the March 8, 1944, mission to Berlin.

Eighth Air Force Combat Chronology
WEDNESDAY, 8 MARCH 1944
STRATEGIC OPERATIONS (Eighth Air Force): Mission 252: The primary target is the ball bearing plant at Erkner, a suburb of Berlin; enemy opposition is fierce and 37 bombers and 16 fighters are lost; 320 of 414 B-17s and 150 of 209 B-24s dispatched hit the primary; 36 B-17s hit Wildau and targets of opportunity; 33 B-24s hit Berlin and targets of opportunity; the bombers claim 63-17-19 Luftwaffe aircraft; 28 B-17s and 9 B-24s are lost, 1 B-17 and 2 B-24s are damaged beyond repair; casualties are 4 KIA, 14 WIA and 364 MIA. Escort is provided by 104 P-38s, 613 Eighth and Ninth Air Force P-47s and 174 Eighth and Ninth Air Force P-51s; claims/losses are:

1. P-38s claim 9-2-5 *Luftwaffe* aircraft; 3 P-38s are lost, 1 is damaged beyond repair and 2 damaged; casualties are 1 KIA and 4 MIA.

2. P-47s claim 49-6-18 *Luftwaffe* aircraft; 10 P-47s are lost, 13 damaged beyond repair and 4 damaged; casualties are 2 KIA, 2 WIA and 10 MIA.

3. P-51s claim 29-4-9 *Luftwaffe* aircraft; 5 P-51s are lost, 2 damaged beyond repair and 1 damaged; casualties are 4 MIA.

An additional 8-4-7 *Luftwaffe* aircraft are claimed on the ground.

Berlin[38]
a poem by
Robert Shoens

T'was dark when they woke us for briefing
And the air was cold and damp
You could hear the engines running up
Out in the blackness of the ramp.

The sky was clear and moon was bright
As it sailed its silvery way
The Heavens were black and flecked with stars
And there was a peace that predicts the coming
of day.

Briefing was short and to the point
And each detail was expertly told
The target was new and had never been hit
By us the Day Bombers, so bold.

Yes we were bold they told us
We were going to this one at last
And we knew from their words that those were
a cinch
Those "rough ones" we had flown in the past.

Our faces were sober and our voices were silent
As we filed out into the night
We wondered about flak and our escorts too
And we prayed that the timing was right.

We collected our gear and rode to the ship
And put in the guns with a grin
For they were the ones that would save our lives
When the fighters began to come in.

We took off that morning in the sombre gray
That precedes a winters dawn
Soon there was the channel below
Next we'd be in enemy skies and then,
the "first curtain" on a really big show.

We crossed the coast without so much
As a burst of flak to greet us
But don't get me wrong that didn't mean
They weren't prepared to meet us.

The sky was bright and the earth below
Was etched clear for miles around
Here and there a cloud was hung
Like a giant cotton mound.

Suddenly we saw the situation was bad
Our escort was nowhere in sight
And we knew at once without second thought
That they had been drawn away in a fight.

The inter phone ceased its witty chatter
And the bolts on the "50s" banged home
The ship was tensed and ready to fight
As all eyes searched that stratosphere dome.

It wasn't long before we saw
Those Contrails scratching the blue
Just thin white lines, no planes could be seen
But it was "Jerry" we knew.

We didn't know who they would tackle
It might be any group in the force
We prayed that it wouldn't be ours;
So far the were holding their course.

Our thoughts were absorbed by their movements
And the turrets were tracking them too
Any moment now, if they were coming
A battle to the finish was due.

A wing flashed and sunlight down from above us
They were turning to prepare for attack
We wished we were over the target
They never come in thru the flak.

A life time passed before they came
Within the range of our guns
It was seconds' tho' instead of years
And it was either us or the Huns.

They came in on a vital spot
It was level and dead ahead
Now our guns were firing
Firing a hail of lead.

Their aim was good and we all thought
They surely couldn't miss
Their range was short and they came thru fast
Would we get ours like this?

There were gone as quick as they came
And for now the danger was past
But we couldn't relax because we knew
That attack would not be their last.

Three attacks in all they made
Twisting and slashing they came
Each time they took their toll on us
And each time they felt our aim.

For forty five minutes it lasted
Death was up in the blue
Around us the sight was tragic
The sky was a fire red hue.

Parachutes were thick down below us
And Forts blew up with a roar
They were flaming smoking coffins
It was Hell as never before.

Like a nightmare it had unfolded before us
Like a fantastic "Hollywood Play"
It was beyond the mind's comprehension
The destruction in the sky that day.

The day was once more peaceful
But our Group was gone from the sky
Of the 20 that had started the mission
A mere "4" had somehow got by.

Four Forts of a 20 ship force
Still flew in a proud salute
To the Sixteen they had left behind them
Whose engines were forever more mute.

We joined another formation
And as our target came into view
A most beautiful sight confronted us
Our escort had at last gotten thru.

Yes they were there to meet us
And as we dropped our bombs thru the flak
We knew our trip home would be a safe one
We knew we would make it back

They circled above and besides us
And the earth slid swiftly by
The rest of the trip was quiet
Peach again ruled the sky.

Then we were over the channel
And the strain of the battle was over
We had chalked up another mission
And we lived to fight on some more.

There was the field below us
And as we prepared to leave the sky
We breathed a prayer of thankfulness
Then the wheels touched the ground with a sigh.

Epilogue

Was Berlin worth the cost? How do you put a price on the guts and sheer resolve of the Bomber crews and Fighter pilots of the 8AF? On March 6, 1944, it was not about the strategic targets, it was about continuing General Doolittle's edict to rid the skies of the *Luftwaffe* and cripple Germany's economy. It is difficult to assess just how many crewmembers sensed that they were just "bait." Certainly, Doolittle was making a statement to the German high command and the German people, who had been told they were winning the war, that they could have their "guns and butter." Yet, because of the "Round the Clock" 8AF and 15AF raids during the day and the RAF Bomber Command at night, no city was safe in Germany. Even if the head of the *Luftwaffe* still clung to the Nazi cause, the steady, unrelenting stream of heavy bombers over Berlin influenced the German citizens and critics of Göring to begin realizing that for them the war would soon be over. The 8AF made Albert Speer realize no industrial target was immune from Allied bombers. The *Luftwaffe* realized that their men and machines, no matter how determined, could not turn back the massive armadas from their homeland and capital city. The cost was high. From 3-8 March 1944, the 100BG lost a total of 20 B-17s—200 men missing in action, either killed, taken prisoner, or interned in a neutral country. Ten months later, on January 12, 1945, the Group received its second Distinguished Unit Citation for the 4, 6, and 8 March 1944 missions to Berlin.[39] They earned this recognition, to borrow a quotation from British Prime Minister Winston Churchill: "Through blood, sweat, and tears."

In 1947, the massive bomber fleet that once ruled the skies over Europe now baked under the hot Arizona sun at Kingman, waiting to be broken up. Famous planes with names like *Ole Gappy*, *5 Grand*, and *Our Gal Sal* were amongst them. She had flown over 100 missions, bringing the crewmembers home safely, if not shaken by the experience. The war was over and the world was moving on. There is no more need for her four-engine service. The aluminum and other metal used to create this and other Second World War aircraft would soon be recast into stoves, refrigerators, and other needed household utensils. She was just waiting her turn for the breakers and smelters to do what the *Luftwaffe* could not.

Our Gal Sal accomplished what many other B-17s could not—return to the United States. The 8AF had lost more than 6,000 bombers and fighters altogether during World War II. This loss of

Our Gal Sal in the Kingman, AZ, aircraft boneyard in 1947. (photo by Jerry McLain)

Kingman, Arizona, 1947. (Photo: Mohave Museum of History & Arts, Kingman Arizona - Photo #5858.)

5 Grand, the 5000th Boeing built B-17G Served with the 96th BG and is seen here in Kingman, AZ, 1947.

Thorpe Abbotts, Station 139, at dusk. (photo by M.P. Faley)

aircraft involved more than 26,000 airmen dying in the European skies. Still, today 5,126 of these souls are still classified as Missing in Action. At Thorpe Abbotts, the wartime home of *Our Gal Sal*, the runways and hardstands have fallen silent and are almost gone. The base has reverted to farmland, but the history remains in the wonderful 100th Bomb Group Museum, housed in the old control tower. The Rolls Royce of 8AFBG museums, it sets the standard for excellence as a lasting tribute to "our boys" who failed to return. Stand on any derelict control tower in East Anglia and peer out into the distance, squinting, listening for the faint drone of engines and dare to imagine. If you happen to feel a cold chill, or develop an eerie sense you are not alone, do not worry! This may be one of those ghosts Roger Freeman warned us about, reminding you that this is hallowed ground and walk softly.

East Anglia no longer resonates with the "around-the-clock" activities of men and machines preparing for aerial combat. England will never again shudder with the powerful thunder of thousands of Wright Cyclone and Pratt and Whitney engines reverberating over the countryside. She will only feel the soft slow steps of graying veterans traveling back to England for One Last Look. It was here where they lost their youth. It was here where they lost so many good friends. They never forgot the struggle between man and machine over occupied Europe, nor their young comrades who died 5 miles high. However, most of all, they never forgot BERLIN!

When you're looking for heroes, you won't have to go far, look only to your Father, Uncle, Grandfather, or Grandmother. They all helped fight tyranny and injustice when we needed it the most. Ordinary people, doing extraordinary jobs. We must never forget them and their sacrifices.

Thorpe Abbotts Control Tower in 1970.

Thorpe Abbotts Control Tower in 2007. (photo M.P. Faley)

The High Cost of Berlin on March 6, 1944, for the 100th Bomb Group

Date:	Last Name:	First Name:	Rank:	Sqdn:	Pos:	Stat:	Target:
3/6/1944	AGUILA	Reginaldo	SGT	418TH	BTG	KIA	Berlin
3/6/1944	ALSUP	Angus A.	SGT	351ST	TG	KIA	Berlin
3/6/1944	AMIERO	Albert F.	LT	349TH	P	KIA	Berlin
3/6/1944	ANTHONY	Charles C.	SGT	418TH	WG	KIA	Berlin
3/6/1944	AVEN	Matthew C.	S/SGT	418TH	WG	KIA	Berlin
3/6/1944	BAER	Thomas D.	S/SGT	349TH	TG	KIA	Berlin
3/6/1944	BRIDGES	Raymond L.	SGT	418TH	RWG	KIA	Berlin
3/6/1944	BROWN	Glenn D.	S/SGT	350TH	RWG	KIA	Berlin
3/6/1944	BUTLER	Varden I	S/SGT	418TH	BTG	KIA	Berlin
3/6/1944	COTTER	Ralph G.	LT	418TH	BOM	KIA	Berlin
3/6/1944	DALE	Clyde R.	LT	351ST	NAV	KIA	Berlin
3/6/1944	DEWEY	John W.	LT	351ST	NAV	KIA	Berlin
3/6/1944	ELLIOTT	Thomas S.	LT	349TH	BOM	KIA	Berlin
3/6/1944	ESSARY	Dewey	SGT	351ST	BTG	KIA	Berlin
3/6/1944	FORD	Charles H.	T/SGT	351ST	TTE	KIA	Berlin
3/6/1944	FRANKEL	Arthur	A/SGT	349TH	LWG	KIA	Berlin
3/6/1944	GILBERT	Russell G.	T/SGT	349TH	TTE	KIA	Berlin
3/6/1944	GOWEN	Clifford L.	LT	418TH	BOM	KIA	Berlin
3/6/1944	GVEROVICH	John J.	SGT	351ST	WG	KIA	Berlin
3/6/1944	HALL	Matilon A.	S/SGT	349TH	TG	KIA	Berlin
3/6/1944	HAMPTON	Carl D.	SGT	418TH	TG	KIA	Berlin
3/6/1944	HANDORF	Edward P.	LT	351ST	P	KIA	Berlin
3/6/1944	HICKMAN	Melvin A.	S/SGT	418TH	TTE	KIA	Berlin
3/6/1944	HORN	John R.	SGT	418TH	WG	KIA	Berlin
3/6/1944	HORTON	Allen D.	S/SGT	351ST	BTG	KIA	Berlin
3/6/1944	HOWELL	Richard P.	SGT	418TH	ROG	KIA	Berlin
3/6/1944	JONES	George R.	LT	418TH	BOM	KIA	Berlin
3/6/1944	KENDALL	Zeb	LT	418TH	P	KIA	Berlin
3/6/1944	KILMER	Howard L.	LT	349TH	CP	KIA	Berlin
3/6/1944	KINSELLA	George E.	LT	418TH	CP	KIA	Berlin
3/6/1944	KOPER	Robert C.	LT	349TH	P	KIA	Berlin
3/6/1944	KOVACS	John J.	T/SGT	349TH	ROG	KIA	Berlin
3/6/1944	KRUSIENSKI	Joseph C.	SGT	418TH	BTG	KIA	Berlin
3/6/1944	LESLIE	Thomas R.	LT	351ST	CP	KIA	Berlin
3/6/1944	LOUGHRAN	Edwin J.	LT	418TH	CP	KIA	Berlin
3/6/1944	LUQUETTE	Charles J.	S/SGT	349TH	BTG	KIA	Berlin
3/6/1944	MINER	David	LT	418TH	P	KIA	Berlin
3/6/1944	MONTGOMERY	Coy I.	LT	349TH	P	KIA	Berlin
3/6/1944	MURRAY	William B.	LT	349TH	P	KIA	Berlin
3/6/1944	PETERSON	William L.	LT	418TH	CP	KIA	Berlin
3/6/1944	RASSMUSSEN	Norman L.	LT	351ST	BOM	KIA	Berlin
3/6/1944	RISH	Merril T.	LT	351ST	P	KIA	Berlin
3/6/1944	RULE	Albert P.	LT	349TH	NAV	KIA	Berlin
3/6/1944	SCHILLINGER	Fred C.	S/SGT	349TH	ROG	KIA	Berlin
3/6/1944	SCOTT	Grant	T/SGT	350TH	ROG	KIA	Berlin
3/6/1944	SMITH	Frank A.	LT	351ST	CP	KIA	Berlin
3/6/1944	SPENCE	Frederick G.	LT	351ST	CP	KIA	Berlin
3/6/1944	SPIRES	Hobart H.	S/SGT	349TH	WG	KIA	Berlin
3/6/1944	STOFFREGEN	Victon	SGT	418TH	TG	KIA	Berlin
3/6/1944	STRYJESKI	John	S/SGT	350TH	ROG	KIA	Berlin
3/6/1944	SUMMERS	Virgil F.	S/SGT	349TH	BTG	KIA	Berlin
3/6/1944	SUNDIN	Bernhard	S/SGT	349TH	TG	KIA	Berlin
3/6/1944	TANOWIGCH	Michael J.	T/SGT	418TH	ROG	KIA	Berlin
3/6/1944	TEAFF	William F.	T/SGT	351ST	ROG	KIA	Berlin

Cause:	Aircraft:	Notes:
EAC & Explosion	"Sly Fox" (42-30278)	
EAC & Explosion	"Spirit of 44" (42-39044)	Chute Failed
EAC & Explosion	(42-31731)	
EAC	"Terry and the Pirates" (42-97482	
EAC & Explosion	"Sly Fox" (42-30278)	
EAC & Explosion	(42-31731)	Original 100th, Crew #8
EAC & Explosion	"Sly Fox" (42-30278)	
EAC & FLAK	"Rubber Check" (42-39872)	Killed by fighters
EAC	(42-38059)	Mission 250
EAC	"Terry and the Pirates" (42-97482	
EAC & Explosion	"Lucky Lee" (42-31735)	
ME-109 & Explosion	"Kind-A-Ruff" (42-38011)	
EAC & Explosion	(42-31731)	
EAC & Explosion	"Spirit of 44" (42-39044)	
ME-109 & Explosion	"Kind-A-Ruff" (42-38011)	
EAC & Explosion	"Goin Jessies" (42-31051)	
EAC & Explosion	(42-31731)	
EAC & Explosion	"Sly Fox" (42-30278)	
ME-109 & Explosion	"Kind-A-Ruff" (42-38011)	
EAC	"The Bigassbird II" (42-30799)	Mission 250
EAC	"Terry and the Pirates" (42-97482	
ME-109 & Explosion	"Kind-A-Ruff" (42-38011)	
EAC & Explosion	"Sly Fox" (42-30278)	
EAC	"Terry and the Pirates" (42-97482	
ME-109 & Explosion	"Kind-A-Ruff" (42-38011)	
EAC	"Terry and the Pirates" (42-97482	
EAC	(42-38059)	Slipped or thrown from nose without chute.
EAC & Explosion	"Sly Fox" (42-30278)	
EAC & Explosion	(42-31731)	
EAC	(42-38059)	Mission 250
EAC & Explosion	"Goin Jessies" (42-31051)	
EAC & Explosion	(42-31731)	Original 100th, Crew #A2
EAC	"Ronnie R" (42-97491)	
EAC & Explosion	"Lucky Lee" (42-31735)	
EAC & Explosion	"Sly Fox" (42-30278)	Mission 250
EAC & Explosion	"Goin Jessies" (42-31051)	
EAC	(42-38059)	Mission 250
EAC	"Torchy 2nd" (42-30170)	Died in Crash
EAC	"The Bigassbird II" (42-30799)	Not a duplicate
EAC	"Terry and the Pirates" (42-97482	Crashed at Quakenbruck
ME-109 & Explosion	"Kind-A-Ruff" (42-38011)	
EAC & Explosion	"Spirit of 44" (42-39044)	
EAC & Explosion	"Goin Jessies" (42-31051)	
EAC	"The Bigassbird II" (42-30799)	
EAC & FLAK	"Rubber Check" (42-39872)	Killed by fighters
EAC & Explosion	"Spirit of 44" (42-39044)	
ME-109 & Explosion	"Kind-A-Ruff" (42-38011)	
EAC & Explosion	(42-31731)	Original 100th, Crew #4
EAC & Explosion	"Sly Fox" (42-30278)	
EAC & FLAK	"Half and Half" (42-38197)	
EAC & Explosion	(42-31731)	
EAC & Explosion	"Goin Jessies" (42-31051)	
EAC & Explosion	"Goin Jessies" (42-31051)	Original 100th, Crew #4, 2nd Tour.
EAC & Explosion	"Lucky Lee" (42-31735)	Died of wounds as POW/12 JUL 44

Date:	Last Name:	First Name:	Rank:	Sqdn:	Pos:	Stat:	Target:
3/6/1944	TERRY	William A.	LT	418TH	P	KIA	Berlin
3/6/1944	THORPE	William R.	LT	418TH	NAV	KIA	Berlin
3/6/1944	TUTOR	Leman E.	S/SGT	418TH	ROG	KIA	Berlin
3/6/1944	VERDEUR	Henry C.	T/SGT	351ST	ROG	KIA	Berlin
3/6/1944	WING	George H.	LT	349TH	NAV	KIA	Berlin
3/6/1944	ZARZECKI	R.V.	S/SGT	349TH	WG	KIA	Berlin

Cause:	Aircraft:	Notes:
EAC	"Terry and the Pirates" (42-97482	
EAC & Explosion	"Sly Fox" (42-30278)	
EAC & Explosion	"Sly Fox" (42-30278)	
ME-109 & Explosion	"Kind-A-Ruff" (42-38011)	
EAC & Explosion	"Goin Jessies" (42-31051)	
EAC & Explosion	"Goin Jessies" (42-31051)	

WILLIAM A. TERRY
1 LT 418 BOMB SQ 100 BOMB GP (H)
OHIO MAR 6 1944

GEORGE H. WING
2 LT 349 BOMB SQ 100 BOMB GP (H)
NEW HAMPSHIRE MAR 6 1944

GEORGE W. WOOD
S SGT 349 BOMB SQ 100 BOMB GP (H)
NEW JERSEY MAR 3 1944

RALPH V. ZARZECKI
SGT 349 BOMB SQ 100 BOMB GP (H)
PENNSYLVANIA MAR 6 1944

Color Gallery

"Clash at Haseleunne" by Robert Bailey (See p 77)

"First Strike on Berlin" by Nicolas Trudgian (See p 62)

"High Noon" by Robert Bailey

"Fortress Engaged" by Keith Ferris (See p 61)

"Seatons Sad Sack" by Ron Leigh (See p 21)

"The Hunter Becomes The Hunted," copyright 2008 William S. Phillips (See pp 78-79)

A History

100th Bomb Group (H)
13th Combat Wing
Third Air Division
Eighth Air Force

Harry Crosby, Jan Riddling, and Michael P. Faley

From Inception to Combat

The Hundredth Bombardment Group (100BG) came into being "on paper" at Orlando Army Base, Florida, on June 1, 1942. Not until October 27, 1942, in Boise, Idaho, did Special Order 300 transfer 230 enlisted men and 24 officers to the 100BG. Activation of the group occurred on November 14, 1942, and Colonel Darr Alkire became the first Commanding Officer. In December, during their second phase training, the total strength of the Group was 37 crews, with ten men on each crew. At that time, Captain John Egan was Operations Officer with the following Squadron Commanding Officers:

Captain William Veal 349th Bomb Squadron
Captain Gale 'Bucky' Cleven 350th Bomb Squadron
Captain John 'Jack' Kidd 351st Bomb Squadron
Captain Robert Flesher 418th Bomb Squadron

The 100th BG trained at Army Air Fields located in Walla Walla, Washington; Wendover, Field, Utah; Sioux City, Iowa; and Kearney, Nebraska. On April 20, 1943, at Kearney all 37 original crews took off on a practice mission for Hamilton Field, California, a distance of almost 1,300 miles. The results were very poor. Colonel Alkire shouldered this responsibility and was relieved of command of the 100BG.[40] On April 26, 1943, Colonel Howard Turner assumed command, and on May 1, 1943, the air echelon took off for Wendover Field, Utah, for 20 days of advanced training in navigation, gunnery, bombing, and formation flying while aircraft combat modifications were being done at Ogden, Utah. With training completed, 35 crews flew to England on May 25, 1943, and arrived at Station 139, Thorpe Abbotts, England, on June 8, 1943. Three days later Colonel Turner was assigned to the First Bombardment Wing and was replaced by Colonel Harold Huglin, who made the following changes: Major Egan to 418 CO, Captain Flesher to Air Executive, Captain Kidd to Operations Officer, and Captain Ollie Turner to 351 CO. The 100BG, flying the B-17 Flying Fortress on June 22, 1943, participated in a decoy mission, but on 25 June participated in its first combat operational sortie. Any sense of adventure and bravado came to a halt on that first mission; three planes and 30 men were lost over Bremen. The average life of an VIII Bomber Command—renamed in January 1944 the 8th Air Force—B-17 crewman in 1943 was eleven missions! On July 2, 1943, Colonel Neil B. 'Chick' Harding assumed command of the 100BG with Colonel Huglin being reassigned to 4th Combat Wing HQ. 'Chick' commanded the 100BG until March 7, 1944, and by that time the group had already become legendary.

From June 25, 1943, until April 20, 1945, the 100BG never went off operational status due to losses. Throughout its stay at Thorpe Abbotts, the Ground Echelon of the 100BG was cited frequently for its excellent maintenance and preparation activity. The 100BG did not stand alone at Thorpe Abbotts. Throughout their stay they were supported by the following units:

1776th Ordnance Company
18th Weather Detachment
869th Chemical Company
216th Finance Section
592nd Postal Unit
1285th Military Police
2110th Fire Fighting Platoon
1141st Quartermaster Company
83rd Service Group
    456th Sub-Depot
    412th Air Service Group
    838th Air Engineering Squadron
    662nd Air Material Squadron
American Red Cross
Royal Air Force Detachment

Combat Narrative

The 100BG from June 1943 to January 1944 concentrated its efforts against airfields, submarine facilities, and aircraft industries in France and Germany. During this time the Group participated in the epic air battles over Regensburg on August 17, 1943, where it received the first of two Presidential Unit Citations, and during Black Week, October 8-14, 1943, with missions to Bremen, Munster, Marienburg, and Schweinfurt.[41] The Group also lead the bombing of Rujkan, Norway, which delayed the manufacture of heavy water and ostensibly denied Germany the atomic bomb.

January through May 1944 the Group bombed enemy airfields, industries, marshalling yards, and V-1 missile sites, including participation in the Allied campaign against enemy aircraft factories during Big Week, February 20-25, 1944. The Group participated in the first daylight raid against Berlin on March 4, 1944, and completed a series of attacks against Berlin March 6-8, 1944, for which the 100BG received its second Presidential Unit Citation. The Group lost their beloved Colonel Harding, who was relieved of command due to illness, and his replacement, Colonel Robert H. Kelly, was shot down and killed in action on his first mission April 28, 1944, one week after taking command. The Group also engaged in support and interdiction missions, hitting bridges and gun positions in preparation for the Normandy invasion in June 1944. On June 6, 1944 (D-Day), the Group flew 3 missions in support of the ground troops. Later that month the 100BG participated in the First Frantic Operation, a shuttle mission to the Soviet Union led by new Group CO Colonel Thomas S. Jeffrey.

In the summer of 1944 oil installations became the major target. July though September 1944 saw the 100BG strike at enemy positions in St. Lo and Brest and concentrated on the oil refineries at Merseburg, Ruhland, Politz, and Hamburg, as well as conduct a Second Russian Shuttle Mission, along with two low level supply drops to the French Maquis. The 100BG received the French *Croix de Guerre* with Palm for attacking heavily defended German installations and for dropping supplies to the French Forces of the Interior.

In October through December 1944, the "Century Bombers" attacked transportation, oil refineries, and ground defences in the drive against the Siegfried Line. They were involved in the December 24, 1944, mission to attack communication centers and airfields in the Ardennes sector during the Battle of the Bulge. On February 2, 1945, Colonel Frederick J. Sutterlin took command of the 100BG and would remain there until after the end of the war. On February 3, 1945, the 100BG led the entire Third Air Division on a mission to *Big B*. Leading the group was Major Robert 'Rosie' Rosenthal flying his 52nd mission.

January to April 1945 the Group concentrated on marshalling yards, bridges, factories, docks, oil refineries, and ground support, including the airborne assault across the Rhine in March 1945. By March 1945 the *Luftwaffe* was limited in strength and overall effectiveness. Even so, the *Luftwaffe* did manage at times to make its presence known by deploying its Me 262 jet fighters, and used ramming techniques on the April 7, 1945, Buchen mission in a futile effort to thwart the 100BG and the Eighth Air Force (8AF). On April 20, 1945, the 100BG flew its last combat mission to Oranienburg, a suburb of Berlin, with no losses.

Statistical Summary and Awards
First mission: June 25 1943
Last mission: April 20 1945
Total missions: 306
Total credit sorties: 8,630
Total bomb tonnage: 19,257
184 Missing Air Crew Reports
229 planes were Lost or Salvaged
785 men KIA/MIA
894 men POW
6 Chowhound missions in May 1945, dropping 137.8 tons of food to Dutch citizens.

Campaign Credits
Air Offensive Europe
Air Offensive Normandy
Air Offensive Northern France
Air Offensive Rhineland
Air Offensive Ardennes-Alsace
Air Offensive Central Europe

Awards and Decorations
Presidential Distinguished Unit Citation
Regensburg, Germany - August 17, 1943
Berlin, Germany - March 4, 6, 8, 1944
French *Croix de Guerre* with Palm
Attacking heavily defended installations in Germany and for dropping supplies to French Forces of the Interior, June 25, 1944 through December 31, 1944.

Commanding Officers:
Colonel Darr H. Alkire
Nov 14, 1942 - Apr 25, 1943
Colonel Howard M. Turner
Apr 26, 1943 - Jun 10, 1943
Colonel Harold Q. Huglin
Jun 11, 1943 - Jul 1, 1943
Colonel Neil B. 'Chick' Harding
Jul 2, 1943 - Mar 6, 1944
Lt. Colonel John M. Bennett (temporary command)
Mar 7, 1944 - Apr 19, 1944
Colonel Robert H. Kelly
Apr 20, 1944 - Apr 28, 1944
Lt. Colonel John M. Bennett (temporary command)
Apr 29, 1944 - May 6, 1944
Colonel Thomas S. Jeffrey
May 7, 1944 - Feb 1, 1945
Colonel Frederick J. Sutterlin
Feb 2, 1945 - Jun 23, 1945
Colonel John B. Wallace
Jun 24, 1945 - Aug 1, 1945
Colonel Harry F. Cruver
Aug 1, 1945 - Dec 1945

The Moniker

The 100BG did not have the highest overall group loss rate in the 8AF, but it did have heavy losses during eight missions to Germany. As Group Navigator Harry Crosby stated, "when we lost, we lost BIG!" Thus earning the 100 Bomb Group the monikers the *Hard Luck* group and the *Bloody Hundredth.*

August 17, 1943	9 B-17s lost at Regensburg
October 8, 1943	7 B-17s lost at Bremen
October 10, 1943	12 B-17s lost at Munster
March 6, 1944	15 B-17s lost at Berlin
May 24, 1944	9 B-17s lost at Berlin
July 29, 1944	8 B-17s lost at Merseburg
September 11, 1944	12 B-17s lost at Ruhland
December 31, 1944	12 B-17s lost at Hamburg

Appendices

by **Paul M. Andrews**

There are three appendices. Appendix **A** provides an array of historical data on the 100 BG aircrews and aircraft as they apply to the Berlin missions discussed in this monograph. Where appropriate additional information is provided regarding relevant 95 BG and 390 BG aircrews and aircraft. Appendix **B** provides a selection of historical documentation. Finally, Appendix **C** provides data regarding German Air Force claims and Eighth Air Force losses.

These appendices reflect the continual effort by the 100 BG Association to compile data relevant to the group's history from its dwindling number of veterans so as to preserve the past for future generations. Data has also been compiled from published sources, as well as from the documentation held by the National Archives at College Park, Maryland; the Air Force Historical Research Agency at Maxwell Air Force Base, Alabama; Air Force History Office at Bolling Air Force Base, Washington, D.C.; and the Smithsonian Air and Space Museum at Washington, D.C.

Archival research poses many challenges. Some of the records are hand written, and even though most of the records are typed, it is often difficult to read microfilmed copies of second and third generation carbon copies of the original document. Surviving Eighth Air Force and 100 BG records have limitations. Each unit had to prepare a series of reports to satisfy the apparently neverending thirst of "HQ" for information and statistics—how many aircrews and aircraft are missing, how many returning crews were either wounded or killed in action, how many aircraft are operational, how long will it take to turn damaged aircraft to operational status, how many gallons of gasoline were consumed, how many bombs were dropped, and how many rounds of machine gun ammunition were expended. This information was necessary to ensure that the logistical requirements for the Eighth Air Force were identified and satisfied.

Unit records, accomplished in a timely manner under a stressful environment, and before there was white out or computers, do contain errors: names are misspelled, serial numbers transposed, and even "facts" contradict "facts." Despite these limitations in quality, consistency, specificity, and availability, the following appendices provide a "snap shot" and place into a larger historical context the events of 3, 4, 6, and 8 March 1944.

Finally, these appendices would not have been possible without the support from the staff of the above cited research facilities, as well as the generous support from countless veterans, and the meticulous efforts by aviation enthusiasts to explore and understand the past—those who are still with us today, and those who have made the journey to the other side of the clouds.

Appendix A
Historical Data: Participating 100 BG Aircrews and Aircraft

Participating 100 BG Aircrew Matrix

This section identifies to the greatest extent possible each 100 BG participant on any of the 3, 4, 6, and 8 March 1944 missions to Berlin. From left to right each entry details the air crew member's rank and full name, squadron assignment, crew position, and the serial number of the aircraft flown in for each of the respective dates.

Those cells highlighted in light blue indicate that the aircraft did not complete the mission (recalled, returned early because the aircraft was a scheduled spare, mechanical issues, personnel related issues, or failed to take off). Those cells highlighted in green indicate that the aircraft was damaged as a result of completing the sortie. Cells highlighted in red indicate that the aircraft failed to return and the fate of the crew member is noted. Cells highlighted in yellow indicate that the information needs to be confirmed

Name	Sqd	Position	3-Mar	4-Mar	6-Mar	8-Mar	FATE
S/Sgt. Robert D. Abney	418	Tail Gunner	240056			231412	
2Lt. Charles E. Adams	349	Copilot	230170	23534	23534	231710	
2Lt. John W. Adams III	349	Copilot	239817				KIA
Lt. William B. Agnetti	418	Bombardier		297491	297491		POW
S/Sgt. Reginaldo Aguila	418	Ball Turret Gunner	230091	230278	230278		KIA
T/Sgt. James P. Aitken	418	Top Turret - Engineer	297482	297482	297482		POW
T/Sgt. Clifford E. Akin	418	Top Turret - Engineer	238059	26087	26087		
S/Sgt. Charles F. Allen	418	Left Waist Gunner		297491	297491		POW
S/Sgt. Bruce E. Alshouse	349	Tail Gunner		230152	231710		
Sgt. Angus Alsup	351	Tail Gunner	238044	238044	238044		KIA
Lt. Albert F. Amiero	349	Pilot			231731		KIA
S/Sgt. Charles L. Anglin	351	Ball Turret Gunner	240056			231066	
S/Sgt. Charles C. Anthony	418	Left Waist Gunner	297482	297482	297482		KIA
T/Sgt. Ira L. Arnold	350	Top Turret - Engineer	231220	239830	231968	231968	
T/Sgt. Walter S. Austin	351	Top Turret - Engineer	231735	231735	231735		POW
S/Sgt. Matthew G. Aven Jr	418	Right Waist Gunner	230091	230278	230278		KIA
S/Sgt. Thomas D. Baer	349	Tail Gunner			231731		KIA
Lt. Ronald C. Bailey	418	Navigator	231504	231504			
2Lt. Robert W. Bailie	350	Copilot	231049	231049	231049		
S/Sgt. James A. Bain	418	Ball Turret Gunner	297482	297482	297482		POW
Lt. Howard G. Ball	349	Bombardier	238017				POW
Lt. Samuel L. Barrick	418	Pilot	239994	239994	239994		INT
T/Sgt. Robert C. Barrie	350	Radio Operator - Gunner	231049	231049			
S/Sgt. John J. Barry	350	Right Waist Gunner	239934	239934	231981		
S/Sgt. Clifford E. Barton	418	Radio Operator - Gunner	239994	239994	239994		INT
Lt. Sherwin L. Barton	418	Pilot	230061	231800	231800		POW
S/Sgt. Robert T. Bashaw	350	Top Turret - Engineer		238197	238197		POW
S/Sgt. Donald W. Becker	349	Right Waist Gunner	239817				KIA
T/Sgt. Anthony J. Beechey	349	Top Turret - Engineer		230152	231710		
Sgt. William T. Behr	418	Ball Turret Gunner	297491	23508	23508		
S/Sgt. George A. Benedict	350	Ball Turret Gunner	23413	23413	23413		
T/Sgt. Dorsett C. Bennett	351	Toggler	240056			231066	
Lt.Col. John M. Bennett	HQ	Command Pilot				297542	
Lt. L. D. Berthof	418	Bombardier		238059			
S/Sgt. Henry W. Bieze	418	Radio Operator - Gunner	231895	231895	231895		
S/Sgt. Louis G. Black	351	Ball Turret Gunner	231066	231708	231389		
S/Sgt. Don L. Blair	351	Tail Gunner	231767	231767	231767	237936	
2Lt. Sterling B. Blakeman	350	Bombardier	231220	239830			
T/Sgt. Michael Boccuzzi	418	Radio Operator - Gunner	231504	231504		231504	
Sgt. Matthew H. Boguminski	418	Ball Turret Gunner	231895	231895	231895		
T/Sgt. Harry A. Bonn	351	Radio Operator - Gunner				231066	
Sgt. John B. Bowers	350	Left Waist Gunner	231537	231537	232009	231074	
T/Sgt. James O. Brady	418	Toggler			239994		INT
S/Sgt. Richard F. Brady	349	Radio Operator - Gunner	237783				
T/Sgt. Emory L. Brandt	349	Top Turret - Engineer	231731	231731	230799		POW
Lt. George W. Brannan	351	Pilot	231735	231735	231735		POW
Sgt. Robert L. Braswell	418	Tail Gunner	231895	231895	231895		
2Lt. Herbert J. Brice	418	Navigator	238059	26087	26087		
Sgt. Raymond L. Bridges	418	Left Waist Gunner	230091	230278	230278		KIA
S/Sgt. George W. Briggs	349	Tail Gunner	231970				POW
Sgt. Carleton E. Brown	351	Ball Turret Gunner	232018	232018		232018	
S/Sgt. Glenn D. Brown	350	Right Waist Gunner	239872	239872	239872		KIA
T/Sgt. Guy L. Brown Jr	349	Radio Operator - Gunner	231970				POW
T/Sgt. James C. Brown	350	Top Turret - Engineer	239934		231981		
2Lt. Louis Brownstein	418	Bombardier	238059	26087	26087		
S/Sgt. Raymond Bryan	350	Tail Gunner		231968	237807		
Lt. Festus E. *'Shorty'* Bryant	350	Navigator	231074	231968	237807		
S/Sgt. Junior L. Bucher	349	Left Waist Gunner	237783	231249	230170		POW
S/Sgt. Peter J. Buck	418	Radio Operator - Gunner	238175	238175	238175	238175	
Captain Leonard Bull	HQ	Navigator				297542	
S/Sgt. Lawrence A. Burk	350	Tail Gunner	239830				
Sgt. Archie W. Bunting	350	Tail Gunner	231220	239830	231968	231968	
S/Sgt. Seth L. Burkland	351	Right Waist Gunner	231066				
Sgt. Delbert J.H. Burns	350	Left Waist Gunner		23413			
S/Sgt. Delbert J.H. Burns	350	Right Waist Gunner	23413		23413		
Sgt. Armand C. Burt	351	Right Waist Gunner	238044	238044	238044		POW
Lt. John L. Burtch	418	Navigator	230061	231800	231800		POW

T/Sgt. George W. Burton	349	Top Turret - Engineer	237783	231249	230170		POW
2Lt. Anthony J. Busalacchi	349	Navigator		230152	231710	231504	
Sgt. Frank W. Buschmeier	350	Left Waist Gunner	231220	239830	231968	231968	
S/Sgt. Edward C. Butchino	350	Left Waist Gunner	239830				
S/Sgt. James M. Butler	349	Left Waist Gunner	231970				POW
T/Sgt. Varden I. Butler	418	Ball Turret Gunner		238059	238059		KIA
T/Sgt. Daniel J. Cahill	350	Radio Operator - Gunner	239830				
Lt. Maurice H. Cain	350	Navigator	238016	232009	231074	231968	
T/Sgt. Chester J. Carknard	351	Top Turret - Engineer	231389	231389	231389		
2Lt. Edward P. Carr	418	Bombardier	231895	231895	231895		
2Lt. William G. Carr	349	Bombardier	231731	231731	230799		POW
T/Sgt. Wallace S. Carter	418	Top Turret - Engineer	231800			231895	
2Lt. Joseph A. Carty	350	Bombardier	23413	23413	23413		
T/Sgt. Sidney A. Cary	351	Top Turret - Engineer	238047	238047	232018		
2Lt. James N. Cathey	351	Bombardier		231708			
2Lt. Randall T. Chadwick	350	Pilot	23413	23413	23413		
2Lt. Norman L. Chapman	351	Pilot	239983	237936	239983	240056	POW
S/Sgt. George C. Christian	350	Tail Gunner	239872	239872	239872		POW
T/Sgt. Ernest B. Clark	349	Bombardier	239817				KIA
2Lt. Wilson D. Clark	351	Bombardier	239983	237936	239983	240056	POW
2Lt. William F. Clayton	350	Copilot	238016	238016			POW
Sgt. John A. Codoluto	418	Right Waist Gunner	238175	238175	238175	238175	
S/Sgt. Arthur V.R. Congrove	349	Tail Gunner	238017				POW
2Lt. Robert F. Connaway	349	Copilot	237783	231249	230170		POW
S/Sgt. George M. Conrad	351	Left Waist Gunner	231066				
S/Sgt. Robert H. Cook	350	Ball Turret Gunner	238016	238016			POW
T/Sgt. Arthur A. Cooper	349	Top Turret - Engineer	238017				POW
T/Sgt. John P. Cooper	349	Radio Operator - Gunner		231723	231723		
Captain Mark Cope	350	Pilot		231968	237807		
T/Sgt. Charles P. Corea	349	Top Turret - Engineer	230487	230170	231051		POW
S/Sgt. John B. Cortelletty	351	Ball Turret Gunner		231735			
2Lt. Charlie C. Cowing	418	Navigator	231800			231895	
Lt. Ralph G. Cotter	418	Bombardier	297482	297482	297482		KIA
S/Sgt. Chester P. Coulam	351	Tail Gunner			237936		
S/Sgt. Chester P. Coulam	351	Toggler	231256	231256		237936	
Lt. Clement H. Cowan	349	Pilot	231723	231723	231723		
2Lt. Arthur E. Cox	350	Bombardier	231537	231537	237807	231074	
T/Sgt. Neil J. Coyle	349	Radio Operator - Gunner		230152	231710		
S/Sgt. John L. Craven	349	Toggler			231968	231710	
2Lt. Thomas Cryan	350	Copilot			23413		
Sgt. Austin P. Curlee	350	Ball Turret Gunner	231537	231537	232009	231074	
Lt. Clyde F. Dale	351	Navigator	231735	231735	231735		KIA
Sgt. James J. Daly	418	Left Waist Gunner	231895	231895	231895		
T/Sgt. George F. Danehower	351	Radio Operator - Gunner	238044	238044	238044		POW
S/Sgt. Richard L. David	349	Right Waist Gunner	231970				POW
Lt. George W. Davidson	418	Copilot	230061	231800	231800		POW
Sgt. Cecil G. Davis	349	Tail Gunner	230170	23534	23534	231710	
Lt. Paul T. Davis	349	Bombardier	231970				POW
S/Sgt. William J. DeBlassio	418	Tail Gunner	231504	231504		231504	
S/Sgt. John M. Delaney	351	Right Waist Gunner				231066	
S/Sgt. Nicholas Delcimmuto	350	Ball Turret Gunner	239934	239934	231981		
Lt. Louis J. Denisco	351	Bombardier	231735	231735	231735		POW
Lt. Gordon E. Devault	418	Copilot		297491	297491		POW
Sgt. Benjamin J. Devine	418	Right Waist Gunner			23508		
Sgt. Benjamin J. Devine	418	Left Waist Gunner	297491	23508			
Lt. Herbert G. Devore	350	Pilot	239934	239934	231981		
Lt. John W. Dewey	351	Navigator	237936	231066	238011		KIA
2Lt. Charles F. DeWolfe Jr	350	Navigator	238016	238016			POW
Lt. Hank A. Dibbern	349	Copilot	231723	231723	231723		
S/Sgt. Darrell R. Dickenson	350	Left Waist Gunner	239934	239934	231981		
S/Sgt. George E. Dobbs	351	Tail Gunner	239983	237936	239983	240056	POW
Sgt. Wiley A. Dobbs	350	Right Waist Gunner	231537	231537	232009	231074	
S/Sgt. Jack W. Domenig	350	Left Waist Gunner	237807			239830	
Sgt. George B. Donahue	349	Left Waist Gunner	230170	23534	23534	231710	
Sgt. Richard E. Donnelly	350	Ball Turret Gunner		231968	237807		
T/Sgt. Floyd O. Douglas	350	Top Turret - Engineer	237807				
Lt. Thomas O. Drinkwater	349	Bombardier	230487	230170	231051		POW
Lt. Robert L. Dunham	350	Copilot	239872	239872	239872		POW
2Lt. Robert Dykeman	350	Copilot	231220	239830	231968	231968	

2Lt. Robert K. Edgley	351	Copilot	240056				
Sgt. John C. Eling	350	Radio Operator - Gunner		231968	237807		
S/Sgt. Charles F. Elliott	351	Left Waist Gunner	231735	231735	231735		POW
S/Sgt. Thomas S. Elliott	349	Toggler			231731		KIA
2Lt. Rex M. Ellis	351	Copilot	239983	237936	239983	240056	POW
Major Albert *'Bucky'* Elton	350	Command Pilot			231981		
T/Sgt. William Eresman	351	Top Turret - Engineer	231767	231767	231767	237936	
Sgt. Dewey Essary	351	Ball Turret Gunner	238044	238044	238044		KIA
Sgt. Myron J. Ettus	350	Right Waist Gunner	231220	239830	231968	231968	
2Lt. Stuart W. Feely	350	Bombardier				239830	
S/Sgt. Hugh F. Fantone Jr	418	Tail Gunner	239994	239994	239994		INT
Lt. Jerry Felsenstein	350	Copilot	239934				
Lt. Jerry Felsenstein	350	Formation Control Officer		239934	231981		
Lt. Elmer E. Ferbrache	418	Pilot	297491	23508	23508		
S/Sgt. Herbert D. Fern	351	Tail Gunner	232018	232018		232018	
T/Sgt. George L. Ferron	351	Top Turret - Engineer	240056				
Lt. Leland C. Fink	350	Navigator		238197	238197		POW
S/Sgt. Walter E. Fisher	351	Radio Gunner		231708			
2Lt. Robert S. Flannigan	350	Copilot	231537	231537	232009	231074	
S/Sgt. Frank J. Foldy	418	Right Waist Gunner	230061	231800	231800		POW
S/Sgt. Joe S. Folson	351	Right Waist Gunner	231389	231389	231389		
T/Sgt. Charles H. Ford	351	Top Turret - Engineer	237936	231066	238011		KIA
2Lt. Wallace C. Forsythe	418	Pilot	238175	238175	238175	238175	
Sgt. Anderson R. Frank Jr	350	Tail Gunner	231537	231537	232009	231074	
S/Sgt. Arthur Frankel	349	Left Waist Gunner	230487	230170	231051		KIA
2Lt. Albert Franklin	351	Navigator	231389	231389	231389		
2Lt. Frederick D. Fuller	351	Navigator	240056	231708			
Captain Magee C. Fuller	349	Command Pilot		239934			
2Lt. James W. Fulton	349	Bombardier	237783	231249	230170		POW
S/Sgt. Robyn P. Fulton	351	Ball Turret Gunner	231735		231735		POW
Sgt. Hogan Fussell Jr	350	Tail Gunner		238197	238197		POW
2Lt. Charles J. Galligan	351	Navigator	232018	232018		232018	
S/Sgt. Newman E. Garmon	351	Tail Gunner	238047	238047	232018	238047	
S/Sgt. John R. Gensel	418	Top Turret - Engineer	231895	231895	231895		
S/Sgt. William A. Geigle	349	Ball Turret Gunner	231723	231723	231723		
Lt. Murray Geisler	350	Navigator	239872	239872	239872		POW
Sgt. Lorenzo Genovese	350	Tail Gunner	231049	231049	231049		
S/Sgt. John R. Gensel	418	Top Turret - Engineer			231895		
2Lt. John P. Gibbons	350	Pilot	231220	239830	231968	231968	
T/Sgt. Russell G. Gilbert	349	Top Turret - Engineer			231731		KIA
T/Sgt. Sidney A. Goldenburg	349	Top Turret - Engineer	231970				POW
S/Sgt. Ernest R. Gomez	349	Tail Gunner	25957	25957	25957	237783	
T/Sgt. John J. Good	350	Radio Operator - Gunner	23413	23413	23413		
Lt. Jonah Goodbread	351	Copilot	231066			231066	
2Lt. John G. Gossage	349	Pilot	238017				POW
2Lt. George H. Gough	350	Pilot	239830			239830	
2Lt. Clifford L. Gowen	418	Bombardier	230091	230278	230278		KIA
T/Sgt. Sidney Graboyes	351	Radio Operator		231708			
Sgt. Colbert W. Graham	350	Left Waist Gunner					
S/Sgt. Ralph T. Graham	350	Tail Gunner	237807			239830	
Lt. Frank A. Granack	350	Pilot	239872	239872	239872		POW
2Lt. Harold D. Granger	351	Copilot	238047	238047	232018	238047	
Lt.Emmanuel Greasmare	418	Formation Control Officer	231306		231306		
Lt. Walter Green	418	Bombardier	231306		231306		
2Lt. Herbert R. Greenberg	418	Navigator	231767		237936	231412	
S/Sgt. Harry H. Greenfield	418	Radio Operator	231306		231306		
S/Sgt. Robert L. Greenleaf	351	Tail Gunner	231735	231735	231735		POW
S/Sgt. James W. Gregg	349	Right Waist Gunner	238017				POW
2Lt. Frank C. Gregory	351	Bombardier	231066	231389	231389		
Lt. James G. Guerrini	418	Navigator	239994	239994	239994		INT
S/Sgt. Andrew J. Guglieri	351	Right Waist Gunner	240056				
2Lt. Ralph W. Guida	350	Bombardier	231049	231049	231049		
2Lt. Mark G. Gummersall	418	Pilot	231895	231895	231895		
S/Sgt. Don Gutherie	349	Ball Turret Gunner	239817				POW
S/Sgt. John J Gverovich	351	Left Waist Gunner	237936	231066	238011		KIA
T/Sgt. Clarence C. Hall	418	Top Turret - Engineer	231504	231504		231504	
S/Sgt. Mahlon A. Hall	349	Tail Gunner	231731	231731	230799		KIA
Sgt. Nick E. Hamalack	349	Left Waist Gunner	231731	231731	230799		POW
T/Sgt. Donald B. Hammond	351	Radio Operator - Gunner	231767	231767	231767	237936	

S/Sgt. Carl D. Hampton	418	Tail Gunner	297482	297482	297482		KIA
Lt. Edward Handorf	351	Pilot	237936	231066	238011		KIA
S/Sgt. Palmer J. Hanson	349	Right Waist Gunner	231731	231731	230799		POW
2Lt. Prescott H. Haralson	418	Copilot	238175	238175	238175	238175	
2Lt. Charles T. Hardiman	350	Navigator	231537	231537	232009	231074	
2Lt. Celesta B. *'Red'* Harper	350	Pilot	231537	231537	232009	231074	
2Lt. James C. Harper	418	Pilot	231800			231895	
S/Sgt. Edwin T. Harrell	350	Left Waist Gunner	239872	239872	239872		POW
Lt. John A. Harrison	349	Pilot		230152	231710		
T/Sgt. Thompas P. Hastings	351	Radio Operator - Gunner	240056				
S/Sgt. William R. Heathman	418	Right Waist Gunner	231306		231306		
Lt. David N. Hegge	418	Bombardier	297491	23508	23508		
2Lt. Orrin H. Heinrich	349	Navigator	231731	231731	230799		POW
2Lt. Richard Helmick	351	Pilot	231256	231256	237936	231412	
S/Sgt. Kenneth C. Helming	418	Left Waist Gunner	231800			231895	
Lt. James M. Henry	418	Bombardier	239994				
Lt. Harold L. Heyneman	349	Bombardier	231723	231723	231723		
T/Sgt. Melvin A. Hickman	418	Top Turret - Engineer	230091	230278	230278		KIA
2Lt. Norman T. High	351	Bombardier	232018	232018		232018	
Sgt. Leon E. Hill	351	Left Waist Gunner	239983	237936	239983	240056	POW
Sgt. William F. Hoffman Jr	351	Left Waist Gunner	232018				
T/Sgt. Peter A. Hogan	350	Top Turret - Engineer	238016	238016			POW
T/Sgt. Murray W. Holditch	349	Top Turret - Engineer	231723	231723	231723		
2Lt. Reginald C. Holliday	418	Copilot	231895	231895	231895		
S/Sgt. Charlie J. Hopkins	349	Ball Turret Gunner			23534	231710	
S/Sgt. John R. Horn	418	Right Waist Gunner	297482	297482	297482		KIA
Lt. Emory Horvath	418	Navigator	231306		231306		
S/Sgt. Allen D. Horton	351	Ball Turret Gunner	237936	231066	238011		KIA
S/Sgt. Joseph A. Howell	351	Tail Gunner	231389	231389	231389		
T/Sgt. Richard P. Howell	418	Radio Operator - Gunner	297482	297482	297482		KIA
Lt. Glenn Hudson	351	Navigator				237936	
Lt. Glenn Hudson	351	Bombardier - Navigator		231767	231767		
Lt. Glenn Hudson	351	Bombardier	231767				
T/Sgt. Robert E. Hudson	418	Radio Operator - Gunner	231800			231895	
Lt. Burton S. Hufsey	418	Navigator	297491	23508	23508		
2Lt. Robert L. Hughes	351	Command Pilot		231708			
S/Sgt. Leming Hull	350	Tail Gunner	238016	238016			KIA
2Lt. Tony L. Hulsey	418	Copilot	231800			231895	
T/Sgt. William S. Humphrey	349	Top Turret - Engineer	239817				POW
Sgt. Durward E. Hutchings	351	Ball Turret Gunner	239983	237936	239983	240056	POW
Lt. Louis R. Jaebker	350	Bombardier	239934	239934			
T/Sgt. Alvin E. James	350	Radio Operator - Gunner	231537	231537	232009	231074	
2Lt. Carl A. Janssen	351	Pilot		231708			
T/Sgt. Eliad M. Johnson	349	Radio Operator - Gunner	239817				KIA
2Lt. Everett M. Johnson	350	Navigator	231220	239830	231968	231968	
S/Sgt. Henry W. Johnson	351	Right Waist Gunner	231256			231412	
S/Sgt. Loren G. Johnson	351	Right Waist Gunner		231256	237936		
S/Sgt. Loren G. Johnson	351	Left Waist Gunner	240056			231066	
T/Sgt. Walfred J. Johnson	418	Top Turret - Engineer	239994	239994	239994		INT
2Lt. John T. Johnston	349	Navigator	230170	23534	23534	231710	
S/Sgt. Percy J. Johnston	418	Top Turret - Engineer	238175	238175	238175	238175	
Lt. George R. Jones	418	Navigator		238059	238059		KIA
Lt. Burton M. Joseph	350	Navigator	239934	239934			
T/Sgt. Joseph A. Judd	350	Radio Operator - Gunner	238016	238016			POW
Lt. Joseph F. Kawiecki	350	Bombardier	239872	239872	239872		POW
Captain Howard E. Keel	351	Pilot	240056				
2Lt. Donald K. Kehm	351	Bombardier	238044	238044	238044		POW
T/Sgt. Joseph G. Kelly	351	Radio Operator - Gunner	231256	231256	237936	231412	
S/Sgt. Horace R. Kemble	349	Tail Gunner	231723	231723	231723		
Lt. Zeb Kendall	418	Pilot	230091	230278	230278		KIA
S/Sgt. Francis X. Kerin	350	Ball Turret Gunner	231074	232009	231074		
S/Sgt. Richard L. Kerwin	418	Right Waist Gunner		297491	297491		POW
Captain Ernest A. Kiessling	418	Command Pilot	231306				
FO Howard L. Kilmer	349	Copilot			231731		KIA
2Lt. Edward C. King Jr	351	Navigator	238047	238047	232018	238047	
Lt. George E. Kinsella	418	Copilot		238059	238059		KIA
Lt. Thomas R. Kizak	351	Navigator	231066			231066	
S/Sgt. Roger Kirkpatrick	351	Tail Gunner	231066				
S/Sgt. Hugo C. Kleckner	349	Right Waist Gunner	25957	25957	25957	237783	

S/Sgt. Knute Knudson	350	Tail Gunner	239934				
S/Sgt. Knute Knudson	350	Radio Gunner		239934	231981		
Lt. Robert G. Koper	349	Pilot	230487	230170	231051		KIA
T/Sgt. John J. Kovacs	349	Radio Operator - Gunner			231731		KIA
2Lt. Sol S. Kranzler	418	Navigator	231256	231256	237936	231412	
2Lt. Adam Krezo	349	Bombardier			231710		
2Lt. Ralph A. Kroenke	349	Bombardier	230170	23534	23534		
2Lt. Robert R. Kroske	350	Copilot	239830	23413			
S/Sgt. Joseph B. Kyrc	418	Ball Turret Gunner	231800			231895	
S/Sgt. Joseph C. Krusienski	418	Ball Turret Gunner		297491	297491		KIA
S/Sgt. Arthur J. Labreque	350	Right Waist Gunner	238016	238016			POW
Lt. Lucius G. Lacy	351	Pilot	231389	231389	231389		
S/Sgt. Sam J. LaFace	349	Toggler	25957	25957	25957	237783	
Lt. Richard M. Lambiotte	349	Copilot		231731	230799		POW
S/Sgt. Howard T. Larimore	351	Right Waist Gunner			231735		POW
S/Sgt. Kenneth R. Lash Jr	349	Left Waist Gunner	25957	25957	25957	237783	
Captain Frank Lauro	418	Pilot	231306		231306		
Lt. John Lautenschlager	350	Pilot		238197	238197		POW
2Lt. Frank C. Laver	349	Navigator	237783	231249	230170		POW
S/Sgt. Fair C. Lawrence	351	Tail Gunner	237936	231066	238011		POW
S/Sgt. Charles A. Leavitt	418	Radio Operator - Gunner	238059	26087	26087		
T/Sgt. John Lee	350	Top Turret – Engineer	239830				
2Lt. Jerome F. Leirich	351	Copilot	231256	231256	237936	231412	
Sgt. Clifford H. Leming	418	Left Waist Gunner			23508		
Sgt. Clifford H. Leming	418	Right Waist Gunner	297491	23508			
T/Sgt. Harry S. Lenk	350	Radio Operator - Gunner	239934				
T/Sgt. Harry S. Lenk	350	Radio Operator		239934	231981		
Lt. Thomas R. Leslie	351	Copilot	231735	231735	231735		KIA
Lt. Winifred *'Pappy'* Lewis	418	Copilot	231504	231504		231504	
Lt. Gordon C. Lien	349	Copilot	230487	230170	231051		POW
T/Sgt. William C. Libbert	418	Radio Operator - Gunner		238059	238059		POW
2Lt. Glenn G. Lindom	351	Navigator	239983	237936	239983	240056	POW
S/Sgt. Vera R. Lines	349	Ball Turret Gunner	231970				POW
2Lt. Royal W. Lingenfelter	351	Navigator	238044	238044	238044		POW
Sgt. Nelson C. Linke	418	Left Waist Gunner	238175	238175	238175	238175	
T/Sgt. Maynard L. Lobb	349	Top Turret - Engineer	25957	25957	25957	237783	
Captain Robert H. Lohof	349	Pilot	231970				POW
2Lt. Jack E. Longenecker	350	Navigator	23413	23413	23413		
T/Sgt. Harrison L. Longhi	350	Top Turret - Engineer		239934			
T/Sgt. Robert D. Longworth	350	Radio Operator - Gunner			231049	231968	
2Lt. Edwin J. Loughran	418	Copilot	230091	230278	230278		KIA
Captain John Love	351	Pilot	231066				
Sgt. John P. Lucarelli	418	Radio Operator - Gunner	297491	23508	23508		
2Lt. Wilbert D. Lund	350	Copilot	231074	232009	231074		
T/Sgt. Clarence P. Luquet	350	Top Turret - Engineer	231537	231537	232009	231074	
Sgt. Charles J. Luquette	349	Ball Turret Gunner	230487	230170	231051		KIA
S/Sgt. David C. Lyon Jr	349	Ball Turret Gunner	25957	25957	25957	237783	
S/Sgt. James P. Mack	418	Right Waist Gunner	231504	231504		231504	
T/Sgt. Callen F. MacKenzie	351	Radio Operator - Gunner	231066				
S/Sgt. Joseph L. Mackey	350	Ball Turret Gunner	239830				
T/Sgt. George E. Madden	351	Top Turret - Engineer	231256	231256	237936	231412	
S/Sgt. D. J. Maddra Jr	351	Right Waist Gunner	231735	231735			
S/Sgt. Leonard D. Malcuit	418	Left Waist Gunner		238059	238059		POW
2Lt. Thomas H. Mallen	350	Copilot				239830	
S/Sgt. Loydell Malone	350	Left Waist Gunner	238016	238016			POW
2Lt. Francis J. Malooly	350	Pilot	231049	231049	231049		
S/Sgt. Theodore E. Mangum	418	Tail Gunner		297491	297491		POW
S/Sgt. Edward J. Marlen	418	Ball Turret Gunner	239994	239994	239994		INT
Lt. John F. Massol	351	Pilot	238047	238047	232018	238047	
S/Sgt. John L. Mauk	418	Tail Gunner	231800			231895	
2Lt. Charles H. Mauvais	350	Navigator	231049	231049	231049		
2Lt. Robert W. McAtee	418	Bombardier	238175	238175	238175	238175	
T/Sgt. John W. McAuliffe	349	Top Turret - Engineer	230170	23534	23534	231710	
S/Sgt. Oliver N. McCartney	351	Right Waist Gunner	238047	238047	232018	238047	
2Lt. Robert E. McCormick	349	Navigator	25957	25957	25957	237783	
2Lt. Warren G. McCoy	351	Copilot	232018	232018		232018	
2Lt. Stuart W. McFeely	350	Bombardier	237807				
S/Sgt. Daniel S. McGill	418	Right Waist Gunner	238059	26087	26087		
S/Sgt. Estil V. McGuffee	351	Left Waist Gunner	238044	238044	238044		POW

2Lt. Edward N. McKay	350	Pilot	237807				
S/Sgt. Robert L. McKimmy	351	Left Waist Gunner	231256	231256			
S/Sgt. Vernon T. McNabb	351	Right Waist Gunner		231708			
2Lt. Bertrand D. McNeil	349	Copilot	238017				POW
Sgt. Charles E. McSpadden	351	Right Waist Gunner	232018	232018		232018	
T/Sgt. Sherwyn W. Meyers	349	Radio Operator - Gunner	231723				
Lt. Clifford Milburn	418	Bombardier	231504	231504		231504	
Sgt. Willard H. Miller	350	Right Waist Gunner	231049	231049	231049		
Captain David L. Miner	418	Pilot		238059	238059		KIA
S/Sgt. Raymond J. Mitchell	351	Left Waist Gunner	231389	231389	231389		
Lt. Raymond V.E. Monrad	351	Pilot				231066	
2Lt. Coy I. Montgomery	349	Pilot	237783	231249	230170		KIA
T/Sgt. Harvey A. Moore	418	Top Turret - Engineer	230061	231800	231800		POW
S/Sgt. Willard W. Moore	418	Ball Turret Gunner	238059	26087	26087		
S/Sgt. John A. Miller	349	Right Waist Gunner	231723				
Sgt. William E. Moreland	349	Right Waist Gunner	230170	23534	23534	231710	
S/Sgt. Edwin I. Morgan	418	Left Waist Gunner			237936	231412	
2Lt. George R. Morgan	349	Bombardier		230152			
Lt. Leon R. Morgan	349	Pilot	25957	25957	25957	237783	
S/Sgt. Paul H. Morris	418	Left Waist Gunner	230061	231800	231800		POW
S/Sgt. James E. Morrison	350	Left Waist Gunner		231968	237807		
2Lt. Thomas J. Mullen	350	Copilot	237807				
S/Sgt. Thomas H. Mullenix	349	Left Waist Gunner	239817				POW
Lt. Ira A. Munn	418	Copilot	239994	239994	239994		INT
Lt. William B. Murray	349	Pilot	231731	231731	230799		KIA
S/Sgt. Robert M. Myers	351	Ball Turret Gunner	231256	231256	237936	231412	
2Lt. Charles W. Mylius Jr	351	Pilot	232018	232018		232018	
Sgt. Luke E. Nachatilo	349	Ball Turret Gunner		230152	231710		
2Lt. William A. Naegele	418	Bombardier	231800			231895	
Sgt. Glover Nall	349	Left Waist Gunner		230152	231710		
S/Sgt. Lucien E. Neveu	350	Tail Gunner			23413		
T/Sgt. George N. Ofiesh	351	Bombardier	231389	238016			POW
S/Sgt. Frederick A. Padstawski	418	Right Waist Gunner	231800			231895	
2Lt. Augustus H. Paine	418	Navigator	238175	238175	238175	238175	
T/Sgt. Louis P. Paltrineri	350	Radio Operator - Gunner	237807			239830	
Sgt. Nelson A.S. Pardee	350	Ball Turret Gunner	231049	231049	231049		
S/Sgt. Robert Patrick	349	Right Waist Gunner		231723	231723		
S/Sgt. Harold H. Patterson	418	Top Turret - Engineer	297491	23508	23508		
Captain Joseph *'Bubbles'* Payne	350	Navigator			231981		
S/Sgt. Jim Peace	349	Ball Turret Gunner	231731	231731	230799		POW
Lt. Robert L. Phillips	349	Copilot	231731				
2Lt. Delbert S. Pearson	350	Pilot	231074	232009	231074		
Captain Robert K. Peel	350	Bombardier			231981		
Sgt. James T. Penny	418	Right Waist Gunner	231895	231895	231895		
T/Sgt. Arthur J. Perry	350	Top Turret - Engineer	231049	231049	231049		
Lt. William L. Peterson	418	Copilot	297482	297482	297482		KIA
T/Sgt. Van D. Pinner	418	Top Turret - Engineer		297491	297491		POW
T/Sgt. Michael G. Polanick	349	Radio Operator - Gunner	238017				POW
T/Sgt. Edwin E. Postel	350	Top Turret - Engineer	23413	23413	23413		
S/Sgt. C. L. Powell	351	Ball Turret Gunner		231389			
S/Sgt. James W. Powell	418	Tail Gunner	230061	231800	231800		POW
S/Sgt. Sam Pry	418	Right Waist Gunner		238059	238059		POW
Lt. Herbert G. Pryor	350	Bombardier		231968			
Captain Gerald R. Putnam	349	Command Pilot	231970				POW
Lt. Dean M. Radtke	418	Pilot		297491	297491		POW
2Lt. John J. Raring	418	Copilot	238059	26087	26087		
Lt. Norman L. Rasmussen	351	Bombardier	237936	231066	238011		KIA
T/Sgt. Robert Ray	418	Radio Operator - Gunner		297491	297491		POW
Lt. Robert M. Reilly	418	Navigator		297491	297491		POW
T/Sgt. Ernest J. Rene	350	Top Turret - Engineer	231074	232009	231074		
S/Sgt. William L. Reneau	351	Left Waist Gunner	238047	238047	232018	238047	
Lt. Earl L. Richardson	418	Bombardier		239994	238059		POW
Lt. Merril T. Rish	351	Pilot	238044	238044	238044		KIA
S/Sgt. Earl W. Ritter	349	Tail Gunner	237783	231249	230170		POW
Sgt. Lawrence A. Robbins	349	Right Waist Gunner		230152	231710		
S/Sgt. June E. Roberson	418	Tail Gunner		238059	238059		POW
S/Sgt. Austin B. Roberts	350	Left Waist Gunner	23413		23413		
Sgt. Austin B. Roberts	350	Right Waist Gunner		23413			
2Lt. Frank W. Roberts Jr	418	Navigator	231895	231895	231895		

Lt. Fred W. Robertson	349	Navigator	231723	231723	231723		
T/Sgt. Jack M. Robins	418	Radio Operator - Gunner	230061	231800	231800		POW
Sgt. Ray H. Robinson	418	Ball Turret Gunner	231504	231504		231504	
T/Sgt. Cuertis W. Rockhill	351	Top Turret - Engineer	231066				
S/Sgt. Lloyd H. Rodgers Jr	350	Ball Turret Gunner	239872	239872	239872		POW
S/Sgt. W. H. Rodkey	349	Radio Operator - Gunner	230487				
S/Sgt. Donald M. Rohasek	349	Ball Turret Gunner	230170	23534			
Lt. David Rolnick	350	Bombardier		238197	238197		POW
Lt. Robert *'Rosie'* Rosenthal	418	Pilot	231504	231504		231504	
S/Sgt. Michael Rotz	351	Tail Gunner	231256	231256			
Sgt. Anthony E. Ruda	349	Right Waist Gunner	237783	231249	230170		POW
Lt. Albert P. Rule	349	Navigator			231731		KIA
S/Sgt. John Rupnick	351	Tail Gunner				231066	
S/Sgt. James R. Russel	351	Top Turret - Engineer	232018	232018		232018	
S/Sgt. Donald B. Sackrider	349	Left Waist Gunner	238017				POW
T/Sgt. Nunziato Sansevero	350	Radio Operator - Gunner	231074	232009	231074		
S/Sgt. William D. Sapp	418	Right Waist Gunner	239994	239994	239994		INT
S/Sgt. Louis P. Savell	349	Ball Turret Gunner	237783	231249	230170		POW
Sgt. Richard D. Schad	418	Tail Gunner	238175	238175	238175	238175	
S/Sgt. Milton Scharf	351	Radio Operator - Gunner	239983	237936	239983	240056	POW
T/Sgt. Fred C. Schillinger	349	Radio Operator - Gunner	231731	231731	230799		KIA
2Lt. Claude E. Schindler	351	Copilot	231389	231389	231389		
Lt. Robert P. Schremser	418	Navigator	297482	297482	297482		POW
S/Sgt. Murray Schrier	418	Ball Turret Gunner	231306		231306		
S/Sgt. Carl F. Schuster	350	Ball Turret Gunner	237807			239830	
T/Sgt. Grant H. L. Scott	350	Radio Operator – Gunner	239872	239872	239872		KIA
S/Sgt. Harold J. Scrivener	350	Left Waist Gunner	231074	232009	231074	239830	
Lt. Stanley M. Seaton	350	Pilot	238016	238016			POW
Lt. Duncan R. Shand	351	Copilot	231767	231767	231767	237936	
S/Sgt. James L. Simmons	350	Right Waist Gunner	239830				
Sgt. Harold L. Sheldon	350	Ball Turret Gunner		238197	238197		POW
S/Sgt. Marion J. Sheldon	418	Left Waist Gunner	231504	231504		231504	
2Lt. William D. Sheridan	350	Navigator	239830				
T/Sgt. Bernard G. Siegal	351	Top Turret - Engineer				238047	
Lt. Robert J. Shoens	351	Pilot	231767	231767	231767	237936	
S/Sgt. George W. Silvermann	351	Top Turret - Engineer	239983	237936	239983	240056	POW
S/Sgt. Edward Silverstone	351	Ball Turret Gunner	231767	231767	231767	237936	
T/Sgt. Howard T. Skaggs Jr	351	Top Turret - Engineer	238044	238044	238044		POW
Lt. Anthony D. Slatinsky	418	Copilot	297491	23508	23508		
T/Sgt. Hugh A. Smallwood	351	Top Turret - Engineer				231066	
S/Sgt. Ronald E. Smeall	351	Left Waist Gunner		231708			
2Lt. Frank A. Smith	351	Copilot	238044	238044	238044		KIA
Lt. Lester N. Smith	350	Bombardier	231074	232009	231074		
Lt. Bernard J. Smolens	418	Bombardier	230061	231800	231800		POW
S/Sgt. John D. Smoot	418	Left Waist Gunner	238059	26087	26087		
2Lt. Frederick G. Spence	351	Copilot	237936	231066	238011		KIA
T/Sgt. Asa A. Spengler	351	Radio Operator - Gunner	238047	238047	232018	238047	
S/Sgt. Hobart H. Spires	349	Right Waist Gunner			231731		KIA
Sgt. Bernard L. Spragg	350	Ball Turret Gunner	231220	239830	231968	231968	
Lt. Charles S. Stapleton	349	Formation Control Officer				297542	
Lt. Charles S. Stapleton	349	Copilot		230152	231710		
T/Sgt. Harold Stearns	350	Top Turret - Engineer	239872	239872	239872		POW
2Lt. Edwin A. Stern Jr	351	Bombardier	238047	238047	232018	238047	
S/Sgt. Owen D. Stockton	349	Left Waist Gunner			231731		POW
S/Sgt. Victor Stoffregen	418	Tail Gunner	230091	230278	230278		KIA
S/Sgt. Adam C. Stoppel	349	Left Waist Gunner	231723	231723	231723		
S/Sgt. John Stryjeski	350	Radio Operator - Gunner		238197	238197		KIA
Lt. William J. Sugg	350	Copilot		238197	238197		POW
Sgt. Edmond J. Sullivan	351	Left Waist Gunner		232018		232018	
2Lt. Edward G. Sullivan	349	Navigator	239817				POW
S/Sgt. Virgil F. Summers	349	Ball Turret Gunner			231731		KIA
Sgt. Bernard Sundin	349	Tail Gunner	230487	230170	231051		KIA
Captain Jack Swartout	418	Copilot			231306		
T/Sgt. Eugene V. Sweeney	349	Radio Operator - Gunner	230170	23534	23534	231710	
T/Sgt. Earl L. Symes	351	Top Turret - Engineer	238047	231708			
S/Sgt. S. M. Szekely	351	Ball Turret Gunner	231389				
S/Sgt. Michael J. Tanowigch	349	Radio Operator - Gunner		230170	231051		KIA
2Lt. Martin Tashjian	350	Copilot	23413	231968	237807		
S/Sgt. Robert J. Taylor	418	Ball Turret Gunner		231800	231800		POW

T/Sgt. William F. Teaff	351	Radio Operator - Gunner	231735	231735	231735		POW
Lt. William A. Terry	418	Pilot	297482	297482	297482		KIA
2Lt. William H. Thomas	418	Pilot	238059	26087	26087		
T/Sgt. Chester Thompson	350	Top Turret - Engineer				239830	
T/Sgt. Dewey Thompson	418	Top Turret - Engineer	231306		231306		
S/Sgt. Frederick C. Thorpe	418	Left Waist Gunner	239994	239994	239994		INT
2Lt. William R. Thorpe Jr	418	Navigator	230091	230278	230278		KIA
S/Sgt. Arthur R. Tirrell	418	Radio Gunner	231306		231306		
T/Sgt. Wilbur I. Trembley Jr	349	Radio Operator - Gunner		231249	230170		POW
S/Sgt. Philip K. Troetschel	350	Tail Gunner	23413	23413			
S/Sgt. John E. Trout	350	Right Waist Gunner	237807			239830	
S/Sgt. Bradford F. Truesdell	350	Right Waist Gunner	231074	232009	231074		
T/Sgt. Leman E. Tutor	418	Radio Operator - Gunner	230091	230278	230278		KIA
Lt. William E. Vaden	349	Navigator	231970				POW
Sgt. Peter VanSlyck	418	Ball Turret Gunner	238175	238175	238175	238175	
Sgt. John Verbovski	350	Top Turret - Engineer		231968	237807		
T/Sgt. Henry C. Verdeur Jr	351	Radio Operator - Gunner	237936	231066	238011		KIA
T/Sgt. Tony L. Verdusco	349	Radio Operator - Gunner	25957	25957	25957	237783	
S/Sgt. Edward A. Vollmer	418	Tail Gunner	238059	26087	26087		
2Lt. Robert C. Vollmer	349	Pilot	239817				POW
S/Sgt. Donald E. Walker	350	Right Waist Gunner		231968	237807		
T/Sgt. Edward Walker Jr	350	Radio Operator - Gunner	231220	239830	231968		
T/Sgt. John H. Walters	350	Bombardier			232009		
2Lt. Ralph O. Ward	349	Copilot	25957	25957	25957	237783	
S/Sgt. Virgil H. Warders	351	Right Waist Gunner	231767	231767	231767	237936	
FO Edward A. Warner	349	Navigator	238017				POW
S/Sgt. John H. White	350	Left Waist Gunner		238197	238197		POW
S/Sgt. Samuel Wilenski	350	Right Waist Gunner		238197	238197		POW
S/Sgt. Gerald J. Will	418	Left Waist Gunner	231306		231306		
2Lt. Earl R. Williams	351	Formation Control Officer		231708			
Sgt Howard O. Williams	418	Tail Gunner	297491	23508	23508		
S/Sgt. Winfred C. Williams	351	Ball Turret Gunner	238047	238047	232018	238047	
S/Sgt. John L. Willsey	351	Right Waist Gunner	237936	231066	238011		POW
2Lt. Mark V. Wilson	349	Pilot	230170	23534	23534	231710	
2Lt. George H. Wing	349	Navigator	230487	230170	231051		KIA
2Lt. Paul R. Winters	350	Bombardier	239830				
S/Sgt. George W. Wood	349	Tail Gunner	239817				KIA
S/Sgt. Vincent J. Wood	351	Radio Operator - Gunner	232018	232018		232018	
T/Sgt. Clarence H. Wood Jr	351	Radio Operator - Gunner	231389	231389	231389		
S/Sgt. Thomas R. Wooderson	349	Ball Turret Gunner	238017				POW
S/Sgt. William W. Wright	351	Left Waist Gunner	231767	231767	231767	237936	
Sgt. Leonard W. Yeager	350	Left Waist Gunner	231049	231049	231049		
2Lt. Jack A. Young	350	Navigator	237807			239830	
S/Sgt. Frank A. Yzenas	351	Right Waist Gunner	239983	237936	239983	240056	POW
Sgt. Ralph V. Zarzecki	349	Right Waist Gunner	230487	230170	231051		KIA
S/Sgt. George P. Zigo	350	Tail Gunner	231074	232009	231074		
T/Sgt. Albert Zikorus	418	Top Turret - Engineer		238059	238059		POW

Participating 100 BG Aircraft Matrix

This section identifies to the greatest extent possible each 100 BG aircraft on any of the 3, 4, 6, and 8 March 1944 missions to Berlin. From left to right each entry details of the aircraft serial number, aircraft nickname, squadron assignment and codes, as well as the last name of the pilot for each of the respective dates. In some instances there are two "pilots" listed; the first name is usually the regular pilot for the crew and the second name is that of the "command pilot" who usually occupied the "right" seat on the B-17.

Those cells highlighted in light blue indicate that the aircraft did not complete the mission (returned early because the aircraft was a scheduled spare, mechanical issues, personnel related issues, or failed to take off). Those cells highlighted in green indicate that the aircraft was damaged as a result of completing the sortie. Cells highlighted in red indicate that the aircraft failed to return. Where relevant to 100 BG aircraft, information is also included on 95 BG and 390 BG aircraft.

Related 100 BG Aircraft

Serial	Name	Squadron	03-Mar-44	04-Mar-44	06-Mar-44	08-Mar-44
23413	*Hard Luck*	350 LN V	Chadwick	Chadwick	Chadwick	
23508	*Bastard's Bungalow*	418 LD P		Ferbrache	Ferbrache	
23534	*Ol' Dad*	349 XR N		Wilson	Wilson	
25957	*Horny*	349 XR D	Morgan	Morgan	Morgan	
26087	*Royal Flush*	418 LD Z		Thomas	Thomas	
230061	*Wolf Pack*	418 LD T	Barton			
230091	*Blivit*	418 LD S	Kendall			
230152	*Messie Bessie*	418 LD X		Harrison		
230170	*The Pride of the Century*	349 XR G	Wilson	Koper	Montgomery	
230278	*Sly Fox*	418 LD R		Kendall	Kendall	
230487	*Torchy 3*	349 XR P	Koper			
230799	*The Bigassbird II*	349 XR J			Murray	
231049	*Superstitious Aloysious*	350 LN U	Malooly	Malooly	Malooly	
231051	*Goin Jessies*	351 EP K			Koper	
231066	*Fools Rush In*	351 EP H	Love	Handorf		Monrad
231074	*Cahepit*	350 LN Q	Pearson		Pearson	C.B. Harper
231220	*Fletcher's Castoria*	350 LN P	Gibbons			
231249	*Miss Carriage*	349 XR L		Montgomery		
231256	*King Bee II*	351 EP S	Helmick	Helmick		
231306	*Nelson King*	418 LD V	Lauro		Lauro-Swartout	
231389	*Luscious Lucy*	351 EP J	Lacy	Lacy	Lacy	
231412	*Mason And Dixon*	351 EP G				Helmick
231504	*Rosie's Riveters*	418 LD E	Rosenthal	Rosenthal		Rosenthal
231537	*Buffalo Gal*	349 LN S	C.B. Harper	C.B. Harper		
231708	*Skipper II*	351 EP N		Hughes-Janssen		
231710	*The Savage*	349 XR P			Harrison	Wilson
231723	*"Sparky"*	349 XR R	Cowan	Cowan	Cowan	
231731		349 XR M	Murray	Murray	Amiero	
231735	*Lucky Lee*	351 EP B	Brannan	Brannan	Brannan	
231767	*Our Gal Sal*	351 EP E	Shoens	Shoens	Shoens	
231800		418 LD U	Harper	Barton	Barton	
231895	*Miss Chief*	418 LD Y	Gummersall	Gummersall	Gummersall	Harper
231968	*Miss Irish*	350 LN D		Cope	Gibbons	Gibbons
231970	*Berth'a the Blues*	349 XR	Lohof-Putnam			
231981		350 LN E			Devore-Elton	
232009	*Black Cat 13*	350 LN X		Pearson	C.B. Harper	
232018	*Waticare*	351 EP L	Mylius	Mylius	Massol	Mylius
237783	*Dobie*	349 XR B	Montgomery			Morgan
237807	*Alice From Dallas II*	350 LN O	McKay		Cope	
237936	*Our Mark*	351 EP M	Handorf	Chapman	Helmick	Shoens
238011	*Kind-a-Ruff*	351 EP P			Handorf	
238016	*Seaton's Sad Sack*	350 LN B	Seaton	Seaton		
238017	*One Mission Lulu*	349 XR O	Gossage			
238044	*Spirit of 44*	351 EP R	Rish	Rish	Rish	
238047	*Feaver Beaver*	351 EP O	Mossol	Massol		Massol
238059		418 LD A	Thomas	Miner	Miner	
238175		418 LD Q	Forsythe	Forsythe	Forsythe	Forsythe
238197	*Half and Half*	350 LN T		Lautenschlager	Lautenschlager	
239817	*Murderer's Row*	349 XR A	Vollmer			
239830	*Berlin Playboy*	350 LN Y	Gough	Gibbons		Gough
239872	*Rubber Check*	350 LN A	Granack	Granack	Granack	
239934	*My Achin' Back*	350 LN Z	Devore	Devore-Fuller		
239983	*Katie*	351 EP F	Chapman			
239994	*Snort Stuff*	418 LD D	Barrick	Barrick	Barrick	
240056	*Holy Terror III* *Katie's Boys*	351 EP F	Keel			Chapman
297482	*Terry and the Pirates*	418 LD W	Terry	Terry	Terry	
297491	*Ronnie R*	418 LD B	Ferbrache	Radtke	Radtke	
297542	*City of Savannah* 388BG	563 B PFF				Bennett

Related 95 BG Aircraft

Serial	Name	Squadron	03-Mar-44	04-Mar-44	06-Mar-44	08-Mar-44
23153	*The Devil's Daughter*	336 ET A				
23263	*Slightly Dangerous*	334 BG V		Harris		
23529		336 ET F			Frantz	
229943		334 BG K		Vansant	Mailman	
230120	*Patches*	334 BG D		Herman	Herman	
230233	*Rhapsody in Flak*	412 QW X				
230235	*The Zoot Suiters*	412 QW U				
230342	*Taint A Bird*	334 BG B		Mailman	Woodcock	
231205		336 ET E				
231251		334 BG P			Keasbey	
231299	*She's My Gal II*	334 BG M		Lloyd	Lloyd	
231320	*I'll Be Around*	412 QW M		Brown		
231329		334 BG H		Infield	Stern	
231410	*I Dood It*	336 ET G		Jeffers		
231565		335 OE U		Roehm		
231589		334 BG O		Fagan		
231600	*Spirit of New Mexico*	334 BG M		Powers		
231632		335 OE Z		Woodcock		
231675	*Berlin Bessie*	412 QW W			Gunn	
231681		412 QW G		Haitt		
231734		412 QW H		Worthy		
231785	*Slightly Dangerous*	335 OE N		Dunham		
231798		412 QW J		Gunn	McLane	
231876	*Fire Ball*	412 QW Q		Newson		
231887	*Big Casino*	336 ET K			Biesecker	
231910		336 ET P		Brownlow		
231920	*Able Mabel*	334 BG G		Geib	Harris	
231924	*Ol' Dog*	334 BG Q		Brink		
231939		336 ET J		Kroeger		
232002	*Berlin First*	335 OE X		Barksdale	Barksdale	
232019		336 ET R		Abbott		
237882	*A Good Bet*	412 QW T			Brown	
237889	*Pride of Vhelhalis*	336 ET L		Hagenbaugh	Hagenbaugh	
237929		334 OE Y		Henderson	Henderson	
237988	*Flagship*	336 ET M		Dean	Dean	
238024		336 ET Q			Russell	
238140	*Dolly's Daughter*	335 OE W		Rourke	Rourke	
238151		336 ET L			Cavalier	
239793		412 QW V			Read	
239884		336 ET N		Reis		
239924	*Tornado*	334 BG N		Huie		
239989		334 BG F		Edwards	Newson	
297495		336 ET C		Westmyer	Conley	

Related 390 BG Aircraft

Serial	Name	Squadron	03-Mar-44	04-Mar-44	06-Mar-44	08-Mar-44
231892	*I'll Be Around*	570 DI H			Sterr	
231971	*Twenty-One or Bust*	570 DI E			Sutters	
231974	*Bomboogie*	570 DI G			Wilkinsom	
232089		570 DI W			Dower	
238130		570 DI B			Reich	
239821	*Hey Motile*	570 DI J			Warren	

Formation Charts and Aircrew Data

This section identifies to the greatest extent possible the position of 100 BG aircraft in the planned formation for any of the 3, 4, 6, and 8 March 1944 missions to Berlin. Information is provided for relevant 95 BG and 390 BG B-17s. Where possible information is provided about the formation as it appeared "Over the Target."

In *The Mighty Eighth War Manual* (Jane's 1984), Roger A. Freeman traces the variety of heavy bomber formations employed by the Eighth Air Force. In March 1944 there generally existed a 21-plane formation, though various groups did experiment with this basic formation. Each formation, referred to as a group, contained three squadrons: lead, high, and low. Some "groups" even had a trail squadron, which flew directly behind and below the "lead" squadron. The term "group" refers to a formation not necessarily composed of aircraft assigned to the same numbered unit. This caveat applies to the term "squadron." The terms "high" and "low" refer to the altitude of the "squadron" in relation to the altitude of the lead "squadron." Each "squadron" consists of smaller three aircraft "V" formations. The numbering system is straightforward. The first aircraft of the squadron is #1, the aircraft to the right is #2, and the aircraft to the left is #3. The lead aircraft of the next "V" is #4, and the aircraft to its right is #5 and so on. The same numbering system is employed for the high and low squadron. Each cell will provide information about the pilot's last name, the aircraft serial number, and the squadron and individual aircraft letter codes.

Those cells highlighted in light blue indicate that the aircraft did not complete the mission (recall, returned early because the aircraft was a scheduled spare, mechanical issues, personnel related issues, or failed to take off). Those cells highlighted in green indicate that the aircraft was damaged as result of completing the sortie. Cells highlighted in red indicate that the aircraft failed to return.

Under each formation chart information will appear for each aircraft. This information will correspond to the position of the aircraft in the formation. The first line of the entry will provide the aircraft serial number, aircraft nick name, and the squadron assignment and code letters, as well as the last name of the pilot as it appears on the formation chart. The following entries detail from left to right the last name of the pilot (e.g. Smith incidates "The Smith crew"), rank and full name of the crew member, squadron assignment, and any notes about the crew member. In some crews, identity of each crew member has yet to be determined. Unless otherwise noted, the crewmen listed participated on the mission, whether or not their aircraft was recalled from the mission, as many were on 3 and 4 March and March, or returned early either as a scheduled spare or for mechniacal or other reasons. The notation TBC indicates that data remains to be confirmed, while a name (e.g. Smith crew) indicates the individual was borrowed from another crew.

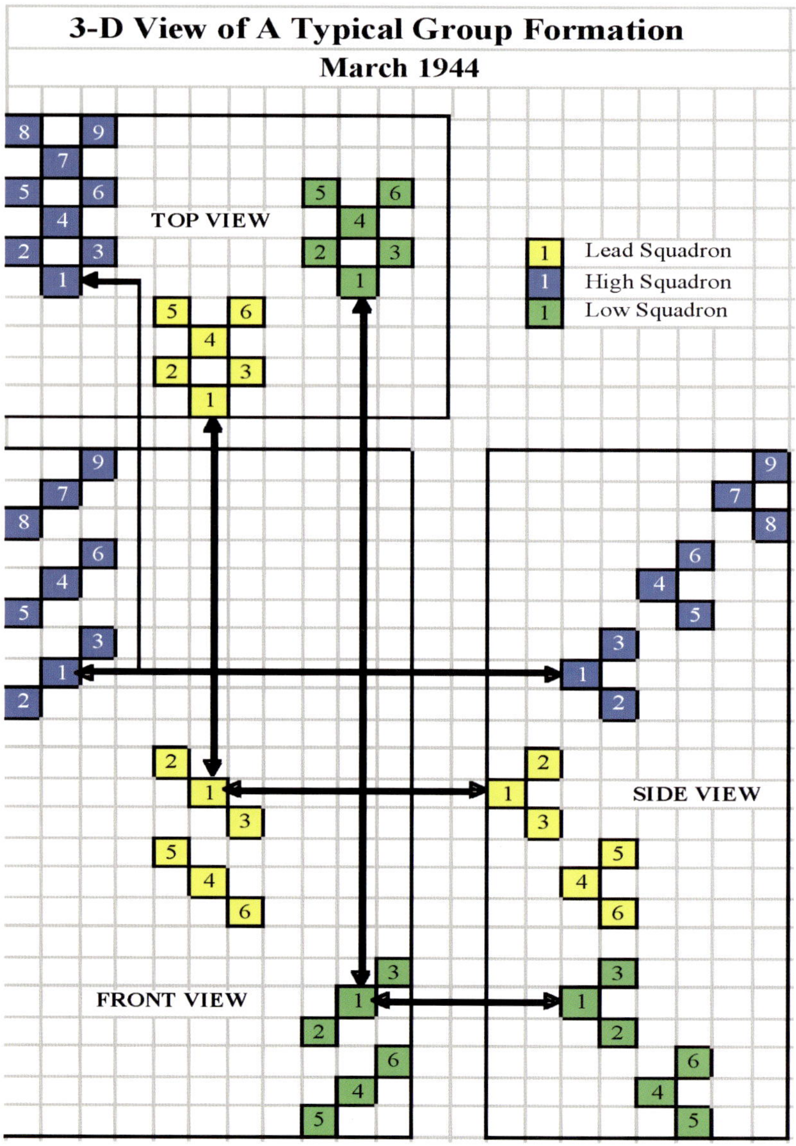

March 3, 1944, Berlin

100 A Group

Lead Squadron

Lohof-Putnam 231970 XR

Vollmer 239817 XR A
Gossage 238017 XR O

Cowan 231723 XR R

Montgomery 237783 XR B
Morgan 25957 XR D

Low Squadron

Murray 231731 XR M

Koper 230487 XR F
Wilson 230170 XR G

Granack 239872 LN A

Thomas 238059 LD A

High Squadron

Devore 239934 LN Z

Pearson 231074 LN Q
Gibbons 231220 LN P

Gough 239830 LN Y

McKay 237807 LN O
Chadwick 23413 LN V

Seaton 238016 LN B

Malooly 231049 LN U
Harper 231537 LN S

100 A Lead Squadron

231970 ***Berth'a the Blues*** **349 XR Lohof / Putnam**

Lohof-Putnam	Captain Robert H. Lohof	349	Pilot	POW
Lohof-Putnam	Captain Gerald R. Putnam	349	Command Pilot	POW
Lohof-Putnam	Lt Paul T. Davis	349	Bombardier	POW
Lohof-Putnam	Lt William E. Vaden	349	Navigator	POW
Lohof-Putnam	T/Sgt Sidney A. Goldenburg	349	Top Turret - Engineer	POW
Lohof-Putnam	T/Sgt Guy L. Brown Jr	349	Radio Operator-Gunner	POW
Lohof-Putnam	S/Sgt Vera R. Lines	349	Ball Turret Gunner	POW
Lohof-Putnam	S/Sgt James M. Butler	349	Left Waist Gunner	POW
Lohof-Putnam	S/Sgt Richard L. David	349	Right Waist Gunner	POW
Lohof-Putnam	S/Sgt George W. Briggs	349	Tail Gunner	POW Died in captivity

238017 ***One Mission Lulu*** **349 XR O Gossage**

Gossage	2Lt. John G. Gossage	349	Pilot	POW
Gossage	2Lt Bertrand D. McNeil	349	Copilot	POW
Gossage	Lt. Howard G. Ball	349	Bombardier	POW
Gossage	FO Edward A. Warner	349	Navigator	POW
Gossage	T/Sgt Arthur A. Cooper	349	Top Turret - Engineer	POW
Gossage	T/Sgt Michael G. Polanick	349	Radio Operator - Gunner	POW
Gossage	S/Sgt Thomas R. Wooderson	349	Ball Turret Gunner	POW
Gossage	S/Sgt Donald B. Sackrider	349	Left Waist Gunner	POW
Gossage	S/Sgt James W. Gregg	349	Right Waist Gunner	POW
Gossage	S/Sgt Arthur V.R. Congrove	349	Tail Gunner	POW

239817 ***Murderer's Row*** **349 XR A Vollmer**

Vollmer	2Lt. Robert C. Vollmer	349	Pilot	POW
Vollmer	2Lt John W. Adams III	349	Copilot	KIA
Vollmer	T/Sgt Ernest B. Clark	349	Bombardier	KIA
Vollmer	2Lt. Edward G. Sullivan	349	Navigator	POW
Vollmer	T/Sgt William S. Humphrey	349	Top Turret - Engineer	POW
Vollmer	T/Sgt Eliad M. Johnson	349	Radio Operator - Gunner	KIA
Vollmer	S/Sgt Don Gutherie	349	Ball Turret Gunner	POW
Vollmer	S/Sgt Thomas H. Mullenix	349	Left Waist Gunner	POW
Vollmer	S/Sgt Donald W. Becker	349	Right Waist Gunner	KIA
Vollmer	S/Sgt George W. Wood	349	Tail Gunner	KIA

231723	***"Sparky"***	**349**	**XR R Cowan**
Cowan	Lt. Clement H. Cowan	349	Pilot
Cowan	Lt. Hank A. Dibbern	349	Copilot
Cowan	Lt. Harold L. Heyneman	349	Bombardier
Cowan	Lt. Fred W. Robertson	349	Navigator
Cowan	T/Sgt. Murray W. Holditch	349	Top Turret - Engineer
Cowan	T/Sgt. Sherwyn W. Meyers	349	Radio Operator - Gunner
Cowan	S/Sgt. William A. Geigle	349	Ball Turret Gunner
Cowan	S/Sgt. Adam C. Stoppel	349	Left Waist Gunner
Cowan	S/Sgt. John A. Miller	349	Right Waist Gunner
Cowan	S/Sgt Horace R. Kemble	349	Tail Gunner
25957	***Horny***	**349**	**XR D Morgan**
Morgan	Lt. Leon R. Morgan	349	Pilot
Morgan	2Lt. Ralph O. Ward	349	Copilot
Morgan	S/Sgt. Sam J. LaFace	349	Toggler
Morgan	2Lt. Robert E. McCormick	349	Navigator
Morgan	T/Sgt. Maynard L. Lobb	349	Top Turret - Engineer
Morgan	T/Sgt. Tony L. Verdusco	349	Radio Operator - Gunner
Morgan	S/Sgt. David C. Lyon Jr	349	Ball Turret Gunner
Morgan	S/Sgt. Hugo C. Kleckner	349	Waist Gunner
Morgan	S/Sgt. Kenneth R. Lash Jr	349	Waist Gunner
Morgan	S/Sgt. Ernest R. Gomez	349	Tail Gunner
237783	***Dobie***	**349**	**XR B Montgomery**
Montgomery	2Lt. Coy I. Montgomery	349	Pilot
Montgomery	2Lt. Robert F. Connaway	349	Copilot
Montgomery	2Lt. James W. Fulton	349	Bombardier
Montgomery	2Lt. Frank C. Laver	349	Navigator
Montgomery	T/Sgt. George W. Burton	349	Top Turret - Engineer
Montgomery	S/Sgt. Richard F. Brady	349	Radio Operator - Gunner
Montgomery	S/Sgt. Louis P. Savell	349	Ball Turret Gunner
Montgomery	S/Sgt. Junior L. Bucher	349	Left Waist Gunner
Montgomery	Sgt. Anthony E. Ruda	349	Right Waist Gunner
Montgomery	S/Sgt. Earl W. Ritter	349	Tail Gunner

100 A High Squadron

239934	***My Achin' Back***	**350**	**LN Z Devore**
Devore	Lt. Herbert G. Devore	350	Pilot
Devore	Lt. Jerry Felsenstein	350	Copilot
Devore	Lt. Louis R. Jaebker	350	Bombardier
Devore	Lt. Burton M. Joseph	350	Navigator
Devore	T/Sgt. James C. Brown	350	Top Turret – Engineer
Devore	T/Sgt. Harry S. Lenk	350	Radio Operator – Gunner
Devore	S/Sgt. Nicholas Delcimmuto	350	Ball Turret Gunner
Devore	S/Sgt. Darrell R. Dickenson	350	Left Waist Gunner
Devore	S/Sgt. John J. Barry	350	Right Waist Gunner
Devore	S/Sgt Knute Knudson	350	Tail Gunner
231220	***Fletcher's Castoria***	**350**	**LN P Gibbons**
Gibbons	2Lt. John P. Gibbons	350	Pilot
Gibbons	2Lt. Robert Dykeman	350	Copilot
Gibbons	2Lt. Sterling B. Blakeman	350	Bombardier
Gibbons	2Lt. Everett M. Johnson	350	Navigator
Gibbons	T/Sgt. Ira L. Arnold	350	Top Turret - Engineer
Gibbons	T/Sgt. Edward Walker Jr	350	Radio Operator - Gunner
Gibbons	Sgt. Bernard L. Spragg	350	Ball Turret Gunner
Gibbons	Sgt. Frank W. Buschmeier	350	Left Waist Gunner
Gibbons	Sgt. Myron J. Ettus	350	Right Waist Gunner
Gibbons	Sgt. Archie W. Bunting	350	Tail Gunner

231074 *Cahepit* 350 LN Q Pearson

Pearson	2Lt. Delbert S. Pearson	350	Pilot
Pearson	2Lt. Wilbert D. Lund	350	Copilot
Pearson	Lt. Lester N. Smith	350	Bombardier
Pearson	Lt. Festus E. *'Shorty'* Bryant	350	Navigator
Pearson	T/Sgt. Ernest J. Rene	350	Top Turret - Engineer
Pearson	T/Sgt. Nunziato Sansevero	350	Radio Operator - Gunner
Pearson	S/Sgt. Francis X. Kerin	350	Ball Turret Gunner
Pearson	S/Sgt. Harold J. Scrivener	350	Left Waist Gunner
Pearson	S/Sgt. Bradford F. Truesdell	350	Right Waist Gunner
Pearson	S/Sgt. George P. Zigo	350	Tail Gunner

239830 *Berlin Playboy* 350 LN Y Gough

Gough	2Lt. George H. Gough	350	Pilot
Gough	2Lt. Robert R. Kroske	350	Copilot
Gough	2Lt. Paul R. Winters	350	Bombardier
Gough	2Lt. William D. Sheridan	350	Navigator
Gough	T/Sgt John Lee	350	Top Turret – Engineer
Gough	T/Sgt Daniel J. Cahill	350	Radio Operator – Gunner
Gough	S/Sgt Joseph L. Mackey	350	Ball Turret Gunner
Gough	S/Sgt Edward C. Butchino	350	Left Waist Gunner
Gough	S/Sgt James L. Simmons	350	Right Waist Gunner
Gough	S/Sgt Lawrence A. Burk	350	Tail Gunner

23413 *Hard Luck* 350 LN V Chadwick

Chadwick	2Lt. Randall T. Chadwick	350	Pilot
Chadwick	2Lt. Mark Tashjian	350	Copilot
Chadwick	2Lt. Joseph A. Carty	350	Bombardier
Chadwick	2Lt. Jack E. Longenecker	350	Navigator
Chadwick	T/Sgt. Edwin E. Postel	350	Top Turret - Engineer
Chadwick	T/Sgt. John J. Good	350	Radio Operator - Gunner
Chadwick	S/Sgt. George A. Benedict	350	Ball Turret Gunner
Chadwick	S/Sgt. Austin B. Roberts	350	Left Waist Gunner
Chadwick	S/Sgt. Delbert J.H. Burns	350	Right Waist Gunner
Chadwick	S/Sgt Philip K. Troetschel	350	Tail Gunner

237807 *Alice From Dallas II* 350 LN O McKay

McKay	2Lt Edward N. McKay	350	Pilot
McKay	2Lt.Thomas J. Mullen	350	Copilot
McKay	2Lt. Stuart W. McFeely	350	Bombardier
McKay	2Lt. Jack A. Young	350	Navigator
McKay	T/Sgt Floyd O. Douglas	350	Top Turret - Engineer
McKay	T/Sgt Louis P. Paltrineri	350	Radio Operator - Gunner
McKay	S/Sgt Carl F. Schuster	350	Ball Turret Gunner
McKay	S/Sgt Jack W. Domenig	350	Left Waist Gunner
McKay	S/Sgt John E. Trout	350	Right Waist Gunner
McKay	S/Sgt Ralph T. Graham	350	Tail Gunner

238016 *Seaton's Sad Sack* 350 LN B Seaton

Seaton	Lt. Stanley M. Seaton	350	Pilot
Seaton	2Lt. William F. Clayton	350	Copilot
Seaton	Lt Maurice H. Cain	350	Bombardier
Seaton	2Lt. Charles F. DeWolfe Jr	350	Navigator
Seaton	T/Sgt. Peter A. Hogan	350	Top Turret - Engineer
Seaton	T/Sgt. Joseph A. Judd	350	Radio Operator - Gunner
Seaton	S/Sgt. Robert H. Cook	350	Ball Turret Gunner
Seaton	S/Sgt. Loydell Malone	350	Left Waist Gunner
Seaton	S/Sgt. Arthur J. Labreque	350	Right Waist Gunner
Seaton	S/Sgt Leming Hull	350	Tail Gunner

231537 *Buffalo Gal* 350 LN S C.B. *'Red'* Harper

Harper, CB	2Lt. Celesta B. *'Red'* Harper	350	Pilot
Harper, CB	2Lt. Robert S. Flannigan	350	Copilot
Harper, CB	2Lt Arthur E. Cox	350	Bombardier
Harper, CB	2Lt. Charles T. Hardiman	350	Navigator
Harper, CB	T/Sgt. Clarence P. Luquet	350	Top Turret - Engineer
Harper, CB	T/Sgt. Alvin E. James	350	Radio Operator - Gunner
Harper, CB	Sgt. Austin P. Curlee	350	Ball Turret Gunner
Harper, CB	Sgt. John B. Bowers	350	Left Waist Gunner
Harper, CB	Sgt. Wiley A. Dobbs	350	Right Waist Gunner
Harper, CB	Sgt. Anderson R. Frank Jr	350	Tail Gunner

231049 *Superstitious Aloysious* 350 LN U Malooly

Malooly	2Lt. Francis J. Malooly	350	Pilot
Malooly	2Lt. Robert W. Bailie	350	Copilot
Malooly	2Lt. Ralph W. Guida	350	Bombardier
Malooly	2Lt. Charles H. Mauvais	350	Navigator
Malooly	T/Sgt. Arthur J. Perry	350	Top Turret - Engineer
Malooly	T/Sgt. Robert C. Barrie	350	Radio Operator - Gunner
Malooly	Sgt. Nelson A.S. Pardee	350	Ball Turret Gunner
Malooly	Sgt. Leonard W. Yeager	350	Left Waist Gunner
Malooly	Sgt. Willard H. Miller	350	Right Waist Gunner
Malooly	Sgt. Lorenzo Genovese	350	Tail Gunner

100 A Low Squadron

231731 349 XR M Murray

Murray	Lt. William B. Murray	349	Pilot
Murray	Lt. Robert L. Phillips	349	Copilot
Murray	2nd William G. Carr	349	Bombardier
Murray	2Lt. Orrin H. Heinrich	349	Navigator
Murray	T/Sgt. Emory L. Brandt	349	Top Turret – Engineer
Murray	T/Sgt. Fred C. Schillinger	349	Radio Operator - Gunner
Murray	S/Sgt. Jim Peace	349	Ball Turret Gunner
Murray	Sgt. Nick E. Hamalack	349	Left Waist Gunner
Murray	S/Sgt. Palmer J. Hanson	349	Right Waist Gunner
Murray	S/Sgt. Mahlon A. Hall	349	Tail Gunner

230170 *The Pride of the Century* 349 XR G Wilson

Wilson	2Lt. Mark V. Wilson	349	Pilot
Wilson	2Lt. Charles E. Adams	349	Copilot
Wilson	2Lt. Ralph A. Kroenke	349	Bombardier
Wilson	2Lt. John T. Johntson	349	Navigator
Wilson	T/Sgt. John W. McAuliffe	349	Top Turret - Engineer
Wilson	T/Sgt. Eugene V. Sweeney	349	Radio Operator - Gunner
Wilson	S/Sgt. Donald M.Rohasek	349	Ball Turret Gunner
Wilson	Sgt. George B. Donahue	349	Left Waist Gunner
Wilson	Sgt. William E. Moreland	349	Right Waist Gunner
Wilson	Sgt. Cecil G. Davis	349	Tail Gunner

230487 *Torchy 3* 349 XR P Koper

Koper	Lt. Robert G. Koper	349	Pilot
Koper	Lt. Gordon C. Lien	349	Copilot
Koper	Lt. Thomas O. Drinkwater	349	Bombardier
Koper	2Lt. George H. Wing	349	Navigator
Koper	T/Sgt. Charles P. Corea	349	Top Turret - Engineer
Koper	S/Sgt. W. H. Rodkey	349	Radio Operator - Gunner
Koper	Sgt. Charles J. Luquette	349	Ball Turret Gunner
Koper	S/Sgt. Arthur Frankel	349	Left Waist Gunner
Koper	Sgt. Ralph V. Zarzecki	349	Right Waist Gunner
Koper	Sgt. Bernard Sundin	349	Tail Gunner

239872	***Rubber Check***	**350**	**LN A Granack**
Granack	Lt. Frank A. Granack	350	Pilot
Granack	Lt. Robert L. Dunham	350	Copilot
Granack	Lt. Joseph F. Kawiecki	350	Bombardier
Granack	Lt. Murray Geisler	350	Navigator
Granack	T/Sgt. Harold Stearns	350	Top Turret - Engineer
Granack	T/Sgt. Grant H. L. Scott	350	Radio Operator - Gunner
Granack	S/Sgt. Lloyd H. Rodgers Jr	350	Ball Turret Gunner
Granack	S/Sgt. Edwin T. Harrell	350	Left Waist Gunner
Granack	S/Sgt. Glenn D. Brown	350	Right Waist Gunner
Granack	S/Sgt. George C. Christian	350	Tail Gunner

238059		**418**	**LD A Thomas**
Thomas	2Lt. William H. Thomas	418	Pilot
Thomas	2Lt. John J. Raring	418	Copilot
Thomas	2Lt. Louis Brownstein	418	Bombardier
Thomas	2Lt. Herbert J. Brice	418	Navigator
Thomas	T/Sgt. Clifford E. Akin	418	Top Turret – Engineer
Thomas	S/Sgt. Charles A. Leavitt	418	Radio Operator – Gunner
Thomas	S/Sgt. Willard W. Moore	418	Ball Turret Gunner
Thomas	Sgt. John D. Smoot	418	Left Waist Gunner
Thomas	S/Sgt. Daniel S. McGill	418	Right Waist Gunner
Thomas	S/Sgt. Edward A. Vollmer	418	Tail Gunner

100 B Group

Lead Squadron

	Lauro-Kiessling 231306 LD V	
Harper 231800 LD U		**Terry** 297482 LD W
	Gummersall 231895 LD Y	
Ferbrache 297491 LD B		**Barrick** 239994 LD D

Low Squadron

	Rosenthal 231504 LD Q	
Kendall 230091 LD S		**Barton** 2300061 LD T
	Forsythe 238175 LD Q	
Lacy 231389 EP J		**Brannan** 231735 EP B

High Squadron

	Love 231066 EP H	
Handorf 237936 EP M		**Helmick** 231256 EP S
	Keel 240056 EP F	
Massol 238047 EP O		**Shoens** 231767 EP E
	Chapman 239983 EP F	
Mylius 232018 LN L		**Rish** 238044 EP R

100 B Lead Squadron

231306 *Nelson King* **418 LD V** **Lauro / Kiessling**

Lauro-Kiessling	Captain Frank Lauro	418	Pilot
Lauro-Kiessling	Captain Ernest A. Kiessling	418	Command Pilot
Lauro-Kiessling	Lt. Walter Green	418	Bombardier
Lauro-Kiessling	Lt. Emory Horvath	418	Navigator
Lauro-Kiessling	T/Sgt. Dewey Thompson	418	Top Turret - Engineer
Lauro-Kiessling	S/Sgt. Harry H. Greenfield	418	Radio Operator
Lauro-Kiessling	S/Sgt Arthur R. Tirrell	418	Radio Gunner
Lauro-Kiessling	S/Sgt. Murray Schrier	418	Ball Turret Gunner
Lauro-Kiessling	S/Sgt. Gerald J. Will	418	Left Waist Gunner
Lauro-Kiessling	S/Sgt. William R. Heathman	418	Right Waist Gunner
Lauro-Kiessling	Lt Emanuel E. Greasmare	418	Formation Control Officer

297482 *Terry and the Pirates* **418 LD W** **Terry**

Terry	Lt. William A. Terry	418	Pilot
Terry	Lt. William L. Peterson	418	Copilot
Terry	Lt. Ralph G. Cotter	418	Bombardier
Terry	Lt. Robert P. Schremser	418	Navigator
Terry	T/Sgt. James P. Aitken	418	Top Turret - Engineer
Terry	T/Sgt. Richard P. Howell	418	Radio Operator - Gunner
Terry	S/Sgt. James A. Bain	418	Ball Turret Gunner
Terry	S/Sgt. Charles C. Anthony	418	Left Waist Gunner
Terry	S/Sgt. John R. Horn	418	Right Waist Gunner
Terry	S/Sgt. Carl D. Hampton	418	Tail Gunner

231800 **418 LD U** **Harper**

Harper, J	2Lt. James C. Harper	418	Pilot
Harper, J	2Lt. Tony L. Hulsey	418	Copilot
Harper, J	2Lt. William A. Naegele	418	Bombardier
Harper, J	2Lt. Charlie C. Cowing	418	Navigator
Harper, J	T/Sgt Wallace S. Carter	418	Top Turret – Engineer
Harper, J	T/Sgt Robert E. Hudson	418	Radio Operator - Gunner
Harper, J	S/Sgt Joseph B. Kyrc	418	Ball Turret Gunner
Harper, J	S/Sgt Kenneth C. Helming	418	Left Waist Gunner
Harper, J	S/Sgt Frederick A. Padstawski	418	Right Waist Gunner
Harper, J	S/Sgt John L. Mauk	418	Tail Gunner

231895 ***Miss Chief*** **418 LD Y Gummersall**

Gummersall	2Lt. Mark G. Gummersall	418	Pilot
Gummersall	2Lt. Reginald C. Holliday	418	Copilot
Gummersall	2Lt. Edward P. Carr	418	Bombardier
Gummersall	2Lt. Frank W. Roberts Jr	418	Navigator
Gummersall	S/Sgt. John R. Gensel	418	Top Turret - Engineer
Gummersall	S/Sgt. Henry W. Bieze	418	Radio Operator - Gunner
Gummersall	Sgt. Matthew H. Boguminski	418	Ball Turret Gunner
Gummersall	Sgt. James J. Daly	418	Left Waist Gunner
Gummersall	Sgt. James T. Penny	418	Right Waist Gunner
Gummersall	Sgt. Robert L. Braswell	418	Tail Gunner

239994 ***Snort Stuff*** **418 LD D Barrick**

Barrick	Lt. Samuel L. Barrick	418	Pilot
Barrick	Lt. Ira A. Munn	418	Copilot
Barrick	Lt. James M. Henry	418	Bombardier
Barrick	Lt. James G. Guerrini	418	Navigator
Barrick	T/Sgt. Walfred J. Johnson	418	Top Turret - Engineer
Barrick	S/Sgt. Clifford E. Barton	418	Radio Operator - Gunner
Barrick	S/Sgt. Edward J. Marlen	418	Ball Turret Gunner
Barrick	S/Sgt. Frederick C. Thorpe	418	Left Waist Gunner
Barrick	S/Sgt. William D. Sapp	418	Right Waist Gunner
Barrick	S/Sgt Hugh F. Fantone Jr	418	Tail Gunner

297491 ***Ronnie R*** **418 LD B Ferbrache**

Ferbrache	Lt. Elmer E. Ferbrache	418	Pilot
Ferbrache	Lt. Anthony D. Slatinsky	418	Copilot
Ferbrache	Lt. David N. Hegge	418	Bombardier
Ferbrache	Lt. Burton S. Hufsey	418	Navigator
Ferbrache	S/Sgt. Harold H. Patterson	418	Top Turret - Engineer
Ferbrache	Sgt. John P. Lucarelli	418	Radio Operator - Gunner
Ferbrache	Sgt. William T. Behr	418	Ball Turret Gunner
Ferbrache	Sgt. Benjamin J. Devine	418	Left Waist Gunner
Ferbrache	Sgt. Clifford H. Leming	418	Right Waist Gunner
Ferbrache	Sgt Howard O. Williams	418	Tail Gunner

100 B High Squadron

231066 ***Fools Rush In*** **351 EP H Love**

Love	Captain John Love	351	Pilot	
Love	2Lt Jonah Goodbread	351	Copilot	
Love	2Lt Frank C. Gregory	351	Bombardier	
Love	2Lt Thomas R. Kizak	351	Navigator	
Love	T/Sgt Curtis W. Rockhill	351	Top Turret – Engineer	
Love	T/Sgt Callen F. MacKenzie	351	Radio Operator - Gunner	
Love	S/Sgt Louis G. Black	351	Ball Turret Gunner	Vallesh Crew
Love	S/Sgt George M. Conrad	351	Left Waist Gunner	
Love	S/Sgt Seth L. Burklund	351	Right Waist Gunner	
Love	S/Sgt Roger Kirkpatrick	351	Tail Gunner	

231256 ***King Bee II*** **351 EP S Helmick**

Helmick	2ndLt. Richard Helmick	351	Pilot	
Helmick	2ndLt. Jerome F. Leirich	351	Copilot	
Helmick	S/Sgt Chester P. Coulam	351	Toggler	
Helmick	2ndLt. Sol S. Kranzler	351	Navigator	
Helmick	T/Sgt. George E. Madden	351	Top Turret – Engineer	
Helmick	T/Sgt. Joseph G. Kelly	351	Radio Operator - Gunner	
Helmick	S/Sgt. Robert M. Myers	351	Ball Turret Gunner	
Helmick	S/Sgt. Robert L. McKimmy	351	Left Waist Gunner	Hughes Crew
Helmick	S/Sgt Henry W. Johnson	351	Right Waist Gunner	
Helmick	S/Sgt Michael Rotz	351	Tail Gunner	

237936 ***Our Mark*** **351 EP M** **Handorf**

Handorf	Lt. Edward Handorf	351	Pilot	
Handorf	2Lt. Frederick G. Spence	351	Copilot	
Handorf	Lt. Norman L. Rasmussen	351	Bombardier	
Handorf	Lt. John W. Dewey	351	Navigator	
Handorf	T/Sgt. Charles H. Ford	351	Top Turret - Engineer	
Handorf	T/Sgt. Henry C. Verdeur Jr	351	Radio Operator - Gunner	
Handorf	S/Sgt. Allen D. Horton	351	Ball Turret Gunner	
Handorf	S/Sgt. John J Gverovich	351	Left Waist Gunner	
Handorf	S/Sgt John L. Willsey	351	Right Waist Gunner	
Handorf	S/Sgt Fair C. Lawrence	351	Tail Gunner	
240056	***Holy Terror III / Katie's Boys***	**351 EP F**	**Keel**	
Keel	Captain Howard E. Keel	351	Pilot	
Keel	2Lt. Robert K.Edgley	351	Copilot	
Keel	T/Sgt. Dorsett. C. Bennett	351	Toggler	
Keel	Lt. Frederick D. Fuller	351	Navigator	
Keel	T/Sgt. George L. Ferron	351	Top Turret – Engineer	
Keel	T/Sgt. Thomas P. Hastings	351	Radio Operator – Gunner	
Keel	S/Sgt. Charlie L.Anglin	351	Ball Turret Gunner	
Keel	S/Sgt.Loren G. Johnson	351	Left Waist Gunner	
Keel	S/Sgt. Andrew J.Guglieri	351	Right Waist Gunner	
Keel	S/Sgt. Robert D.Abney	351	Tail Gunner	
231767	***Our Gal Sal***	**351 EP E**	**Shoens**	
Shoens	Lt. Robert J. Shoens	351	Pilot	
Shoens	Lt. Duncan R. Shand	351	Copilot	
Shoens	Lt Glenn Hudson	351	Bombardier	
Shoens	Lt. Herbert R. Greenberg	351	Navigator	
Shoens	T/Sgt. William Eresman	351	Top Turret - Engineer	
Shoens	T/Sgt. Donald B. Hammond	351	Radio Operator - Gunner	
Shoens	S/Sgt. Edward Silverstone	351	Ball Turret Gunner	
Shoens	S/Sgt. William W. Wright	351	Left Waist Gunner	
Shoens	S/Sgt. Virgil H. Warders	351	Right Waist Gunner	
Shoens	S/Sgt. Don L. Blair	351	Tail Gunner	
238047	***Feaver Beaver***	**351 EP O**	**Massol**	
Massol	Lt. John F. Massol	351	Pilot	
Massol	2Lt. Harold D. Granger	351	Copilot	
Massol	2. Edwin A. Stern Jr	351	Bombardier	
Massol	2Lt. Edward C. King Jr	351	Navigator	
Massol	T/Sgt. Sidney A. Cary	351	Top Turret – Engineer	TBC
Massol	T/Sgt. Earl L. Symes	351	Top Turret - Engineer	TBC
Massol	T/Sgt. Asa A. Spengler	351	Radio Operator - Gunner	
Massol	S/Sgt. Winfred C. Williams	351	Ball Turret Gunner	
Massol	S/Sgt. William L. Reneau	351	Left Waist Gunner	
Massol	S/Sgt. Oliver N. McCartney	351	Right Waist Gunner	
Massol	S/Sgt. Newman E. Garmon	351	Tail Gunner	
239983	***Katie***	**351 EP F**	**Chapman**	
Chapman	2Lt. Norman L. Chapman	351	Pilot	
Chapman	2Lt. Rex M. Ellis	351	Copilot	
Chapman	2Lt. Wilson D. Clark	351	Bombardier	
Chapman	2Lt. Glenn G. Lindom	351	Navigator	
Chapman	S/Sgt. George W. Silvermann	351	Top Turret – Engineer	
Chapman	S/Sgt. Milton Scharf	351	Radio Operator – Gunner	
Chapman	Sgt. Durward E. Hutchings	351	Ball Turret Gunner	
Chapman	Sgt. Leon E. Hill	351	Left Waist Gunner	
Chapman	S/Sgt Frank A. Yzenas	351	Right Waist Gunner	
Chapman	S/Sgt George E. Dobbs	351	Tail Gunner	

238044 *Spirit of 44* 351 EP R Rish

Rish	Lt. Merril T. Rish	351	Pilot	
Rish	2Lt. Frank A. Smith	351	Copilot	
Rish	2Lt. Donald K. Kehm	351	Bombardier	
Rish	2Lt. Royal W. Lingehfelter	351	Navigator	
Rish	T/Sgt. Howard T. Skaggs Jr	351	Top Turret – Engineer	
Rish	T/Sgt. George F. Danehower	351	Radio Operator - Gunner	
Rish	Sgt. Dewey Essary	351	Ball Turret Gunner	Spare Gunner Pool
Rish	S/Sgt. Estil V. McGuffee	351	Left Waist Gunner	
Rish	Sgt. Armand C. Burt	351	Right Waist Gunner	
Rish	Sgt. Angus Alsup	351	Tail Gunner	

232018 *Waticare* 351 EP L Mylius

Mylius	2Lt Charles W. Mylius Jr	351	Pilot
Mylius	2Lt. Warren G. McCoy	351	Copilot
Mylius	2Lt Norman T. High	351	Bombardier
Mylius	2Lt Charles J. Galligan	351	Navigator
Mylius	S/Sgt James R. Russel	351	Top Turret - Engineer
Mylius	S/Sgt Vincent J. Wood	351	Radio Operator - Gunner
Mylius	Sgt Carleton E. Brown	351	Ball Turret Gunner
Mylius	Sgt William F. Hoffman Jr	351	Left Waist Gunner
Mylius	Sgt Charles E. McSpadden	351	Right Waist Gunner
Mylius	S/Sgt Herbert D. Fern	351	Tail Gunner

100 B Low Squadron

231504 *Rosie's Riveters* 418 LD E Rosenthal

Rosenthal	Capt. Robert *'Rosie'* Rosenthal	418	Pilot
Rosenthal	Lt Winifred *'Pappy'* Lewis	418	Copilot
Rosenthal	Lt Clifford Milburn	418	Bombardier
Rosenthal	Lt Ronald C. Bailey	418	Navigator
Rosenthal	T/Sgt Clarence C. Hall	418	Top Turret - Engineer
Rosenthal	T/Sgt Michael Boccuzzi	418	Radio Operator - Gunner
Rosenthal	Sgt Ray H. Robinson	418	Ball Turret Gunner
Rosenthal	S/Sgt Marion J. Sheldon	418	Left Waist Gunner
Rosenthal	S/Sgt James P. Mack	418	Right Waist Gunner
Rosenthal	S/Sgt William J. DeBlasio	418	Tail Gunner

230061 *Wolf Pack* 418 LD T Barton

Barton	Lt. Sherwin L. Barton	418	Pilot
Barton	Lt. George W. Davidson	418	Copilot
Barton	Lt. Bernard J. Smolens	418	Bombardier
Barton	Lt. John L. Burtch	418	Navigator
Barton	T/Sgt. Harvey A. Moore	418	Top Turret - Engineer
Barton	T/Sgt. Jack M. Robins	418	Radio Operator - Gunner
Barton	S/Sgt. Robert J. Taylor	418	Ball Turret Gunner
Barton	S/Sgt. Paul H. Morris	418	Left Waist Gunner
Barton	S/Sgt. Frank J. Foldy	418	Right Waist Gunner
Barton	S/Sgt James W. Powell	418	Tail Gunner

230091 *Blivit* 418 LD S Kendall

Kendall	Lt. Zeb Kendall	418	Pilot
Kendall	2Lt. Edwin J. Loughran	418	Copilot
Kendall	2Lt. Clifford L. Gowen	418	Bombardier
Kendall	2Lt. William R. Thorpe Jr	418	Navigator
Kendall	T/Sgt. Melvin A. Hickman	418	Top Turret - Engineer
Kendall	T/Sgt. Leman E. Tutor	418	Radio Operator - Gunner
Kendall	S/Sgt. Reginaldo Aguila	418	Ball Turret Gunner
Kendall	Sgt. Raymond L. Bridges	418	Left Waist Gunner
Kendall	S/Sgt. Matthew G. Aven Jr	418	Right Waist Gunner
Kendall	S/Sgt. Victor Stoffregen	418	Tail Gunner

238175		**418 LD X**	**Forsythe**
Forsythe	2Lt. Wallace C. Forsythe	418	Pilot
Forsythe	2Lt. Prescott H. Haralson	418	Copilot
Forsythe	2Lt. Robert W. McAtee	418	Bombardier
Forsythe	2Lt. Augustus H. Paine	418	Navigator
Forsythe	S/Sgt. Percy J. Johnston	418	Top Turret - Engineer
Forsythe	S/Sgt. Peter J. Buck	418	Radio Operator - Gunner
Forsythe	Sgt. Peter VanSlyck	418	Ball Turret Gunner
Forsythe	Sgt. Nelson C. Linke	418	Left Waist Gunner
Forsythe	Sgt. John A. Codoluto	418	Right Waist Gunner
Forsythe	Sgt. Richard D. Schad	418	Tail Gunner
231735	***Lucky Lee***	**351 EP B**	**Brannan**
Brannan	Lt. George W. Brannan	351	Pilot
Brannan	Lt. Thomas R. Leslie	351	Copilot
Brannan	Lt. Louis J. Denisco	351	Bombardier
Brannan	Lt. Clyde F. Dale	351	Navigator
Brannan	T/Sgt. Walter S. Austin	351	Top Turret - Engineer
Brannan	T/Sgt. William F. Teaff	351	Radio Operator - Gunner
Brannan	S/Sgt. Robyn P. Fulton	351	Ball Turret Gunner
Brannan	S/Sgt. Charles F. Elliott	351	Left Waist Gunner
Brannan	S/Sgt. D. J. Maddra Jr	351	Right Waist Gunner
Brannan	S/Sgt Robert L. Greenleaf	351	Tail Gunner
231389	***Luscious Lucy***	**351 EP J**	**Lacy**
Lacy	Lt. Lucius G. Lacy	351	Pilot
Lacy	2Lt. Claude E. Schindler	351	Copilot
Lacy	T/Sgt. George N. Ofiesh	351	Bombardier
Lacy	2Lt. Albert Franklin	351	Navigator
Lacy	T/Sgt. Chester J. Carknard	351	Top Turret - Engineer
Lacy	T/Sgt. Clarence H. Wood Jr	351	Radio Operator - Gunner
Lacy	S/Sgt. S. M. Szekely	351	Ball Turret Gunner
Lacy	S/Sgt. Raymond J. Mitchell	351	Left Waist Gunner
Lacy	S/Sgt. Joe S. Folson	351	Right Waist Gunner
Lacy	S/Sgt. Joseph A. Howell	351	Tail Gunner

March 4, 1944, Berlin

100 A Group[42]

Lead Squadron

	Devore-Fuller 239934 LN Z	
Chadwick 23413 LN V		**Granack** 239872 LN A
	Lautenschlager 238197 LN T	
Pearson 232009 LN X		**Harper** 231537 LN S

Low Squadron

	Harrison 230152 LD X	
Morgan 25957 XR D		**Murray** 231731 XR M
	Cowan 231723 XR R	
Koper 230170 XR G		**Montgomery** 231249 XR L

High Squadron

	Cope 231968 LN D	
Malooly 231049 LN U		**Gibbons** 239830 LN Y
	Seaton 238016 LN B	
Handorf 231066 EP H		**Wilson** 23534 XR N
	Lacy 231389 EP J	

Over Target

Lead Squadron

	Devore - Fuller 239934 LN Z	
Chadwick 23413 LN V		**Granack** 239872 LN A
	Lautenschlager 238197 LN T	
Pearson 232009 LN X		**Wilson** 23534 XR N

Low Squadron

	Barrick 239994 LD D	

High Squadron

	Cope 231968 LN D	
Malooly 231049 LN O		**Gibbons** 239830 LN Y
	Seaton 238016 LN B	
		Montgomery 231249 XR L

100 A Lead Squadron

239934 ***My Achin' Back*** **350 LN Z** **Devore-Fuller**

Devore/Fuller	Lt. Herbert G. Devore	350	Pilot
Devore/Fuller	Captain Magee C. Fuller	349	Command Pilot
Devore/Fuller	Lt. Louis R. Jaebker	350	Bombardier
Devore/Fuller	Lt. Burton M. Joseph	350	Navigator
Devore/Fuller	T/Sgt. Harrison L. Longhi	350	Top Turret - Engineer
Devore/Fuller	T/Sgt. Harry S. Lenk	350	Radio Operator
Devore/Fuller	S/Sgt Knute Knudson	350	Radio Gunner
Devore/Fuller	S/Sgt. Nicholas Delcimmuto	350	Ball Turret Gunner
Devore/Fuller	S/Sgt. Darrell R. Dickenson	350	Left Waist Gunner
Devore/Fuller	S/Sgt. John J. Barry	350	Right Waist Gunner
Devore/Fuller	Lt. Jerry Felsenstein	350	Formation Control Officer

239872 ***Rubber Check*** **350 LN A** **Granack**

Granack	Lt. Frank A. Granack	350	Pilot
Granack	Lt. Robert L. Dunham	350	Copilot
Granack	Lt. Joseph F. Kawiecki	350	Bombardier
Granack	Lt. Murray Geisler	350	Navigator
Granack	T/Sgt. Harold Stearns	350	Top Turret – Engineer
Granack	T/Sgt. Grant H.L. Scott	350	Radio Operator – Gunner
Granack	S/Sgt. Lloyd H. Rodgers Jr	350	Ball Turret Gunner
Granack	S/Sgt. Edwin T. Harrell	350	Left Waist Gunner
Granack	S/Sgt. Glenn D. Brown	350	Right Waist Gunner
Granack	S/Sgt. George C. Christian	350	Tail Gunner

23413 ***Hard Luck*** **350 LN V** **Chadwick**

Chadwick	2Lt. Randall T. Chadwick	350	Pilot	
Chadwick	2Lt. Robert R. Kroske	350	Copilot	Gough Crew
Chadwick	2Lt. Joseph A. Carty	350	Bombardier	
Chadwick	2Lt. Jack E. Longenecker	350	Navigator	
Chadwick	S/Sgt. Edwin E. Postel	350	Top Turret - Engineer	
Chadwick	S/Sgt. John J. Good	350	Radio Operator - Gunner	
Chadwick	Sgt. George A. Benedict	350	Ball Turret Gunner	
Chadwick	Sgt. Delbert J.H. Burns	350	Left Waist Gunner	
Chadwick	Sgt. Austin B. Roberts	350	Right Waist Gunner	
Chadwick	Sgt Philip K. Troetschel	350	Tail Gunner	

238197 ***Half and Half*** **350 LN T** **Lautenschlager**

Lautenschlager	Lt. John Lautenschlager	350	Pilot
Lautenschlager	Lt. William J. Sugg	350	Copilot
Lautenschlager	Lt. David Rolnick	350	Bombardier
Lautenschlager	Lt. Leland C. Fink	350	Navigator
Lautenschlager	S/Sgt. Robert T. Bashaw	350	Top Turret - Engineer
Lautenschlager	S/Sgt. John Stryjeski	350	Radio Operator - Gunner
Lautenschlager	Sgt. Harold L. Sheldon	350	Ball Turret Gunner
Lautenschlager	S/Sgt. John H. White	350	Left Waist Gunner
Lautenschlager	S/Sgt. Samuel Wilenski	350	Right Waist Gunner
Lautenschlager	Sgt. Hogan Fussell Jr	350	Tail Gunner

231537 ***Buffalo Gal*** **349 LN S** **C.B. '*Red*' Harper**

Harper, CB	2Lt. Celesta B. '*Red*' Harper	350	Pilot
Harper, CB	2Lt. Robert S. Flannigan	350	Copilot
Harper, CB	2Lt. Arthur E. Cox	350	Bombardier
Harper, CB	2Lt. Charles T. Hardiman	350	Navigator
Harper, CB	T/Sgt. Clarence P. Luquet	350	Top Turret - Engineer
Harper, CB	T/Sgt. Alvin E. James	350	Radio Operator - Gunner
Harper, CB	Sgt. Austin P. Curlee	350	Ball Turret Gunner
Harper, CB	Sgt. John B. Bowers	350	Left Waist Gunner
Harper, CB	Sgt. Wiley A. Dobbs	350	Right Waist Gunner
Harper, CB	Sgt. Anderson R. Frank Jr	350	Tail Gunner

232009 ***Black Cat 13*** **350 LN X** **Pearson**

Pearson	2Lt. Delbert S. Pearson	350	Pilot	
Pearson	2Lt. Wilbert D. Lund	350	Copilot	
Pearson	Lt. Lester N. Smith	350	Bombardier	
Pearson	Lt. Maurice H. Cain	350	Navigator	Gibbons Crew
Pearson	T/Sgt. Ernest J. Rene	350	Top Turret - Engineer	
Pearson	T/Sgt. Nunziato Sansevero	350	Radio Operator - Gunner	
Pearson	S/Sgt. Francis X. Kerin	350	Ball Turret Gunner	
Pearson	S/Sgt. Harold J. Scrivener	350	Left Waist Gunner	
Pearson	S/Sgt. Bradford F. Truesdell	350	Right Waist Gunner	
Pearson	S/Sgt. George P. Zigo	350	Tail Gunner	

100 A High Squadron

231968 ***Miss Irish*** **350 LN D** **Cope**

Cope	Captain Mark Cope	350	Pilot
Cope	Lt. Martin Tashjian	350	Copilot
Cope	Lt. Herbert G. Pryor	350	Bombardier
Cope	Lt. Festus E. *'Shorty'* Bryant	350	Navigator
Cope	Sgt. John Verbovski	350	Top Turret - Engineer
Cope	Sgt. John C. Eling	350	Radio Operator - Gunner
Cope	Sgt. Richard E. Donnelly	350	Ball Turret Gunner
Cope	S/Sgt. James E. Morrison	350	Left Waist Gunner
Cope	S/Sgt. Donald E. Walker	350	Right Waist Gunner
Cope	S/Sgt Raymond Bryan	350	Tail Gunner

239830 ***Berlin Playboy*** **350 LN Y** **Gibbons**

Gibbons	2Lt. John P. Gibbons	350	Pilot
Gibbons	2Lt. Robert Dykeman	350	Copilot
Gibbons	2Lt. Sterling B. Blakeman	350	Bombardier
Gibbons	2Lt. Everett M. Johnson	350	Navigator
Gibbons	T/Sgt. Ira L. Arnold	350	Top Turret - Engineer
Gibbons	T/Sgt. Edward Walker Jr	350	Radio Operator - Gunner
Gibbons	Sgt. Bernard L. Spragg	350	Ball Turret Gunner
Gibbons	Sgt. Frank W. Buschmeier	350	Left Waist Gunner
Gibbons	Sgt. Myron J. Ettus	350	Right Waist Gunner
Gibbons	Sgt. Archie W. Bunting	350	Tail Gunner

231049 ***Superstitious Aloysious*** **350 LN U** **Malooly**

Malooly	2Lt. Francis J. Malooly	350	Pilot
Malooly	2Lt. Robert W. Bailie	350	Copilot
Malooly	2Lt. Ralph W. Guida	350	Bombardier
Malooly	2Lt. Charles H. Mauvais	350	Navigator
Malooly	T/Sgt. Arthur J. Perry	350	Top Turret - Engineer
Malooly	T/Sgt. Robert C. Barrie	350	Radio Operator - Gunner
Malooly	Sgt. Nelson A.S. Pardee	350	Ball Turret Gunner
Malooly	Sgt. Leonard W. Yeager	350	Left Waist Gunner
Malooly	Sgt. Willard H. Miller	350	Right Waist Gunner
Malooly	Sgt. Lorenzo Genovese	350	Tail Gunner

238016 ***Seaton's Sad Sack*** **350 LN B** **Seaton**

Seaton	Lt. Stanley M. Seaton	350	Pilot	POW
Seaton	2Lt. William F. Clayton	350	Copilot	POW
Seaton	T/Sgt. George N. Ofiesh	350	Bombardier	POW
Seaton	2Lt. Charles F. DeWolfe Jr	350	Navigator	POW
Seaton	T/Sgt. Peter A. Hogan	350	Top Turret - Engineer	POW
Seaton	T/Sgt. Joseph A. Judd	350	Radio Operator - Gunner	POW
Seaton	S/Sgt. Robert H. Cook	350	Ball Turret Gunner	POW
Seaton	S/Sgt. Loydell Malone	350	Left Waist Gunner	POW
Seaton	S/Sgt. Arthur J. Labreque	350	Right Waist Gunner	POW
Seaton	S/Sgt Leming Hull	350	Tail Gunner	KIA

23534	***Ol' Dad***	**349 XR N**	**Wilson**	
Wilson	2Lt. Mark V. Wilson	349	Pilot	
Wilson	2Lt. Charles E. Adams	349	Copilot	
Wilson	2Lt. Ralph A. Kroenke	349	Bombardier	
Wilson	2Lt. John T. Johnston	349	Navigator	
Wilson	T/Sgt. John W. McAuliffe	349	Top Turret - Engineer	
Wilson	T/Sgt. Eugene V. Sweeney	349	Radio Operator - Gunner	
Wilson	S/Sgt. Charlie J. Hopkins	349	Ball Turret Gunner	Raring Crew
Wilson	Sgt. George B. Donahue	349	Left Waist Gunner	
Wilson	Sgt. William E. Moreland	349	Right Waist Gunner	
Wilson	Sgt. Cecil G. Davis	349	Tail Gunner	

231066	***Fools Rush In***	**351 EP H**	**Handorf**	
Handorf	Lt. Edward Handorf	351	Pilot	
Handorf	2Lt. Frederick G. Spence	351	Copilot	
Handorf	Lt. Norman L. Rasmussen	351	Bombardier	
Handorf	Lt. John W. Dewey	351	Navigator	
Handorf	T/Sgt. Charles H. Ford	351	Top Turret - Engineer	
Handorf	T/Sgt. Henry C. Verdeur Jr	351	Radio Operator - Gunner	
Handorf	S/Sgt. Allen D. Horton	351	Ball Turret Gunner	
Handorf	S/Sgt. John J. Gverovich	351	Left Waist Gunner	
Handorf	S/Sgt John L. Willsey	351	Right Waist Gunner	
Handorf	S/Sgt Fair C. Lawrence	351	Tail Gunner	

231389	***Luscious Lucy***	**351 EP J**	**Lacy**	
Lacy	Lt. Lucius G. Lacy	351	Pilot	
Lacy	2Lt. Claude E. Schindler	351	Copilot	
Lacy	2Lt. Frank C. Gregory	351	Bombardier	
Lacy	2Lt. Albert Franklin	351	Navigator	
Lacy	T/Sgt. Chester J. Carknard	351	Top Turret - Engineer	
Lacy	T/Sgt. Clarence H. Wood Jr	351	Radio Operator - Gunner	
Lacy	S/Sgt. C. L. Powell	351	Ball Turret Gunner	Rish Crew
Lacy	S/Sgt. Raymond J. Mitchell	351	Left Waist Gunner	
Lacy	S/Sgt. Joe S. Folson	351	Right Waist Gunner	
Lacy	S/Sgt. Joseph A. Howell	351	Tail Gunner	

100 A Low Squadron

230152	***Messie Bessie***	**418 LD X**	**Harrison**	
Harrison	Lt. John A. Harrison	349	Pilot	
Harrison	2Lt. Charles S. Stapleton	349	Copilot	
Harrison	2Lt. George R. Morgan	349	Bombardier	Mason Crew
Harrison	2Lt. Anthony J. Busalacchi	349	Navigator	
Harrison	T/Sgt. Anthony J. Beechey	349	Top Turret – Engineer	
Harrison	T/Sgt. Neil J. Coyle	349	Radio Operator - Gunner	
Harrison	Sgt. Luke E. Nachatilo	349	Ball Turret Gunner	
Harrison	Sgt. Glover Nall	349	Left Waist Gunner	
Harrison	Sgt. Lawrence A. Robbins	349	Right Waist Gunner	
Harrison	S/Sgt Bruce E. *Curly* Alshouse	349	Tail Gunner	

231731		**349 XR M**	**Murray**	
Murray	Lt. William B. Murray	349	Pilot	
Murray	Lt. Richard M. Lambiotte	349	Copilot	
Murray	2nd William G. Carr	349	Bombardier	
Murray	2Lt. Orrin H. Heinrich	349	Navigator	
Murray	T/Sgt. Emory L. Brandt	349	Top Turret - Engineer	
Murray	T/Sgt. Fred C. Schillinger	349	Radio Operator - Gunner	
Murray	S/Sgt. Jim Peace	349	Ball Turret Gunner	
Murray	Sgt. Nick E. Hamalack	349	Left Waist Gunner	
Murray	S/Sgt. Palmer J. Hanson	349	Right Waist Gunner	
Murray	S/Sgt. Mahlon A. Hall	349	Tail Gunner	

25957	***Horny***	**349 XR D**	**Morgan**
Morgan	Lt. Leon R. Morgan	349	Pilot
Morgan	2Lt. Ralph O. Ward	349	Copilot
Morgan	S/Sgt. Sam J. LaFace	349	Toggler
Morgan	2Lt. Robert E. McCormick	349	Navigator
Morgan	T/Sgt. Maynard L. Lobb	349	Top Turret - Engineer
Morgan	T/Sgt. Tony L. Verdusco	349	Radio Operator - Gunner
Morgan	S/Sgt. David C. Lyon Jr	349	Ball Turret Gunner
Morgan	S/Sgt. Kenneth R. Lash Jr	349	Left Waist Gunner
Morgan	S/Sgt. Hugo C. Kleckner	349	Right Waist Gunner
Morgan	S/Sgt. Ernest R. Gomez	349	Tail Gunner

231723	***"Sparky"***	**349 XR R**	**Cowan**
Cowan	Lt. Clement H. Cowan	349	Pilot
Cowan	Lt. Hank A. Dibbern	349	Copilot
Cowan	Lt. Harold L. Heyneman	349	Bombardier
Cowan	Lt. Fred W. Robertson	349	Navigator
Cowan	T/Sgt. Murray W. Holditch	349	Top Turret - Engineer
Cowan	T/Sgt. John P. Cooper	349	Radio Operator - Gunner
Cowan	S/Sgt. William A. Geigle	349	Ball Turret Gunner
Cowan	S/Sgt. Adam C. Stoppel	349	Left Waist Gunner
Cowan	S/Sgt. Robert Patrick	349	Right Waist Gunner
Cowan	S/Sgt Horace R. Kemble	349	Tail Gunner

231249	***Miss Carriage***	**349 XR L**	**Montgomery**	
Montgomery	2Lt. Coy I. Montgomery	349	Pilot	
Montgomery	2Lt. Robert F. Connaway	349	Copilot	
Montgomery	2Lt. James W. Fulton	349	Bombardier	
Montgomery	2Lt. Frank C. Laver	349	Navigator	
Montgomery	T/Sgt. George W. Burton	349	Top Turret - Engineer	
Montgomery	T/Sgt. Wilbur I. Trembley Jr	349	Radio Operator - Gunner	Stout Crew
Montgomery	S/Sgt. Louis P. Savell	349	Ball Turret Gunner	
Montgomery	S/Sgt. Junior L. Bucher	349	Left Waist Gunner	
Montgomery	Sgt. Anthony E. Ruda	349	Right Waist Gunner	Spare Gunner Pool
Montgomery	S/Sgt. Earl W. Ritter	349	Tail Gunner	

230170	***The Pride of the Century***	**349 XR G**	**Koper**
Koper	Lt. Robert G. Koper	349	Pilot
Koper	Lt. Gordon C. Lien	349	Copilot
Koper	Lt. Thomas O. Drinkwater	349	Bombardier
Koper	2Lt. George H. Wing	349	Navigator
Koper	T/Sgt. Charles P. Corea	349	Top Turret - Engineer
Koper	S/Sgt. Michael J. Tanowigch	349	Radio Operator - Gunner
Koper	Sgt. Charles J. Luquette	349	Ball Turret Gunner
Koper	S/Sgt. Arthur Frankel	349	Left Waist Gunner
Koper	Sgt. Ralph V. Zarzecki	349	Right Waist Gunner
Koper	Sgt. Bernard Sundin	349	Tail Gunner

100 B Group

100 B Lead Squadron

231708 ***Skipper II*** **351 EP N** **Hughes-Janssen**

Hughes/Janssen	Captain Robert L. Hughes	351	Command Pilot
Hughes/Janssen	2Lt. Carl A. Janssen	351	Pilot
Hughes/Janssen	2Lt James N. Cathey	351	Bombardier
Hughes/Janssen	2Lt Frederick D. Fuller	351	Navigator
Hughes/Janssen	T/Sgt Earl L. Symes	351	Top Turret – Engineer
Hughes/Janssen	T/Sgt Sidney Graboyes	351	Radio Operator
Hughes/Janssen	S/Sgt Walter E. Fisher	351	Radio Gunner
Hughes/Janssen	S/Sgt Louis G. Black	351	Ball Turret Gunner
Hughes/Janssen	S/Sgt Ronald E. Smeall	351	Left Waist Gunner
Hughes/Janssen	S/Sgt Vernon T. McNabb	351	Right Waist Gunner
Hughes/Janssen	2Lt. Earl R. Williams	351	Formation Control Officer

Valesh Crew

231767 ***Our Gal Sal*** **351 EP E** **Shoens**

Shoens	Lt. Robert J. Shoens	351	Pilot
Shoens	Lt. Duncan R. Shand	351	Copilot
Shoens	Lt. Glenn Hudson	351	Bombardier / Navigator
Shoens	T/Sgt. William Eresman	351	Top Turret - Engineer
Shoens	T/Sgt. Donald B. Hammond	351	Radio Operator - Gunner
Shoens	S/Sgt. Edward Silverstone	351	Ball Turret Gunner
Shoens	S/Sgt. William W. Wright	351	Left Waist Gunner
Shoens	S/Sgt. Virgil H. Warders	351	Right Waist Gunner
Shoens	S/Sgt. Don L. Blair	351	Tail Gunner

238044 ***Spirit of 44*** **351 EP R** **Rish**

Rish	Lt. Merril T. Rish	351	Pilot
Rish	2Lt. Frank A. Smith	351	Copilot
Rish	2Lt. Donald K. Kehm	351	Bombardier
Rish	2Lt. Royal W. Lingenfelter	351	Navigator
Rish	T/Sgt. Howard T. Skaggs Jr	351	Top Turret - Engineer
Rish	T/Sgt. George F. Danehower	351	Radio Operator - Gunner
Rish	Sgt. Dewey Essary	351	Ball Turret Gunner
Rish	S/Sgt. Estil V. McGuffee	351	Left Waist Gunner
Rish	Sgt. Armand C. Burt	351	Right Waist Gunner
Rish	Sgt. Angus Alsup	351	Tail Gunner

237936 *Our Mark* 351 EP M Chapman

Chapman	2Lt. Norman L. Chapman	351	Pilot
Chapman	2Lt. Rex M. Ellis	351	Copilot
Chapman	2Lt. Wilson D. Clark	351	Bombardier
Chapman	2Lt. Glenn G. Lindom	351	Navigator
Chapman	S/Sgt. George W. Silvermann	351	Top Turret - Engineer
Chapman	S/Sgt. Milton Scharf	351	Radio Operator - Gunner
Chapman	Sgt. Durward E. Hutchings	351	Ball Turret Gunner
Chapman	Sgt. Leon E. Hill	351	Left Waist Gunner
Chapman	S/Sgt Frank A. Yzenas	351	Right Waist Gunner
Chapman	S/Sgt George E. Dobbs	351	Tail Gunner

231256 *King Bee II* 351 EP S Helmick

Helmick	2Lt. Richard Helmick	351	Pilot
Helmick	2Lt. Jerome F. Leirich	351	Copilot
Helmick	S/Sgt Chester P. Coulam	351	Toggler
Helmick	2Lt. Sol S. Kranzler	351	Navigator
Helmick	T/Sgt. George E. Madden	351	Top Turret - Engineer
Helmick	T/Sgt. Joseph G. Kelly	351	Radio Operator - Gunner
Helmick	S/Sgt. Robert M. Myers	351	Ball Turret Gunner
Helmick	S/Sgt. Robert L. McKimmy	351	Left Waist Gunner
Helmick	S/Sgt. Loren G. Johnson	351	Right Waist Gunner
Helmick	S/Sgt. Michael Rotz	351	Tail Gunner

238047 *Feaver Beaver* 351 EP O Massol

Massol	Lt. John F. Massol	351	Pilot
Massol	2Lt. Harold D. Granger	351	Copilot
Massol	2Lt. Edwin A. Stern Jr	351	Bombardier
Massol	2Lt. Edward C. King Jr	351	Navigator
Massol	T/Sgt. Sidney A. Cary	351	Top Turret - Engineer
Massol	T/Sgt. Asa A. Spengler	351	Radio Operator - Gunner
Massol	S/Sgt. Winfred C. Williams	351	Ball Turret Gunner
Massol	S/Sgt. William L. Reneau	351	Left Waist Gunner
Massol	S/Sgt. Oliver N. McCartney	351	Right Waist Gunner
Massol	S/Sgt. Newman E. Garmon	351	Tail Gunner

100 B High Squadron

238059 418 LD A Miner

Miner	Captain David L. Miner	418	Pilot
Miner	Lt. George E. Kinsella	418	Copilot
Miner	Lt. D. F. Berthof	418	Bombardier
Miner	Lt. George R. Jones	418	Navigator
Miner	T/Sgt. Albert Zikorus	418	Top Turret – Engineer
Miner	T/Sgt. William C. Libbert	418	Radio Operator – Gunner
Miner	T/Sgt. Varden I. Butler	418	Ball Turret Gunner
Miner	S/Sgt. Leonard D. Malcuit	418	Left Waist Gunner
Miner	S/Sgt. Sam Pry	418	Right Waist Gunner
Miner	S/Sgt. June E. Roberson	418	Tail Gunner

26087 *Royal Flush* 418 LD Z Thomas

Thomas	2Lt. William H. Thomas	418	Pilot
Thomas	2Lt. John J. Raring	418	Copilot
Thomas	2Lt. Louis Brownstein	418	Bombardier
Thomas	2Lt. Herbert J. Brice	418	Navigator
Thomas	T/Sgt. Clifford E. Akin	418	Top Turret - Engineer
Thomas	S/Sgt. Charles A. Leavitt	418	Radio Operator - Gunner
Thomas	S/Sgt. Willard W. Moore	418	Ball Turret Gunner
Thomas	Sgt. John D. Smoot	418	Left Waist Gunner
Thomas	S/Sgt. Daniel S. McGill	418	Right Waist Gunner
Thomas	S/Sgt. Edward A. Vollmer	418	Tail Gunner

23508	***Bastard's Bungalow***	**418 LD P**	**Ferbrache**	
Ferbrache	Lt. Elmer E. Ferbrache	418	Pilot	
Ferbrache	Lt. Anthony D. Slatinsky	418	Copilot	
Ferbrache	Lt. David N. Hegge	418	Bombardier	
Ferbrache	Lt. Burton S. Hufsey	418	Navigator	
Ferbrache	S/Sgt. Harold H. Patterson	418	Top Turret - Engineer	
Ferbrache	Sgt. John P. Lucarelli	418	Radio Operator - Gunner	
Ferbrache	Sgt. William T. Behr	418	Ball Turret Gunner	
Ferbrache	Sgt. Benjamin J. Devine	418	Left Waist Gunner	
Ferbrache	Sgt. Clifford H. Leming	418	Right Waist Gunner	
Ferbrache	Sgt Howard O. Williams	418	Tail Gunner	
231895	***Miss Chief***	**418 LD Y**	**Gummersall**	
Gummersall	2Lt. Mark G. Gummersall	418	Pilot	
Gummersall	2Lt. Reginald C. Holliday	418	Copilot	
Gummersall	2Lt. Edward P. Carr	418	Bombardier	
Gummersall	2Lt. Frank W. Roberts Jr	418	Navigator	
Gummersall	S/Sgt. John R. Gensel	418	Top Turret - Engineer	
Gummersall	S/Sgt. Henry W. Bieze	418	Radio Operator - Gunner	
Gummersall	Sgt. Matthew H. Boguminski	418	Ball Turret Gunner	
Gummersall	Sgt. James J. Daly	418	Left Waist Gunner	
Gummersall	Sgt. James T. Penny	418	Right Waist Gunner	
Gummersall	Sgt. Robert L. Braswell	418	Tail Gunner	
230278	***Sly Fox***	**418 LD R**	**Kendall**	
Kendall	Lt. Zeb Kendall	418	Pilot	
Kendall	2Lt. Edwin J. Loughran	418	Copilot	
Kendall	2Lt. Clifford L. Gowen	418	Bombardier	
Kendall	2Lt. William R. Thorpe Jr	418	Navigator	
Kendall	T/Sgt. Melvin A. Hickman	418	Top Turret - Engineer	
Kendall	T/Sgt. Leman E. Tutor	418	Radio Operator - Gunner	
Kendall	S/Sgt. Reginaldo Aguila	418	Ball Turret Gunner	
Kendall	Sgt. Raymond L. Bridges	418	Left Waist Gunner	
Kendall	S/Sgt. Matthew G. Aven Jr	418	Right Waist Gunner	
Kendall	S/Sgt. Victor Stoffregen	418	Tail Gunner	
232018	***Waticare***	**351 EP L**	**Mylius**	
Mylius	2Lt Charles W. Mylius Jr	351	Pilot	
Mylius	2Lt. Warren G. McCoy	351	Copilot	
Mylius	2Lt Norman T. High	351	Bombardier	
Mylius	2Lt Charles J. Galligan	351	Navigator	
Mylius	S/Sgt James R. Russel	351	Top Turret - Engineer	
Mylius	S/Sgt Vincent J. Wood	351	Radio Operator - Gunner	
Mylius	Sgt Carleton E. Brown	351	Ball Turret Gunner	
Mylius	Sgt Edmond J. Sullivan	351	Left Waist Gunner	
Mylius	Sgt Charles E. McSpadden	351	Right Waist Gunner	
Mylius	S/Sgt Herbert D. Fern	351	Tail Gunner	
231735	***Lucky Lee***	**351 EP B**	**Brannan**	
Brannan	Lt. George W. Brannan	351	Pilot	
Brannan	Lt. Thomas R. Leslie	351	Copilot	Lacy Crew
Brannan	Lt. Louis J. Denisco	351	Bombardier	
Brannan	Lt. Clyde F. Dale	351	Navigator	
Brannan	T/Sgt. Walter S. Austin	351	Top Turret - Engineer	
Brannan	T/Sgt. William F. Teaff	351	Radio Operator - Gunner	
Brannan	S/Sgt. John B. Cortelletty	351	Ball Turret Gunner	Clark Crew
Brannan	S/Sgt. Charles F. Elliott	351	Left Waist Gunner	
Brannan	S/Sgt. D. J. Maddra Jr	351	Right Waist Gunner	Spare Gunner Pool
Brannan	S/Sgt Robert L. Greenleaf	351	Tail Gunner	

100 B Low Squadron

231504 *Rosie's Riveters* 418 LD E Rosenthal

Rosenthal	Capt. Robert *'Rosie'* Rosenthal	418	Pilot
Rosenthal	Lt Winifred "Pappy" Lewis	418	Copilot
Rosenthal	Lt Clifford Milburn	418	Bombardier
Rosenthal	Lt Ronald C. Bailey	418	Navigator
Rosenthal	T/Sgt Clarence C. Hall	418	Top Turret – Engineer
Rosenthal	T/Sgt Michael Boccuzzi	418	Radio Operator – Gunner
Rosenthal	Sgt Ray H. Robinson	418	Ball Turret Gunner
Rosenthal	S/Sgt Marion J. Sheldon	418	Left Waist Gunner
Rosenthal	S/Sgt James P. Mack	418	Right Waist Gunner
Rosenthal	S/Sgt William J. DeBlasio	418	Tail Gunner

297491 *Ronnie R* 418 LD B Radtke

Radtke	Lt. Dean M. Radtke	418	Pilot
Radtke	Lt. Gordon E. Devault	418	Copilot
Radtke	Lt. William B. Agnetti	418	Bombardier
Radtke	Lt. Robert M. Reilly	418	Navigator
Radtke	T/Sgt. Van D. Pinner	418	Top Turret - Engineer
Radtke	T/Sgt. Robert Ray	418	Radio Operator - Gunner
Radtke	S/Sgt. Joseph C. Krusienski	418	Ball Turret Gunner
Radtke	S/Sgt. Charles F. Allen	418	Left Waist Gunner
Radtke	S/Sgt. Richard L. Kerwin	418	Right Waist Gunner
Radtke	S/Sgt. Theodore E. Mangum	418	Tail Gunner

231800 418 LD U Barton

Barton	Lt. Sherwin L. Barton	418	Pilot
Barton	Lt. George W. Davidson	418	Copilot
Barton	Lt. Bernard J. Smolens	418	Bombardier
Barton	Lt. John L. Burtch	418	Navigator
Barton	T/Sgt. Harvey A. Moore	418	Top Turret - Engineer
Barton	T/Sgt. Jack M. Robins	418	Radio Operator - Gunner
Barton	S/Sgt. Robert J. Taylor	418	Ball Turret Gunner
Barton	S/Sgt. Paul H. Morris	418	Left Waist Gunner
Barton	S/Sgt. Frank J. Foldy	418	Right Waist Gunner
Barton	S/Sgt James W. Powell	418	Tail Gunner

238175 418 LD Q Forsythe

Forsythe	2Lt. Wallace C. Forsythe	418	Pilot
Forsythe	2Lt. Prescott H. Haralson	418	Copilot
Forsythe	2Lt. Robert W. McAtee	418	Bombardier
Forsythe	2Lt. Augustus H. Paine	418	Navigator
Forsythe	S/Sgt. Percy J. Johnston	418	Top Turret - Engineer
Forsythe	S/Sgt. Peter J. Buck	418	Radio Operator - Gunner
Forsythe	Sgt. Peter VanSlyck	418	Ball Turret Gunner
Forsythe	Sgt. Nelson C. Linke	418	Left Waist Gunner
Forsythe	Sgt. John A. Codoluto	418	Right Waist Gunner
Forsythe	Sgt. Richard D. Schad	418	Tail Gunner

297482 *Terry and the Pirates* 418 LD W Terry

Terry	Lt. William A. Terry	418	Pilot
Terry	Lt. William L. Peterson	418	Copilot
Terry	Lt. Ralph G. Cotter	418	Bombardier
Terry	Lt. Robert P. Schremser	418	Navigator
Terry	T/Sgt. James P. Aitken	418	Top Turret - Engineer
Terry	T/Sgt. Richard P. Howell	418	Radio Operator - Gunner
Terry	S/Sgt. James A. Bain	418	Ball Turret Gunner
Terry	S/Sgt. Charles C. Anthony	418	Left Waist Gunner
Terry	S/Sgt. John R. Horn	418	Right Waist Gunner
Terry	S/Sgt. Carl D. Hampton	418	Tail Gunner

239994 ***Snort Stuff*** **418 LD D** **Barrick**

Barrick	Lt. Samuel L. Barrick	418	Pilot
Barrick	Lt. Ira A. Munn	418	Copilot
Barrick	Lt. Earl L. Richardson	418	Bombardier
Barrick	Lt. James G. Guerrini	418	Navigator
Barrick	T/Sgt. Walfred J. Johnson	418	Top Turret - Engineer
Barrick	S/Sgt. Clifford E. Barton	418	Radio Operator - Gunner
Barrick	S/Sgt. Edward J. Marlen	418	Ball Turret Gunner
Barrick	S/Sgt. Frederick C. Thorpe	418	Left Waist Gunner
Barrick	S/Sgt. William D. Sapp	418	Right Waist Gunner
Barrick	S/Sgt Hugh F. Fantone Jr	418	Tail Gunner

95 A Group

Lead Squadron

	Powers 231600 BG M	
Barksdale 232002 OE X		**Woodcock** 231632 OE Z
	Dunham 231785 OE N	
Hagenbaugh 237889 ET L		**Roehm** 231565 OE U

Low Squadron

	Brink 231924 BG Q	
Edwards 239989 BG F		**Lloyd** 231299 BG M
	Geib 231920 BG G	
		Herman 230120 BG D

High Squadron

	Infield 231329 BG H	
Mailman 230342 BG B		**Harris** 23263 QW V
	Huie 239924 BG N	
Henderson 237929 OE Y		**Fagan** 231589 BG O
	Rourke 238140 OE W	
Vansant 229943 BG K		

95 B Group

Lead Squadron

	Brown-Mumford 231320 QW M	
	Gunn 231798 QW J	
Newson 231876 QW Q		

Low Squadron

	Haitt 231681 QW G	
		Worthy 231734 QW H

High Squadron

	Westmyer 297495 ET C	
Jeffers 231410 ET C		**Abbott** 232019 ET R
	Dean 237988 ET M	
Brownlow 231910 ET P		**Reis** 239884 ET N
	Kroeger 231939 ET J	

March 6, 1944, Berlin

100 A Group

Lead Squadron

	Devore – Elton 231981 LN E	
Chadwick 23413 LN V		**Granack** 239872 LN A
	Cope 237807 LN O	
Pearson 231074 LN Q		**Malooly** 231049 LN U

Low Squadron

	Wilkinson 239927 DI R	
Warren 239821 DI J		**Dower** 232089 DI W
	Sutters 231971 DI E	
Reich 238130 DI B		**Sterr** 231892 DI H

High Squadron

	Harrison 231710 XR P	
Murray 230799 XR J		**Amiero** 231731 XR M
	Cowan 231723 XR R	
Wilson 23534 XR N		**Morgan** 25957 XR D
	Lautenschlager 238197 LN T	
Gibbons 231968 LN D		**Harper** 232009 LN X

Over Target

Lead Squadron

	Devore – Elton 231981 LN E	
Chadwick 23413 LN V		**Granack** 239872 LN A
	Malooly 231049 LN U	
Pearson 231074 LN Q		**Gibbons** 231968 LN D

Low Squadron

	Wilkinson 239927 DI R	
Warren 239821 DI J		**Dower** 232089 DI W
	Sutters 231971 DI E	
Reich 238130 DI B		**Sterr** 231892 DI H

High Squadron

	Harrison 231710 XR P	
Wilson 23534 XR N		**Morgan** 25957 XR D
	Cowan 231723 XR R	

100 A Lead Squadron

231981 — 350 LN E — Devore-Elton

Devore	Lt. Herbert G. Devore	350	Pilot	
Devore	Major Albert *'Bucky'* Elton	350	Command Pilot	
Devore	Captain Robert K. Peel	350	Bombardier	
Devore	Captain Joseph *'Bubbles'* Payne	350	Navigator	
Devore	T/Sgt. James C. Brown	350	Top Turret - Engineer	Spare Gunner Pool
Devore	T/Sgt. Harry S. Lenk	350	Radio Operator	
Devore	S/Sgt Knute Knudson	350	Radio Gunner	
Devore	S/Sgt. Nicholas Delcimmuto	350	Ball Turret Gunner	
Devore	S/Sgt. Darrell R. Dickenson	350	Left Waist Gunner	
Devore	S/Sgt. John J. Barry	350	Right Waist Gunner	
Devore	Lt. Jerry Felsenstein	350	Formation Control Officer	

239872 *Rubber Check* — 350 LN A — Granack

Granack	Lt. Frank A. Granack	350	Pilot	POW
Granack	Lt. Robert L. Dunham	350	Copilot	POW
Granack	Lt. Joseph F. Kawiecki	350	Bombardier	POW
Granack	Lt. Murray Geisler	350	Navigator	POW
Granack	T/Sgt. Harold Stearns	350	Top Turret - Engineer	POW
Granack	T/Sgt. Grant H. L. Scott	350	Radio Operator - Gunner	KIA
Granack	S/Sgt. Lloyd H. Rodgers Jr	350	Ball Turret Gunner	POW
Granack	S/Sgt. Edwin T. Harrell	350	Left Waist Gunner	POW
Granack	S/Sgt. Glenn D. Brown	350	Right Waist Gunner	KIA
Granack	S/Sgt. George C. Christian	350	Tail Gunner	POW

23413 *Hard Luck* — 350 LN V — Chadwick

Chadwick	2Lt. Randall T. Chadwick	350	Pilot	
Chadwick	2Lt. Thomas Cryan	350	Copilot	Cope Crew
Chadwick	2Lt. Joseph A. Carty	350	Bombardier	
Chadwick	2Lt. Jack E. Longenecker	350	Navigator	
Chadwick	S/Sgt. Edwin E. Postel	350	Top Turret - Engineer	
Chadwick	S/Sgt. John J. Good	350	Radio Operator - Gunner	
Chadwick	Sgt. George A. Benedict	350	Ball Turret Gunner	
Chadwick	Sgt. Austin B. Roberts	350	Left Waist Gunner	
Chadwick	Sgt. Delbert J.H. Burns	350	Right Waist Gunner	
Chadwick	S/Sgt Lucien E. Neveu	350	Tail Gunner	

237807 *Alice From Dallas II* — 350 LN O — Cope

Cope	Captain Mark Cope	350	Pilot	
Cope	Lt. Martin Tashjian	350	Copilot	
Cope	2Lt. Arthur E. Cox	350	Bombardier	*'Red'* Harper Crew
Cope	Lt. Festus E. *'Shorty'* Bryant	350	Navigator	
Cope	T/Sgt. John Verbovski	350	Top Turret - Engineer	
Cope	T/Sgt. John C. Eling	350	Radio Operator - Gunner	
Cope	Sgt. Richard E. Donnelly	350	Ball Turret Gunner	
Cope	S/Sgt. James E. Morrison	350	Left Waist Gunner	
Cope	S/Sgt. Donald E. Walker	350	Right Waist Gunner	
Cope	S/Sgt Raymond Bryan	350	Tail Gunner	

231049 *Superstitious Aloysious* — 350 LN U — Malooly

Malooly	2Lt. Francis J. Malooly	350	Pilot	
Malooly	2Lt. Robert W. Bailie	350	Copilot	
Malooly	2Lt. Ralph W. Guida	350	Bombardier	
Malooly	2Lt. Charles H. Mauvais	350	Navigator	
Malooly	T/Sgt. Arthur J. Perry	350	Top Turret - Engineer	
Malooly	T/Sgt. Robert D. Longworth	350	Radio Operator - Gunner	Tashjian Crew
Malooly	Sgt. Nelson A.S. Pardee	350	Ball Turret Gunner	
Malooly	Sgt. Leonard W. Yeager	350	Left Waist Gunner	
Malooly	Sgt. Willard H. Miller	350	Right Waist Gunner	
Malooly	Sgt. Lorenzo Genovese	350	Tail Gunner	

231074 *Cahepit* 350 LN Q Pearson

Pearson	2Lt. Delbert S. Pearson	350	Pilot	
Pearson	2Lt. Wilbert D. Lund	350	Copilot	
Pearson	Lt. Lester N. Smith	350	Bombardier	
Pearson	Lt. Maurice H. Cain	350	Navigator	Gibbons Crew
Pearson	T/Sgt. Ernest J. Rene	350	Top Turret - Engineer	
Pearson	T/Sgt. Nunziato Sansevero	350	Radio Operator - Gunner	
Pearson	S/Sgt. Francis X. Kerin	350	Ball Turret Gunner	
Pearson	S/Sgt. Harold J. Scrivener	350	Left Waist Gunner	
Pearson	S/Sgt. Bradford F. Truesdell	350	Right Waist Gunner	
Pearson	S/Sgt. George P. Zigo	350	Tail Gunner	

100 A High Squadron

231710 *The Savage* 349 XR P Harrison

Harrison	Lt. John A. Harrison	349	Pilot
Harrison	2Lt. Charles S. Stapleton	349	Copilot
Harrison	2Lt. Adam Krezo	349	Bombardier
Harrison	2Lt. Anthony J. Busalacchi	349	Navigator
Harrison	T/Sgt. Anthony J. Beechey	349	Top Turret - Engineer
Harrison	T/Sgt. Neil J. Coyle	349	Radio Operator - Gunner
Harrison	Sgt. Luke E. Nachatilo	349	Ball Turret Gunner
Harrison	Sgt. Glover Nall	349	Left Waist Gunner
Harrison	Sgt. Lawrence A. Robbins	349	Right Waist Gunner
Harrison	S/Sgt Bruce E. Alshouse	349	Tail Gunner

231731 349 XR M Amiero (pick up crew)

Amiero	Lt. Albert F. Amiero	349	Pilot	KIA
Amiero	FO Howard L. Kilmer	349	Copilot	KIA
Amiero	S/Sgt. Thomas S. Elliott	349	Toggler	KIA
Amiero	Lt. Albert P. Rule	349	Navigator	KIA
Amiero	T/Sgt. Russell G. Gilbert	349	Top Turret – Engineer	KIA
Amiero	T/Sgt. John J. Kovacs	349	Radio Operator – Gunner	KIA
Amiero	S/Sgt. Virgil F. Summers	349	Ball Turret Gunner	KIA
Amiero	S/Sgt. Owen D. Stockton	349	Left Waist Gunner	POW
Amiero	S/Sgt. Hobart H. Spires	349	Right Waist Gunner	KIA
Amiero	S/Sgt Thomas D. Baer	349	Tail Gunner	KIA

230799 *The Bigassbird II* 349 XR J Murray

Murray	Lt. William B. Murray	349	Pilot	KIA
Murray	Lt. Richard M. Lambiotte	349	Copilot	POW
Murray	2nd William G. Carr	349	Bombardier	POW
Murray	2Lt. Orrin H. Heinrich	349	Navigator	POW
Murray	T/Sgt. Emory L. Brandt	349	Top Turret - Engineer	POW
Murray	T/Sgt. Fred C. Schillinger	349	Radio Operator - Gunner	KIA
Murray	S/Sgt. Jim Peace	349	Ball Turret Gunner	POW
Murray	Sgt. Nick E. Hamalack	349	Left Waist Gunner	POW
Murray	S/Sgt. Palmer J. Hanson	349	Right Waist Gunner	POW
Murray	S/Sgt. Mahlon A. Hall	349	Tail Gunner	KIA

231723 *"Sparky"* 349 XR R Cowan

Cowan	Lt. Clement H. Cowan	349	Pilot
Cowan	Lt. Hank A. Dibbern	349	Copilot
Cowan	Lt. Harold L. Heyneman	349	Bombardier
Cowan	Lt. Fred W. Robertson	349	Navigator
Cowan	T/Sgt. Murray W. Holditch	349	Top Turret - Engineer
Cowan	T/Sgt. John P. Cooper	349	Radio Operator - Gunner
Cowan	S/Sgt. William A. Geigle	349	Ball Turret Gunner
Cowan	S/Sgt. Adam C. Stoppel	349	Left Waist Gunner
Cowan	S/Sgt. Robert Patrick	349	Right Waist Gunner
Cowan	S/Sgt Horace R. Kemble	349	Tail Gunner

25957 ***Horny*** **349 XR D** **Morgan**

Morgan	Lt. Leon R. Morgan	349	Pilot	
Morgan	2Lt. Ralph O. Ward	349	Copilot	
Morgan	S/Sgt. Sam J. LaFace	349	Toggler	
Morgan	2Lt. Robert E. McCormick	349	Navigator	
Morgan	T/Sgt. Maynard L. Lobb	349	Top Turret - Engineer	
Morgan	T/Sgt. Tony L. Verdusco	349	Radio Operator - Gunner	
Morgan	S/Sgt. David C. Lyon Jr	349	Ball Turret Gunner	
Morgan	S/Sgt. Kenneth R. Lash Jr	349	Left Waist Gunner	
Morgan	S/Sgt. Hugo C. Kleckner	349	Right Waist Gunner	
Morgan	S/Sgt. Ernest R. Gomez	349	Tail Gunner	

23534 ***Ol' Dad*** **349 XR N** **Wilson**

Wilson	2Lt. Mark V. Wilson	349	Pilot	
Wilson	2Lt. Charles E. Adams	349	Copilot	
Wilson	2Lt. Ralph A. Kroenke	349	Bombardier	
Wilson	2Lt. John T. Johnston	349	Navigator	
Wilson	T/Sgt. John W. McAuliffe	349	Top Turret - Engineer	
Wilson	T/Sgt. Eugene V. Sweeney	349	Radio Operator - Gunner	
Wilson	S/Sgt. Charlie J. Hopkins	349	Ball Turret Gunner	Raring Crew
Wilson	Sgt. George B. Donahue	349	Left Waist Gunner	
Wilson	Sgt. William E. Moreland	349	Right Waist Gunner	
Wilson	Sgt. Cecil G. Davis	349	Tail Gunner	

238197 ***Half and Half*** **350 LN T** **Lautenschlager**

Lautenschlager	Lt. John Lautenschlager	350	Pilot	POW
Lautenschlager	Lt. William J. Sugg	350	Copilot	POW
Lautenschlager	Lt. David Rolnick	350	Bombardier	POW
Lautenschlager	Lt. Leland C. Fink	350	Navigator	POW
Lautenschlager	T/Sgt. Robert T. Bashaw	350	Top Turret - Engineer	POW
Lautenschlager	T/Sgt. John Stryjeski	350	Radio Operator - Gunner	KIA
Lautenschlager	Sgt. Harold L. Sheldon	350	Ball Turret Gunner	POW
Lautenschlager	S/Sgt. John H. White	350	Waist Gunner	POW Tashjian Crew
Lautenschlager	S/Sgt. Samuel Wilenski	350	Waist Gunner	POW
Lautenschlager	Sgt. Hogan Fussell Jr	350	Tail Gunner	POW

232009 ***Black Cat 13*** **350 LN X** **C.B. *'Red'* Harper**

Harper, CB	2Lt. Celesta B. *'Red'* Harper	350	Pilot	
Harper, CB	2Lt. Robert S. Flannigan	350	Copilot	
Harper, CB	T/Sgt. John H. Walters	350	Toggler	
Harper, CB	2Lt. Charles T. Hardiman	350	Navigator	
Harper, CB	T/Sgt. Clarence P. Luquet	350	Top Turret - Engineer	
Harper, CB	T/Sgt. Alvin E. James	350	Radio Operator - Gunner	
Harper, CB	Sgt. Austin P. Curlee	350	Ball Turret Gunner	
Harper, CB	Sgt. John B. Bowers	350	Left Waist Gunner	
Harper, CB	Sgt. Wiley A. Dobbs	350	Right Waist Gunner	
Harper, CB	Sgt. Anderson R. Frank Jr	350	Tail Gunner	

231968 ***Miss Irish*** **350 LN D** **Gibbons**

Gibbons	2Lt. John P. Gibbons	350	Pilot	
Gibbons	2Lt. Robert Dykeman	350	Copilot	
Gibbons	S/Sgt. John L. Craven	350	Toggler	
Gibbons	2Lt. Everett M. Johnson	350	Navigator	
Gibbons	T/Sgt. Ira L. Arnold	350	Top Turret - Engineer	
Gibbons	T/Sgt. Edward Walker Jr	350	Radio Operator - Gunner	
Gibbons	Sgt. Bernard L. Spragg	350	Ball Turret Gunner	
Gibbons	Sgt. Frank W. Buschmeier	350	Left Waist Gunner	
Gibbons	Sgt. Myron J. Ettus	350	Right Waist Gunner	
Gibbons	Sgt. Archie W. Bunting	350	Tail Gunner	

100 A Low Squadron
(390th Bomb Group Crews)

239927 *The Skillet* 570 DI R Wilkinson

Wilkinson	Lt James E. Wilkinson	570	Pilot
Wilkinson	Lt. Peter A. Dobrus	570	Copilot
Wilkinson	Lt. Howard C. Hitz	570	Navigator
Wilkinson	Lt. Emil J. Brinkman	570	Bombardier
Wilkinson	T/Sgt. John A. Heasley	570	Top Turret – Engineer
Wilkinson	T/Sgt. Michael Sheragy	570	Radio Operator
Wilkinson	Sgt. William Q, McLendon	570	Ball Turret Gunner
Wilkinson	Sgt. Norman J. Stein	570	Waist Gunner
Wilkinson	Sgt. Edward Kabo	570	Waist Gunner
Wilkinson	Sgt. Jack Miller	570	Tail Gunner

239821 *HeyMoitle* 570 DI J Warren

Warren	Lt James L. Warren	570	Pilot
Warren	Lt. Arthur E. Fillmore	570	Copilot
Warren	Lt. Richard S. Ingham	570	Navigator
Warren	Lt. Hugh J. McCarthy	570	Bombardier
Warren	T/Sgt. Robert House	570	Top Turret – Engineer
Warren	T/Sgt. Jack H. Hagan	570	Radio Operator
Warren	Sgt. Merle D. Childress	570	Ball Turret Gunner
Warren	Sgt. Clemons O. Larker	570	Waist Gunner
Warren	Sgt. John B. Kennedy	570	Waist Gunner
Warren	Sgt. Robert E. Netling	570	Tail Gunner

232089 570 DI W Dower

Dower	Lt Philip J. Dower	570	Pilot
Dower	Lt. Gordon S. Brown	570	Copilot
Dower	Lt. John R. Mooney	570	Navigator
Dower	Lt. William F. Burke	570	Bombardier
Dower	T/Sgt. Cosmo D. Tavella	570	Top Turret – Engineer
Dower	T/Sgt. Joseph W. Thompson	570	Radio Operator
Dower	Sgt. James E. Dawes	570	Ball Turret Gunner
Dower	Sgt. Donald O. Anstrom	570	Waist Gunner
Dower	Sgt. Albert W. Weymouth	570	Waist Gunner
Dower	Sgt. Harry B. Finn	570	Tail Gunner

231971 *Twenty-one or Bust* 570 DI E Sutters

Sutters	Lt Thomas J. Sutters	570	Pilot
Sutters	Lt. Paul R. Cooper	570	Copilot
Sutters	Lt. Theodore O. Kaplen	570	Navigator
Sutters	Lt. Charles J. Ell	570	Bombardier
Sutters	T/Sgt. Otto B. Fugett	570	Top Turret – Engineer
Sutters	T/Sgt. Albert J. Selvidio	570	Radio Operator
Sutters	Sgt. Joseph M. Collector	570	Ball Turret Gunner
Sutters	Sgt. Ernest H. Peiffer	570	Waist Gunner
Sutters	Sgt. Kenneth E. Pyle	570	Waist Gunner
Sutters	Sgt. Bernard J. Jensen	570	Tail Gunner

238130 570 DI B Reich

Reich	Lt Harold E. Reich	570	Pilot
Reich	Lt. Lester W. Bergeman	570	Copilot
Reich	Lt. John A. Arvin	570	Navigator
Reich	Lt. John W. Fredy	570	Bombardier
Reich	T/Sgt. Horace Huron	570	Top Turret – Engineer
Reich	T/Sgt. Carl E. Marsini	570	Radio Operator
Reich	Sgt. Peter M. Filippone	570	Ball Turret Gunner
Reich	Sgt. George F. Rocchio	570	Waist Gunner
Reich	Sgt. Frank Link	570	Waist Gunner
Reich	Sgt. John M. Zediak	570	Tail Gunner

231892 ***BI'll Be Around*** **570 DI H** **Sterr**

Sterr	Lt Roger J. Sterr	570	Pilot
Sterr	Lt. Earl F. Schmidt	570	Copilot
Sterr	Lt. Charles J. Pecorella	570	Navigator
Sterr	Lt. Robert H. DeWalt	570	Bombardier
Sterr	T/Sgt. Willard B. Warren	570	Top Turret – Engineer
Sterr	T/Sgt. Roland J. Malfitano	570	Radio Operator
Sterr	Sgt. Charles A. Baker	570	Ball Turret Gunner
Sterr	Sgt. James T. Curtis	570	Waist Gunner
Sterr	Sgt. Adam S. Oleksiak	570	Waist Gunner
Sterr	Sgt. Othel B. Steele	570	Tail Gunner

100 B Group

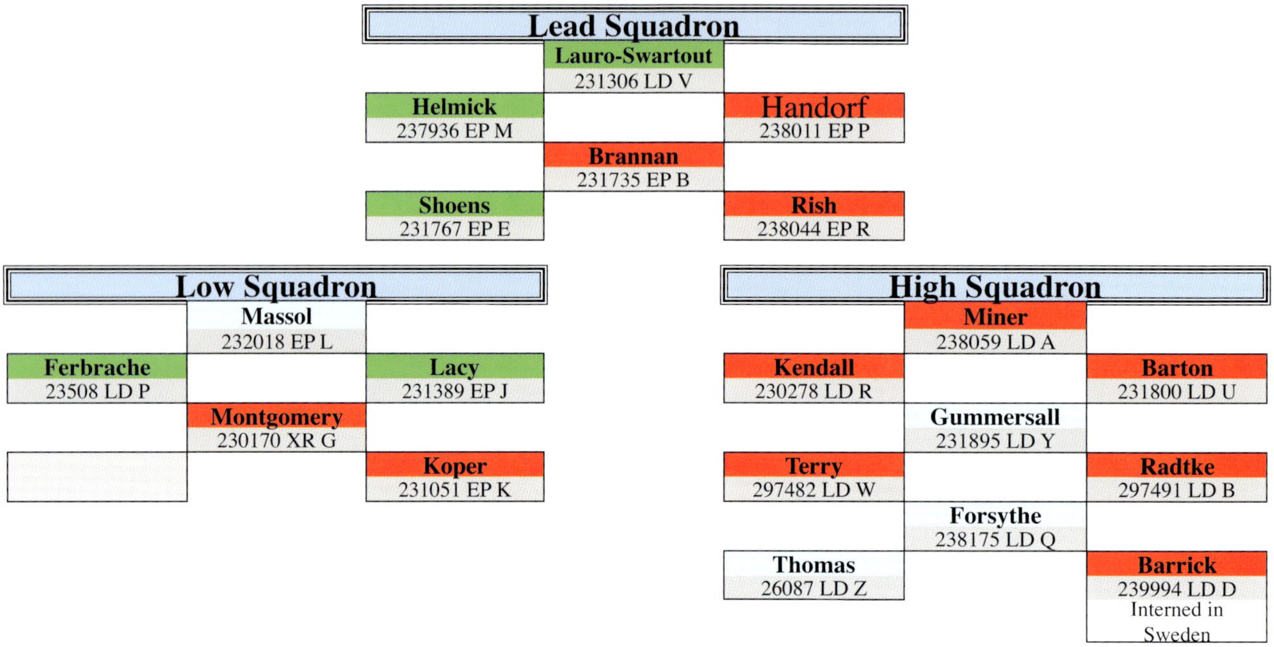

Over Target[43]

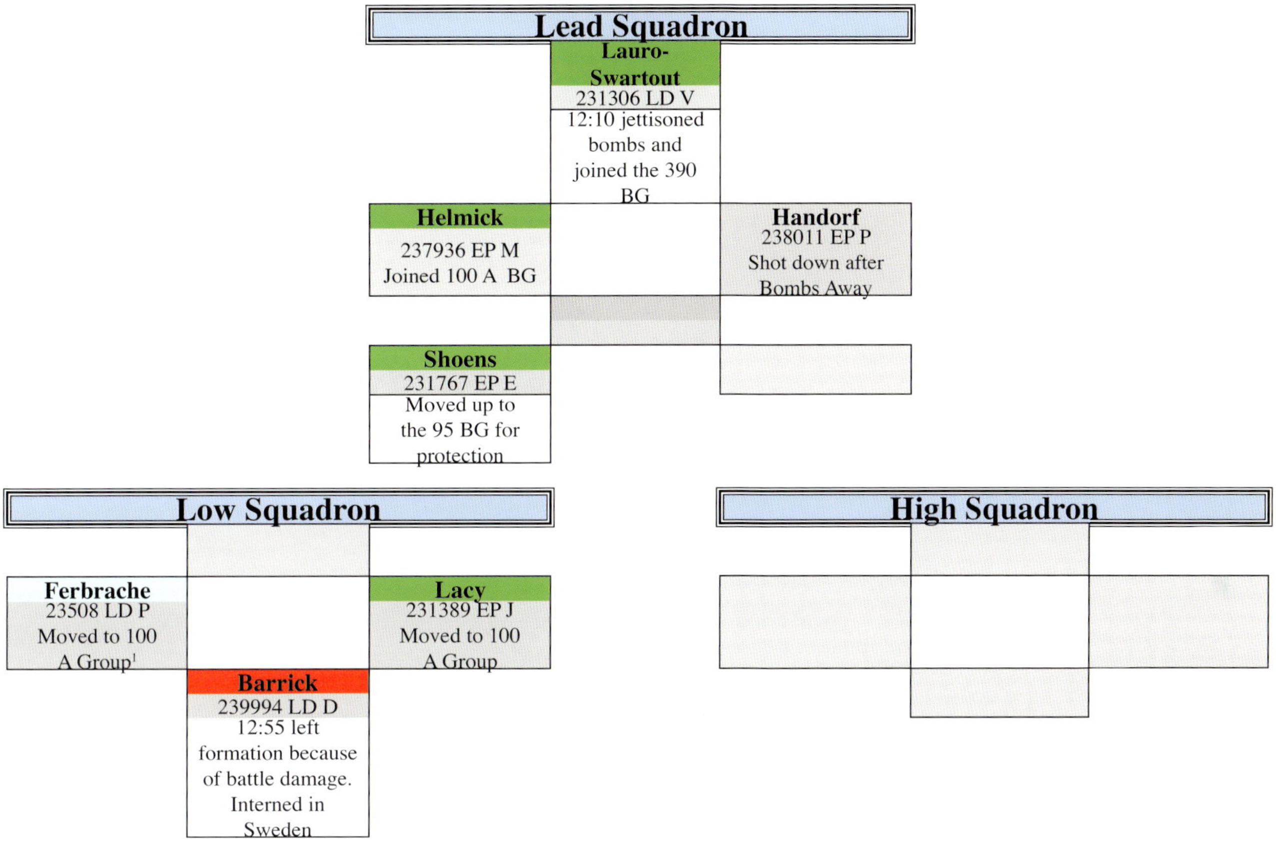

100 B Lead Squadron

231306 ***Nelson King*** **418 LD V** **Lauro-Swartout**

Lauro	Captain Frank Lauro	418	Pilot
Lauro	Captain Jack Swartout	418	Copilot
Lauro	Lt. Walter Green	418	Bombardier
Lauro	Lt. Emory Horvath	418	Navigator
Lauro	T/Sgt. Dewey Thompson	418	Top Turret - Engineer
Lauro	S/Sgt. Harry H. Greenfield	418	Radio Operator - Gunner
Lauro	S/Sgt Arthur R. Tirrell	418	Radio Gunner
Lauro	S/Sgt. Murray Schrier	418	Ball Turret Gunner
Lauro	S/Sgt. Gerald J. Will	418	Left Waist Gunner
Lauro	S/Sgt. William R. Heathman	418	Right Waist Gunner
Lauro	Lt.Emmanuel Greasmare	418	Formation Control Officer

238011 **Kind-a-Ruff** **351 EP P** **Handorf**

Handorf	Lt. Edward Handorf	351	Pilot	KIA
Handorf	2Lt. Frederick G. Spence	351	Copilot	KIA
Handorf	Lt. Norman L. Rasmussen	351	Bombardier	KIA
Handorf	Lt. John W. Dewey	351	Navigator	KIA
Handorf	T/Sgt. Charles H. Ford	351	Top Turret - Engineer	KIA
Handorf	T/Sgt. Henry C. Verdeur Jr	351	Radio Operator - Gunner	KIA
Handorf	S/Sgt. Allen D. Horton	351	Ball Turret Gunner	KIA
Handorf	S/Sgt. John J Gverovich	351	Left Waist Gunner	KIA
Handorf	S/Sgt John L. Willsey	351	Right Waist Gunner	POW
Handorf	S/Sgt Fair C. Lawrence	351	Tail Gunner	POW

237936	***Our Mark***	**351 EP M**	**Helmick**	
Helmick	2Lt. Richard Helmick	351	Pilot	
Helmick	2Lt. Jerome F. Leirich	351	Copilot	
Helmick	2Lt. Herbert R. Greenberg	351	Bombardier	
Helmick	2Lt. Sol S. Kranzler	351	Navigator	
Helmick	T/Sgt. George E. Madden	351	Top Turret - Engineer	
Helmick	T/Sgt. Joseph G. Kelly	351	Radio Operator - Gunner	
Helmick	S/Sgt. Robert M. Myers	351	Ball Turret Gunner	
Helmick	S/Sgt. Edwin I. Morgan	351	Left Waist Gunner	Barker Crew
Helmick	S/Sgt. Loren G. Johnson	351	Right Waist Gunner	
Helmick	S/Sgt. Chester P. Coulam	351	Tail Gunner	

231735	***Lucky Lee***	**351 EP B**	**Brannan**	
Brannan	Lt. George W. Brannan	351	Pilot	POW
Brannan	Lt. Thomas R. Leslie	351	Copilot	KIA Lacy Crew
Brannan	Lt. Louis J. Denisco	351	Bombardier	POW
Brannan	Lt. Clyde F. Dale	351	Navigator	KIA
Brannan	T/Sgt. Walter S. Austin	351	Top Turret - Engineer	POW
Brannan	T/Sgt. William F. Teaff	351	Radio Operator - Gunner	POW
Brannan	S/Sgt. Robyn P. Fulton	351	Ball Turret Gunner	POW
Brannan	S/Sgt. Charles F. Elliott	351	Waist Gunner	POW
Brannan	S/Sgt. Howard T. Larimore	351	Waist Gunner	POW
Brannan	S/Sgt Robert L. Greenleaf	351	Tail Gunner	POW

238044	***Spirit of 44***	**351 EP R**	**Rish**	
Rish	Lt. Merril T. Rish	351	Pilot	KIA
Rish	2Lt. Frank A. Smith	351	Copilot	KIA
Rish	2Lt. Donald K. Kehm	351	Bombardier	POW
Rish	2Lt. Royal W. Lingenfelter	351	Navigator	POW
Rish	T/Sgt. Howard T. Skaggs Jr	351	Top Turret - Engineer	POW
Rish	T/Sgt. George F. Danehower	351	Radio Operator - Gunner	POW
Rish	Sgt. Dewey Essary	351	Ball Turret Gunner	KIA
Rish	S/Sgt. Estil V. McGuffee	351	Left Waist Gunner	POW
Rish	Sgt. Armand C. Burt	351	Right Waist Gunner	POW
Rish	Sgt. Angus Alsup	351	Tail Gunner	KIA

231767	***Our Gal Sal***	**351 EP E**	**Shoens**
Shoens	Lt. Robert J. Shoens	351	Pilot
Shoens	Lt. Duncan R. Shand	351	Copilot
Shoens	Lt. Glenn Hudson	351	Bombardier
Shoens	T/Sgt. William Eresman	351	Top Turret - Engineer
Shoens	T/Sgt. Donald B. Hammond	351	Radio Operator - Gunner
Shoens	S/Sgt. Edward Silverstone	351	Ball Turret Gunner
Shoens	S/Sgt. William W. Wright	351	Left Waist Gunner
Shoens	S/Sgt. Virgil H. Warders	351	Right Waist Gunner
Shoens	S/Sgt. Don L. Blair	351	Tail Gunner

100 B High Squadron

238059		**418 LD A**	**Miner**	
Miner	Captain David L. Miner	418	Pilot	KIA
Miner	Lt. George E. Kinsella	418	Copilot	KIA
Miner	Lt. Earl L. Richardson	418	Bombardier	POW
Miner	Lt. George R. Jones	418	Navigator	KIA
Miner	T/Sgt. Albert Zikorus	418	Top Turret - Engineer	POW
Miner	T/Sgt. William C. Libbert	418	Radio Operator - Gunner	POW
Miner	T/Sgt. Varden I. Butler	418	Ball Turret Gunner	KIA
Miner	S/Sgt. Leonard D. Malcuit	418	Left Waist Gunner	POW
Miner	S/Sgt. Sam Pry	418	Right Waist Gunner	POW
Miner	S/Sgt. June E. Roberson	418	Tail Gunner	POW

231800 — 418 LD U — Barton

Barton	Lt. Sherwin L. Barton	418	Pilot	POW
Barton	Lt. George W. Davidson	418	Copilot	POW
Barton	Lt. Bernard J. Smolens	418	Bombardier	POW
Barton	Lt. John L. Burtch	418	Navigator	POW
Barton	T/Sgt. Harvey A. Moore	418	Top Turret - Engineer	POW
Barton	T/Sgt. Jack M. Robins	418	Radio Operator - Gunner	POW
Barton	S/Sgt. Robert J. Taylor	418	Ball Turret Gunner	POW
Barton	S/Sgt. Paul H. Morris	418	Left Waist Gunner	POW
Barton	S/Sgt. Frank J. Foldy	418	Right Waist Gunner	POW
Barton	S/Sgt James W. Powell	418	Tail Gunner	POW

230278 *Sly Fox* — 418 LD R — Kendall

Kendall	Lt. Zeb Kendall	418	Pilot	KIA
Kendall	2Lt. Edwin J. Loughran	418	Copilot	KIA
Kendall	2Lt. Clifford L. Gowen	418	Bombardier	KIA
Kendall	2Lt. William R. Thorpe Jr	418	Navigator	KIA
Kendall	T/Sgt. Melvin A. Hickman	418	Top Turret - Engineer	KIA
Kendall	T/Sgt. Leman E. Tutor	418	Radio Operator - Gunner	KIA
Kendall	S/Sgt. Reginaldo Aguila	418	Ball Turret Gunner	KIA
Kendall	Sgt. Raymond L. Bridges	418	Left Waist Gunner	KIA
Kendall	S/Sgt. Matthew G. Aven Jr	418	Right Waist Gunner	KIA
Kendall	S/Sgt. Victor Stoffregen	418	Tail Gunner	KIA

231895 *Miss Chief* — 418 LD Y — Gummersall

Gummersall	2Lt. Mark G. Gummersall	418	Pilot
Gummersall	2Lt. Reginald C. Holliday	418	Copilot
Gummersall	2Lt. Edward P. Carr	418	Bombardier
Gummersall	2Lt. Frank W. Roberts Jr	418	Navigator
Gummersall	S/Sgt. John R. Gensel	418	Top Turret - Engineer
Gummersall	S/Sgt. Henry W. Bieze	418	Radio Operator - Gunner
Gummersall	Sgt. Matthew H. Boguminski	418	Ball Turret Gunner
Gummersall	Sgt. James J. Daly	418	Left Waist Gunner
Gummersall	Sgt. James T. Penny	418	Right Waist Gunner
Gummersall	Sgt. Robert L. Braswell	418	Tail Gunner

297491 *Ronnie R* — 418 LD B — Radtke

Radtke	Lt. Dean M. Radtke	418	Pilot	POW
Radtke	Lt. Gordon E. Devault	418	Copilot	POW
Radtke	Lt. William B. Agnetti	418	Bombardier	POW
Radtke	Lt. Robert M. Reilly	418	Navigator	POW
Radtke	T/Sgt. Van D. Pinner	418	Top Turret - Engineer	POW
Radtke	T/Sgt. Robert Ray	418	Radio Operator - Gunner	POW
Radtke	S/Sgt. Joseph C. Krusienski	418	Ball Turret Gunner	KIA
Radtke	S/Sgt. Charles F. Allen	418	Left Waist Gunner	POW
Radtke	S/Sgt. Richard L. Kerwin	418	Right Waist Gunner	POW
Radtke	S/Sgt. Theodore E. Mangum	418	Tail Gunner	POW

297482 *Terry and the Pirates* — 418 LD W — Terry

Terry	Lt. William A. Terry	418	Pilot	KIA
Terry	Lt. William L. Peterson	418	Copilot	KIA
Terry	Lt. Ralph G. Cotter	418	Bombardier	KIA
Terry	Lt. Robert P. Schremser	418	Navigator	POW
Terry	T/Sgt. James P. Aitken	418	Top Turret - Engineer	POW
Terry	T/Sgt. Richard P. Howell	418	Radio Operator - Gunner	KIA
Terry	S/Sgt. James A. Bain	418	Ball Turret Gunner	POW
Terry	S/Sgt. Charles C. Anthony	418	Left Waist Gunner	KIA
Terry	S/Sgt. John R. Horn	418	Right Waist Gunner	KIA
Terry	S/Sgt. Carl D. Hampton	418	Tail Gunner	KIA

238175 | **418 LD Q** | **Forsythe**

Forsythe	2Lt. Wallace C. Forsythe	418	Pilot	
Forsythe	2Lt. Prescott H. Haralson	418	Copilot	
Forsythe	2Lt. Robert W. McAtee	418	Bombardier	
Forsythe	2Lt. Augustus H. Paine	418	Navigator	
Forsythe	S/Sgt. Percy J. Johnston	418	Top Turret - Engineer	
Forsythe	S/Sgt. Peter J. Buck	418	Radio Operator - Gunner	
Forsythe	Sgt. Peter VanSlyck	418	Ball Turret Gunner	
Forsythe	Sgt. Nelson C. Linke	418	Left Waist Gunner	
Forsythe	Sgt. John A. Codoluto	418	Right Waist Gunner	
Forsythe	Sgt. Richard D. Schad	418	Tail Gunner	

239994 ***Snort Stuff*** | **418 LD D** | **Barrick**

Barrick	Lt. Samuel L. Barrick	418	Pilot	INT
Barrick	Lt. Ira A. Munn	418	Copilot	INT
Barrick	T/Sgt. James O. Brady	418	Toggler	INT Wolf Crew
Barrick	Lt. James G. Guerrini	418	Navigator	INT
Barrick	T/Sgt. Walfred J. Johnson	418	Top Turret - Engineer	INT
Barrick	S/Sgt. Clifford E. Barton	418	Radio Operator - Gunner	INT
Barrick	S/Sgt. Edward J. Marlen	418	Ball Turret Gunner	INT
Barrick	S/Sgt. Frederick C. Thorpe	418	Left Waist Gunner	INT
Barrick	S/Sgt. William D. Sapp	418	Right Waist Gunner	INT
Barrick	S/Sgt Hugh F. Fantone Jr	418	Tail Gunner	INT

26087 ***Royal Flush*** | **418 LD Z** | **Thomas**

Thomas	2Lt. William H. Thomas	418	Pilot
Thomas	2Lt. John J. Raring	418	Copilot
Thomas	2Lt. Louis Brownstein	418	Bombardier
Thomas	2Lt. Herbert J. Brice	418	Navigator
Thomas	T/Sgt. Clifford E. Akin	418	Top Turret - Engineer
Thomas	S/Sgt. Charles A. Leavitt	418	Radio Operator - Gunner
Thomas	S/Sgt. Willard W. Moore	418	Ball Turret Gunner
Thomas	Sgt. John D. Smoot	418	Left Waist Gunner
Thomas	S/Sgt. Daniel S. McGill	418	Right Waist Gunner
Thomas	S/Sgt. Edward A. Vollmer	418	Tail Gunner

100 B Low Squadron

232018 ***Waticare*** | **351 EP L** | **Massol**

Massol	Lt. John F. Massol	351	Pilot	
Massol	2Lt. Harold D. Granger	351	Copilot	
Massol	2Lt. Edwin A. Stern Jr	351	Bombardier	
Massol	2Lt. Edward C. King Jr	351	Navigator	
Massol	T/Sgt. Sidney A. Cary	351	Top Turret - Engineer	
Massol	T/Sgt. Asa A. Spengler	351	Radio Operator - Gunner	
Massol	S/Sgt. Winfred C. Williams	351	Ball Turret Gunner	
Massol	S/Sgt. William L. Reneau	351	Left Waist Gunner	Lacy Crew
Massol	S/Sgt. Oliver N. McCartney	351	Right Waist Gunner	
Massol	S/Sgt. Newman E. Garmon	351	Tail Gunner	

231389 ***Luscious Lucy*** | **351 EP J** | **Lacy**

Lacy	Lt. Lucius G. Lacy	351	Pilot
Lacy	**2Lt. Claude E. Schindler**	**351**	**Copilot**
Lacy	**2Lt. Frank C. Gregory**	**351**	**Bombardier**
Lacy	**2Lt. Albert Franklin**	**351**	**Navigator**
Lacy	**T/Sgt. Chester J. Carknard**	**351**	**Top Turret - Engineer**
Lacy	T/Sgt. Clarence H. Wood Jr	351	Radio Operator - Gunner
Lacy	S/Sgt. Louis G. Black	351	Ball Turret Gunner
Lacy	S/Sgt. Raymond J. Mitchell	351	Left Waist Gunner
Lacy	S/Sgt. Joe S. Folson	351	Right Waist Gunner
Lacy	S/Sgt. Joseph A. Howell	351	Tail Gunner

23508 ***Bastard's Bungalow*** **418 LD P** **Ferbrache**

Ferbrache	Lt. Elmer E. Ferbrache	418	Pilot	
Ferbrache	Lt. Anthony D. Slatinsky	418	Copilot	
Ferbrache	Lt. David N. Hegge	418	Bombardier	
Ferbrache	Lt. Burton S. Hufsey	418	Navigator	
Ferbrache	S/Sgt. Harold H. Patterson	418	Top Turret - Engineer	
Ferbrache	Sgt. John P. Lucarelli	418	Radio Operator - Gunner	
Ferbrache	Sgt. William T. Behr	418	Ball Turret Gunner	
Ferbrache	Sgt. Benjamin J. Devine	418	Left Waist Gunner	
Ferbrache	Sgt. Clifford H. Leming	418	Right Waist Gunner	
Ferbrache	Sgt Howard O. Williams	418	Tail Gunner	

230170 ***The Pride of the Century*** **349 XR G** **Montgomery**

Montgomery	2Lt. Coy I. Montgomery	349	Pilot	KIA	
Montgomery	2Lt. Robert F. Connaway	349	Copilot	POW	
Montgomery	2Lt. James W. Fulton	349	Bombardier	POW	
Montgomery	2Lt. Frank C. Laver	349	Navigator	POW	
Montgomery	T/Sgt. George W. Burton	349	Top Turret - Engineer	POW	
Montgomery	T/Sgt. Wilbur I. Trembley Jr	349	Radio Operator - Gunner	POW	Stout Crew
Montgomery	S/Sgt. Louis P. Savell	349	Ball Turret Gunner	POW	
Montgomery	S/Sgt. Junior L. Bucher	349	Left Waist Gunner	POW	
Montgomery	Sgt. Anthony E. Ruda	349	Right Waist Gunner	POW	Spare Gunner Pool
Montgomery	S/Sgt. Earl W. Ritter	349	Tail Gunner	POW	

231051 ***Goin Jessies*** **351 EP K** **Koper**

Koper	Lt. Robert G. Koper	349	Pilot	KIA
Koper	Lt. Gordon C. Lien	349	Copilot	POW
Koper	Lt. Thomas O. Drinkwater	349	Bombardier	POW
Koper	2Lt. George H. Wing	349	Navigator	KIA
Koper	T/Sgt. Charles P. Corea	349	Top Turret - Engineer	POW
Koper	S/Sgt. Michael J. Tanowigch	349	Radio Operator - Gunner	KIA
Koper	Sgt. Charles J. Luquette	349	Ball Turret Gunner	KIA
Koper	S/Sgt. Arthur Frankel	349	Left Waist Gunner	KIA
Koper	Sgt. Ralph V. Zarzecki	349	Right Waist Gunner	KIA
Koper	Sgt. Bernard Sundin	349	Tail Gunner	KIA

[1]March 6, 1944, Berlin[2]
13 B Wing
100 A Group
Mission Summary

Lead Squadron

Devore – Elton
231981 LN E
No Name
No Battle Damage

Chadwick
23413 LN V
Hard Luck!
A Battle Damage

Granack
239872 LN A
Rubber Check
Failed to Return – 2 KIA, 8 POW

Cope
237807 LN O
Alice from Dallas II
Returned Early – AC Battle Damage

Pearson
231074 LN Q
Cahepit
A Battle Damage

Malooly
231049 LN U
Superstitious Aloysious
No Battle Damage

High Squadron

Harrison
231710 XR P
The Savage
A Battle Damage

Murray
230799 XR J
The Bagassbird II
Failed to Return – 10 KIA

Amiero
231731 XR M
No Name
Failed to Return – 9 KIA, 1 POW

Cowan
231723 XR R
Sparky
No Battle Damage

Wilson
23534 XR N
Ol' Dad
A Battle Damage

Morgan
25957 XR D
Horny
No Battle Damage

Lautenschlager
238197 LN T
Half and Half
Failed to Return – 1 KIA, 9 POW

Gibbons
231968 LN D
Miss Irish
A Battle Damage

Harper
232009 LN X
Black Cat 13
Returned Early – AC Battle Damage

Low Squadron 390th BG A/C

Wilkinson
239927 DI R
The Skillet

Warren
239821 DI J
Hey Moitle
AC Battle Damage

Dower
232089 DI W
No Name

Sutters
231971 DI E
Twenty-One or Bust
AC Battle Damage

Reich
238130 DI B
No Name
AC Battle Damage

Sterr
231892 DI H
I'll Be Around
AC Battle Damage

Nine Aircraft returned from the 100 A Group that hit the Target. All six 390 BG aircraft returned to Framlingham after the mission.

100 B Group[3]

Mission Summary

Lead Squadron

Lauro-Swartout
231306 LD V
Nelson King
B Battle Damage

Helmick
237936 EP M
Our Mark
A Battle Damage

Handorf
238011 EP P
Kind-a-Ruff
Failed to Return – 2 POW, 8 KIA

Brannan
231735 EP B
Lucky Lee
Failed to Return – 8 POW, 2 KIA

Shoens
231767 EP E
Our Gal Sal
A Battle Damage

Rish
238044 EP R
Spirit of 44
Failed to Return – 7 POW, 3 KIA

High Squadron

Miner
238059 LD A
No Name
Failed to Return – 6 POW, 4 KIA

Kendall
230278 LD R
Sly Fox
Failed to Return – 10 KIA

Barton
231800 LD U
No Name
Failed to Return – 10 POW

Gummersall
231895 LD Y
Miss Chief
Returned Early

Terry
297482 LD W
Terry and the Pirates
Failed to Return – 3 POW, 7 KIA

Radtke
297491 LD B
Ronnie R
Failed to Return – 9 POW, 1 KIA

Forsythe
238175 LD Q
No Name
Returned Early

Thomas
26087 LD Z
Royal Flush
Returned Early

Barrick
239994 LD D
Snort Stuff
Failed to Return – Landed in Sweden

Low Squadron

Massol
232018 EP L
Waticare
Returned Early

Ferbrache
23508 LD P
Bastard's Bungalow II
A Battle Damage

Lacy
231389 EP J
Luscious Lucy
A Battle Damage

Montgomery
230170 XR G
Pride of the Century
Failed to Return – 9 POW, 1 KIA

Koper
231051 EP K
Goin Jessies
Failed to Return – 3 POW, 7 KIA

95 A Group

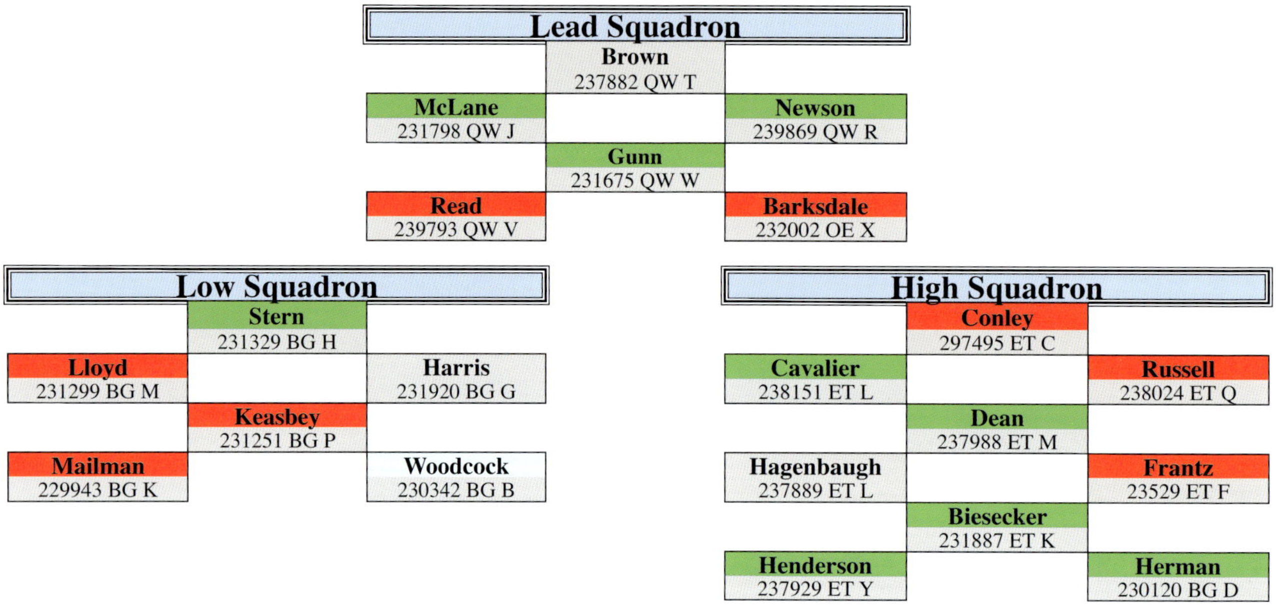

[1] 231968 ***Miss Irish*** moved down from High Squadron and then to the slot to the right of to 231981 when 239872 ***Rubber Check*** was hit by flak over the target.

[2] 231306 ***Nelson King*** Captain Jack Swartout, 351st Bomb Squadron Operations Officer was designated as low **B** Group leader and fly "right seat" to Captain Frank Lauro, 418th Bomb Squadron, as lead aircraft to the group's 20 B-17s. At 1200 over Haseluenne, this B-17 was struck by a FW 190 but continued with the mission, making a forced landing at Honnington Sub Depot.

231767 ***Our Gal Sal*** bombed with the 95 BG.

239994 ***Snort Stuff*** moved from High Squadron to Low squadron when Massol (232018) left the formation with mechanical problems.

March 8, 1944, Berlin

100 A Group

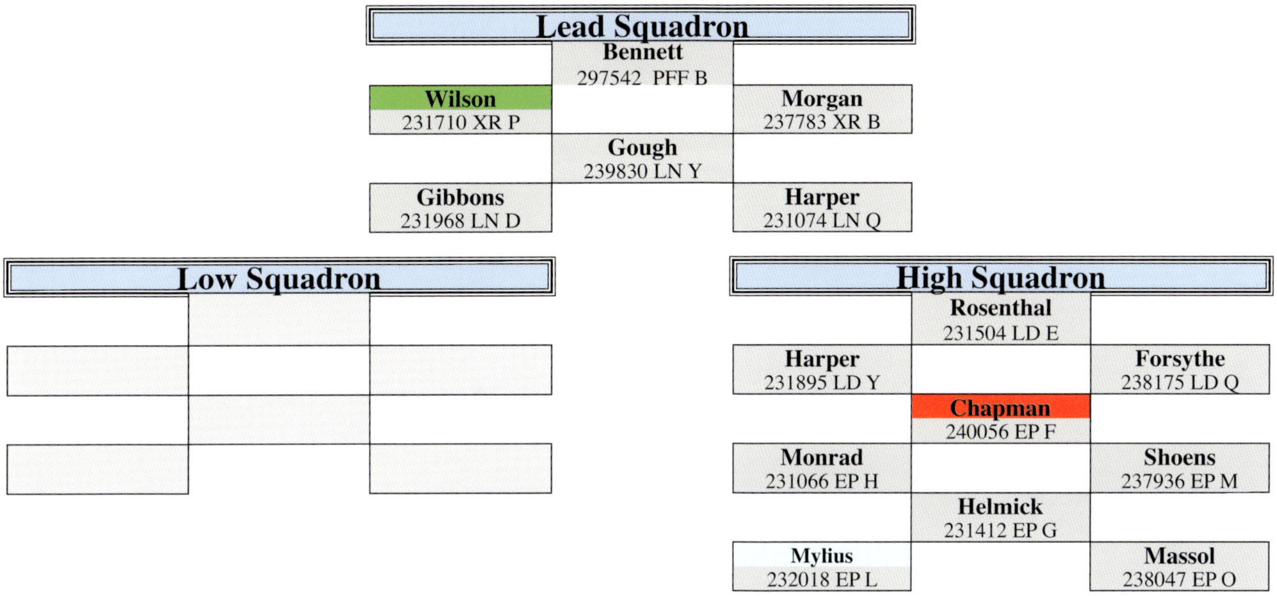

100 A Lead Squadron

297542 *City of Savannah* 388 BG 563 BS B Bennett

Bennett	Lt Col John M. Bennett	HQ	Command Pilot
Bennett	To Be Determined		Pilot
Bennett	To Be Determined		Bombardier
Bennett	Captain Leonard Bull	HQ	Navigator
Bennett	To Be Determined		Top Turret – Engineer
Bennett	To Be Determined		Radio Operator - Gunner
Bennett	To Be Determined		Ball Turret Gunner
Bennett	To Be Determined		Left Waist Gunner
Bennett	To Be Determined		Right Waist Gunner
Bennett	Lt. Charles S. Stapleton	349	Formation Control Officer

237783 *Dobie* 349 XR B Morgan

Morgan	Lt. Leon R. Morgan	349	Pilot
Morgan	2Lt. Ralph O. Ward	349	Copilot
Morgan	S/Sgt. Sam J. LaFace	349	Toggler
Morgan	2Lt. Robert E. McCormick	349	Navigator
Morgan	T/Sgt. Maynard L. Lobb	349	Top Turret - Engineer
Morgan	T/Sgt. Tony L. Verdusco	349	Radio Operator - Gunner
Morgan	S/Sgt. David C. Lyon Jr	349	Ball Turret Gunner
Morgan	S/Sgt. Kenneth R. Lash Jr	349	Left Waist Gunner
Morgan	S/Sgt. Hugo C. Kleckner	349	Right Waist Gunner
Morgan	S/Sgt. Ernest R. Gomez	349	Tail Gunner

231710 *The Savage* 349 XR P Wilson

Wilson	2Lt. Mark V. Wilson	349	Pilot
Wilson	2Lt. Charles E. Adams	349	Copilot
Wilson	S/Sgt.John L. Craven	349	Toggler
Wilson	2Lt. John T. Johnston	349	Navigator
Wilson	T/Sgt. John W. McAuliffe	349	Top Turret - Engineer
Wilson	T/Sgt. Eugene V. Sweeney	349	Radio Operator - Gunner
Wilson	S/Sgt. Charlie J. Hopkins	349	Ball Turret Gunner
Wilson	Sgt. George B. Donahue	349	Left Waist Gunner
Wilson	Sgt. William E. Moreland	349	Right Waist Gunner
Wilson	Sgt. Cecil G. Davis	349	Tail Gunner

239830 *Berlin Playboy* 350 LN Y Gough

Gough	2Lt. George H. Gough	350	Pilot
Gough	2Lt Thomas H. Mallen	350	Copilot
Gough	2 Lt. Stuart W. Feely	350	Bombardier
Gough	2Lt. Jack A. Young	350	Navigator
Gough	T/Sgt Chester Thompson	350	Top Turret - Engineer
Gough	T/Sgt Louis P. Paltrineri	350	Radio Operator - Gunner
Gough	S/Sgt Carl F. Schuster	350	Ball Turret Gunner
Gough	S/Sgt Jack W. Domenig	350	Left Waist Gunner
Gough	S/Sgt John E. Trout	350	Right Waist Gunner
Gough	S/Sgt Ralph T. Graham	350	Tail Gunner

231074 *Cahepit* 350 LN Q C.B. *'Red'* Harper

Harper, CB	2Lt. Celesta B. *'Red'* Harper	350	Pilot
Harper, CB	2Lt. Robert S. Flannigan	350	Copilot
Harper, CB	2Lt. Arthur E. Cox	350	Bombardier
Harper, CB	2Lt. Charles T. Hardiman	350	Navigator
Harper, CB	T/Sgt. Clarence P. Luquet	350	Top Turret - Engineer
Harper, CB	T/Sgt. Alvin E. James	350	Radio Operator - Gunner
Harper, CB	Sgt. Austin P. Curlee	350	Ball Turret Gunner
Harper, CB	Sgt. John B. Bowers	350	Left Waist Gunner
Harper, CB	Sgt. Wiley A. Dobbs	350	Right Waist Gunner
Harper, CB	Sgt. Anderson R. Frank Jr	350	Tail Gunner

231968 *Miss Irish* 350 LN D Gibbons

Gibbons	2Lt. John P. Gibbons	350	Pilot
Gibbons	2Lt. Robert Dykeman	350	Copilot
Gibbons	2Lt. Maurice H. Cain	350	Bombardier
Gibbons	2Lt. Everett M. Johnson	350	Navigator
Gibbons	T/Sgt. Ira L. Arnold	350	Top Turret - Engineer
Gibbons	T/Sgt. Robert D. Longworth	350	Radio Operator - Gunner
Gibbons	Sgt. Bernard L. Spragg	350	Ball Turret Gunner
Gibbons	Sgt. Frank W. Buschmeier	350	Left Waist Gunner
Gibbons	Sgt. Myron J. Ettus	350	Right Waist Gunner
Gibbons	Sgt. Archie W. Bunting	350	Tail Gunner

100 A High Squadron

231504 *Rosie's Riveters* 418 LD E Rosenthal

Rosenthal	Captain Robert *'Rosie'* Rosenthal	418	Pilot
Rosenthal	Lt Winifred *'Pappy'* Lewis	418	Copilot
Rosenthal	Lt Clifford Milburn	418	Bombardier
Rosenthal	Lt Anthony J. Busalacchi	418	Navigator
Rosenthal	T/Sgt Clarence C. Hall	418	Top Turret - Engineer
Rosenthal	T/Sgt Michael Boccuzzi	418	Radio Operator - Gunner
Rosenthal	Sgt Ray H. Robinson	418	Ball Turret Gunner
Rosenthal	S/Sgt Marion J. Sheldon	418	Left Waist Gunner
Rosenthal	S/Sgt James P. Mack	418	Right Waist Gunner
Rosenthal	S/Sgt William J. DeBlasio	418	Tail Gunner

238175 418 LD X Forsythe

Forsythe	2Lt. Wallace C. Forsythe	418	Pilot
Forsythe	2Lt. Prescott H. Haralson	418	Copilot
Forsythe	2Lt. Robert W. McAtee	418	Bombardier
Forsythe	2Lt. Augustus H. Paine	418	Navigator
Forsythe	S/Sgt. Percy J. Johnston	418	Top Turret - Engineer
Forsythe	S/Sgt. Peter J. Buck	418	Radio Operator - Gunner
Forsythe	Sgt. Peter VanSlyck	418	Ball Turret Gunner
Forsythe	Sgt. Nelson C. Linke	418	Left Waist Gunner
Forsythe	Sgt. John A. Codoluto	418	Right Waist Gunner
Forsythe	Sgt. Richard D. Schad	418	Tail Gunner

231895 ***Miss Chief*** **418 LD Y** **Harper**

Harper, J	2Lt. James C. Harper	418	Pilot	
Harper, J	2 Lt. Tony L. Hulsey	418	Copilot	
Harper, J	2Lt. William A. Naegele	418	Bombardier	
Harper, J	2Lt. Charlie C. Cowing	418	Navigator	
Harper, J	T/Sgt Wallace S. Carter	418	Top Turret - Engineer	
Harper, J	T/Sgt Robert E. Hudson	418	Radio Operator - Gunner	
Harper, J	S/Sgt Joseph B. Kyrc	418	Ball Turret Gunner	
Harper, J	S/Sgt Kenneth C. Helming	418	Left Waist Gunner	
Harper, J	S/Sgt Frederick A. Padstawski	418	Right Waist Gunner	
Harper, J	S/Sgt John L. Mauk	418	Tail Gunner	

240056 ***Holy Terror III – Katie's Boys*** **351 EP F** **Chapman**

Chapman	2Lt. Norman L. Chapman	351	Pilot	
Chapman	2Lt. Rex M. Ellis	351	Copilot	POW
Chapman	2Lt. Wilson D. Clark	351	Bombardier	POW
Chapman	2Lt. Glenn G. Lindom	351	Navigator	POW
Chapman	S/Sgt. George W. Silvermann	351	Top Turret - Engineer	POW
Chapman	S/Sgt. Milton Scharf	351	Radio Operator - Gunner	POW
Chapman	Sgt. Durward E. Hutchings	351	Ball Turret Gunner	POW
Chapman	Sgt. Leon E. Hill	351	Left Waist Gunner	POW
Chapman	S/Sgt Frank A. Yzenas	351	Right Waist Gunner	POW
Chapman	S/Sgt George E. Dobbs	351	Tail Gunner	POW

237936 ***Our Mark*** **351 EP M** **Shoens**

Shoens	Lt. Robert J. Shoens	351	Pilot
Shoens	Lt. Duncan R. Shand	351	Copilot
Shoens	S/Sgt. Chester P. Coulam	351	Toggler
Shoens	Lt Glenn Hudson	351	Navigator
Shoens	T/Sgt. William Eresman	351	Top Turret – Engineer
Shoens	T/Sgt. Donald B. Hammond	351	Radio Operator – Gunner
Shoens	S/Sgt. Edward Silverstone	351	Ball Turret Gunner
Shoens	S/Sgt. William W. Wright	351	Left Waist Gunner
Shoens	S/Sgt. Virgil H. Warders	351	Right Waist Gunner
Shoens	S/Sgt. Don L. Blair	351	Tail Gunner

231066 ***Fools Rush In*** **351 EP H** **Monrad** (pick up crew)

Monrad	Lt Raymond V.E. Monrad	351	Pilot
Monrad	Lt J. Goodbread	351	Copilot
Monrad	T/Sgt Dorsett C. Bennett	351	Toggler
Monrad	Lt. Thomas R. Kizak	351	Navigator
Monrad	T/Sgt Hugh A. Smallwood	351	Top Turret – Engineer
Monrad	T/Sgt Harry A. Bonn	351	Radio Operator – Gunner
Monrad	S/Sgt Charlie L. Anglin	351	Ball Turret Gunner
Monrad	S/Sgt Loren G. Johnson	351	Left Waist Gunner
Monrad	S/Sgt John M. Delaney	351	Right Waist Gunner
Monrad	S/Sgt John Rupnick	351	Tail Gunner

231412 ***Mason And Dixon*** **351 EP G** **Helmick**

Helmick	2Lt. Richard Helmick	351	Pilot
Helmick	2Lt. Jerome F. Leirich	351	Copilot
Helmick	2Lt. Herbert R. Greenberg	351	Bombardier
Helmick	2Lt. Sol S. Kranzler	351	Navigator
Helmick	T/Sgt. George E. Madden	351	Top Turret – Engineer
Helmick	T/Sgt. Joseph G. Kelly	351	Radio Operator - Gunner
Helmick	S/Sgt. Robert M. Myers	351	Ball Turret Gunner
Helmick	S/Sgt. Edwin I. Morgan	351	Left Waist Gunner
Helmick	S/Sgt. Henry W. Johnson	351	Right Waist Gunner
Helmick	S/Sgt. Robert D. Abney	351	Tail Gunner

238047	*Feaver Beaver*	351 EP O	Massol
Massol	Lt. John F. Massol	351	Pilot
Massol	2Lt. Harold D. Granger	351	Copilot
Massol	2Lt. Edwin A. Stern Jr	351	Bombardier
Massol	2Lt. Edward C. King Jr	351	Navigator
Massol	T/Sgt. Bernard G. Siegel	351	Top Turret - Engineer
Massol	T/Sgt. Asa A. Spengler	351	Radio Operator - Gunner
Massol	S/Sgt. Winfred C. Williams	351	Ball Turret Gunner
Massol	S/Sgt. William L. Reneau	351	Left Waist Gunner
Massol	S/Sgt. Oliver N. McCartney	351	Right Waist Gunner
Massol	S/Sgt. Newman E. Garmon	351	Tail Gunner

232018	*Waticare*	351 EP L	Mylius
Mylius	2Lt Charles W. Mylius Jr	351	Pilot
Mylius	2Lt. Warren G. McCoy	351	Copilot
Mylius	2Lt. Norman T. High	351	Bombardier
Mylius	2Lt. Charles J. Galligan	351	Navigator
Mylius	S/Sgt James R. Russel	351	Top Turret – Engineer
Mylius	S/Sgt Vincent J. Wood	351	Radio Operator – Gunner
Mylius	S/Sgt Carleton E. Brown	351	Ball Turret Gunner
Mylius	S/Sgt Edmond J. Sullivan	351	Left Waist Gunner
Mylius	S/Sgt Charles E. McSpadden	351	Right Waist Gunner
Mylius	S/Sgt Herbert D. Fern	351	Tail Gunner

Thumbnail History of Participating 100 BG Aircraft

This section provides to the greatest extent possible an operational history of each participating 100 BG aircraft. For each aircraft information is provided about when the aircraft was accepted into the USSAF inventory, stateside assignments, when assigned the UK, details about known missions, and the ultimate fate of the aircraft. The key at the end of this section provides details to the various codes used (e.g. REM, RES, P, A, just to name a few).

Activated - 1 June 1942
AF Stations:
Podington 2 June 1943
Thorpe Abbotts 9 June 1943
First Operational Sortie - 25 June 1943
Last Operational Sortie - 20 April 1945
Markings:
Air Division Group Letter -- **D**.
349 XR
350 LN
351 EP
418 LD

23413 350 V *Hard Luck!*

8 Jun 43	Accepted into Inventory
10 Jun 43	Dallas
18 Aug 43	Dow
19 Aug 43	Assigned to UK
3 Sep 43	A
15 Sep 43	P
23 Sep 43	REO
26 Sep 43	P
2 Oct 43	P
4 Oct 43	P
9 Oct 43	P
10 Oct 43	REO - Arrived at AF Framlingham Too late to pick up 390BG crew
20 Oct 43	P
7 Nov 43	P
13 Nov 43	P
30 Nov 43	REM
11 Dec 43	RES
13 Dec 43	RES
16 Dec 43	P
22 Dec 43	P
24 Dec 43	P
31 Dec 43	P
21 Jan 44	AC
3 Mar 44	P
4 Mar 44	P
6 Mar 44	A - f - 100A Lead #3
16 Mar 44	P
13 Apr 44	AC - f
7 May 44	RFO - Pilot Lt Loren G. Van Steenis 1 KIA, 8 RTD, 1 WIA
15 May 44	Returned to operations
14 Aug 44	FTR - Flak crashed Falkengesass, Germany 2Lt Donald E. Cielewich – 9 POW - MACR 7899

23508 418 P ***Bastard's Bungalow***

13 Jul 43	Denver
14 Jul 43	Accepted into Inventory
15 Aug 43	Scott
24 Aug 43	Assigned to UK
26 Sep 43	P
2 Oct 43	P
4 Oct 43	A
20 Oct 43	A
5 Nov 43	REM
7 Nov 43	P
16 Nov 43	P
19 Nov 43	REM
30 Nov 43	REM
11 Dec 43	P
13 Dec 43	P
16 Dec 43	A
22 Dec 43	P
30 Dec 43	AC
11 Jan 44	AC
4 Mar 44	P
6 Mar 44	A - f, c - Lt Ferbrache Crew
18 Mar 44	FTR - Fighters Crash landed Ulm, Germany - 2Lt Robert J. Horn – 10 POW - MACR 3232

NOTE: Also named ***Jersey Lily***

23534 349 N ***Ol' Dad***

23 Jul 43	Accepted into Inventory
24 Jul 43	Denver
31 Aug 43	Dyersburg
8 Sep 43	Assigned to UK
10 Oct 43	REM - #2 and #3 high temperature could not keep up with formation
22 Dec 43	RES
25 Feb 44	A
4 Mar 44	P
6 Mar 44	P
15 Mar 44	P
16 Mar 44	P
22 Mar 44	AC
27 Apr 44	FTR - Flak crashed Ardoye, France Lt Winans C. Shaddix - 1 EVD, 9 POW - E&E 1692 - MACR 4268 A/C code was L at this point

25957 349 D ***Horny***

24 May 43	Accepted into Inventory
31 May 43	Long Beach
5 Jul 43	Gore
20 Jul 43	Dow
25 Jul 43	Assigned to UK
2 Oct 43	P
4 Oct 43	FTO-Blew tail wheel
8 Oct 43	A
14 Oct 43	A - xmg
20 Oct 43	FL - AF Framlingham
3 Nov 43	REO
13 Nov 43	P
30 Nov 43	REO
11 Dec 43	P
13 Dec 43	P
16 Dec 43	REM - electric controls failed
20 Dec 43	REM - # 2 failed
22 Dec 43	P
24 Dec 43	P
30 Dec 43	A
3 Mar 44	P
4 Mar 44	P
6 Mar 44	P
15 Mar 44	P
16 Mar 44	P
25 Apr 44	A - f
9 May 44	Salvaged

26087 418 Z ***Royal Flush/Harper's Ferry***

16 Jul 43	Accepted into Inventory
18 Jul 43	Long Beach
19 Jul 43	Cheyenne
4 Sep 43	Assigned to UK
00 Sep 43	Named ***Harper's Ferry***
23 Sep 43	P
27 Sep 43	P
2 Oct 43	P
4 Oct 43	A
9 Oct 43	P
10 Oct 43	AC - f, c, xmg, s
30 Nov 43	P
11 Dec 43	P
13 Dec 43	P
16 Dec 43	P
20 Dec 43	REM - # 4 failed, # 3 supercharger failed
22 Dec 43	P
24 Dec 43	P
30 Dec 43	P
31 Dec 43	P
4 Mar 44	P
6 Mar 44	REM
9 Mar 44	P
18 Mar 44	A
13 Apr 44	A - f
29 May 44	A - f
18 Jun 44	A - f
11 Aug 44	FTR - Flak - Destroyed by flak, hits between No. 3 engine and the fuselage immediately after bombs away. The aircraft exploded over the Foret de Neudon near Clamart and crashed in a harvest field near the target. Six of the crew bailed out. 2Lt Alfred Aske Jr - 4 KIA, 5 POW -

E&E 1238, 2124 -MACR 8074
NOTE: Also named ***Harper's Ferry***

230061 418 T ***Wolf Pack***
3 Apr 43 Accepted into Inventory
6 Apr 43 Cheyenne
15 Apr 43 Kearney
2 May 43 Wendover
22 May 43 Kearney
30 May 43 Dow
1 Jun 43 Assigned to UK
? Jun 43 Named *Just-a-Snappin'*
14 Jul 43 REM - runaway prop
? Aug 43 Named *Wolf Pack*
15 Aug 43 A -
17 Aug 43 E -
10 Oct 43 REO – Could not test fire guns
5 Nov 43 REO
7 Nov 43 P
13 Nov 43 REO – Could not find formation
11 Dec 43 P
13 Dec 43 P
16 Dec 43 P
20 Dec 43 P
22 Dec 43 P
24 Dec 43 P
30 Dec 43 P
3 Mar 44 P
28 Jun 44 RZOI
17 Apr 45 Brookley
28 Jun 44 Returned Zone of the Interior
17 Apr 45 Brookley

230091 418 S ***Blivit***
6 Apr 43 Accepted into Inventory
9 Apr 43 Denver
10 Apr 43 Gore
27 Apr 43 Denver
1 May 43 Tinker
25 May 43 Great Falls
29 May 43 Kearney
16 Jun 43 Dow
16 Jun 43 Assigned to UK
2 Oct 43 P
4 Oct 43 P
8 Oct 43 A -
7 Nov 43 P
13 Nov 43 P
30 Nov 43 P
13 Dec 43 P
16 Dec 43 P
20 Dec 43 P
22 Dec 43 P
24 Dec 43 P
31 Dec 43 P
3 Mar 44 P
21 Apr 44 NCS - crashed - AF Eye
2Lt Myron D. Richman - 10 KIS
5 May 44 Salvaged

230152 418 X ***Messie Bessie***
15 Apr 43 Accepted into Inventory
17 Apr 43 Cheyenne
24 Apr 43 Smoky Hill
30 Apr 43 Walla Walla
20 May 43 Smoky Hill
28 May 43 Dow
31 May 43 Assigned to UK
25 Jun 43 REM - # 4 engine burned up
25 Jul 43 REM - ball turret
12 Aug 43 REM - flap trouble
17 Aug 43 RES
16 Sep 43 FTO - # 4 magneto out
7 Nov 43 REM
21 Jan 44 AC
4 Mar 44 P
19 Mar 44 A
28 Apr 44 A - f
24 May 44 AC - c
28 Apr 45 Salvaged

230170 349 G ***The Pride of the Century***
17 Apr 43 Accepted into Inventory
21 Apr 43 Cheyenne
27 Apr 43 Tinker
5 May 43 Smoky Hill
28 May 43 Kearney
7 Jun 43 Dow
9 Jun 43 Assigned to UK
7 Jul 43 Named ***Torchy 2***
17 Aug 43 P
15 Sep 43 RFO - Lt Sam L. Barr - 1 WIA
(Lt James Brown)
23 Sep 43 P
27 Sep 43 P
? Oct 43 Named ***Hot Spit***
? Oct 43 Named ***Miss Carriage***
? Oct 43 Named ***Oh Nausea***
2 Oct 43 P
8 Oct 43 A
? Nov 43 Named ***Ten Batty Boys***
5 Nov 43 REO
13 Nov 43 P
16 Nov 43 P
19 Nov 43 REM
11 Dec 43 P
13 Dec 43 FTO
16 Dec 43 P
20 Dec 43 P
22 Dec 43 P

24 Dec 43 P
30 Dec 43 FTO
31 Dec 43 P
? Mar 44 Named ***The Pride of the Century***
3 Mar 44 P
4 Mar 44 P
6 Mar 44 FTR Fighters crashed Colnrode, Germany Lt Coy I. Montgomery – 1 KIA, 9 POW - MACR 3015

230278 418 R ***Sly Fox***
4 May 43 Accepted into Inventory
8 May 43 Denver
9 May 43 Gore
29 May 43 Kearney
19 Jun 43 Dow
19 Jun 43 Assigned to UK
20 Jun 43 Assigned to 385th Bomb Group
28 Jul 43 Damaged by Flak over Oschersleben
24 Aug 43 Damaged in North Africa with 385thBG taxi accident, a/c slipped off steel matting, Tail Fin chopped off by another bomber. Lt Hutchison Crew left in North Africa for repairs.
? Sept 43 Return to England, assigned to 418th BS, 100BG
4 Mar 44 P
6 Mar 44 FTR - Fighters crashed Haseluenne, Germany 2Lt Zeb Kendall – 10 POW - MACR 3016

230487 349 F **Torchy 3**
8 Jun 43 Accepted into Inventory
9 Jun 43 Dallas
11 Jun 43 Gore
28 Jul 43 Love
11 Aug 43 Scott
17 Aug 43 Presque Isle
19 Aug 43 Assigned to UK
2 Oct 43 FTO
20 Oct 43 REM
26 Sep 43 P
2 Oct 43 FTO -
4 Oct 43 P
8 Oct 43 P
20 Oct 43 REM – interphone failed
7 Nov 43 P
13 Nov 43 P
16 Nov 43 P
26 Nov 43 AC -
22 Dec 43 P
24 Dec 43 P
31 Dec 43 P
3 Mar 44 P
22 Mar 44 A -
13 Apr 44 A - f
20 Apr 44 A - f

230799 349 J ***The Bigassbird II***
27 Jul 43 Accepted into Inventory
29 Jul 43 Cheyenne
9 Aug 43 Gore
10 Aug 43 Scott
16 Aug 43 Presque Isle
19 Aug 43 Assigned to UK
15 Sep 43 P
23 Sep 43 P
26 Sep 43 P
9 Oct 43 REM - #3 high oil pressure
20 Oct 43 P
6 Mar 44 FTR - Fighters crashed Haseluenne, Germany Lt William E. Murray – 3 KIA, 7 POW

231049 350 U ***Superstitious Aloysious***
10 Sep 43 Accepted into Inventory
10 Sep 43 Cheyenne
23 Sep 43 Grand Island
4 Oct 43 Assigned to UK
5 Nov 43 REM
7 Nov 43 REM
13 Nov 43 P
26 Nov 43 REM
13 Dec 43 RES
16 Dec 43 P
20 Dec 43 P
24 Dec 43 P
21 Jan 44 AC
3 Mar 44 P
4 Mar 44 P
6 Mar 44 P
9 Mar 44 P
19 Mar 44 AC
11 Apr 44 A - f
29 Apr 44 A - f
24 May 44 AC - f, c
12 Jan 45 Returned Zone of the Interior
18 Sep 45 Altus, Oklahoma
NOTE: Also named ***Section Eight***

231051 351 K ***Goin Jessies***
9 Sep 43 Accepted into Inventory
11 Sep 43 Cheyenne
21 Sep 43 Grand Island
24 Oct 43 Assigned to UK
7 Nov 43 P
13 Nov 43 P
16 Nov 43 P
29 Nov 43 REM
11 Dec 43 P

	13 Dec 43	P
	16 Dec 43	P
	20 Dec 43	P
	22 Dec 43	P
	30 Dec 43	REM
	4 Mar 44	P
	6 Mar 44	FTR - Fighters- Jump near Oldenburg. 2Lt Robert C. Koper – 7 KIA, 3 POW - MACR 3018

231066	351 H	***Fools Rush In***
	10 Sep 43	Accepted into Inventory
	14 Sep 43	Cheyenne
	29 Sep 43	Scott
	3 Oct 43	Assigned to UK
	5 Nov 43	REO
	13 Nov 43	RFO - Lt John Love
	30 Nov 43	P
	13 Dec 43	P
	16 Dec 43	P
	20 Dec 43	P
	22 Dec 43	P
	24 Dec 43	P
	30 Dec 43	P
	31 Dec 43	P
	3 Mar 44	P
	8 Mar 44	P
	31 Dec 44	FTR - Flak - Radegast, Germany Lt Floyd E. Henderson 6 KIA, 3 POW - MACR 11366

NOTE: Aircraft flew 65 missions. Also named ***Dixie Baby***

231074	350 Q	***Cahepit***
	13 Sep 43	Accepted into Inventory
	15 Sep 43	Cheyenne
	28 Sep 43	Scott
	3 Oct 43	Assigned to UK
	30 Nov 43	REM
	22 Dec 43	RES
	30 Dec 43	RES
	5 Nov 43	A
	16 Nov 43	P
	11 Dec 43	P
	16 Dec 43	P
	20 Dec 43	P
	24 Dec 43	P
	31 Dec 43	P
	21 Jan 44	AC
	3 Mar 44	P
	6 Mar 44	A - f, smg
	8 Mar 44	P
	15 Mar 44	P
	16 Mar 44	P
	19 Mar 44	A
	20 Apr 44	A - f
	25 Jun 44	A - f
	13 Jul 44	FTRINT - Flak Crash landed Emmen, Switzerland. 2Lt Donald A. Waters - 10 INT - MACR 7501

231220	350 P	***Fletcher's Castoria***
	29 Sep 43	Accepted into Inventory
	4 Oct 43	Denver
	16 Oct 43	Grand Island
	21 Oct 43	Wilmington
	4 Nov 43	Assigned to UK
	20 Dec 43	REM - # 2 leaking oil
	22 Dec 43	P
	24 Dec 43	P
	30 Dec 43	RES
	31 Dec 43	P
	3 Mar 44	P
	27 Apr 45	Returned Zone of the Interior - Rome
	2 Oct 45	Salvaged

231249	349 L	***Miss Carriage***
	5 Oct 43	Accepted into Inventory
	8 Oct 43	Cheyenne
	22 Oct 43	Grand Island
	28 Oct 43	Memphis
	1 Nov 43	Assigned to UK
	4 Mar 44	P
	9 Mar 44	P
	16 Mar 44	P
	22 Mar 44	AC
	11 Apr 44	AC - f, smg
	27 Apr 44	A - f
	28 Apr 44	AC - f, z fragments from an exploded aircraft
	10 May 44	RFO - crash landed
	20 May 44	Salvaged

NOTE: Also named ***Section Eigh***t by Cowan Crew

231256	351 S	***King Bee II***
	6 Oct 43	Accepted into Inventory
	12 Oct 43	Cheyenne
	20 Oct 43	Grand Island
	6 Nov 43	Memphis
	10 Nov 43	Assigned to UK
	3 Mar 44	P
	4 Mar 44	P
	16 Mar 44	RES
	11 Apr 44	A - f
	? Jul 44	NCS - Training crash landed
	13 Jul 44	Salvaged

231306	351 V	***Nelson King***
	14 Oct 43	Accepted into Inventory
	20 Oct 43	Cheyenne
	3 Nov 43	Grand Island

10 Nov 43 Romulus
14 Nov 43 Assigned to UK
24 Dec 43 P
31 Dec 43 P
4 Mar 44 P
6 Mar 44 B Forced landing at Honington,
11 May 44 A - f
19 May 44 A - f
24 May 44 FTR - Fighters crashed Wittstock, Germany. Lt Emil J. Siewart - 3 KIA, 7 POW - MACR 5165

231389 351 J ***Lucious Lucy***
25 Oct 43 Accepted into Inventory
28 Oct 43 Cheyenne
13 Nov 43 Grand Island
26 Nov 43 Wilmington
30 Nov 43 Assigned to UK
3 Mar 44 P
4 Mar 44 P
6 Mar 44 A - f, s - Lt Lucious G. Lacy
15 Mar 44 P
16 Mar 44 P
23 Mar 44 A
20 Apr 44 A - f
24 May 44 A - c
28 May 44 FTR - Fighters crashed Barleben, Germany. Lt Lucius G. Lacy – 3 KIA, 7 POW - MACR 5382

NOTE: ***Lacy's Lushes*** (nickname for crew)

231412 351 G ***Mason And Dixon***
27 Oct 43 Accepted into Inventory
31 Oct 43 Cheyenne
12 Nov 43 Grand Island
19 Nov 43 Long Beach
26 Nov 43 Assigned to UK
45 WW Salvaged
30 Jun 45 Returned Zone of the Interior - Bradley
1 Jul 45 Greensboro
2 Jul 45 Tinker
21 Oct 45 South Plains
19 Dec 45 Kingman, Arizona

NOTE: B-17 flew 100+ sorties

231504 418 E ***Rosie's Riveters***
9 Nov 43 Accepted into Inventory
13 Nov 43 Cheyenne
28 Nov 43 Kearney
4 Dec 43 Romulus
8 Dec 43 Presque Isle
15 Dec 43 Assigned to UK
21 Jan 44 AC
3 Mar 44 P
4 Mar 44 P
8 Mar 44 P
15 Mar 44 P
16 Mar 44 P
18 Mar 44 AC
23 Mar 44 A
13 Apr 44 A - f
7 May 44 AC - f
12 May 44 FTR - Flak crashed Goarshausen, ? Lt Alexander W. Kinder - 10 POW MACR 4865

231537 350 S ***Buffalo Gal***
13 Nov 43 Accepted into Inventory
19 Nov 43 Cheyenne
2 Dec 43 Kearney
10 Dec 43 Presque Isle
22 Dec 43 Assigned to UK
23 Dec 43 Gained by 94BG
3 Mar 44 P
4 Mar 44 P
9 Mar 44 P
15 Mar 44 AC
16 Mar 44 P
18 Mar 44 AC
13 Apr 44 AC - f
20 Apr 44 A - f
24 Apr 44 A - f
28 Apr 44 A - f
6 Jun 44 A – f
29 Jul 44 FTR - Fighters crashed Pauschrau, ? Lt William T. Fitzroy - 4 KIA, 5 POW - MACR 7809

231708 351 N ***Skipper II***
6 Dec 43 Accepted into Inventory
9 Dec 43 Cheyenne
20 Dec 43 Kearney
15 Jan 44 Prestwick
16 Jan 44 Assigned to UK
4 Feb 44 AC - f
4 Mar 44 P
16 Mar 44 P
22 Mar 44 AC
13 Apr 44 A - f
21 Jun 44 P-Ruhland, Lt Simmons, Ran out of Gas, landed near Kiev, Ukraine, Soviet Union
2 Mar 45 Carried individual letter **R,** assigned to hard stand #10
5 Jul 45 Returned Zone of the Interior - Bradley
6 Jul 45 Love
7 Jul 45 South Plains
6 Dec 45 Kingman, Arizona

NOTE: B-17 flew 100+ sorties

231710 349 P ***The Savage***
6 Dec 43 Accepted into Inventory
9 Dec 43 Cheyenne
24 Dec 43 Kearney
7 Jan 44 Romulus
19 Jan 44 Assigned to UK
25 Feb 44 AC
6 Mar 44 A - f, xmg
8 Mar 44 A
15 Mar 44 P
16 Mar 44 P
19 Mar 44 AC
28 Mar 44 AC
20 Apr 44 A - f
8 May 44 FTR - Fighters crashed Holingen, ? 2Lt Donald E. Riggle - 2 KIA, 8 POW MACR 4578

231723 349 R ***"Sparky"***
7 Dec 43 Accepted into Inventory
12 Dec 43 Cheyenne
31 Dec 43 Kearney
14 Feb 44 Assigned to UK
3 Mar 44 P
6 Mar 44 P
15 Mar 44 P
16 Mar 44 RFO - Lt Clement H. Cowan - 1 KIA
18 Mar 44 AC
27 Apr 44 A - f
19 May 44 AC - f, z collision with E/A Lt John P. Keys
29 Jul 44 FTR - Fighters crashed Bad Kosen, Germany. 2Lt Jackson E. Phelps – 8 KIA, 1 POW - MACR 7810

231731 349 M
7 Dec 43 Accepted into Inventory
11 Dec 43 Cheyenne
24 Dec 43 Grand Island
24 Jan 44 Romulus
26 Jan 44 Grenier
30 Jan 44 Presque Isle
3 Feb 44 Assigned to UK
3 Mar 44 P
4 Mar 44 P
6 Mar 44 FTR - Fighters crashed Quackenbruck, Germany. Lt Albert F. Amiero 9 KIA, 1 POW – MACR 3019

231735 351 B ***Lucky Lee***
8 Dec 43 Accepted into Inventory
11 Dec 43 Cheyenne
30 Dec 43 Kearney
15 Jan 44 RAF Nutts Corner
16 Jan 44 Assigned to UK
3 Mar 44 P
4 Mar 44 P
6 Mar 44 FTR - Fighters crashed Hausstette, ? Lt George W. Brannan - 3 KIA, 7 POW - MACR 3020

231767 351 E ***Our Gal Sal***
11 Dec 43 Accepted into Inventory
12 Dec 43 Denver
31 Dec 43 Kearney
16 Jan 44 Assigned to UK
16 Jan 44 RAF Nutts Corner
3 Mar 44 P
4 Mar 44 P
6 Mar 44 A - f, smg, s
15 Mar 44 A
16 Mar 44 RES
11 Apr 44 AC - f, smg
7 May 44 A - f
24 May 44 AC - f, c
20 May 45 482BG
31 May 45 Returned Zone of the Interior – Bradley
3 Jun 45 South Plains
8 Nov 45 Kingman, Arizona
NOTE: B-17 flew 100+ sorties

231800 418 U
15 Dec 43 Accepted into Inventory
16 Dec 43 Denver
21 Dec 43 Great Falls
2 Jan 44 Kearney
28 Jan 44 Assigned to UK
29 Jan 44 Presque Isle
3 Mar 44 P
4 Mar 44 P
6 Mar 44 FTR– Fighters crashed Oldenburg, Germany. 2Lt Sherwin L. Barton – 10 POW - MACR 3021

231895 418 Y
28 Dec 43 Accepted into Inventory
3 Jan 44 Cheyenne
14 Jan 44 Kearney
3 Feb 44 Presque Isle
15 Feb 44 Assigned to UK
6 Mar 44 REM
8 Mar 44 A
9 Mar 44 P
16 Mar 44 A
18 Mar 44 A
22 Mar 44 A
11 Apr 44 AC - xmg, smg
15 Jun 44 A - f

25 Jun 44 A - f
31 Dec 44 FTR - Fighters crashed Wesermunde, Germany. 2Lt Paul L. Carroll 9 POW - MACR 11365

231968 350 D ***Miss Irish***
7 Jan 44 Accepted into Inventory
11 Jan 44 Cheyenne
21 Jan 44 Savannah
2 Feb 44 Morrison
2 Feb 44 Assigned to UK
4 Mar 44 P
6 Mar 44 A - f
8 Mar 44 P
9 Mar 44 P
15 Mar 44 P
19 Mar 44 RFO - Flak crash landed RAF Raydon Lt John P. Gibbons - 1 KIA, 9 RTD Salvaged

231970 349 ***Berth'a the Blues***
7 Jan 44 Accepted into Inventory
10 Jan 44 Cheyenne
22 Jan 44 Savannah
2 Feb 44 Assigned to UK
27 Feb 44 Assigned to Lt Murray Crew, who named A/C
3 Mar 44 FTR-Fighters - Iztehoe, Germany Capt Robert H. Lohof - 10 POW – MACR 3022

231981 350 E
10 Jan 44 Accepted into Inventory
12 Jan 44 Cheyenne
25 Jan 44 Savannah
5 Feb 44 Assigned to UK
6 Mar 44 P Lead Plane Devore/Elton
19 Mar 44 AC
20 Apr 44 A - f
24 Apr 44 A - f
15 May 44 Crash Landed at Honington Salvaged
NOTE: On the pilot's side of the B-17, the "N" in the squadron code "LN" was reversed "LИ"

231991 351 D ***Raiford's Raiders***
? Jan 44 Accepted into Inventory
13 Jan 44 Cheyenne
31 Jan 44 Kearney
? Feb 44 Assigned to UK
22 Feb 44 Grenier
6 Mar 44 REM
00 Apr 44 Named ***Miss-Chief***
11 Apr 44 A - f, x
20 Apr 44 A - f
28 Apr 44 A - f
2 Nov 44 RFO - Lt David C. Raiford - 1 KIA
10 Jan 45
26 Feb 45 Salvaged
30 Mar 45 Regained
14 May 45 Taxi accident
14 May 45 Salvaged
NOTE: ***Railford'S Raiders*** not painted on the B-17

232009 350 X ***Black Cat 13***
? Jan 44 Accepted into Inventory
15 Jan 44 Denver
29 Jan 44 Grand Island
? Feb 44 Assigned to UK
4 Mar 44 A
6 Mar 44 AC - f, c
16 Mar 44 A
18 Mar 44 AC
23 Mar 44 A
13 Apr 44 A - f
24 Apr 44 A - f
27 Apr 44 A - f
28 Apr 44 AC - f
11 May 44 AC - f
28 Jul 44 FTR - Mid-Air with 297621. 2Lt Albert S. Spear – 8 KIA, 1 POW - MACR 8174:

232018 351 L ***Waticare***
12 Jan 44 Accepted into Inventory
15 Jan 44 Cheyenne
28 Jan 44 Grand Island
10 Feb 44 Assigned to UK
6 Mar 44 P
9 Mar 44 A
16 Mar 44 P
22 Mar 44 A
23 Mar 44 A
13 Apr 44 AC - f
18 Apr 44 A - f
20 Apr 44 A - f
1 May 44 AC - f
21 Jun 44 LAG Poltava, USSR Lt Mylius Crew ran out gas and crash landed near Kiev

237783 349 B ***Dobie***
26 Aug 43 Accepted into Inventory
26 Aug 43 Denver
29 Sep 43 Scott
3 Oct 43 Assigned to UK
7 Nov 43 P
13 Nov 43 P
16 Nov 43 P
29 Nov 43 A -

16 Dec 43 P
30 Dec 43 A -
3 Mar 44 P
8 Mar 44 P
20 Apr 44 A - f
22 Apr 44 FTR - Fighters - Obersholden Lt Frank W. Harte - 3 KIA, 7 POW – MACR 4166

237807 350 O ***Alice from Dallas II***
3 Sep 43 Accepted into Inventory
7 Sep 43 Long Beach
27 Sep 43 Assigned to UK
7 Nov 43 P
11 Dec 43 P
22 Dec 43 P
24 Dec 43 FTO - # 1 would not start
31 Dec 43 P
21 Jan 44 AC
21 Jan 44 AC
3 Mar 44 P
6 Mar 44 AC - f, c - Mark Cope - 1 WIA
19 May 44 FTR - DIT North Sea - 10 RTD – No MACR
NOTE: ***Rogers Raiders*** not painted on B-17

237936 351 M ***Our Mark***
19 Oct 43 Accepted into Inventory
19 Oct 43 Denver
5 Nov 43 Grand Island
10 Nov 43 Assigned to UK
00 Dec 43 Named ***Our Mark***
3 Mar 44
4 Mar 44 P
6 Mar 44 A - f, z 20mm brass casing
8 Mar 44 P
9 Mar 44 A
16 Mar 44 RES
18 Mar 44 A
22 Mar 44 A
00 Apr 44 Named ***Hang the Expense***
00 Apr 44 Named ***The All American Girl***
00 Apr 44 Dubbed ***Berlin Boys*** by Lt Eichen
22 Jun 44 A - f
10 Jan 45 FTR - Flak crashed Gladbach, Germany. Lt John J. Dodrill - 9 KIA MACR 11744
NOTE: B-17 flew 98 sorties

238011 351 P ***Kind-a-Ruff***
15 Nov 43 Accepted into Inventory
12 Nov 43 Cheyenne
7 Dec 43 New Castle
11 Dec 43 Presque Island
16 Dec 43 Assigned to UK
28 Feb 44 AC
4 Mar 44 P
6 Mar 44 FTR - Fighters crashed Exploded Diepholz, Germany Lt Edward Handorf - 8 KIA, 2 POW – MACR 3023

238016 350 B ***Seaton's Sad Sack***
16 Nov 43 Accepted into Inventory
14 Nov 43 Cheyenne
8 Dec 43 Kearney
9 Dec 43 Presque Island
15 Dec 43 Assigned to UK
3 Mar 44 P
4 Mar 44 FTR - Fighters crashed Berlin, Germany. Lt Stanley M. Seaton – 1 KIA, 9 POW - MACR 3024

238017 349 O ***One Mission LuLu***
16 Nov 43 Accepted into Inventory
15 Nov 43 Cheyenne
7 Dec 43 Syracuse
15 Dec 43 Presque Island
27 Dec 43 Assigned to UK
24 Feb 44 AC
3 Mar 44 FTR - Fighters Schesweg, Germany Lt John G. Gossage - 10 POW – MACR 3025 Mistakenly landed at German Airfield instead of Sweden
NOTE: Name not painted on the aircraft

238044 351 R ***Spirit of '44***
24 Nov 43 Accepted into Inventory
24 Nov 43 Cheyenne
16 Dec 43 Romulus
24 Dec 43 Presque Island
26 Dec 43 Assigned to UK
4 Feb 44 AC - f
3 Mar 44 P
4 Mar 44 P
6 Mar 44 FTR - Fighters crashed Quackenbruck, Germany Lt Merril T. Rish - 4 KIA, 6 POW - MACR 3026

238047 351 O ***Fever Beaver***
25 Nov 43 Accepted into Inventory
25 Nov 43 Cheyenne
6 Dec 43 Kearney
19 Dec 43 Grenier
3 Jan 44 Presque Island
8 Jan 44 Assigned to UK
? Jan 44 Named ***Fever Beaver***
4 Feb 44 A - f
3 Mar 44 P
6 Mar 44 P
9 Mar 44 P

15 Mar 44 P
11 Apr 44 AC - c
20 Apr 44 AC - f
24 Apr 44 AC - f
13 May 44 AC - f
19 May 44 AC - f, smg
21 Jul 45 Returned Zone of the Interior – Independence
10 Nov 45 Independence
21 Dec 45 Kingman, Arizona

NOTE: B-17 flew 125+ sorties; named ***Melancholy Baby*** by Ransom Crewcon; named ***Shady Lady*** by Massol Crew, but not painted on B-17.

238059 418 A
29 Nov 43 Cheyenne
1 Dec 43 Accepted into Inventory
11 Dec 43 Kearney
19 Dec 44 Presque Island
24 Dec 43 Assigned to UK
3 Mar 44 P-
4 Mar 44 P
6 Mar 44 FTR - Fighters crashed Quackenbruck, Germany. Capt David L. Miner - 4 KIA, 6 POW - MACR 3027

238175 418 Q
5 Jan 44 Cheyenne
8 Jan 44 Accepted into Inventory
22 Jan 44 Savannah
14 Feb 44 Assigned to UK
3 Mar 44 P
4 Mar 44 P
6 Mar 44 REM
8 Mar 44 P
15 Mar 44 P
16 Mar 44 P
23 Mar 44 AC
13 Apr 44 AC – f
31 Dec 44 Carried letter code **X**
2 Jan 45 Salvaged

238197 350 T ***Half and Half***
12 Jan 44 Cheyenne
13 Jan 44 Accepted into Inventory
27 Jan 44 Grand Island
9 Feb 44 Assigned to UK
4 Mar 44 P
6 Mar 44 FTR - Fighters crashed Haltern, Germany Lt John Lautenschlager 1 KIA, 9 POW - MACR 3028

239817 349 A ***Murderer's Row***
8 Sep 43 Accepted into Inventory
9 Sep 43 Long Beach
26 Sep 43 Assigned to UK
5 Nov 43 A -
16 Nov 43 P
19 Nov 43 REM -
11 Dec 43 P
13 Dec 43 P
22 Dec 43 P
24 Dec 43 P
30 Dec 43 P
31 Dec 43 P
3 Mar 44 FTR-Fighters- Iztehoe, Germany Lt Robert D. Vollmer - 5 KIA, 5 POW – MACR 3029

239830 350 Y ***Berlin Playboy***
11 Sep 43 Accepted into Inventory
21 Sep 43 Long Beach
3 Oct 43 Grand Island
7 Oct 43 Assigned to UK
30 Dec 43 RES
4 Mar 44 AC
18 Mar 44 FTR - Mid-Air with 237913 crashed Les Defends, France 2Lt Paul A. Martin - 9 KIA, 1 POW – E&E 556 - MACR 3234:

239872 350 A ***Rubber Check***
24 Sep 43 Accepted into Inventory
24 Sep 43 Long Beach
24 Oct 43 Grand Island
18 Nov 43 Assigned to UK
4 Jan 44 RFO - Lt Frank A. Granack
4 Mar 44 TTE Sgt Stearns shot down the 1st Fighter over Berlin
6 Mar 44 FTR- Flak Fighters –Halenbeck, Germany Lt Frank A. Granack – 2 KIA, 8 POW -MACR 3030

NOTE: Also named ***Old Vibration***

239934 350 Z ***My Achin' Back!***
11 Oct 43 Accepted into Inventory
21 Oct 43 Long Beach
31 Oct 43 Grand Island
20 Nov 43 Assigned to UK
4 Mar 44 A
15 Mar 44 FTR - Flak Exploded - Watenbuetel, Germany. Lt Herbert G. Devore – 7 KIA, 3 POW - MACR 3915

239983 351 F ***Katie***
25 Oct 43 Accepted into Inventory
26 Oct 43 Long Beach
3 Dec 43 Assigned to UK
3 Mar 44 P
6 Mar 44 FTO -
15 Mar 44 P
23 Mar 44 A -
13 Apr 44 AC - f
11 May 44 FTR
11 May 44 FTR - Flak Exploded -Ougree, Belgium. 2Lt Jack Hunter – 7 KIA, 3 POW - MACR 4866

239994 418 D ***Snort Stuff***
29 Oct 43 Accepted into Inventory
29 Oct 43 Long Beach
15 Dec 43 Assigned to UK
3 Mar 44 P
4 Mar 44 P
6 Mar 44 FTRINT - Fighters Bulltofta, Sweden Lt Samuel L. Barrick - 10 INT – MACR 3031

NOTE: Some sources cite the name was ***Barrick's Bag;*** Sam Barrick, the pilot, states the B-17 never had that name.

240056 351 F ***Holy Terror III / Katie's Boys***
15 Nov 43 Accepted into Inventory
16 Nov 43 Long Beach
24 Nov 43 Kearney
8 Dec 43 Assigned to UK
? Jan 44 Named ***Call Her Savage***, not painted on B-17
? Feb 44 Named ***Holy Terror III***, painted on B-17
4 Feb 44 AC - f
3 Mar 44 P
8 Mar 44 FTR - Fighters - Juterbog approximately 50 kilometers south of Berlin, Germany. Lt Norman L. Chapman - 10 POW – MACR 3032

297482 418 W ***Terry and the Pirates***
29 Nov 43 Accepted into Inventory
29 Nov 43 Denver
16 Dec 43 Kearney
2 Jan 44 Romulus
10 Jan 44 Westover
14 Jan 44 Presque Isle
15 Jan 44 Assigned to UK
3 Mar 44 P
4 Mar 44 P
6 Mar 44 FTR - Fighters crashed Quackenbruck, Germany. Lt William A. Terry – 7 KIA, 3 POW - MACR 3033

297491 418 B ***Ronnie R***
30 Nov 43 Cheyenne
2 Dec 43 Accepted into Inventory
16 Dec 43 Kearney
31 Dec 43 Romulus
5 Jan 44 Assigned to UK
3 Mar 44 P
4 Mar 44 P
6 Mar 44 FTR - Fighters crashed Twirstringen, Germany. Lt Dean M. Radtke – 1 KIA, 9 POW - MACR 3043

Key

A – Minor battle damage reparable at nearest unit
AC – Major battle damage reparable on site by Maintenance repair Unit
AF - Air Field
B – Significant battle damage reparable by a salvage unit
DIT - Ditched
E – Serious battle damage, beyond economic repair
E&E – Escape and Evasion Report number
EVD – Evaded capture
FTO - Failed to Takeoff
FTR - Failed to Return
KIA – Killed in action
KIS – Killed in service, not operational
MACR - Missing Aircrew Report number
NCS – Non-Combat Sortie
P- Participated on sortie, no reported damage
REM - Returned Early, mechanical reasons
REO - Returned Early, other than mechanical reasons
RES - Returned Early, scheduled spare
RFO - Returned From Operation
RTD – Returned to duty
WIA – Wounded in action

c - 20 mm cannon
f - flak
s - empty shell casings
smg - self-inflicted

Appendix B
Lead Navigator's Narrative

HEADQUARTERS
ONE HUNDREDTH BOMBARDMENT GROUP (H) AAF
Office of the Operations Officer
APO 634

5 March 1944

SUBJECT: Lead Navigator's Narrative for Berlin Mission, 4 March 1944.
TO : Commanding Officer, 100th Bomb group (H), Army Air Forces.

1. The 100th "A" group. Flew as high group in 13 A Combat Wing, which was in the center of the Third Air Division.

2. Takeoff was accomplished approximately 30 minute's late duo to snow squalls in local area. There was no notification of delay in control times. 100th "A" Group attempted to reach briefed alt. (- 19,000') in local area, but high clouds cover prevented this as a re- sult. The first two control points, Felixstowe and Spl. #6 were cut off. Since the circling to flt. alt. was achieved in the area around Colchester, Spl. #7 was crossed 4 minutes early at 1015 hours. The group then was essed to slow down for Clacton, the last control point. At 1030 hours the group left the English coast 10 miles south of Clacton and 95th groups came in under us to accomplish the rendezvous. The wing was in a depleted condition. At 1051 hours 13 "A" Combat Wing crossed the enemy coast 3 miles north of course. Gee fix 1106 hours 5055N - 0343E. DR position at 1126 hours 5018N - DR position 1148 hours 5026N - 0721, after which point the other divisions were observed abandoning Ops. At 1230 hours Dr position 5208N 1012E. At 1235 hours flak was encountered (believed from Brunswick according to DR) At 1301 hours started turning on IP, DR position 5255N - 1300E. At 1524 hours bombs away on lead PFF e estimated position 5223N - 1310E. After swinging on RP at 1330 hours A gradual descent was started, letting down to a minimum of 11,000/. At 1404 hours DR position 5048N - 1230E. At Which point a westerly heading was picked up (273°Mag.). At 1430 hours DR position 5042N - 1038E; At 1500 hours DR position 5035N - 0810E DR position 1540 hours DR position 5030N 0520E. At which point a Mag. heading of 300° was picked up on the turn towards the coast. At 1629 hours Gee position. (10.30 – 35.11); At 1638 hours departed enemy coast on friefed [sic] course. At 1700 hours crossed English coast 5 Mi. north of Felixstowe. Landed at base, Thorpe Abbotts, at 1725 hours.

3. Bombing Data - Approach, arbitrary I.P. selected by PFF, no visible flare notification, time 1301 hours, Bombs away at 1324 hours.

4. Navigation instruments functioned well.

5. Difficulties: - Rendezvous times were almost impossible to make because of weather and failure to delay control times. Otherwise the only major difficulty encountered was adverse weather.

BURTON M. JOSEPH
1st Lt., Air Corps,
Lead Navigator

Lead Bombardier's Narrative

HEADQUARTERS
ONE HUNDREDTH BOMBARDMENT GROUP (H) AAF
Office of the Operations Officer
APO 634

5 March 1944

SUBJECT: Lead Bombardier's Narrative for Berlin Mission, 4 March 1944.
TO : Commanding Officer, 100th Bomb group (H), Army Air Forces.

1. Bombs were dropped on the PFF aircraft.

2. We made a turn at the I.P. of 60°. It was too sharp. We remained in Combat Wing formation on the bomb run.

3. Bomb bay doors were opened at 1301 hours 52°55'N & 13°00'E.

4. The AFCE was on until we reached the I.P., where it was found that this was going to be PFF. The AFCE was then disengaged and the bomb run was made manually. There were several fighter attacks on the run.

5. Fighter attacks interfered with the bombing run.

6. There was a solid under cast, with the exception of several small openings near the target.

7. There were no unusual tactics used by the enemy.

8. We could not observe the results of the bombing.

9. Aiming point was not used.

10. There are no suggested tactical changes.

L. R. JAEBKER
1st Lt., Air Corps,
Lead Bombardier

"The Big B"

Following World War II, I was fortunate to become acquainted with Grif Mumford and Harry Conley. They were both pilots in the original cadre of the 95th Bomb Group, 8th Air Force. I was a waist gunner in a replacement crew assigned to the 95th in the latter part of the war, so I didn't know either one of them in England. In the post war years, Grif and I served on the governing board of our Association, and since the three of us lived in the Bay Area of California, we often got together and became close friends.

It became our custom to meet for lunch once a month to discuss the business of the 95th BG Association and our favorite subject: "How we won the Air War." We usually met at The Circus Club of Menlo Park where Harry, a devoted horseman, was a member. After one or two "Beefeater cocktails," the stories would begin to flow.

Often we would talk about the first daylight bombing of Berlin. Grif was the mission commander for that great event, and I relished hearing the story from him; however, Harry would never fail to lament the fact that bad weather had prevented him from completing the same mission! He was a Squadron Commander and had been selected to lead nine groups from the Third Air Division on 3 March 1944, but they were all turned back when they encountered bad weather in the area above Hamburg. In the spring of 1944, everyone who flew with the 8th Air Force felt the frustration in not bombing Berlin. Harry, as mission commander of that first aborted attempt, felt it most keenly; furthermore, it was to have been his 25th mission!

The next day, 4 March, Berlin was selected again as the prime target for the 13th Combat Wing. The weather was predicted as better than the previous day, and Lt. Colonel Grif Mumford, Commanding Officer of the 412th squadron and Base Operations Officer, was selected to lead the mission. Something new was to take place. A "Pathfinder" aircraft piloted by Lt. Bill Owen of the 482nd BG was to accompany the mission. It was equipped with radar navigational equipment to help see through the clouds to the target below. Because radar was considered "top secret" at the time no publicity was allowed for the crew. Grif as mission commander was to fly the right seat of a B-17 231320, piloted by Lt. Alvin Brown, 412th Squadron. His plane was named "I'll BE AROUND." There was to be P-51 fighter support from the 4th and 357th Fighter Groups. Grif would lead the Wing and Lt. Hal Powers, also of the 412th, was to lead Flight A.

Crews were wakened at 0300 hours. They dressed, ate breakfast, and assembled for briefing. The curtain was drawn revealing the big familiar map of the continent and a line from East Anglia to Berlin. There was the usual mix of whistles and groans that reflected the different attitudes about going to Berlin. Major "Jigs" Donohue, the silver tongued briefing officer, gave a detailed description of the expected fighter opposition and flak, weather, and assembly and takeoff times, then ended the briefing referring to the mission as a "gallant adventure." Harry attended the briefing as usual, but his job that day was to stay at Headquarters and "sweat it out."

Just prior to takeoff time, the perimeter at Horham airfield was buzzing with activity. The "Forts" sitting on their hardstands were being loaded with 500 lb bombs as light snow showers swept across the runways. In the eerie dawn light the gunners were mounting their 50 caliber Browning guns, and the Chaplains could be seen passing among the hardstands giving their blessings to the crews. As takeoff time approached, you could hear the B-17 engines "coughing" and then roaring to life. Then a line of olive drab planes began to lumber around the perimeter towards the runway to find their place for take off. At 0700 hours a green flare from the control tower signaled the first plane to take off. The mission to Big B was on its way! The 95th had put up thirty-eight planes, including two Pathfinder planes.

The assembly in the skies above East Anglia had its usual frightening moments as the Forts from all the surrounding bomb groups jockeyed for their appointed places in the formation. One bomb group from the 3rd Air Division was unable to attain combat formation and aborted before we left England. Another was scattered all over the sky while crossing the North Sea and abandoned the mission before reaching the coast of Belgium, but all the other groups of the 13th Combat Wing pressed on towards Berlin.

The formations leveled off at 27,000 feet over Eastern Belgium, but there was a solid layer of clouds that prohibited any view of the continent. Ahead was a huge wall of dark clouds that rose to an altitude of 29,000 feet as though it were a barrier to Hitler's Third Reich. About this time Harry, anxiously waiting for reports at Base Headquarters, received a message saying that several flights had turned back and were headed for secondary targets. But then a second message said that the 95th Group led by Grif Mumford had completed their bombing run on Berlin and were headed home! What happened? According to Grif, his radio operator, T/Sergeant Frank Atterbury, received an encrypted bomber code message that read, "ABANDON OPS. RETURN TO BASE, 1200 HOURS RZNC." Atterbury informed Grif that the message did not follow standard operating procedure, and Grif concluded the message probably came from an enemy transmitter; he made the courageous decision to continue to the assigned target! But there was a state of confusion among the other Flights. They had all received the message to turn back, and there was much intercom chatter about Grif's decision to continue. Some claimed that Division had instructed all Combat Wing Leaders to use their discretion on continuing to the target or to bomb other targets of opportunity. Many formations could be seen making 180° turns and breaking radio silence with the remark "you'll be sorry." But Grif and Al Brown, leading 19 planes of the 95th and 12 from the 100th Bomb Group, flew eastward through the towering wall of clouds toward Berlin.

A new menace appeared! About twenty ME 109s and FW 190s appeared and immediately began their attack on our bombers. They were attacking from 12 o'clock high, and sometimes our pilots could see the faces of their attackers. The attack no sooner started than our P 51s appeared from nowhere and chased them away. This was a great morale booster, for many of the crews thought our escort fighters had returned to England with the other bombers. They stayed with the mission and saved the lives of the crews! Finally our formations reached the I.P., and German anti-aircraft guns began a flak barrage that burst well above our formations, but eventually they honed in on us. When the lead plane attempted to open its bomb bay doors the doors wouldn't open! They were frozen shut because the heating system in the plane had malfunctioned; the temperature outside was minus 65° Fahrenheit! The Pathfinder plane was ordered to pull alongside Grif's plane and a dialog ensued with the pilot, Bill Owen, about what to do. It was agreed that the Pathfinder Bombardier, Lt. Marshal Thixton, would find the target using both visual and radar methods, then drop his bombs and a marker flare for the rest of the formations to follow. The plan worked! The bombs were released at 1335 hours in spite of lousy weather, German fighters, and flak. Our P 51s destroyed five German Me 109s and FW 190s. Chuck Yeager was flying a Mustang that day and shot down his first German fighter! But sixteen P51s from the 4th and 357th Fighter Groups were lost—some to weather! The 95th lost four planes and the 100th lost one. In all, fourteen planes of the 95th and eleven of the 100th completed the mission. According to Al Brown, "We had proved that Germany's most prized and protected target, Berlin, was no longer safe from 8th Air Force air attacks!

The planes of the 95th Bomb Group returned to Horham at 1705 hours. General Curtis LeMay personally greeted Grif and the crew of "I'LL BE AROUND." This dispelled the fear of some that the "brass" had come to our base to discipline Colonel Mumford for failing to comply with the order to return home. It was quite the opposite! Grif was awarded the Silver Star by General LeMay as news correspondents crowded around to ask questions and get the story. One of those correspondents was Andy Rooney of Sixty Minutes fame. Lt. Al Brown, the pilot of the lead plane, and Lt Bill Owen were both awarded the Distinguished Flying Cross. A commendation of high praise was given to 1st Lt. Malcolm Durr for his outstanding job of navigating the first mission to Big B.

For the mission on 4 March 1944, the 95th Bombardment Group (H) was given its third Presidential Unit Citation.

Maynard D. Stewart, 335th Sq., 95th Bomb Group (H),
8th Air Force
Major USAF ret

Notes to **The Big B**:
After the war, Grif continued to serve in the United States Air Force and finally retired a Colonel USAF. He died on 2 July 2007. Harry left the service after the war and returned to his original love of horses and the "wide open spaces" of the west as a cattleman. He died on 9 July 2002. I flew my missions as a S/Sgt waist gunner. After the war and a good education on the GI Bill, I was commissioned in the AF Reserve and was finally retired as Major USAF.

For more detailed information on the first daylight bombing of Berlin, I have found two publications valuable: *B-17s Over Berlin, Personal Stories from the 95th Bomb Group (H)* by Ian L. Hawkins, and *No Foxholes in the Sky* by Harry Conley, edited by Mark H. Miller and Stuart G. Whittlsey Jr., FNP Military Division.

Report of Operations Officer
HEADQUARTERS
ONE HUNDREDTH BOMBARDMENT GROUP (H) AAF
Office of the Operations Officer
APO 634

7 March 1944

SUBJECT: Report of the Operations Officer, Mission of, 6 March 1944.

TO : Commanding Officer, 100th Bomb group (H), Army Air Forces.

TO: Commanding Officer, l00th Bomb Group (H), Army Air Forces.

100th"A" Group

1. General Narrative: The l00th"A" Group formation took off from this base at 0754 - 0826 hours. The formation consisted Or 15 aircraft which had assembled in good formation by 0835 hours over the base. The l00th"A" Group led the 13th"B" Combat Wing the 100th "B" filled in the low position, being supplemented by aircraft of the 95th Group*. There was no group in the high position. 15 aircraft of this Group formation were dispatched.

The English Coast was crossed at 1016 hours at Aldeburgh,3 miles north of the briefed course. The formation was good; it continued good throughout the mission. The enemy coast was recrossed on the return trip at 16,000 feet, 1510 hours at 52 40 North, 04 50 East. The English Coast was recrossed at 1537 hours at Great Yarmouth. The lead ship landed at this base at 1602 hours.

The primary target was not located; bombs were away at 1323 hours on a target of opportunity - a factory district near Berlin.

2. Aircraft Not Attacking: 15 aircraft departed this base in formation as shown on the attached formation diagram marked "l00th"A" Group - After Assembly" 15 aircraft were dispatched. Aircraft #42-37807 turned back from the I.P. at 1205 hours, returning to base at 1526 hours. Aircraft #42-32009 turned back from 52 38 North, 08 04 East at 1200 hours, altitude 21,000 feet, landing at this base at 1403 hours.

Four aircraft, namely: 42-3987Z, 42-31731, 42-38197 and 42-30799 are missing in action. No particulars of their fate are known at this time.

11 aircraft of this formation, including the aircraft returning early, returned to this base.

100th"B" Group

1. General Narrative: The 100th "B" Group formation, consisting of 20 aircraft departed this base at 0757 hours A good assembly was made by 0833 hours over the base. The l00th"B" Group assumed the low group position, supplemented by six aircraft of the 95th Group*. The l00th"A" Group led the 13th Combat Wing no group in the high position. The Wing assembled at Splasher #7 at 0956 hours. We were about 8 minutes behind the rest of the Division at all times herein mentioned. We crossed the English Coast at 1019 hours; the enemy coast at 1107 hours, altitude 20,000 feet. The climb to bombing altitude had commenced immediately after leaving the English Coast. After crossing the enemy coast we had 17 aircraft in our group. Flak commenced immediately after crossing the enemy coast moderate to heavy. Fighter attacks commenced at 1200 hours at 52 36 North, 07 46 East. Heavy attacks were made by ME l09s and FW 190s 75 to 100 enemy fighters were seen; 40 to 50 made attacks on our group. They came in head-on and without regard for their safety. The lead aircraft of our formation had its controls shot away. The vertical stabilizer was ripped off by a mid-air collision with an enemy fighter. The lead aircraft returned with the 390th Group after jettisoning its bombs at 1210 hours at approximately 52 40 North, 08 10 East.

After 1200 hours the group was under heavy fighter attack by a great number of FW190s and ME l09s. The group was broken up; most of the high squadron was shot down and the lead ship was knocked out of formation.

Fighter support was good for a time after leaving the enemy coast on the way in; it was poor thereafter. However, from the target back to the coast it was very good.

Over Berlin, showers of red balls were seen from flak bursts. Red flak smoke was also seen - apparently a signal for enemy fighters.

The decent was begun at 1300 hours. The enemy coast was recrossed at 1512 hours at 52 37 North, 04 37 East. The English Coast was recrossed at 1540 hours; base was reached by 1632 hours.

2. Aircraft Not Attacking: 20 aircraft departed this base in formation as shown on the formation chart marked "l00th"B" Group After Assembly" 17 aircraft were dispatched; 16 aircraft attacked the target.

Aircraft #42-32018 turned back at 1032 hours from 14,800 feet, 52 04 North, 02 28 East, landing at 1117 hours. Aircraft #42-31895 turned back at 1132 hours, after being dispatched, from 20,000 feet, 52 28 North, 06 19 East, landing at 1231 hours. #4238175 turned back at 0924 hours from 9,000 feet, 51 57 North, 00 42 East, landing at 1050 hours. #42-6087 turned back at 0910 hours from 9,000 feet over Splasher #6, landing at 1116 hours.

Eleven aircraft, namely: #42-38011, 42-31735, 42-38044, 42-30170,42-38059, 42-30278, 42-31800, 42-97482, 42-97491, 42-31051 and 42-39994 are missing in action. No further particulars of their fate are known at this time. 8 aircraft returned to this base, including the aircraft that returned early. This does not include aircraft #42-31306 which landed at Honington because of battle damage.

JOHN B. KIDD
Lt. Col., Air Corps,
Operations Officer

* This information is in error; the 100 "A" Group was the group augmented by six B-17s and they from the 390th Bomb Group, not the 95th BG. The 100th "B" Group consisted of twenty 100BG aircraft.

Damage Report
HEADQUARTERS
ONE HUNDREDTH BOMBARDMENT GROUP (H), AAF
Office of the Station Engineering Officer
APO 634

6 March 1944

SUBJECT: Damage Report on Mission 6 March 1944
TO : Commanding Officer, 100th Bombardment Group (H), AAF

SHIP # 508
1. Hole in outer wing panel top left wing, Skin damage, flak.
2. Flak hole just forward of astro dome, skin damage.
3. Squadron repair.

SHIP # 074
1. Flak hole in right stress panel, skin damage
2. Flak hole in right inner wing panel top, skin damage
3. Flak hole between stations [?] A and [?]N, skin damage
4. Flak hole in dorsal fin left side, skin damage
5. Flak hole in right horizontal stabilizer, skin damage
6. Flak hole in tail passing thru ammo chute and knocking out signal light
7. Flak hole in left inner wing panel, skin damage
8. Squadron repair.

SHIP # 968
1. Flak hole in right wing, skin damage
2. Flak hole in top of left horizontal stabilizer, skin damage
3. Squadron repair.

SHIP # 413
1. Flak hole in left inner wing panel, skin damage.
2. Flak hole in right outer wing panel, skin damage
3. Flak hole in #3 nacelles ring cowling
4. Squadron repair.

SHIP # 009
1. Hole in right horizontal stabilizer damaging fuselage at station #10, two stringers broken out, framing torn, 20mm. caused damage
2. 20mm hole in #1 nacelle.

3. 30cal. holes in # 2 nacelle.
4. 30 cal hole in right horizontal stabilizer passing thru right elevator
5. Squadron and Sub-Depot repair.

SHIP # 807
1. Badly battle damaged awaiting inspection to be conducted by Honington.

SHIP # 389
1. Flak hole in leading edge of right outer wing panel, skin damage
2. Flak hole in nose fuselage, skin damage
3. Squadron repair.

SHIP # 936
1. Flak holes in right and left stabilizer, skin damage.
2. Flak hole in right inner wing panel, skin damage.
3. Flak hole in fuselage by control access, hydraulic line out.
4. Hole in left inner wing panel, skin damage.
5. Flak hole in bombay left side, skin damage.
6. Squadron repair.

SHIP # 767
1. Flak hole right inner panel supercharger oil tank.
2. Flak hole in stiffener for tank door.
3. Flak hole in left stabilizer, skin damage.
4. Flak hole in vertical stabilizer, skin damage.
5. Flak hole in left outer wing panel leading edge, skin damage.
6. Squadron and Sub-Depot repair.

SHIP # 710
1. Flak hole in chin turret.
2. Flak hole in leading edge of left stabilizer, skin damage.
3. Three Flak holes in left elevator, skin damage.
4. Squadron repair.

SHIP # 534
1. Flak hole in # 4 engine oil pump.
2. Flak hole in plexiglass nose.
3. Flak hole in right bomb bay door.
4. Squadron repair.

EUGENE ROVEGNO,
Major, Air Corps,
Engineering Officer.

Legion of Merit Citation[46]

RESTRICTED
HEADQUARTERS 3RD BOMBARDMENT DIVISION
APO 559

GENERAL ORDERS)

25 MAY 1944

:
NO. 147)

CITATION

The following listed members of an aircraft maintenance crew of the 351st Bombardment Squadron (H), 100th Bombardment Group (H), are cited for meritorious conduct and outstanding service in the maintenance of B-17 aircraft #42-3234, #42-31035, #4239867 and #42-31767, from the period 4 July 1943, to 11 May 1944. During that time the four aircraft completed fifty-six (56) consecutive high altitude bombing operations without having to return because of mechanical difficulty or failure. This record was accomplished through the extraordinary diligent and painstaking care with which these men performed their maintenance and repair work. Battle damage sustained by the aircraft required the replacement of three outer wing panels and three engines; stabilizer, rudder and aileron changes, besides the constant preventative maintenance demanded for continued safe flight. Work had to be done out of doors, often at night, and in bad weather. The devoted attention to detail shown by these enlisted men has enabled their crews to go into battle with the fullest confidence in their aircraft. The high degree of skill and unwavering devotion to duty displayed by this crew reflect highest credit upon themselves and the Armed Forces of the United States.

Official:

Harold C. Wildrick	M/Sgt.	33169105	Crew Chief
Nels O. Davidson	S/Sgt.	39176352	Mechanic
Sherman M. Nelson	S/Sgt.	37174389	Mechanic
Arnold L. Schluter	S/Sgt.	36476574	Mechanic

By command of Major General Le May:

O.T. Dreawell
Major, Air Corps
Adjutant General

A.W. Kissner
Brigadier General, U.S.A.
Chief of Staff.

Distribution: Special Awards

Commendation

HEADQUARTERS
ONE HUNDREDTH BOMBARDMENT GROUP (H) AAF
Office of the Commanding Officer
APO 634

11 March 1944

SUBJECT: Commendation.
TO : 2nd Lt. John P. Gibbons, 350th Bomb. Sqdn (H)

1. Special recognition is merited by you and your entire crew for your superior conduct during a most perilous and strenuous initiation into combat flying.

2. Your first five operational missions were flown in the brief period of twelve days, and all were to targets of very great importance and difficulty of attack. Your inaugural trip was to Regensburg, 25 February 1944; and you participated in each of the first four missions which had Berlin as the objective, including the tentative thrust on 3 March, the limited operation of 4 March, and the great follow-up blows of 6 and 8 March

3. Probably few bomber pilots and crews have had such an epic introduction to battle, and your courage, resolution and effectiveness in the circumstances certainly warrant the highest praise.

4. Please accept, and convey to all members of your crew, my sincere compliments and congratulations.

JOHN M. BENNETT, JR.
Lt. Col., Air Corps,
(Acting) Commander
100th Bomb Group.

Narrative to Captain Swartout's Silver Star
Short summary of the act involved with particular reference to Courage, Skill or Ability displayed.

Captain Jack R. Swartout distinguished himself by extraordinary achievement in a aerial flight while serving as leader of the low group of the 13th Combat Wing "A" formation on a heavy bombardment mission over Berlin, Germany, March 6, 1944. Throughout approximately two hours of constant fighter attacks, Capt. Swartout's group was the principal focal point of the enemy's fire. Early in the encounter west of Hanover [sic], he lost his entire high squadron , three ships of his lead squadron, and three ships of the low squadron, leaving a balance of only five ships to counteract the carefully planned and skilfully executed fighter attacks of the enemy. In this early action an enemy fighter collided with his ship, tearing away a large portion of the vertical stabilizer which immediately knocked his ship out of formation. As soon as the ship was brought under control, Capt. Swartout proceeded to the target area. For three quarters of an hour he attempted to reach Group A's formation but his efforts were futile, due to the necessity of violent evasive action in order to ward off approximately thirty enemy fighters which attacked singley, in pairs, and in groups of four. During this onslaught the following battle damage was received. A 20mm cannon shell penetrated the right side of the fuselage, exploding in the cockpit at the co-pilot's feet, spraying fragments which pierced the left leg of the Group leader. This explosion rendered the hydraulic system useless and started a fire just below the cockpit. A second 20mm shell pierced the number three engine's gas tank, damaging the oil cooler line. Large spouts of oil were thrown back over the ball turret, completely enveloping the turret thus rendering it inoperative. A third 20mm shell pierced the number four engine controls, which shredded the cables to such an extent that no response to the controls could be obtain. The number four fuel shut off switch and booster pump switch were inoperative, all interphone and radio communication in the co-pilot side was smashed. The command transmitter and receiver were nonoperational, the right landing gear motor would not function and the feathering motor on the number four engine was blasted away. Due to the severe damage of the vertical stabilizer by enemy fighters, in addition to the considerable flack holes in the entire ship, the rudder controls vibrated excessively. In spite of this damage and the intense ongoing fighter attacks, Capt. Swartout was able to tack on to the rear echelon of the 390th Bomb Group's formation and proceed to the target. Although the entire oxygen system was smashed with the exception of the pilots – co-pilots [sic] and navigators, the gunners were able to remain at their battle stations and ward off numerous fighter attacks by passing around emergency oxygen bottles, stopping only long enough to enable them to remain conscious. The left waist gunner received a gash in his right hand from an explosion of a twenty mm shell yet he remained at his post in an effort to aid in bringing his crew safely home. Confronted with structural damage, partial loss of control, fire in the air, and injuries to personnel, and faced with fresh waves of fighters still rising to the attack, Capt. Swartout had every justification for abandoning ship. His crew was preparing to bail out, but the order was with held until he [sic] was definitely certain there wasn't the slightest chance of making the trip safely back to his home base. The gunners faithfully stuck to their guns and the crew continued to the target and managed to return safely to their home base despite constant enemy attacks that continued until the formation reached the target and managed to return safely to their home base despite the constant enemy attacks that continued until the formation reached the enemy coast enroute to their home base. Approaching a neighboring field, Capt. Swartout prepared for landing. With the landing gear mechanism destroyed, brakes completely wiped out, and without the aid of flaps a safe landing was made with only partial control of the ship. Capt. Swartout exhibited strength of purpose on this occasion and through his high degree of training and application of self to duty measurably contributed to the operation's success.

NEIL B. HARDING,
Colonel, Air Corps,
Commanding.

Captain Swartout Silver Star

HEADQUARTERS EIGHTH AIR FORCE
Office of the Commanding General
APO 634

20 April 1944

GENERAL ORDERS)

:
NO. 291)

I. Under the provisions of Army Regulations 600-45, 22 September 1943, and pursuant to authority contained in Restricted TT Message #2139, Hq USAFE, 11 January 1944, the SILVER STAR is awarded to the following-named Officers and Enlisted men.

***

JACK R. SWARTOUT, O-728936, Army Air Forces, United States Army.

For gallantry in action, while serving as Air Commander of a Group of B-17 airplanes on a bombardment mission over Germany, 6 March 1944. For approximately two hours, his group was the focal point of concentrated attacks by enemy fighter and during this aerial battle against great odds, suffered serious losses. In the early stages of the battle, an enemy fighter collided with Captain Swartout's plane, shearing off a large portion of the vertical stabilizer. As soon as he regained control of his aircraft, he continued on towards the target, making every effort to join another unit. A large number of enemy fighters, seeing his plane out of formation, pressed their attacks savagely. Though wounded by an exploding cannon shell and with his plane heavily damaged, Captain Swartout valiantly fought on and finally succeeded in joining another group. Still subject to constant attack, he continued on to the target and successfully bombed it. When the loss of his aircraft seemed inevitable during the withdrawal from the target, Captain Swartout refused to give the order to bail out and brought his plane and crew back to England, making a landing at a friendly airbase. The gallantry, indomitable fighting spirit and devotion to duty displayed by Captain

Swartout set an inspiring example for his fellow flyers. Entered military service from California.

***

By command of Lieutenant General DOOLITTLE:

JOHN A SAMFORD

Brigadier General, USA,

Chief of Staff.

OFFICIAL:

/s/ Edward E. Toro
EDWARD E. TORO,
Colonel, A.G.D.
Adjutant General

Operational Narrative for March 8, 1944

100th Bomb Group - Operational Narrative - Erkner - 8 March 1944

1. LEAFLETS - None

2. Bombing Results - All Navigators and Bombardiers were certain that our bombs hit very near the P.T. but were unable to determine the exact spot they hit because of smoke caused by the bombing of formations that bombed ahead of us. Dense smoke and flame was pouring from the target at the time of our bombing. Some Bombardiers believe that our bomb pattern started across the RR track Northeast of the target and walked into the target. Photographs confirm the dense smoke reported. The target was definitely bombed heavily, but it is not possible to ascertain from pictures, the exact spot bombed by A/C of this Group. Smoke was visible from target area when we were over Celle on route home.

3. E/A - 75 to 100 S/E E/A attacked between 5236N - 0805E and the I.P. There were about 15 particular intense attacks beginning at 1259 hours. The 45th CBW caught the heaviest attacks. The 4th CBW was also seen to receive severe attacks. The 13th CBW. Particularly our Group, received comparatively light attacks. Sporadic attacks continued until we rendezvoused with a large number of our escort fighters near the I.P E/A were scattered but remanded with our formation until we left the Berlin area on our route from the target. Withdrawal support was excellent and no E/A were seen along the route from the target. One of our aircraft is missing and thought to have been shot down by E/A. Our claims are 5-4-2.

4. FLAK - Osnabruck - Meager and Inaccurate.
Magdeburg - Moderate Barrage, Inaccurate.
Berlin - Moderate and Inaccurate on our formation, but was very intense over the center of the city. Several rockets seen.
Gifhorn - Meager and Inaccurate.
Diepholz - Meager and Inaccurate.

March. 3/44
Mission to Berlin. On waythere ran into heavy cloud wall at 28,000 ft. Started through in formation. We broke throughat 30,000 ft. alone, others having turned back because of a recall which we didn't receive. A sqdn. of FW were sitting there waiting for us. Saw a small formation of 17's at 20' clock about 5 mi. off. Trying to reach them we were attacked several times. Looked back behind us and saw two B-17's break through cloids and collide exploding. No chutes seen. Made a diveing turn to the left and had to drop bombs to keep from tearing wings off. It also helped us gain a little speed. This was about 20 mi, West of Hamburg. Reached group of 8 ships of the 95th that were split from their group. Turned on heading home, and was attacked again by FW's and Me. 109's Shot our way through, dropping one Me. 109. Our P-47 and P-51 escort finally reached us and from there on didn't have any trouble. On way back saw B-24 ditch in "channel". Circeled ship and radiod position to Air Sea Rescue. Back home learned we lost 4 ships. Two groups ran together in cloids. Only 6 ships got out. Mission not complete and a very serious mistake was made by not recalling it sooner. We were very lucky to get back. I hope they won't all be this rough. It was to be the first time USAAF has ever bombed Berlin. On alert again for tomorrow. Time 7½ hrs. (Of HELL)

March. 4/44
Mission to Berlin again. This time we got through. Over 900 ships started. Near Brunswick jast north, all turned back because of high clouds up to 27,000 to 30,000 ft. All but 31 ships of us. We picked up very heavy and accurate flak at Magdenburg. Many ships were hit badly but manabed to keep up. From I.P. to MPI we were attacked bya large number of FW's and Me. 109's. Made nine passes at our ship alone. The temp. was 60°C. below at 27,000 ft. They cut the tail off of one of our bombers. We saw one FW blow up and two shot down. P-51 escorts shot a lot down. We had 4 head on attacks from 12 o'clock and 5 from 9 and 3 o'clock on our ship alone. Couldn't use chin turret it was froze up at 26,500 ft. As we reached target there was very heavy flak and our low Sqdn. on left caught most of it. We lost one ship (Seaton) at target. He was in my barracks with me. We are the only crew left now in this barracks the rest we have lost. Had a 8/10 undercast at target. After leaving target we picked up a new escort and pick up some more heavy flak, at Magdenburg. We ran through a solid row of flak for 8 min. at Magdenburg. Had a good escort all the way back home. After leaving target we dropped down to 12,000 ft. About a 4/10 undercast we could see small German towns and lots of snow on ground. Oxygen ran out half way back from target. Came out through Belgiem just about 4 mi. north of Dunkirk. Picked up moderate flak at Dunkirk. N ear English coast two FW's came out of clouds and followed a B-17 which dropped out of formation and headed back to Germany. Apparently it was a captured US plane and the Jerrys were just following us in it. Back at the field, they had war corospondents at interrogation and by the looks and sounds of things. We made history. We were only 31 planes out of more than 900 to get to Berlin. We are damn lucky to be here now. At target it was a running gun fight. We just had to shoot out way through. It lasted at the longest point over the target for about 30 min. Nine of the 13 planes from this field in the mission were from my sqdn. One was lost. They took our pictures and we are to have a special interogation by the war corospondants. Adding up everything and from reports I guess we really did something big. The Major said that we would get a special citation but I doubt it. (Stand down tomorrow) This is the first time Berlin has every been bombed in the daylight. The first time USAAF has ever bombed Berlin. A very dangerous mission.

March 5/44
Got 19 letters today. Just like Xmas. One from Will 3 from Mom and 15 from Tommie. On alert for tomorrow.

March 6/44
Mission to Berlin again. All 8thAF. Swell day, sunny and a few scattered clouds below us. We were at 23,000 ft. About the coast of Germany we picked up P-47's and 100 mi. into Germany they left us and another group was to pick us up. P-47's left us and ~~another group~~ a few min. later about 50 FW's attacked us. We were #2 2nd. element lead sqdn. They came in between 10 and 2 o'clock. Knocking down all but two of the high Sqdn. also knocking Copes ship in #1 causing him to drop out of the lead and we moved into his place taking over lead of 2nd element lead sqdn. Tried to get fighter help but couldn't contact them The FW's shot at us for about 30 min. We had no fighter escort from there to target and half way back home. During the end of that fighter attack we ran into heavy and very accurate flak. Several planes hit. Some (2) blew up and 1 caught fire. Saw 8 men bail out of one ship and 6 out of another. Went on to target and ran into flak all along the way. Over the city we saw the Bowl the 1936 Olympics were held in and many other points of interest. On bombs awaym our bombs would not realese. Finally we were able to drop then on the outskirts of Berlin. It was a beautiful day and you could see everything. It reminded me of the times I use to go on drives int the summer time. It was only-30°C. I changed my mind however before we ever reached the targer. Turning back for home our bombbaydoors would not close causing the Ball to be very inefective against the fighters that started attacking us and continued until we were about 150 mi. from the coast, where we met our escort. We were hit in the wing and in the nose by flak one piece coming through and hitting Ralph on the flak vest and going off to the compass. denting the cover. (Lost Mailman from 95th and Koper and Barton from here too.) Another B-17 caught fire and 8 got out. Several FW's were shot down. Our Ball possibly hitting one which blew up and another the pilot bailed out. A B-17 hit in tail cutting it half into. We had heavy flak in some spots. Lading at field with doors open and having to crank our flaps down. Cope's ship off on side of runway all shot to hell. Wing tip shot off, all around waist windows and all over. Quite a few men wounded. One WG kept both WG'sgoing while he gave first aid to another gunner. 16 planes failed to return from this field and 20 more from another Gp. I know of 2 crews lost from my sqdn. This mission is one of the roughest they have had at theis field. I hope we will never have to go on another to Berlin. If only we had fighter escort all the way it wouldn't have been so bad. Most of the ships that got back were shot up ~~that~~ in some way. The whole mission was one long nightmare of burning planes and heavy flak. Guns firing and fighter attackting, Bailouts etc

Lt Robert W. Bailie's Original Diary (Lt Malooly Crew)

Cont.

Alert on for tomorrow, Time on this 10½ hrs.

March 7/44
Mission briefed for Burl, Germany on edge of happy Valley. Scrubed. One hr. earlier we were to have gone back to Berlin. No mission for tomorrow. From all reports we lost 69 bombers. I hope we never have to go back to Berlin.

March. 8/44
Sqdn, went back to Berlin again today. Flew to Bovington and got some clothes. Alert on for tomorrow. Mailed Tommie $200 today.

March. 9/44
Mission to Berlin again. Looks like they will never give up. Trip very tame. Ran into little flak on route. Very heavy barrage of flak we had to fly through over target. 10/10 undercast at 10,000 ft. We bombed from 23,500 ft. and despite the heavy clouds below the fires could be seen started by the bombs. (Lost 7 bombers and 1 fighter in all) Heavy smoke over target from our previous bombings. We bombed railroads, termnails and factories in center of the city. We saw no enemy fighters and our own fighters provided a very wonderful protective cover for us. We led the whole 8th AF. Stand down for tomorrow. Our first two day pass. I guess we will go to London ~~and~~ Time was 10hrs and 20 min.

March. 10/44
Went to London and saw the Tower of London, House of Parlament Big Ben, WestminsterAbbey and many others, Buckingham Pallace. The blitz really wrecked a lot of London. People sleeping in subways. Stayed at ARC Club. (Dutchess Club.

March. 12/44
Came back to field and found we have a stand down. A lot of letters from Tommie.

March. 13/44
Was awakened at 4 am. this morning for mission to St. Omar, France. Scrubed. Flew practice mission for 4hrs. Haad to go over to officers Club tonight. Gen.'s Doolittle, La May Carl Spatz were there. they signed my "short snorter". Got a letter from Col. Bennett for our missions to Berlin. Stand down for tomorrow.

March. 14/44
Stand down.

5. WEATHER - CAVU in the target area.

6. OBSERVATIONS - None.

7. OTHER INFORMATION.

1. A small number of bombs are believed to have hit the small towns of Hangelsberg, 5224N - 1356E, and Gardelegen, 5232N - 1124E. Fire and smoke were observed in both places.

2. On route from target, at 1603 hours, 4 P-38s were seen attacking a train running between Meppel and Zwolle. The engine was seen to explode.

3. It was thought that a smoke screen was seen inside the city of Berlin.

4. Fighter support was weak over the same area as on the previous mission to Berlin, and again a large number of bombers were destroyed. After we reached the I.P. the escort improved and was excellent on the route from the target.

5. At 1332 hours, near 5218N - 1144E, one P-47 operating alone was seen to shoot down two E/A in a space of a few minutes. E/A were so busy attacking bombers it wasn't thought that they knew the P-47 was about. It was last seen headed back toward England, but some crew members believed it was too far in to make the return trip.

Operational Intelligence for March 8, 1944

100th Bomb Group - Operational Intelligence - Erkner (Berlin) - 8 March 1944

A. ENEMY AIR OPPOSITION

1. The 100th Group furnished A/C for the Lead and High Squadrons of the Lead Group in the 13th CBW. There was one direct attack from the nose on our High Squadron. Other E/A that made passes at our formation were recovering from passes made on the wing ahead or apparently preparing to attack formations behind. E/A were first seen at 1155 hours, near 5234N - 0509E, but they remained in the distance away from out formation. At 1239 hours, in the vicinity of Nienburg, the majority of our escort left us and E/A closed in. It is estimated that between 80 and 100 S/E E/A, about evenly divided between FW 190s and ME 109's, attacked our division formation. The first attacks were concentrated on the 45th CBW. E/A were seen to attack the Groups in this CBW by diving through their formations from ahead in groups of 4, 6 and 8 flying wing tip to wing tip. After the first series of attacks, E/A separated into smaller units of 2's and 3's and circled back to attack the front groups for more attacks. There were 40 E/A in the first group attacking. Other units of E/A joined their attack as we continued to the target and there appeared to be about 30 E/A at all times until we reached the I.P. The tactics observed during this series of attacks were almost identical to those reported in our last report when attacks were concentrated on the 13th CBW. From observations of both missions it appears that a new standard attack is now employed by E/A that somewhat resembles the triple threat. In this attack E/A approached in two groups of 3's from 11 and 1 o'clock flying parallel to a Wing formation until about 500 yards out. They then cut sharply to HXX the left and right, one element passing over the other in front of the top Groups to be hit and attacking the group opposite to the one each element first approaches. These are diving attacks. Standard nose attacks of all types were observed against both the 45th and 4th CBWs. Also a few tail attacks were made on the 4th CBW by single A/C and also attacks were seen from 9 and 10 o'clock position. In the initial attacks E/A were not observed to use any unusual armament.

2. One A/C of this Group is believed to have been destroyed by E/A after being forced out of formation because of engine trouble. Also 9 B-17s from the 45th CBW, 1 in the 4th CBW, 2 in the 95th Group, 2 in the 390th Group and 6 unidentified B-17s were seen to be destroyed by E/A. Others were observed that straggled from formation and probably were destroyed. Our claims are 5-4-2.

3. In the target area a large number of E/A were seen by XXX but they were effectively countered by our escort. There were about 25 T/E E/A in this area made up of JU 88s, ME 110s and some ME 210s.

4. On route from the target no attacks were observed on any formations because of excellent fighter escort. E/A were airborne in our vicinity, however, and were seen to shoot down three B-24s that were straggling from formation.

B. OBSERVATIONS:

1. 5 airdromes were reported located as follow: Celle, Quakeneruck, near Brunswick, 5235N - 1002E, and 5234N - 1031E. All were reported as having approximately 30 S/E fighters with the exception of the airfield at Celle which had approximately 30 S/E fighters plus 6 T/E fighters. Also at the fields at Celle and Brunswick, several A/C were observed taxing on runways. The airfield at Brunswick was reported as being well camouflaged.

2. 4 Ships were reported in the Amsterdam harbour. Crews reported that a smoke screen was being put up over the ships. One vessel appeared to be very large and there were two smaller ships nearby.

3. Smoke screens were reported in operation at Hanover, Brunswick,Magdeburg and in the city of Berlin.

4. In the vicinity of Dummer Lake rockets were reported shot up from the ground, which left a trail of smoke behind them. These burst in the air making black smoke puffs like flak and then red flares came out resembling those from a very Pistol.

C. FRIENDLY A/C IN DISTRESS:

1. One of our A/C is missing: A/C No. 056 was seen to have trouble with No. 1 engine in the Dummer Lake area on route to the target. An attempt to feather this engine was unsuccessful and the A/C fell out of it's position in the formation. It is believed that this A/C flew with the Low Squadron of our group until we were near the I.P. where it was seen to lag behind and receive attacks from

three E/A. Escort fighters came to it's rescue and it was last seen some distance behind still in level flight. No chutes were seen.

D. OTHER A/C

1. At 1242 hours near Dummer Lake, a silver B-17 from the 95th Group peeled out of formation and lost altitude. It was under control headed back toward England when last seen. It's difficulties could not be ascertained. Three chutes came out when it peeled from the formation.

2. At 1249 hours near Dummer Lake, two B-17s went down, cause unknown. one was from the 390th Group and the other was unidentified. 6 chutes came out of the 390th A/C.

3. At 1251 hours, near 5228N - 0855E one B-17 pulled out of the lead group of the 45th CBW firing green flares. It went down in a nose dive and started to fall apart before it crashed. 4 chutes were seen.

4. At 1257 hours, near Steinhuder Lake, a P-47 went down apparently out of control. No chutes were seen.

5. At 1300 hours, North of Hanover, 4 B-17s from the 45th CBW were knocked out of formation. They turned back toward England with engines smoking but were jumped by more E/A and all were believed to have been shot down. No chutes were seen.

6. At 1300 hours, 7 miles north of Hanover, a B-17 from the 95th Group was knocked out of formation by E/A. It was last seen losing altitude under control. No chutes were seen.

7. At 1304 hours two more B-17s were seen to be knocked out of the 45th CBW by E/A. N0.#1 engine was on fire and parts of the tail was shot away on one. Six chutes were seen from this one aircraft. The other went straight down and crashed. 1 chute was seen.

8. Missing from Report

9. At 1310 hours, near 5236N - 1014E, a B-17 fell out of the 45th CBW and pulled away with it's wheels down. It was last seen in level flight with E/A circling around it. No chutes were seen.

10. At 1327 hours, near 5229N - 1121E, two B-17s were knocked out of the 45th CBW by E/A. Both went down smoking but apparently under control. Three chutes were seen.

11. At 1337 hours, in the vicinity of Magdeburg a B-17 from the Lead Squadron of 45th CBW was apparently hit by flak and fell out of formation with fire in No #4 engine. As it fell away from it's formation it broke in half at the Ball. 9 chutes were seen.

12. At 1337 hours, near Magdeburg two B-17s from the 95th Group were knocked out of formation by E/A. They were last seen losing altitude under control. No chutes were seen.

13. At 1338 hours, near Madgeburg two B-17s were knocked out of the Wing ahead of us and went down under control but flaming. 4 chutes were seen from one and 3 from the other.

14. At 1408 hours, south of Berlin, a B-17 straggling from the 390th Group (Call Letter "V") was attacked by 3 ME 109s. It went down and was seen to crash. 10 chutes were seen.

15. At 1437 hours, in the target area, two B-24s were seen to go down in a spin after being hit by flak. No chutes were observed.

16. At 1459 hours, near Magdeburg, No #2 in the Low Squadron of the Group to our right (95th) fell out of formation with No #4 engine feathered and headed for cloud cover. 2 E/A were after him. No chutes were seen.

17. At 1515 hours, in the Brunswick area, two B-24s that were thought to have been hit by flak, went down spinning. No chutes were seen.

18. At 1523 hours, near 5235N - 1003E, two B-24s were attacked by 3 E/A and went down. One caught fire and went down in a flat spin. The other turned over on it's back, fell away and was seen to crash. No chutes were observed.

19. At 1550 hours, near Lingen, three chutes were observed but no A/C were known to be in distress.

D. CREW SUGGESTIONS:

1. Gunners request some tracer ammunition.

2. The number of missions per tour of duty should not be increased if recent missions are an index to what is to be expected in the future.

3. Fighter support was again spotty, and E/A took full advantage of the situation.

COBOMGP ONE HUNDRED

Sortie Information

HEADQUARTERS
ONE HUNDREDTH BOMBARDMENT GROUP (H) AAF
Office of the Operations Officer
APO 634

8 March 1944

SUBJECT: SORTIE INFORMATION, MISSION #125, 8 March 1944
TO : S-1 100TH BOMB GROUP (H)

SUBJECT: SORTIE INFORMATION, MISSION #125
TO: S-1, 100TH BOMB GROUP (H)

The following pilots and their crews flew operational mission # 125, 8 Mar 1944

Pilots	Target Bombed	Coordinate Turn Back	E/A Observed
PFF - Lt. Colonel Bennett			
Captain Leonard Bull			
Lt. C. S. Stapleton	yes	Target	Yes
Lt. W. C. Foraythe	yes	Target	Yes
Lt. J. P. Gibbons	yes	Target	Yes
Lt. G. H. Gough	yes	Target	Yes
Lt. C. B. Harper	yes	Target	Yes
Lt. J. C. Harper	yes	Target	Yes
Lt. R. H. Helmick	yes	Target	Yes
Lt. J. F. Massol	yes	Target	Yes
Lt. V. E. Monrad	yes	Target	Yes
Lt. L. R. Morgan	yes	Target	Yes
Lt. E. R. Williams	yes	Target	Yes
Lt. R. Rosenthal	yes	Target	Yes
Lt. R. J. Shoens	yes	Target	Yes
Lt. M. V. Wilson	yes	Target	Yes
Lt. N. L. Chapman	MISSING		

MINOR SHAW
Maj., Air Corps,
Gp Intelligence Officer
100th Bombardment GP (H)

Commendation

HEADQUARTERS
ONE HUNDREDTH BOMBARDMENT GROUP (H) AAF
Office of the Commanding Officer
APO 634

11 March 1944

SUBJECT: Commendation
TO : 2ndLt. Celesta B. Harper, 350th Bomb Sqdn. (H)

1. Special recognition is hereby tendered you and your entire crew for your fine conduct during a most dangerous and strenuous initiation into combat flying.

2. Your first four operational missions have been flown in the brief period of nine days, and all have been deep penetrations of Germany proper. After your inaugural trip, to Brunswick on 29 February 1944, you went on the tentative mission to Berlin on 3 March, and the great attacks on the German capital on 6 and 8 March.

3. Probably few bomber pilots and crews have had such an epic introduction to battle, and your courage, resolution and effectiveness in the circumstances certainly merit the highest praise.

4. Please accept, and convey to all members of your crew, my sincere thanks and congratulations.

WALTER G. BURKE.
1ST Lt., Air Corps,
(Acting) Commander
100th Bomb Group.

A TRUE COPY
/S/ John M. Bennett, Jr.
JOHN M. BENNETT, JR.,
Lt. Col., Air Corps,
(Acting) Commander
100th Bomb Group.

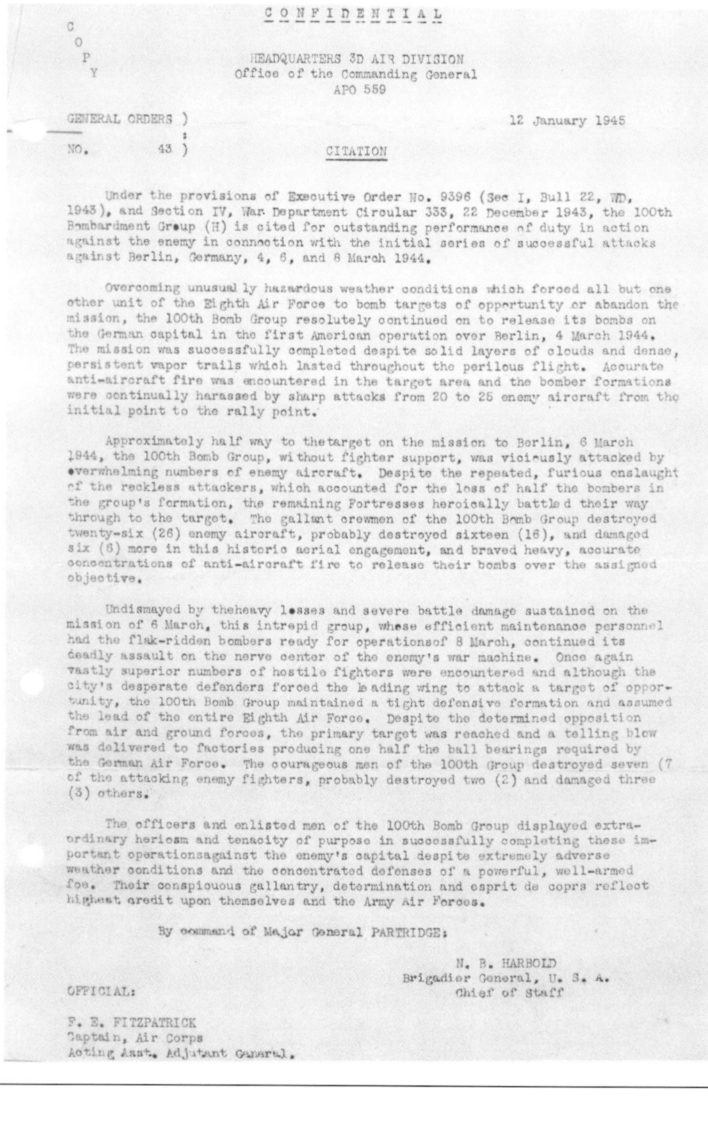

C O N F I D E N T I A L

C O P Y

HEADQUARTERS 3D AIR DIVISION
Office of the Commanding General
APO 559

GENERAL ORDERS)
:
NO. 43)

12 January 1945

CITATION

Under the provisions of Executive Order No. 9396 (Sec I, Bull 22, WD, 1943), and Section IV, War Department Circular 333, 22 December 1943, the 100th Bombardment Group (H) is cited for outstanding performance of duty in action against the enemy in connection with the initial series of successful attacks against Berlin, Germany, 4, 6, and 8 March 1944.

Overcoming unusually hazardous weather conditions which forced all but one other unit of the Eighth Air Force to bomb targets of opportunity or abandon the mission, the 100th Bomb Group resolutely continued on to release its bombs on the German capital in the first American operation over Berlin, 4 March 1944. The mission was successfully completed despite solid layers of clouds and dense, persistent vapor trails which lasted throughout the perilous flight. Accurate anti-aircraft fire was encountered in the target area and the bomber formations were continually harassed by sharp attacks from 20 to 25 enemy aircraft from the initial point to the rally point.

Approximately half way to thetarget on the mission to Berlin, 6 March 1944, the 100th Bomb Group, without fighter support, was viciously attacked by overwhelming numbers of enemy aircraft. Despite the repeated, furious onslaught of the reckless attackers, which accounted for the loss of half the bombers in the group's formation, the remaining Fortresses heroically battled their way through to the target. The gallant crewmen of the 100th Bomb Group destroyed twenty-six (26) enemy aircraft, probably destroyed sixteen (16), and damaged six (6) more in this historic aerial engagement, and braved heavy, accurate concentrations of anti-aircraft fire to release their bombs over the assigned objective.

Undismayed by theheavy losses and severe battle damage sustained on the mission of 6 March, this intrepid group, whose efficient maintenance personnel had the flak-ridden bombers ready for operationsof 8 March, continued its deadly assault on the nerve center of the enemy's war machine. Once again vastly superior numbers of hostile fighters were encountered and although the city's desperate defenders forced the leading wing to attack a target of opportunity, the 100th Bomb Group maintained a tight defensive formation and assumed the lead of the entire Eighth Air Force. Despite the determined opposition from air and ground forces, the primary target was reached and a telling blow was delivered to factories producing one half the ball bearings required by the German Air Force. The courageous men of the 100th Group destroyed seven (7 of the attacking enemy fighters, probably destroyed two (2) and damaged three (3) others.

The officers and enlisted men of the 100th Bomb Group displayed extraordinary heriosm and tenacity of purpose in successfully completing these important operationsagainst the enemy's capital despite extremely adverse weather conditions and the concentrated defenses of a powerful, well-armed foe. Their conspicuous gallantry, determination and esprit de coprs reflect highest credit upon themselves and the Army Air Forces.

By command of Major General PARTRIDGE:

N. B. HARBOLD
Brigadier General, U. S. A.
Chief of Staff

OFFICIAL:

F. E. FITZPATRICK
Captain, Air Corps
Acting Asst. Adjutant General.

Appendix C
German Air Force Claims and Eighth Air Force Losses
March 3-8, 1944, Missions to Berlin

This appendix is a result of intermingling a comprehensive list of *Luftwaffe* claims available on Tony Woods www.lesbutler.ip3.co.uk/tony/tonywood.htm, which provides remarkable detail about the claims made by GAF fighter pilots regarding aircraft and Michael Holm's website www.ww2.dk provides an array of German documentation on many aspects of the GAF. This Appendix is subdivided by American aircraft type and date. Within each sub-division, from left to right data is provided to the extent possible as to what is known about the Time of Event, Pilot's Name (German and American) Unit Assignment (German and American), Type of Aircraft, Serial Number (American), Missing Air Crew Report (MACR), Event Location, and Altitude. The notation "**HSS**" indicates that the aircraft was separated from the protection of its formation and the notation "**e.V.**" indicates Final Destruction i.e. shooting-down of a straggler previously separated and damaged from its formation as a Herausabschüß [HSS]. For entries that involve American aircraft, the time listed is GMT, while for German claims the time is German Time: either CET or CET+1.

B-17 - March 3, 1944

Time	Pilot Name	Unit	Type	Serial	MACR	Location	Altitude
11:25	Capt Robert H. Lohof	100 BG		231970	3022	5410N 0910E	
11:35	Fhj-Fw. Schmidt	2/JG 11	FW 190A			Stader Sand	
11:35	Fhj.Fw. Schmidt	Stab I/JG 11	FW 190A			Stade-rand Elbemündung	7.000 m.
11:37	Ltn. Unger	Stab I/JG 11	FW 190A			nördl. Itzehoe	2.500 m.
12:01	Ltn. Reinhard [sic]	Stab II/NJG 3	Ju 88 C			Magdeburg	6.000 m.
12:02	Hptm. Rolf Hermichen	Stab I/JG 11	FW 190A			westl. Tönning	7.200 m.
12:03	Fw. Karl-Otto Harloff	7/JG 3	Me 109G			südwest. Magdeburg	7.000 m.
12:04	Oblt. Zwernemann	1/JG 11	FW 190A				
12:04	Fw. Alwin Doppler	2/JG 11	FW 190A				
	Lt John G. Gossage	100 BG		238017	3025		
	Lt Robert D. Vollmer	100 BG		239817	3029		
	2Lt Robert H. Rogers	381 BG		237986	2737		
	Lt Francis R. Graham	447 BG		231112	2887		
	Lt Don E. Ralston	447 BG		231148	4436		
	2Lt Walter M. Pickard	91 BG		237965	3222		
	Lt Walter C. Lansford Jr	92 BG		240014	2857		
	Lt Donald L. Ahlwardt	94 BG		238075	2794		

B-17 - March 4, 1944

Time	Pilot Name	Unit	Type	Serial	MACR	Location	Altitude
12:01	Ltn. Johannes Jung	6/JG 27	Me 109G			Raum Koblenz	7.500 m.
13:01	Ltn. Hans Weik	10/JG 3	Me 109G			Neuruppin	7.500 m.
13:03	Uffz. Gerhard Vivroux	Sturmstaffel1				N.W. Rhinow	4.000 m.
13:03	Fw. Hermann Wahlfeldt	Sturmstaffel1				Rotenburg	3.000 m.
13:11	Ltn. Leopold Münster	5/JG 3	Me 109G			E. Stendal	8.000 m.
13:20	Lt Stanley M. Seaton	100 BG		238016	3024	Over Berlin	
13:31	Ltn. Wolfgang Harnisch	8/JG 2	FW 190A			Kaiserslautern	4.000-2.000 m.
14:53	Ltn. Adolf Kneip	2/JG 300	Me 109G			25 km. N.E. Kesseling	2.500 m.
	2Lt David D. Keyes	381 BG		230151	2910		
	Lt Walter R. Carpenter	384 BG		239991	2741		
	Lt Hollie R. Lovvorn	384 BG		231606	2739		
	Lt George Cosentino	384 BG		232007	2740		
	2Lt Philip D. Geyer	447 BG		231165	2888		
	2Lt Arthur Mittman	452 BG		231341	2915		
	2Lt Julius O. Blake	94 BG		239801	2978		
	2Lt Delmar D. Pollack	94 BG		231169	2998		
	2Lt Rodney P. Roehm	95 BG		231565	2795		
	Lt Marvin J. Worthy	95 BG		231734	2796		
Time	Pilot Name	Unit	Type	Serial	MACR	Location	Altitude
	Lt Melvin B. Dunham	95 BG		231785	2797		
	Lt William U. Brownlow	95 BG		231910	2798		
	Lt Paul Herring	96 BG		230412	3425		
	Oblt. Hans Siedel	3/JG 302	Me 109G				
	Lt. Passhaus	5/JG 53	Me 109G				
	Uffz. Maximilian Soentgerath	6/JG 27	Me 109G			Ahrweiler 20 km. S. Bonn	
	Ofw. Ehrenberger	6/JG 53	Me 109G				
	Oblt. Seidel	I/JG 301	Me 109G				
	Obstlt. Wolf-Dietrich Wilcke	Stab/JG 3	Me 109G				
	Obstlt. Wolf-Dietrich Wilcke	Stab/JG 3	Me 109G				
	Oblt. Hermann von Kap-herr	Stab/JG 3	Me 109G	HSS			

B-17 - March 6, 1944

Time	Pilot Name	Unit	Type	Serial	MACR	Location	Altitude
	Ofw. Bach	5/JG 1	FW 190A			südlich Delmenhorst	
	Maj. Heinz Bär	6/JG 1	FW 190A			S. Dinklage	6.000 m.
	Hptm. Rolf Hermichen	Stab I/JG 11	FW 190A			Söge-Cloppenburg	7.400 m.
	Uffz. Rebitz	5/ZG 26	Me 410			nördl. Treuenbrietzen	7.000 m.
	Uffz. Martin	1/JG 1	FW 190A			Emmen-Hardenburg	5.000 m.
	Ofw. Scherer	1/JG 11	FW 190A			S. Assen	5.700 m.
	Uffz. Losch	1/JG 11	FW 190A			S.E. Emmen	5.400 m.
	Lt Albert F. Amiero	100 BG		231731	3019		
	Lt George W. Brannan	100 BG		231735	3020		
	2Lt Sherwin L. Barton	100 BG		231800	3021		
	Lt Charles W. Smith	306 BG		240006	2735		
	Lt Edward E. Haushalter	381 BG		231553	3241		
	2Lt Richard W. Coyle	381 BG		23215	3000		
	Capt Paul E. Brown	388 BG		240054	3092	Mid-Air by 237886	
	Lt Montgomery D. Givens	388 BG		231135	3082	Hpt Frey	
	2Lt Claude M. Kolb	401 BG		238136	2743		
	Lt Arthur R. Socolofsky	447 BG		231227	3657		
	2Lt Howard W. Sweeny	452 BG		231337	2914		
	Lt Robert C. Schimmel	452 BG		231919			
	2Lt Eugene H. Whalen	457 BG		231595	3197	Rammed by Fw W. Bonnecke	Me 410
	2Lt Roy E. Graves	457 BG		231627	3198	Mid-Air with 231595	
	Lt Wallace C. Upson	92 BG		240052	2905		
	Obfhr. Erhard Nolting	11/JG 3	Me 109G				
	Ltn. Berger	2/JG 1	FW 190A				
	Fw. Alwin Doppler	2/JG 11	FW 190A				
	Ofw. Heinz Stöwer	3/JG 11	FW 190A				
	Oblt. Hugo Frey	7/JG 11	FW 190A				
	Oblt. Hugo Frey	7/JG 11	FW 190A				
	Oblt. Hugo Frey	7/JG 11	FW 190A				
	Oblt. Hugo Frey	7/JG 11	FW 190A				
	Fw. Gerhard Slabon	Stab IV/JG 3	Me 109G				
	Hptm. Heinrich Wurzer	1/JG 302	Me 109G				
	Ltn. Dieterle	I/JG 300	Me 109G				
	Ltn. Dieterle	I/JG 300	Me 109G				
	Ltn. Schlüter	I/JG 300	Me 109G				
12:02-10	Fw. Hoës	9/JG 11	FW 190A			Diepholz 090°	6.500 m.
12:03-06	Fw. Born	9/JG 11	FW 190A			Diepholz-Sulingen	6.000 m.
12:08-10	Fw. Rudolf Hübl	2/JG 1	FW 190A			area Diepholz	6.500 m.
11:55	Oblt. Josef Zwernemann	1/JG 11	FW 190A			Raum Haselünne	7.000 m.
11:58	Ltn. Eugen Ludwig Zweigart	7/JG 54	FW 190A			Söge-Cloppenburg	7.000 m.
11:59	Fhj.Fw. Schmid	2/JG 11	FW 190A			Lorup	7.000 m.
11:59	Fw. Hanke	3/JG 11	FW 190A			nördlich Meppen	
12:00	Lt Samuel L. Barrick	100 BG		239994	3031	5230N 0716E	
12:00	2Lt Albert J. Mailman	95 BG		229943	2980		
12:00	Lt James W. Conley	95 BG		297495	2986		
12:01	Ltn. Windbichler	2/JG 1	FW 190A			S.W. Delmenhorst	6.500 m.
12:01	Maj. Heinz Bär	6/JG 1	FW 190A			W. Diepholz	6.000 m.
12:01	Ofw. Siegfried Zick	7/JG 11	FW 190A			Wagenfeld-Sulingen	6.500 m.
12:01	Hptm. Hermann Segatz	Stab II/JG 1	FW 190A			E. Diepholz	6.000 m.
12:02	Ofw. Karl-Emil Demuth	2/JG 1	FW 190A			östlich Lingen	
Time	Pilot Name	Unit	Type	Serial	MACR	Location	Altitude
12:02	Ltn. Erich Dobrick	Stab I/JG 11	FW 190A			N. Hölstedt	7.500 m.
12:03	Gefr. Schultheiss	1/JG 11	FW 190A			S. Friesoythe	7.000 m.
12:03	Hptm. Heinrich Wurzer	1/JG 302	Me 109G			Berlin	
12:04	Uffz. Rolf Rischke	7/ZG 26	Me 110				
12:04	Stabs-Fw. Krausse	9/JG 11	FW 190A			Diepholz-Sulingen	6.500 m.
12:05	Ofw. Karl-Emil Demuth	2/JG 1	FW 190A			Diepholz	6.500 m.
12:05	Fw. Wiegand	2/JG 1	FW 190A			Diepholz	6.500 m.
12:05	Fw. Walter Köhne	3/JG 1	FW 190A			Vechta-Emsdek	6.500 m.
12:05	Uffz. Stiegler	4/JG 1	FW 190A			N. Wildenhausen	6.500 m.
12:06	Oblt. Hans-Heinrich Koenig	3/JG 11	FW 190A			Lindern-Cloppenburg	7.000 m.
12:06	Fw. Hanke	3/JG 11	FW 190A			westlich Cloppenburg	
12:06	Hptm. Rolf Hermichen	Stab I/JG 11	FW 190A			Ahlhorn area	7.200 m.
12:07	Oblt. Rudolf Klemm	7/JG 54	FW 190A			Loningen	5.800 m.
12:08	Hptm. Segatz	II/JG 1	FW 190A			östlich Lingen	
12:10	2Lt Zeb Kendall Jr	100 BG		230278	3016	Northern Germany	

12:10	Lt William B. Murray	100 BG		230799	3017	5237N 0830E	
12:10	Lt Dean M. Radtke	100 BG		297491	3034	Central Germany	
12:10	2Lt Thomas L. Barksdale	95 BG		232002	2982		
12:10	Lt Richard H. Read	95 BG		239793	2985		
12:11	Lt Merril T. Rish	100 BG		238044	3026	N Hannover	
12:13	2Lt Robert C. Koper	100 BG		231051	3018	N Hannover	
12:15	Lt Coy I. Montgomery	100 BG		230170	3015	N Hannover	
12:15	Oblt. Heinz Knoke	5/JG 11	Me 109G			südl. Delmenhorst	
12:15	Uffz. Karl Mertgen	8/JG 54	FW 190A			Diepholz	6.000 m.
12:15-20	Oberst Walter Oesau	Stab/JG 1	FW 190A			Vechta area	3.000 m.
12:15	Lt Robert F. Starks	390 BG		231935	3989		
12:15	Lt Michael B. Russell	95 BG		238024	2984		
12:20-30	Ltn. Klaffenbach	5/JG 11	Me 109G			Emstek-Bassum	8.000 m.
12:20	Lt Thomas A. Keasbey	95 BG		231251	2981		
12:30	2Lt Benjamin J. Fourmy Jr	91 BG		238118	2901		
12:35	Oblt. Herbert Schob	1/ZG 76	Me 110			Gardelegen	7.000 m.
12:35	Ltn. Hans Ehlers	3/JG 1	FW 190A			Vechta	6.500 m.
12:35	Uffz. Kurt Röhrich	Sturmstaffel1				nordl. Hadersleben	6.500 m.
12:35	Gefr. Willi Maximowitz	Sturmstaffel1		HSS		vor Fallersleben	6.500 m.
12:35-45	Oblt. Fritz Stehle	5/ZG 26	Me 410			Gardelegen-Burg	6.500 m.
12:35-45	Uffz. Hock	5/ZG 26	Me 410			Raum Gardelegen	6.500 m.
12:38	Oblt. Herbert Schob	1/ZG 76	Me 110			Gardelegen	7.000 m.
12:38	Ltn. Gerhard Dost	Sturmstaffel1				S. Gardelegen	6.300 m.
12:38	Ofw. Hermann Wahlfeldt	Sturmstaffel1				nördl. Hadersleben	6.500 m.
12:45	Uffz. Walter Agricola	5/JG 3	Me 109G			S.E. Gardelegen	7.000 m.
12:45	Uffz. Juhlanz	FlÜG 1 [N]				2 km. E. Gardelegen	6.000 m.
12:45	Lt Paris R. Coleman	91 BG		231079	2897		
12:45	Lt Clyde V. Mason	91 BG		231869	2899		
12:45	2Lt Bryce S. Evertson	91 BG		297483	2902		
12:46	Oblt. Hermann Greiner	11/NJG 1	Me 110			11 km. S.W. Quakenbrück	60 m.
12:46	Uffz. Otto Erhardt	10/JG 3	Me 109G	HSS		10 km. westl. Genthin	6.800 m.
12:47	Ltn. Hans Weik	10/JG 3	Me 109G			S. Tangerhütte	7.000 m.
12:49	Lt Douglas Harding	91 BG		231911	2900		
12:50	Lt William C. Hendrickson	379 BG		231555	2909		
12:50	Lt Bob Tibbetts Jr	91 BG		231578	2898		
12:50	Lt Frank Krizan	92 BG		231503	2903		
12:52	Ltn. Hans Weik	10/JG 3	Me 109G			nördl. Braunschweig	6.800 m.
12:55	Oblt. Ottmar Zehart	Sturmstaffel1				N. Magdeburg	6.500 m.
12:55	Uffz. Walter Loos	11/JG 3	Me 109G	HSS			
12:58	Oblt. Kirchmayr	5/JG 1	FW 190A	E,V,		östl. Lingen	
13:00	Fw. Schneider	5/ZG 26	Me 410			Raum Brandenburg-Jüterbog	7.000 m.
13:00	Ltn. Kutscher	5/ZG 26	Me 410			Brandenburg	7.000 m.
13:00	Ofw. Frös	5/ZG 26	Me 410			Raum Brandenburg-Jüterbog	7.000 m.
13:00	Ofw. Pennekamp	5/ZG 26	Me 410			in Raum v. Belzig	6.000 m.
13:02	Ofw. Herger	2/NJG 5	Me 110			10 km. N.W. Werneuchen	1.800 m.
13:05	Maj. Friedrich-Karl Müller	Stab IV/JG 3	Me 109G			Klaistow	7.800 m.
13:05	2Lt Milton A. Fastrup	381 BG		231448	3001		
13:12	Capt David L. Miner	100 BG		238059	3027	N Hannover	
13:12	Lt John Lautenschlager	100 BG		238197	3028		
Time	Pilot Name	Unit	Type	Serial	MACR	Location	Altitude
13:14	Uffz. Otto Czermin	11/JG 3	Me 109G			S.W. Berlin	6.800 m.
13:14	Maj. Friedrich-Karl Müller	Stab IV/JG 3	Me 109G			Erkner	4.000 m.
13:15	Gefr. Heinz Jeworrek	12/JG 3	Me 109G			S.E. Berlin	7.800 m.
13:17	Ltn. Karl Bolte	12/JG 3	Me 109G			südl. Zirnsee	6.000 m.
13:26	Maj Fred A. Rabo	482 BG		23491	3362		
13:45	Hptm. Heinrich Sannemann	6/JG 3	Me 109G				
13:59	2Lt Francis J. Frantz	95 BG		23529	2979		
14:00	Lt William A. Terry	100 BG		297482	3033	Western Germany	
14:03	Lt. Hans Iffland	10/JG 3	Me 109G				
14:03	Uffz. Stiegler	4/JG 1	FW 190A			Raum Hilversum.	
14:03	Ofw. Hans Heitmann	4/JG 26	FW 190A			N.W. Osnabrück	
14:03	Ofw. Hans Heitmann	4/JG 26	FW 190A			N.W. Osnabrück	5.500 m.
14:03	Hptm. Iro Ilk	Stab I/JG 300	Me 109G			25 km. nordl. Quackenbrück	4.700 m.
14:03	Ltn. Fritz Potthast	11/NJG 1	Me 110			2 km. S. Wieste	
14:05	Fw. Kahl	4/JG 1	FW 190A			Almelo-Raalte	4.000 m.
14:05	Ltn. Werner Gerth	Sturmstaffel1		e,V,		N.W. Hannover	5.800 m.
14:08	Ltn. Werner Gerth	Sturmstaffel1				S.W. Brandenburg	5.500 m.
14:18	Oblt. Josef Zwernemann	1/JG 11	FW 190A			S.E. Bassum	6.500 m.

14:21	Oblt. Hans-Heinrich Koenig	3/JG 11	FW 190A			Bassum	6.500 m.
14:23	Lt Frank A. Granack	100 BG		239872	3030	Berlin	
14:25	Lt Edward Handorf	100 BG		238011	3023	Diephols	
14:30	Lt Charles E. Johnston	94 BG		238022	2977		
14:31	Lt Rex M. Townsend	92 BG		297527	2996		
14:35	Hptm. Karl Borris	I/JG 26	FW 190A			Garrel-Cloppenburg	
14:40	Ltn. Fritz Harbauer	7/JG 2	FW 190A				6.000 m.
14:41	Ltn. Karl Willius	2/JG 26	FW 190A			Flammersfeld	4.500 m.
14:45	Maj. Heinz Bär	6/JG 1	FW 190A			Raum Deventer	
14:49	Ltn. Eugen Ludwig Zweigart	7/JG 54	FW 190A			Rheinsehlen	500 m.
14:50	2Lt Charles P. Wallace	388 BG		231163	3083		
14:50	Lt A. Christiani	388 BG		238177	?		
14:50	Lt Clarence A. Gridley	388 BG		231194	3084		
14:50	2Lt John W. McLaughlin	388 BG		231240	3086		
14:50	Lt Lowell H. Watts	388 BG		237886	3089		
14:50	Lt Charles F. Wagner	452 BG		231373	2916		
14:50	Lt Elmyran R. Cooper	92 BG		231680	2904		
14:50	Lt Garland B. Lloyd	95 BG		231299	2999		
14:55	Uffz. Wolfgang Ortlepp	7/JG 2	FW 190A				2.500 m.
14:58	Ofw. Leo Schuhmacher	6/JG 1	FW 190A			Ahlhorn-Lorup	6.000 m.
15:01	Uffz. Swoboda	5/JG 1	FW 190A			SW Hoogeveen	
15:05	Oblt. Walter Matoni	5/JG 26	FW 190A			15 km. E. Jülich	4.500-500 m.
15:05	Uffz. Otto Kleinert	7/JG 2	FW 190A			Lorient	7.000 m.
15:05	2Lt Milton A. Fastrup	381 BG		231448	3001		
15:11	Fw. Kurt Knappe	7/JG 2	FW 190A				4.000 m.
15:11	Fw. Erich Kolodzie	9/JG 54	FW 190A			Diepholz	5.000 m.

B-17 - March 8, 1944

Time	Pilot Name	Unit	Type	Serial	MACR	Location	Altitude
12:05	Ofw. Brodbeck	6/JG 1	FW 190A	HSS		Hannover city	
12:52	Uffz. Schulz	4/JG 1	FW 190A			Hannover Peine area	
12:55	Uffz. Swoboda	5/JG 1	FW 190A			N.W. Hannover	7.600 m.
12:59	Fhj.Fw. Schmid	2/JG 11	FW 190A			Nienburg-Wietze	7.000 m.
13:03	Hptm. Karl-Heinz Dietsche	2/JG 302	Me 109G				
13:03	Uffz. Enderle	3/JG 1	FW 190A			FU-7 Neustadt/Rbge	
13:03	Oblt. Walter Matoni	5/JG 26	FW 190A				6.500-300 m.
13:03	Fw. Gerhard Vogt	7/JG 26	FW 190A				7.300 m.
13:03	Ltn. Gustav Nagel	7/ZG 26	Me 110				
13:03	Ofw. Fritz Reinke	7/ZG 26	Me 110				
13:03	Ofw. Fritz Reinke	7/ZG 26	Me 110				
13:03	Ofw. Fritz Reinke	7/ZG 26	Me 110				
13:03	Maj. Karl-Friedrich Müller	Stab IV/JG 3	Me 109G			S.W. Burg	7.000 m.
13:03	Ltn. Hans Weik	10/JG 3	Me 109G	HSS			6.800 m.
13:03	Hptm. Karl-Heinz Dietsche	2/JG 302	Me 109G	HSS			
13:04	Uffz. Enderle	3/JG 1	FW 190A			Nienburg	7.000 m.
13:04	Uffz. Siegfried Teske	8/ZG 26	Me 110				
13:04	Uffz. Siegfried Teske	8/ZG 26	Me 110				
13:04	Oblt. Paul Bley	9/ZG 26	Me 110				
13:04	Oblt. Paul Bley	9/ZG 26	Me 110				
Time	Pilot Name	Unit	Type	Serial	MACR	Location	Altitude
13:04	Uffz. Hans Wittgen	9/ZG 26	Me 110				
13:04	Uffz. Hans Wittgen	9/ZG 26	Me 110				
13:05	Oblt. Josef Zwernemann	1/JG 11	FW 190A			bei Schwarmstedt	8.000 m.
13:05	Fw. Wiegand	2/JG 1	FW 190A			Nienburg-Wunstorf	7.000 m.
13:05	Ltn. Franz Ruhl	4/JG 3	Me 109G				
13:12	Ofw. Haninger	4/JG 1	FW 190A			Neustadt-Winsum area	
13:19	Ltn. Adolf Kneip	Stab I/JG 300	Me 109G			30 km. S. Oldenburg	4.500 m.
13:25	Oblt. Heinz Knoke	5/JG 11	Me 109G				
13:25	Hptm. Klaus Mietusch	Stab III/JG26	Me 109G			Wolfsburg N.E. Braunschwieg	
13:26	Obfhr. Blassing	2/JG 11	FW 190A			Masener Moor	6.000 m.
13:28	Uffz. Walter Loos	11/JG 3	Me 109G	HSS			
13:31	Uffz. Walter Loos	11/JG 3	Me 109G	HSS			
13:32	Ltn. Karl Bolte	12/JG 3	Me 109G			20 km. N.E. Magdeburg	6.800 m.
13:32	Ltn. Franz Ruhl	4/JG 3	Me 109G				7-8.000 m.
13:33	Fw. Gerhard Vogt	7/JG 26	FW 190A				7.500 m.
13:35	Fw. Hans Prager	5/JG 26	FW 190A			80 km. N.Braunschweig	6.000-7.000 m.
13:35	Oblt. Karl-Hainz Bendert	5/JG 27	Me 109G			Magdeburg	8-4.500 m.
13:35	Major Johann Kogler	StabIII/ZG26	Me 110				
13:36	Hptm. Karl-Heinz Dietsche	2/JG 302	Me 109G	HSS		N.E. Magdeburg	7.000 m.
13:37	Ltn. Leopold Münster	5/JG 3	Me 109G			10 km. N. Burg	5.000 m.

Time	Pilot Name	Unit	Type	Serial	MACR	Location	Altitude
13:47	Ltn. Hans Iffland	10/JG 3	Me 109G			10 km. N. Aschersleben	tiefflug
13:54	Ltn. Joachim v. Buddenbrock	Stab II/JG 27	Me 109G			20 km. S.W. Magdeburg	7.000 m.
14:01	Gefr. Horst Witzler	10/JG 3	Me 109G			N.W. Wittenberg	6.500 m.
14:05	Ltn. Karl Paashaus	5/JG 53	Me 109G			10 km. N. Torgau	8 m.
14:17	Fw. Rubel	5/JG 53	Me 109G			18 km. E. Jüterbog	5.000 m.
14:23	Fw. Kübrick	IndSt Erla				12 km. N.W. Cottbus	5.000 m.
14:30	Lt Norman L. Chapman	100 BG		240056	3032	Berlin	
14:42	Ltn. Munsch [sic]	EprKdo 25	FW 190A			W. Osterburg	4.500 m.
14:42	Ofw. Fink	EprKdo 25	FW 190A			W. Osterburg	4.500 m.
15:02	Uffz. Heinz Bolle	1/JG 3	Me 109G			N.W. Magdeburg	4.500 m.
15:36	Hptm. Rolf Hermichen	Stab I/JG 11	FW 190A			W. Celle	6.000 m.
15:45	Uffz. Pleines	7/JG 1	FW 190A			Deventer-Raalte	200 m.
15:47	Hptm. Rolf Hermichen	I/JG 11	FW 190A				
15:48	Oblt. Caleme	Stab III/JG54	Me 109G				6.000 m.
0:00	Fw. Gerhard Guttmann	5/JG 26	FW 190A			N.E. Helmstedt	5.000-6.000 m.
0:00	Fw. Hans Jürgens	5/JG 27	Me 109G			50 km. S.E. Magdeburg	8.000 m.
0:00	Oblt. Hermann von Kap-herr	Stab/JG 3	Me 109G			Zerbst	7.000 m.
13:20	Ofw. Fritz Reinke	7/ZG 26	Me 110			E. Magdeburg	7.000 m.
13:30	Uffz. Teske	8/ZG 26	Me 110			N. Magdeburg	7.000 m.
13:30	Ltn. Gustav Nagel	7/ZG 26	Me 110			N.N.E. Magdeburg	5-7.000 m.
13:30	Uffz. Hans Wittgen	9/ZG 26	Me 110			bei Magdeburg	7.000 m.
13:35	Maj. Johann Kogler	StabIII/ZG26	Me 110			Magdeburg	7.000 m.
13:40	Oblt. Walter Matoni	5/JG 26	FW 190A	HSS		N. Magdeburg	6.500-2.500 m.
	2Lt Leo B. McGrath	351 BG		231471	2908		
	2Lt Thomas A. Pirtle	381 BG		238029	3002		
	2Lt Allan O. Amann	388 BG		230340	3079		
	Lt Leonard T. Tobias	388 BG		237819	3087		
	2Lt William W. Lentz Jr	388 BG		238138	3090		
	2Lt Michael J. Moran	388 BG		230829	3081		
	2Lt Homer B. Pou	388 BG		231214	3085		
	Lt Paul J. Quillin	390 BG		231717	2988		
	2Lt Max J. Quakenbush	390 BG		230713	2987		
	Lt William S. Branum	390 BG		237812	2990		
	2Lt Dale A. Peterson	401 BG		231488	2911		
	2Lt Glenn T. Butterworth Jr	452 BG		231331	3190		
	2Lt Durwald L. Sorenson	452 BG		231354	3191		
	Lt Henry L. Wilson	452 BG		237954	3192		
	2Lt Theodore J. MacDonald	452 BG		238211	3193		
	2Lt Frank S. Stephans	452 BG		297525	3195		
	Lt Vasco E. Gulino	452 BG		297549	3196		
	2Lt Claude M. Williams	91 BG		239892	3223		
	Lt William F. Babington	94 BG		25950	2997		
	Lt Frank P. Scott	94 BG		231141	2976		
	2Lt Frank A. Fagan	95 BG		237929	2983		
	Lt Donald O. Kasch	96 BG		230847	3423		
	2Lt Clark Ross Jr	96 BG		231403	3424		
	Lt Richard F. Lemanski	96 BG		231576	3426		
	2Lt James M. Swendiman	96 BG		231716	3428		
	Capt Norman C. Thomas	96 BG		231912	3429		
	Lt George K. Pond	96 BG		239988	3430		
	Fw. Schueckin	1/JG 11	FW 190A				
	Hptm. Hermann Staiger	12/JG 26	Me 109G			Berlin-Potsdam	
	Hptm. Hermann Staiger	12/JG 26	Me 109G			N. Hannover	
	Oblt. Karl-Hainz Bendert	5/JG 27	Me 109G			W. Coburg 35 km. N.Bamberg	
	Fw. Wischhöfer	I/JG 300	Me 109G				
	Fw. Wischhöfer	I/JG 300	Me 109G				
	Oblt. Sachs	I/JG 300	Me 109G				
	Ltn. Richard Franz	Sturmstaffel1					

B-24 - March 3, 1944

Time	Pilot Name	Unit	Type	Serial	MACR	Location	Altitude
11:42	Hptm. Adalbert Sommer	Stab I/JG 2	FW 190A			5 km. S.W. Tuscania	5.200 m.
11:47	Ofw. Franz Malsch	1/JG 4	Me 109G			25 km. S.W. Viterbo	4.500 m.
11:52	Fw. Herbert Schäfer	2/JG 4	Me 109G				4.500 m.
11:52	Ltn. Detlef Grossfuss	3/JG 2	FW 190A			5 km. W. Tarquinia	4.000 m.
11:58	Ofw. Ludwig Hartmann	3/JG 2	FW 190A			25 km. S. Orbetello	4.800 m.
11:59	Uffz. Clemens Waltherscheid	3/JG 2	FW 190A			15 km. S. Orbetello	4.800 m.
12:08	Uffz. Clemens Waltherscheid	3/JG 2	FW 190A			9 km. S.W. Pitigliano	4.800 m.

	Uffz. Josef Ostrowitski	2/JG 4	Me 109G			7 km. S.W. Montalto di Castro	4.500 m.
	Lt Richard E. Smith	392 BG		27491	2800		
	Lt Frank W. Herzik	458 BG		129298	3347		

B-24 - March 6, 1944

Time	Pilot Name	Unit	Type	Serial	MACR	Location	Altitude
	Lt Kenneth C. Griesel	389 BG		2100424	3249		
CTO	Lt P. F. Shea	392 BG		27473			
	Lt Jack D. Harris	93 BG		2109832	2957		
	Lt Neal J. Serkland	445 BG		2109796	2962	8 miles NE Furstenau	
	Lt Robert E. Paltz	446 BG		2100288	2966		
	2Lt Charles C. York	448 BG		129191	3548		
	Lt Hubert R. Cripe	453 BG		252226	2970		
	2Lt Henry J. Meek	453 BG		252191	2969		
	Lt Elmer B. Crockett	453 BG		264457	2971		
	2Lt Thayer Hopkins	458 BG		129299	3348		
	Obstlt. Hermann Graf	Stab/JG 11	FW 190A	HSS			
	Ltn. Georg Kiefner	1/JG 26	FW 190A			Wierden	800 m.
	Ofw. Herbert Korber	6/JG 2	FW 190A			Cloppenburg	6.000 m.
	Lt. Georg Kiefner	1/JG 26	FW 190A			Almelo	
13:40	Lt George L. Lymburn	445 BG		27586	2960		
13:45	Uffz. Philipp	6/NJG 5	Me 110			20 km. N.W. Berlin	4.000 m.
13:45	2Lt Guy C. Rogers	458 BG		252515	3351		
13:46	Fw. Robert Mayer-Arend	8/JG 3	FW 190A			S. Potsdam	5.500 m.
13:53	Oblt. Hermann Greiner	11/NJG 1	Me 110			N.W. Quakenbrück	no height
14:10	2Lt Jessie L. McMains	458 BG		252306	3349		
Time	Pilot Name	Unit	Type	Serial	MACR	Location	Altitude
14:15	Lt Erling A. Hestad	392 BG		27598	3183		
14:17	Oblt. Döring	2/LBeoSt				Mittelland	400 m.
14:19	Ofw. Rathkamp	6/NJG 5	Me 110			120° 5 km. vor Münster	3.500 m.
14:28	Oblt. Rudolf Klemm	7/JG 54	FW 190A			Söge-Cloppenburg	4.000 m.
14:45	Oblt. Wolfgang Neu	4/JG 26	FW 190A			Quackenbrück 180	no height
14:50	Lt Patrick D. Tobin Jr	453 BG		264460	2972		
Time	Pilot Name	Unit	Type	Serial	MACR	Location	Altitude
14:58	Ltn. Lothar Kabbe	6/JG 2	FW 190A			S. Cloppenburg	5.000 m.
15:01	Ltn. Günther Jahn	Stab II/JG 2	FW 190A			nördl. Rheine	5.000 m.
15:02	Capt Jack L. Bogusch	458 BG		129286	3346		
15:17	2Lt Beverly E. Ballard Jr	458 BG		252450	3350		

B-24 - March 8, 1944

Time	Pilot Name	Unit	Type	Serial	MACR	Location	Altitude
14:02	Hptm. Hermann Segatz	Stab II/JG 1	FW 190A	HSS		Luben N. Luckau	8.000 m.
14:25	Oblt. Rüdiger v. Kirchmayr	5/JG 1	FW 190A			Luben 2 km. N.W. Luckau	no height
14:46	Ltn. Rudolf Thun	6/NJG 5	Me 110			8 km. E. Taterburg	700 m.
14:46	Oblt. Rudolf Thun	II/NJG 5	Me 110				
Time	Pilot Name	Unit	Type	Serial	MACR	Location	Altitude
15:03	Maj. Karl-Friedrich Müller	Stab IV/JG 3	Me 109G				5.000 m.
15:25	Uffz. Pfeffer	Stab/JG 11	FW 190A	HSS		N. Neustadt	6.000 m.
15:26	Hptm. Rolf Hermichen	Stab I/JG 11	FW 190A			N. Großburgwedel	6.000 m.
15:28	Hptm. Rolf Hermichen	Stab I/JG 11	FW 190A			N. Großburgwedel	6.000 m.
15:34	Maj. Karl-Friedrich Müller	Stab IV/JG 3	Me 109G	HSS			5.000 m.
	FO John M. Kendrick Jr	389 BG		299975	2958		
	2Lt James B. McArthur	389 BG		2100375	2959		
	Lt James A. Merriman	446 BG		129292	2964		
	Lt Clifton C. McFar	446 BG		2100231	2965		
	Lt Herbert F. Bohnet Jr	446 BG		27595	2963		
	2Lt John N. Daley	448 BG		2100122	3189		
	Lt John R. Bringardner	448 BG		2100342	2967		
	Lt Everett G. Ehrman	453 BG		252175	2928		
	Hptm. Heinrich Wurzer	1/JG 302	Me 109G				
	Hptm. Heinrich Wurzer	1/JG 302	Me 109G				

P-38 - March 3, 1944

Time	Pilot Name	Unit	Type	Serial	MACR	Location	Altitude
12:23	Maj. Werner Schroer	Stab II/JG 27	Me 109G			Magdeburg	
12:23	Ltn. Fritz-J. von Buddenbrock	Stab II/JG 27	Me 109G			Gegend Braunschwieg	6.000 m.
	2Lt Don D. Goble	20FG		267705	2791		

P-38 - March 4, 1944

Time	Pilot Name	Unit	Type	Serial	MACR	Location	Altitude
14:05	Oblt. Ernst-Georg Altnorthoff	2/JGr Süd				60 km. S. Grenoble	6.000 m.
15:03	Oblt. Ernst-Georg Altnorthoff	2/JGr Süd				N. Marseilles	7.000 m.
15:25	Fw. Gerd Wiegand	4/JG 26	FW 190A			südl. Courtrai	no height
	Lt Harry E. Bisher	20FG		267923	2784		
	Lt James C. Scott	20FG		267864	2782		
	2Lt Edward G. Pfeiffer	20FG		268097	2783		

P-38 - March 6, 1944

Time	Pilot Name	Unit	Type	Serial	MACR	Location	Altitude
14:02	Hptm. Detlev Rohwer	Stab II/JG 3	Me 109G			10 km. W. Wittenberge	7.500 m.
14:10	2Lt Larry N. Ferguson	364FG		267461	3061		

P-38 - March 8, 1944

Time	Pilot Name	Unit	Type	Serial	MACR	Location	Altitude
13:03	Hptm. Siegmund Kahse	IV/JG 3	Me 109G				
15:12	Hptm. Detlev Rohwer	Stab II/JG 3	Me 109G			Hannover	7.500 m.
15:42	Ltn. Ernst-Erich Hirschfeld	5/JG 300	FW 190A			nördl. Twente	7.500 m.
	Hptm. Siegmund Kahse	Stab IV/JG 3	Me 109G			N.E. Magdeburg	30-40 m.
	2Lt Kenneth F. London	364FG		267223	3059		
	2Lt Charles E. Brock	364FG		267233	3060		
	Ofw. Siegfried Zick	7/JG 11	FW 190A				

P-47 - March 3, 1944

Time	Pilot Name	Unit	Type	Serial	MACR	Location	Altitude
11:47	Uffz. Franz Hilbuer	1/JG 2	FW 190A			4 km. S.W. Tuscania	5.500 m.
11:48	Fhj.Ofw. Siegfried Lemke	1/JG 2	FW 190A			5 km. N. Farnese	8.500 m.
11:51	Fhj.Ofw. Siegfried Lemke	1/JG 2	FW 190A			Vallentano	4.800 m.
12:05	Ofhr. Klaus Eugel	1/JG 2	FW 190A			5 km. S. Montalto di Castro	5.800 m.
Time	Pilot Name	Unit	Type	Serial	MACR	Location	Altitude
	Lt George W. Barnes	4FG		36643	3043		
	Lt Glenn A. Herter	4FG		36740	3045		
	Lt Vermont Garrison	4FG		36871	3048		
	Lt Phillip H. Dunn	4FG		36903	3050		
	Uffz. Rudolf Pintsch	11/JG 3	Me 109G				

P-47 - March 4, 1944

Time	Pilot Name	Unit	Type	Serial	MACR	Location	Altitude
	Lt William R. Burkett	353FG		275850	2793		
	Lt Hugh A. Ward	4FG		36810	3047		
	Lt Robert H. Richards	4FG					
Time	Pilot Name	Unit	Type	Serial	MACR	Location	Altitude
	Lt Paul M. Ellington	4FG		37004	3051		
	2Lt Robert V. Lloyd	55FG		268182	2792		
	2Lt Irvin E. Valenta	56FG		27942	2785		
	Lt Everett W. Powell	78FG		16374	2973		

P-47 - March 6, 1944

Time	Pilot Name	Unit	Type	Serial	MACR	Location	Altitude
11:55	Uffz. Wilhelm Fest	5/JG 11	Me 109G			S. Löningen	7.000 m.
12:12	Hptm. Rolf Hermichen	Stab I/JG 11	FW 190A			Alhorn-Emsteck area	
14:47	Ofw. Alfred Heckmann	3/JG 26	FW 190A			3 Almelo	
12:05	Oberst Walter Oesau	Stab/JG 1	FW 190A			Cloppenburg-Vechta	500-800 m.
12:07	Fw. Walter Köhne	3/JG 1	FW 190A			Quakenbrück	2.000-0 m.
14:45	Lt Milton F. Erickson	356FG		275255	3058		
	Maj Frederick J. Nelander	362FG		275635	2714		
	Lt Edward D. Mialen	4FG		36899	2839		
	Lt Edmund D. Whalen	4FG					
	Lt Robert J. Messenger	4FG		36630	3042		
	Maj Henry L. Mills	4FG		36690	3044		
	Lt Cecil E. Manning	4FG		36887	3049		
12:15	2Lt Andrew B. Stauss	56FG		275397	2787		
12:15	FO Edward J. Downey	78FG		27983	2974		
12:15	2Lt Grant M. Turley	78FG		27998	2975		
	Fw. Hans-Gerd Wennekers	5/JG 11	Me 109G			Raum Quakenbrück	

P-47 - March 8, 1944

Time	Pilot Name	Unit	Type	Serial	MACR	Location	Altitude
11:03	Ltn. Fritz Karch	6/JG 2	FW 190A			Amsterdam	6.000 m.
12:27	Uffz. Stiegler	4/JG 1	FW 190A			N.E. Rheine-Hopsten	7.000 m.
13:03	Oblt. Hans Ehlers	3/JG 1	FW 190A			40 km. N.E. Hannover	tiefflug
13:07	Fw. Rudolf Hübl	2/JG 1	FW 190A			Langenhagen tief	200 m.

13:13	Oblt. Hans-Heinrich Koenig	3/JG 11	FW 190A			Ahlhorn	100 m.
13:25	Fw. Gerd Wiegand	4/JG 26	FW 190A			Balkbrug N.E. Zwolle	no height
	Lt John Zolner	353FG		28557	2992		
	Lt Charles H. Sweat	355FG		28441	3055		
	2Lt Daniel S. Rothenberg	355FG		36989	3056		
	Lt Justus D. Henry Jr	356FG		28467	3057		
	2Lt Clyde L. Coldren	358FG		275084	2846		
	2Lt Edward A. Abdallah	362FG		275672	2734		
	Lt Col Selden R. Edner	4FG		36442	2838		
	Lt Anthony R. Carcione	56FG		274697	2B42		
	2Lt Joe W. Icard	56FG		275040	2843		
	2Lt Frederick L. Roy	56FG		275697	2844		
	2Lt John C. Marcotte	56FG		27885	2840		
	Lt Caleb L. Reeder Jr	56FG		274623	2841		
	2Lt George C. Maitland	78FG					
	Obfhr. Dreizehner	1/JG 11	FW 190A				
	Oblt. Zwernemann	1/JG 11	FW 190A				
	Uffz. Otto Erhardt	10/JG 3	Me 109G				
	Fw. Walter Köhne	3/JG 1	FW 190A			Steinhuder Meer	tief
	Uffz. Herhold	4/JG 11	Me 109G				
	Lt. Ernst-Erich Hirschfeld	5/JG 300	FW 190A				

P-51 - March 3, 1944

Time	Pilot Name	Unit	Type	Serial	MACR	Location	Altitude
11:04	Maj. Heinz Bär	6/JG 1	FW 190A			S.E. Soltau	tiefflug
12:05	Oblt. Heinz Knoke	5/JG 11	Me 109G				
	Oblt. Witzmann	6/JG 1	FW 190A			Fassberg/Südheide	2.000 m.
				312264	2919		
	Fw. Hans-Gerd Wennekers	5/JG 11	Me 109G				
	Uffz. Wilhelm Fest	5/JG 11	Me 109G				
	Ofw. Schuhmacher	6/JG 1	FW 190A				

P-51 - March 4, 1944

Time	Pilot Name	Unit	Type	Serial	MACR	Location	Altitude
13:25	Ltn. Leopold Münster	5/JG 3	Me 109G			Raum Brandenburg	7.000 m.
				36366	2805		
				312158	2804		
				36853	2789		
Time	Pilot Name	Unit	Type	Serial	MACR	Location	Altitude
				36435	2849		
				36492	2850		
				36493	2848		
				36619	3072		
				36645	3070		
				36694	2847		
				36814	2852		
				36919	3074		
				36924	3073		
	Lt. Schmiedel	4/JG 53	Me 109G				
	Uffz. Kurt Wahl	5/JG 3	Me 109G				
	Fhj.Ofw. Fritz Yung	I/JG 301	Me 109G				

P-51 - March 6, 1944

Time	Pilot Name	Unit	Type	Serial	MACR	Location	Altitude
13:03	Oblt. Kirchmayr	5/JG 1	FW 190A			Platzne Rheine	
13:24	Uffz. Ferdinand Stretz	10/JG 3	Me 109G			10 km. nördl. Schirnfeld	1.000 m.
13:55	Hptm. Ernst Laube	IndSt Erla				Stendal	7.000 m.
14:01	Hptm. Ernst Laube	IndSt Erla				Stendal	500 m.
14:14	Ofw. Karder	IndSt Erla				bei Meßdorf	no height
12:45	Uffz. Rudolf Klüpfel	StabIII/ZG26	Me 110			Lehmenge Heide	3.000 m.
				312446	2803		

P-51 - March 8, 1944

Time	Pilot Name	Unit	Type	Serial	MACR	Location	Altitude
13:04	Oblt. Hans Schleef	3/JG 3	Me 109G			Loburg-Görzke	7.500 m.
13:35	Fhj.Fw. Rudolf Klüpfel	StabIII/ZG26	Me 110				
13:43	Uffz. Hans Fritz	3/JG 3	Me 109G				9.500 m.
13:56	Ltn. Hans Weik	10/JG 3	Me 109G				
14:02	Ltn. Wilhelm Hofmann	8/JG 26	FW 190A			17 km. W. Torgau	7.500 m.
15:05	Oblt. Hans-Heinrich Koenig	3/JG 11	FW 190A			Raum Hoya	500 m.
13:25	Oblt. Paul Bley	9/ZG 26	Me 110			Burg b. Magdeburg	3.000 m.
13:25	Fw. Rudolf Klüpfel	StabIII/ZG26	Me 110			Burg b. Magdeburg	5.000 m.
				2103041	2994		
				36932			

Appendix D
Eighth Air Force Loss Rate

The table below provides the loss rate; that is how many missions would be conducted for the operational loss of a heavy bomber. For example, the 91BG and 100BG though their losses and number of mission flown were different shared the rate of one heavy bomber per 1.73 missions conducted. This is second only to the 96BG whose rate was 1.70 missions per heavy bomber loss.

GRP	Station	Missions	Losses	Rate
96	Snetterton Heath	321	189	1.70
91	Bassingbourn	340	197	1.73
100	Thorpe Abbots	306	177	1.73
384	Grafton Underwood	314	159	1.97
306	Thurieigh	342	171	2.00
92	Podington	308	154	2.00
95	Horham	320	157	2.04
390	Framlingham	300	144	2.08
94	Bury St. Edmonds	324	153	2.12
388	Knettishall	306	142	2.15
305	Chelveston	337	154	2.19
303	Moleworth	364	165	2.21
44	Shipdham	343	153	2.24
392	Wendling	285	127	2.24
381	Ridgewell	296	131	2.26
452	Deopham Green	250	110	2.27
385	Great Ashfield	296	129	2.29
379	Kimbolton	330	141	2.34
351	Polebrook	311	124	2.51
448	Seething	262	101	2.59
447	Rattlesden	257	97	2.65
401	Deenthrope	256	95	2.69
389	Hethel	321	116	2.77
457	Glatton	237	83	2.86
445	Tibenham	282	95	2.97
398	Nuthampstead	195	58	3.36
489	Halesworth	106	29	3.66
487	Lavenham	185	48	3.85
493	Deebach	158	41	3.85
490	Eye	158	40	3.95
93	Hardwick	396	100	3.96
491	Metfield	187	47	3.98
453	Old Buckenham	259	58	4.47
446	Bungay	273	58	4.71
466	Attlebridge	232	47	4.94
34	Mendelsham	170	34	5.00
458	Horsham St. Faith	240	47	5.11
492	North Pickenham	64	12	5.33
486	Sudbury	188	33	5.70
467	Rackheath	212	29	7.31

Appendix E
Miss Irish Final Flight
March 19, 1944

"MILK RUN REVISITED" March 19, 1944 (No Ball target in France)

by Splasher Six by Harry Crosby

with additional information from Frank Buschmeier and John Gibbons

Having spent their first four missions on daylight bombing strikes over Berlin, the Gibbons' crew hoped their fifth would be a milk run. Flying Tailend Charlie in the high squadron (350th) of the 100th heading for Dungeness, the crew went through the usual routine: test-fire guns, arm bombs, open bomb-bay doors, and prepare to drop. Little black puffs of smoke over the coast of France looked "kind of like the 4th of July."

As Sterling Blakeman (Bombardier) recalls:

"there was a dramatic change in flak . . . All at once we found ourselves surrounded by big black oily smudges with angry red cores, all zeroed in on our plane. The big hit, when it came, created a new directional force on the plane, lifting it straight upward."

Sterling hurried to the cockpit, where pilot JOHN GIBBONS asked for damage assessment. Sterling and flight engineer IRA ARNOLD discovered that "a direct 88mm hit had torn out the whole floor and right side of the radio room, killing radio operator ED WALKER. Six of our twelve 500-lb. G. P. bombs were hung up in their twisted racks."

Frank Buschmeier (Waist Gunner) remembers sitting in the back half of the plane "by my waist gun when I heard a burst of flak in front of the nose, then another one under the tail. There was a terrific explosion in the radio room, blowing the rear door out and sending it to where it ended up between my legs. I looked over at the radio room and Ed looked like he had been hit by a shot gun blast, he was a sieve, blood everywhere. Then he fell through the gaping hole that had been the floor." In the cockpit, John took the news "with amazing calm for a pilot who was now flying an aircraft divided at its middle almost in half."

Bernard Spragg (Ball Turret Gunner): "the flak burst tore the floor out of the radio room and Sgt Walker fell through it." He must have pulled his D-ring, because the remnants of his shredded parachute and lines were tangled in the jagged debris, creating drag on the plane.

According to Sterling:

"aware that the oxygen system had been knocked out, [John] was already nursing the plane down from our 21,000-ft. bomb run altitude. He and co-pilot Bob Dykeman were having trouble with the controls to the shredded right elevator and the rudder."

Fortunately, all four engines were operational. John turned the plane over to Bob and came back to survey the damage. According to Frank Buschmeier, "John's eyes were huge as saucers when I saw him on the catwalk looking at that 88mm damage."

In the ball turret, the side windows were smashed and the front window gone, but the crew got Bernie Spragg safely out. Busch spliced the cables of the elevator and rudder controls and then assisted waist gunner Ty Ettus in holding Bernie's legs while he leaned out over the hole in the radio room to pull back the shroud lines of Ed Walker's "flak-ridden and billowing chute." The trailing lines had snagged a walk-around oxygen bottle and were creating an extra drag factor.

In between repairs, the "Back Half Crew," joined by tail gunner "Bugs" Bunting, began lightening the load by throwing out as much as possible. Having fallen away from the formation and flying without any P-47 escorts, navigator Maz Johnson "set the shortest course to England." But over the Channel only three bombs dropped with the conventional release mechanism. Arnold and Sterling stood on the bomb bay catwalk and worked with pliers and screwdrivers, against time and a heavy draft, to work the other three bombs loose. "Thanks mainly to Arnold's talent for solving mechanical problems not covered in service manuals, all three were finally jettisoned, the last one just moments before we reached the English Coast," recalls Sterling.

In addition to the mid-section slice, *Miss Irish* sustained over 400 flak holes. Her brakes were out, and the crew had no radio communication. Over England no one opted to jump. Flak had rendered several chutes useless, and most of the crew remembered when John had landed them safely at Moses Lake, Washington, with a collapsed right landing gear. They approached a P-47 base at Raydon, near Ipswich, firing red flares. Sterling noted that "since anything but the smoothest of touchdowns would break the plane in half, it had to be a perfect landing. It was." The Raydon personnel could not believe their eyes. Their flight surgeon showed up with bottles of Scotch and gin, which were "put to good use in bringing sleep to nine weary but emotionally keyed up survivors." Someone commented, "If this is what milk runs are like, I'd rather go back to Big B again."

Note: T/Sgt Ed Walker was 20 years old, married, and with a baby girl (Sherrill Jean) on the way when his life tragically ended. His body was never recovered, and his wife Lucille (Walker) Hayes recently reached out to this writer about her young husband wanting closure, but also trying to keep his history and memory alive. We recognize the sacrifice every young man gave to preserve our freedom, and the following Eulogy to Ed Walker, Jr. is appropriate for all those brave men lost:

A Eulogy to a Friend — Junior Walker
By Frank Cox, Jr. Clayton, OK

Yesterday the sun shone down on a little village nestled in the mountains.
And the blood of youth flowed through your vains and mine
And as is the way with all boys we shared our apples and candy together
And told each other our little secrets and further adventures.
Yes, I remember all those things and many more
Even to the night we sat on the creek bank with a fishing pole in hand,
And a cup of coffee in the other singing all the old songs we knew,
And how I wished I could sing like you.

But, as the sun of life rises for us so must it also descend
And you, have left your ambition still unfilled to take up a new way of life;
Where the sun shines forever and the fish will bite unceasingly.
But you in your short span of life gave more to be remembered in the dark recesses of time
Than I can ever hope to leave, even though I should live for countless ages
And I hope that while on the Battlefield you might have thought of the times we spent together and found it in your heart to smile and be glad you knew me.
For I am thankful that I knew you.

So rest easy my friend, for you will never be forgotten as long as the things you died for prevail on earth.
And just as long as we have young men like you who can live and be glad of life or die in the field of battle with a heart still young and gay they shall prevail,
And remember also that some day we will fish again in a stream far better than the one you left behind.

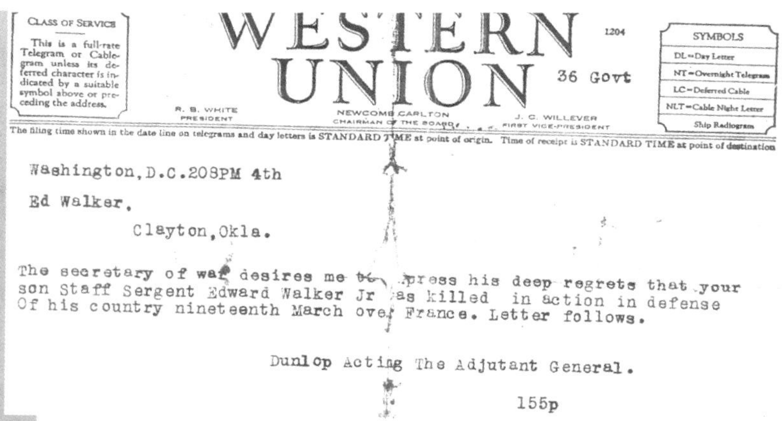

CLASS OF SERVICE
This is a full-rate Telegram or Cablegram unless its deferred character is indicated by a suitable symbol above or preceding the address.

WESTERN UNION

1204

36 Govt

SYMBOLS
DL=Day Letter
NT=Overnight Telegram
LC=Deferred Cable
NLT=Cable Night Letter
Ship Radiogram

R. B. WHITE PRESIDENT — NEWCOMB CARLTON CHAIRMAN OF THE BOARD — J. C. WILLEVER FIRST VICE-PRESIDENT

The filing time shown in the date line on telegrams and day letters is STANDARD TIME at point of origin. Time of receipt is STANDARD TIME at point of destination

Washington,D.C.208PM 4th
Ed Walker,
Clayton,Okla.

The secretary of war desires me to express his deep regrets that your son Staff Sergent Edward Walker Jr was killed in action in defense of his country nineteenth March over France. Letter follows.

Dunlop Acting The Adjutant General.

155p

Sources and Select Bibliography

Primary Sources
Correspondence
The following veterans patiently answered our questions and shared their experiences with the 100th Bomb Group in general and on the Berlin missions in particular.

Charles F. Allen
Bruce E. Alshouse
James A. Bain
Samuel L. Barrick
Frank W. Buschmeier
Joseph A. Carty
Cecil G. Davis
William Sapp (Dixon)
Wiley A. Dobbs
Richard Donnelly
John C. Eling
John R. Gensel
John P. Gibbons
Frank A. Granack
Harold D. Granger
Walter Green
Harry H. Greenfield
Don Hammond
C. B "Red" Harper
John A. Harrison
Richard L. Kerwin
Lucius Lacy
Sam J. LaFace
John P. Lucarelli
John Luckadoo
George E. Madden
Raymond Mitchell
George Ofiesh
Nelson A. Pardee
Delbert S. Pearson
Gerald Putnam
Earl L. Richardson
Robert Shoens
Ed Stone (Silverstone)
Jack Swartout
Peter Van Slyck
Samuel Wilensky
Gerald J. Will
Howard Williams

Additional Interviews
Lt. Robert Vollmer, interviewed in 2000 by Tim Lohof, son of Robert H. Lohof 100th Bomb Group pilot.

Robert Shoens, Don Hammond, Ed Stone (Silverstone) interviewed in Nashville Tennessee at 100th Bomb Group Nashville Reunion 2007

John P. Gibbons & Frank Buschmeier interviewed in Nashville Tennessee at 100th Bomb Group Nashville Reunion 2007

Documentation
Pilot's Flight Operating Instructions for Army Models B-17.
Submitted by Frank Granack
March 6, 1944 excerpts from Diary
March 6, 1944, a written account by Edwin Harrell.
"Target Berlin" by Frank Granack, in "Through the Eye of the Needle."
Submitted by George Madden
March 6, 1944, a written account sent to Jeff Ethell and Alfred Price
Submitted by William Sapp (Dixon)
Lt Samuel Barrick Diary pages on Berlin Missions along with his own personal notes on the mission.
Submitted by Jack Swartout
B Group, Formation position, Lead Squadron.
Pilot's Flimsy March 6, 1944.
Recommendation by Colonel Neil B. Harding to award Silver Star to Captain Jack R. Swartout.

Report of the Operations Officer, Mission of March 6, 1944, John B. Kidd, Lt. Colonel Air Corps, Operations Officer.
Silver Star award to Jack R. Swartout, 20 April 1944.
The Big B – March 6, 1944, by Jack R. Swartout in **Splasher Six** - Summer 1988.
Submitted by 390th Bomb Group Association/Museum
Map 390th Bomb Group, March 6, 1944, Lead 13 "A" Combat Wing, Briefed Route – Route Flown.
Operations Narrative of Mission, March 6 1944.
Crew loading list for Six Crews, March 6, 1944
Submitted by Penn State University Specials Collections Library
James P. Quigel, Head of Historical Collections and Labor Archives
Paul Dzyak, Eighth Air Force specialist,
March 6, 1944 Diary of Sherwin Barton
Submitted by Palm Springs Air Museum
Jack Robins, BTG on Lt Barton Crew, Interview by Dr. David Thompson
Submitted by Scottie (Bailie) McKasson
Diary of her father Lt Robert W. Bailie, CP on Lt Frank Malooly Crew
Submitted by John Adams (Nephew of Lt John Adams III)
Letters from S/Sgt John Miller and Lt Edward Sullivan
Submitted by Joseph D. Heinrich (Son or Orrin Heinrich)
Diary of Lt Orrin Heinrich, Navigator on Lt Murray Crew
Submitted by Mindy Goorchenko (Granddaughter of Earl Richardson)
"My Twenty-Fourth Mission with The Hundredth Bomb Group" by Earl L. Richardson ~ Major USAF Retired
Submitted by Lucille (Walker) Hayes (Widow of Ed Walker, Jr.)
Photos, letters, Western Union telegrams, Eulogy

Photographs
Unless otherwise credited, all photos are courtesy of the 100th Bomb Group Foundation, public domain, personal archive,.USAF.

Our Gal Sal Individual Crew shots courtesy of Donald Hammond via his daughter Donna Buelt-Condon.

231767 *Our Gal Sal* at Kingman. (Photo: Jerry McLain) Every attempt has been made by the authors to locate Mr McLain regarding this use of this photo.

Paintings
"High Noon" courtesy of Robert Bailey http://baileyprints.com
"Clash at Haseleunne" courtesy of Robert Bailey
"Hunter Becomes the Hunted" courtesy of William Phillips http://www.greenwichworkshop.com/phillips/
"Fortress Engaged" courtesy of Keith Ferris http://keithferrisart.com/
"First Strike on Berlin" courtesy of Nicholas Trudgian www.nicolastrudgian.com
"Seatons Sad Sack" courtesy of Ron Leigh ronald.leigh1@ntlworld.com

Secondary Sources
Monographs
Paul M. Andrews
Operational Record of the 95th Bombardment Group (H) World War II: A Supplement to B-17s Over Berlin. US: 95th Bomb Group (H) Association, 1990.
Project Bits & Pieces-Heavy Bombers of the Mighty Eighth
Ray Bowden
Plane Names and Bloody Noses, The 100th Bomb Group. Design Oracle Partnership.
Tales of Noses Over Berlin. Design Oracle Partnership.
Martin W. Bowman
Castles in the Air, Patrick Stephens Limited.
John F. Callahan
Contrails, My War Record, One Hundredth Bomb Group. Contrails Publications.
Jeffrey L. Ethell and Alfred Price
Target Berlin. Mission 250: 6 March 1944. Arms and Armour.
Roger A. Freeman
The Mighty Eighth. Motorsport.
Combat Profile: B-17 G Flying Fortress in World War II. Ian Allan Ltd.
The Mighty Eighth War Diary. Motorsport.
Roger A. Freeman and 'Hub' Zemke.
Personal rememberances as relayed by Col Hub Zemke to Roger A. Freeman.
Grover Hall Jr. Captain.
Mister Tetley's Tenants, Sanders Phillips and Company, Ltd. 1944.
Harry Crosby
"A Wing and A Prayer, Harper Collins Publishers 1993
C. B. 'Red' Harper
The Buffalo Gal, with the Mighty Eighth and the Fifteenth Air Forces in Action over Europe in World War II. Privately Published.
Ian L. Hawkins
B-17s Over Berlin: Personal Stories from the 95th Bomb Group (H) Washington, D.C., 1990 (A reprint of *Courage*Honor*Victory: A First Person History of the 95th Bomb Group (H), 1987*. Used by permission of the 95th Bombardment Group Heritage Association.
William N. Hess
Ill-Fated 8th Air Force Bomb Group Missions, Speciality Press 2000.
Glenn Infield
Big Week, Brassy 1993.
Richard Le Strange (assisted by Jim Brown)
Century Bombers: The Story of the Bloody Hundredth, The 100th Bomb Group Memorial Museum.
Marshall J. Thixton, George E. Moffat, and John O'Neil
Bombs Away, FNP Press.
John R. Nilsson
The Story of the Century. 1947.
James Parton

Air Force Spoken Here, 1986. Alder & Alder Publishers Inc
Hans-Heiri Stapfer.
Strangers in as Strange Land, 1988.
Horace L. Varian
The Bloody Hundredth, 1977.
Eighth Air Force Historical Society
Eighth Air Force Combat Chronology

Articles
Jack Swartout
"The Big B – March 6, 1944," *Splasher Six* - Summer 1988.
Antigo Daily Journal
Antigo, Wisconsin, December 23, 1987.
Stars and Stipes
March 1944
Splasher Six, Vol 26, 1994, "Milk Run Revisited"

Videos
The Hunter Becomes the Hunted April 24, 1990. Courtesy of Greenwich Workshop Inc.
The Yanks Return-Narrated by Roger A. Freeman

Cyber Sources
www.100thbg.com
100th Bomb Group Foundation, Charlie Cole
http://www.trotzimmo.de/B17/
Andreas Trotz, "The Fate of B-17 Bomber Katie's Boys and her Crew" 2001
http://95thbg.org
Janie McKnight,
http://www.390th.org
http://445th-Bomb-Group.com
Michael S. Simpson-Webmaster and Unit Historian, 445th Bomb Group (Heavy)
Tom Brittan, 2nd Air Division & B-24 historian
Linda Dewey-Kassel Mission Historical Society President
http://www.heritageleague.org/
2nd Air Division Heritage League
Reed Hammans-Communications Vice-President
The Heritage League of the Second Air Division
Kelsey McMillan- 389th Bomb Group Official Historian
http://www.jg54greenhearts.com/index.htm
Robert Wartburg JG54 GRUNHERZ
http://www.luftwaffe.cz/index.html
Petr Kacha Aces of the Luftwaffe
http://www.heinzknokewebsite.com/My-Site/Main_Lilo.htm
Franck Ruffino
http://www.geocities.com/luftwaffe_aces/
Pedro Freitas
http://www.littlefriends.co.uk/index.php
Peter Randall
http://www.8thafhs.org/index.htm
Walt Brown, Mark Copeland
http://mighty8thaf.preller.us/
Fred Peller
http://imansolas.freeservers.com/Angelos/blood_red_skies_over_berlin.html
Angelos Thalassinos

Special Thanks Too: Roger A. Freeman, Paul M. Andrews, Martin W. Bowman, Donald L. Miller, Ian Hawkins, Ed Jablonski, Philip Kaplan, Steve Birdsall, Ray Bowden, Jeff Ethell, Russel A. Strong, David R. Osborne, Cliff Bishop, Martin Caiden, Ivo De Jong, Wally Fydenchuk, Geoff Ward, Michael O'Leary, Harry Crosby, Gale "Buck" Cleven, Robert Tienken, Robert "Rosie" Rosenthal, "Cowboy" Owen Roane, Robert Wolff, Gen Thomas Jeffrey, Gen John B. "Jack" Kidd, Hong Kong Wilson, Jim Brown and all the 100th Bomb Group Veterans and Families, Greg Hatzenbuhler, Ron and Carol Batley and everyone at Thorpe Abbotts Tower Museum, Mark Copeland, Gil Cohen, Dawn, Darleen, Diane and Ginger Faley, Patricia Bittle Scarpena, Billy Sheehan, Greta Lichterfeld, Theresa Cameron, Denny Gregory, Jan Riddling, Cindy Goodman, Charlie Cole, Harry Nelson, Jack O'Leary, Curtis Wilson, David and Carol Tallichet, Palm Springs Air Museum, The Carey Family, Maurice Hammond, Brian Slagel, Tracy Vera, Mark Feijo, Matthew Taylor, Dwayne Bennett ('The Chicken Skipper"), George Hoidra, 918th BG Living Memorial, Mighty Eighth Air Force Museum in Savannah-Walt Brown, Ian McLachlan, Russell Zorn, Bob Biondi, Ian Robertson, and Army Air Forces http://www.armyairforces.com/. To the men and women who keep the last flyable Flying Fortress' in the air:

Liberty Belle http://www.libertyfoundation.org/ ,
Aluminum Overcast http://www.b17.org/
Nine-O-Nine http://www.collingsfoundation.org/tour_b-17g.htm
Yankee Lady http://www.yankeeairmuseum.org/
Thunderbird http://www.lsfm.org/
Chuckie http://www.vintageflyingmuseum.org/
Miss Angela http://www.air-museum.org/
Evergreen B-17 http://www.sprucegoose.org/museum/history.html
Sentimental Journey http://www.arizonawingcaf.com/pages/aircraftsj.html
Texas Raiders http://www.gulfcoastwing.org/
Memphis Belle http://www.100thbg.com/specials/tallichetsb17schedule.htm
Fuddy Duddy Martin Aviation, Califorinia
Pink Lady , France http://pink.lady.free.fr/home.html
Sally B, England http://www.sallyb.org.uk/

Endnotes

1 It is not unusual for a Squadron Operations Office to lead missions in place of the Squadron CO.

2 Records show LeMay was Stateside at this time.

3 Upon hearing the story, this request was granted.

4 PINETREE is the code name for VIII Bomber Command Head Quarters.

5 General Hap Arnold and General Tooey Spaatz had also recommended that Eaker be transferred to take over this new position as Commander in Chief of the Mediterranean Allied Air Forces (MAAF). Gen Spaatz was taking over Command of the newly created United States Strategic Air Forces (USSTAF) based in England. His HQ would encompass overall command and target selection of the 8th, 9th, 12th and 15th Air Forces. USSTAF was to be based in England and the USAAF could not afford to have two Commanders with the Expericne of booth Eaker and Spaatz in the same theatre. The MAAF position called for an American commander who had the skill and respect to be in overall command of RAF and USAAF in the MTO. Eaker, although heartbroken by the move, was the perfect choice.

6 Captain Gerald Putnam in a July 29, 1993, letter to Group Navigator Harry Crosby. Lt Vollmer would report after the war that they were hit by six FW 190s.

7 Information provided by Lt Voller, pilot of 239817 *Murderer's Row*, on March 3, 1944.

8 Letter sent in 1980/81

9 Strangers In A Strange Land by Hans-Heiri Stapfer

10 Tale of Noses over Berlin by Ray Bowden.

11 Ian L. Hawkins, *B-17s over Berlin*

12 P-38s were from 55th Fighter Group led by Commanding Officer Col. Jack Jenkins.

13 Standard Operating Procedure called for test firing all the guns on a B-17 over the North Sea to make sure they were operational.

14 Sgt Stearns Quotes courtesy The Greenwich Workshop, Inc.

15 Ian L. Hawkins, *B-17s over Berlin*

16 There is conflict as to the amount of 100th AC that actually went to Berlin with the 95th. The confusion may lie in fact that Red Harper had tagged onto the the 95th/100th BG composite group heading for Berlin but was forced to turn back when his #2 prop ran away and began windmilling. Lt Harper could not feather the prop and headed back to England where he set his B-17 *"Buffalo Gal"* down at a RAF base on the coast. Thus the total number that hit Berlin was in fact twelve 100th Bomb Group planes

17 Second Bombardment Division Deputy Lead was Captain Larson of the 482BG with Lt Albert V. Kirchenbauer, 445 BG, 703 BS Squadron Navigator on board. In the #3 position was the 445BG Deputy Group Commander Major Carl Fleming Jr. flying in B-24 252447 flown by 703 BS Lt Francis W. Conley. 482 BG (P), 814 BS, B-24HSH-15 DT 41-28783 M SI named *FEATHER MERCHANT*. This plane later went to 44 BG and finally 491 BG before being declared war weary and salvaged in Northern Ireland."

18 Prior to take off, the Chapman Crew failed to take off because mechanical problems with 239983. Accordingly, Lt Massol in 232018 *Waticare* took over the lead of the Low Squadron of the 100 **B**, which then constituted only 5 B-17s. This also reduced the total number of 100BG B-17s from 36 to 35.

19 Bufflao Gal by C.B. (Red) Harper

20 Once heading out to their aircraft, how much they wore going out probably depended on the weather, time of day, time of year, how much time before take-off, did they ride in a deuce and a half with a high bed , or a weapons carrier with a low bed to name a few. It is also of note that details of this procedure varied between crews. Information courtesy of John Gilbert, 918th Bomb Group Living Memorial.

21 (Later that day the Group CO, Colonel Neil B. 'Chick' Harding was taken to the hospital with gallstones.

22 Later, Massol and Granger took the plane up to 31,000 feet to test it and found it to be okay.

23 The name Toyko Tanks is said to be associated with adding the range to a B-17 for it to fly one way to Tokyo.

24 Story of the Century by John Nilsson

25 Story of the Century by John Nilsson

26 This is incorrect, the formation chart and Missing Air Crew Report show that Lt Barton was flying 231800

27 In order to keep gunners in the radio room from shooting off the tail of their plane, the 50 cal was blocked from being able to fire at the horizontal and vertical stabilizers.

28 Century Bombers by Richard LeStrange and Jim Brown

29 From Roger A. Freeman 's interview with Col Hub Zemke

30 Courtesy of Greenwich Workshop, Inc.

31 As there is no chart showing the formation over the target, the "over Target" charts are based on information supplied by the survivors of March 6, 1944, and what is Standard Operating Procedure for the 8th AF when a slot in the formation is vacated.

32 Two days before, he had been credited with shooting down the first enemy fighter over Berlin by the 8th AF

33 Letter from 2Lt. Norman Rasmussen, bombardier on the. Handorf Crew, to his sister Velma, February 23, 1944. Less than 2 weeks after this letter was written, Lt. Rasmussen was killed in action over Berlin on March 6, 1944. We thank his Family for sharing this personal insight into this brave young mans last days.

34 See Appendice B for Commondation

35 Marvin Bowman S-2 Diary

36 Castles In The Air by Martin W. Bowman

37 From "Letters From England" by John Bennett

38 After surviving the March 8, 1944, Berlin again, Lt. Robert Shoens sat down and composed this poignant poem.

39 See Appendix B

40 A few weeks later as Colonel Alkire became the Commanding Officer of the 449thBG, which later flew B24s with the 15th Air Force out of Italy. He would see many of his old friends from the 100th BG when he was shot down and became a POW in Stalag Luft III.

41 The October 14, 1943, mission was also known as "Black Thursday" because the 8th Air Force lost 60 bombers).

42 All Crews "Over Target" participated in March 4, 1944, Mission to Berlin while attached to the 95 BG.

43 Lt Lacy could not confirm that he and Ferbrache joined "A" Group but it is the most logical assumption.

44 231968 *Miss Irish* moved down from High Squadron and then to the slot to the right of to 231981 when 239872 *Rubber Check* was hit by flak over the target.

45 231306 *Nelson King* Captain Jack Swartout, 351st Bomb Squadron Operations Officer was designated as low **B** Group leader and fly "right seat" to Captain Frank Lauro, 418th Bomb Squadron, as lead aircraft to the group's 20 B-17s. At 1200 over Haseluenne, this B-17 was struck by a FW 190 but continued with the mission, making a forced landing at Honnington Sub Depot.
231767 *Our Gal Sal* bombed with the 95 BG.
239994 *Snort Stuff* moved from High Squadron to Low squadron when Massol (232018) left the formation with mechanical problems.

46 Note: 42-3234 *Little Mike* Salvaged 10-Oct-43
42-31035 *Hang the Expense* Salvaged 29 Nov '43
42-39867 *Hang the Expense IV* to U.S. June 45*
42-31767 *Our Gal Sal* to U.S. May 45
* Later renamed *Boeing Belle* with Louis Montgomery as Crew Chief.

Call for information

Despite the wealth of information available and the thousands, if not tens of thousands of man-hours spent in compiling the data and resolving conflicting information, it is the nature of any historical endeavor that there are missing "bits and pieces" to be filled in. Any one having additional information or corrections to what is presented in this monograph are encourage to contact the 100th Bomb Group Foundation at www.100thbg.com.

The Authors

Luce Dewez

The son of Belgian resistance fighters, who risked their lives in the fight against tyranny during the Second World War, Luc Dewez lives and works in Belgium. He enjoys a recognized passion for studying and understanding the air war over Europe. His accomplishments as a historian and researcher received laudable comments from air war veterans, fellow researchers, as well as the late Roger Freeman. In addition to this monogram he has written on the 44th BG and the August 1, 1943 Ploesti raid, as well as a detailed account of the 445th Bomb Group's disastrous September 27, 1944, Kassel mission where 25 of the Group's B-24s failed to return to base. His accounts rely heavily on personal interviews with the veterans. In addition to his work and research interests, he enjoys life with his wife, Sophie, and their lively young girls, Marie and Lisa.

Michael P. Faley

Son of a WW II Navy Veteran, Michael P. Faley resides and works in Los Angeles, California. He is no stranger to those interested in the history of the 8th Air Force during the Second World War. During the past 15 years his research has appeared in *Air Classics*, *Warbirds,* and *Bomber Legends*. In addition to being a featured speaker in the video *B-17 Flying Legend*, he provided historical material and proof read many published works on the 8th Air Force. His unique talents are also focused on his position as the Historian for the 100th Bomb Group and 13th Combat Wing. He relishes the conversations with veterans, their families and many friends, documenting their stories. In his effort to better appreciate what these young men of yesterday endured during the Seocnd World War, he has also made numerous visits to Europe and has flown in a Harvard T6, the B-17Gs *Liberty Belle* and *Nine O Nine,* as well as while in England in Maurice Hammonds' P-51D *Janie.*

Don't Send My Boy to Berlin

Don't send my boy to Berlin
The dying Mother Said,

Don't send my boy to Berlin,
I'd rather see him Dead,

For when the flak starts poppin
With fighters all around,

Don't send my boy to Berlin,
Just keep him on the ground.

"Bought the Farm." This dramatic photograph captures the demise of Lt. Robert E. Fuller's *Wee Willie* (231333, 91 Bomb Group, 322 Bomb Squadron) moments after being struck by flak over Stendal, Germany, on April 8, 1945. Only two survived. (Photo: USAF)